D1523936

Dimensions of a Creole Continuum

Dimensions of a Creole Continuum

History, Texts, &
Linguistic Analysis of
Guyanese Creole

John R. Rickford

 Stanford University Press / Stanford, California

Stanford University Press
Stanford, California
© 1987 by the Board of Trustees of the
Leland Stanford Junior University

Printed in the United States of America

CIP data appear at the end of the book

To the memory of my parents,
Russell Howell Rickford and
Eula Sylvia Rickford (née Wade)

Acknowledgments

This project was originally begun at the suggestion of Manfred Görlach, and I am grateful to him for providing support and commentary over several years. Without financial support from the following sources, the book would never have become a reality: the University of Guyana Research and Publications Fund (particularly Dennis Irvine, former Vice Chancellor), the Stanford University Department of Linguistics (particularly Elizabeth Closs Traugott, former Chair), the Spencer Foundation (for a seed grant awarded through the Stanford School of Education, allocated by Myron Atkin, former Dean), and the Dean's Award for Teaching at Stanford (particularly Norman Wessells, Dean of Humanities and Sciences).

Much of the nitty-gritty of transcription, computer processing, typing, library research, indexing, and bibliographical checking was done by various research assistants and secretaries who worked on this project, including Christopher Aird, Michael Bankay, Shelton King, Jacqueline Kowtko, Genine Lentine, Nannette Morgan, Melissa Moyer, Sonia Oliva, Sharon Veach, and Jerri Willett (in particular). The administrative support of Gina Wein and Elke Jones was invaluable, as was the computer training and advice provided by Randy Melen and Tom Goodrich. John Rawlings of Green Library at Stanford provided superb bibliographic support.

I am grateful to the many scholars who read and commented on earlier versions of the manuscript. Among these, Derek Bickerton, Frederic Cassidy, Ian Hancock, and Elizabeth Closs Traugott deserve special thanks for reading the entire manuscript (or most of it) and offering detailed feedback. In addition, the following people provided valuable commentary on various subsections, and/or provided useful references and suggestions: Mervyn Alleyne, Dwight Bolinger, Hazel Carter, Bernard Comrie, Chris Corne, Jean D'Costa, St. Clair Drake, Walter Edwards, Charles A. Ferguson, Glenn Gilbert, Talmy Givón, Morris Goodman, John Holm, Sr., Noel Menezes, Karl Reisman, Ian Robertson, Daizal Samad, Debbie Schiffrin, John Szwed,

Deborah Tannen, Ewart Thomas, Peter Trudgill, and Lise Winer. As usual, none of them should be held responsible for any limitations of the current version.

I thank Wordsworth McAndrew for providing Text sets 22, 26, and 28 and for his constant interest and encouragement. Text 30 I owe to a recording made by Fitzroy Lewis, and Text set 31 to a recording made by Lennox Foster and Francis Callender (with the kind permission of presiding justice Audrey Bishop). I am grateful also to Jan Carew, Hubert Devonish, Lilith Haynes von Mutius, and Robert Le Page for permission to quote from various publications of theirs. To the many Guyanese whose willingness to be interviewed and tape-recorded provided the textual material in this volume, I am especially grateful. If there is anyone whose contributions are not specifically mentioned, I ask their forgiveness.

William Carver and the staff at Stanford University Press provided invaluable assistance throughout the preparation of this book; I am particularly indebted to Barbara Mnookin for her editorial input.

Finally, I wish to remember and thank my father and mother, to whom this book is lovingly dedicated, and my brother Edward, my wife Angela, and our children, Shiyama, Russell, Anakela, and Luke, for their unstinting support and their shared pleasure in seeing this project bear out the Guyanese proverb: "De longes' road gat a en'; de longes' prayer gat Amen."

J.R.R.

Contents

Part I   Background

Part II   Texts and Analysis

Figures & Tables

Texts

Early Written Texts

1. Pinckard, 1797
   1a. From Letter XX, Demerara, Feb. 11, 1797, 87.   1b. From Letter XXI, Demerara, February 1797, 87.

2. Bolingbroke, 1799–1805
   2a. Choice of wives by slaves at Stabroek "sale-room," 90.   2b. Mandingo slave's claim to have seen Mungo Park in Africa, 91.

3. St. Clair, 1806–1808
   3a. Choice of wives by Old Catz's slaves, 94.   3b. Miss Fanny's views on "buckra," 94.   3c. Little Johnny's comments while hunting, 95.   3d. Words of a slave whose right hand has just been cut off, 95.   3e. Comments of "one of the pretty little Black Venuses" about life in the white household, 95.

4. Kirke, 1872–1897
   4a. A "fancy talk" wedding toast, 98.   4b. Comments of three "black men" on the wording of the colony arms, 98.   4c. "Wordy war" between two "black girls," 99.

5. McTurk, 1881/1899
   5a. From "Repote ob de Meeting ob de Kullad Gen'lmans Aglicultulal and Debating Society," 103.   5b. "Muddu Hubbard," 103.

6. C. S. Argus, ca. 1891–1896
   6a. "Every Man Has His Price," 106.   6b. "Insult and Injury," 108.

7. Van Sertima, 1905
   7a. From his translation of *The Pilgrim's Progress*, 112.   7b. From his translation of "The Parable of the Sower," 112.

Modern Texts from Diverse Domains

Foreword

It gives me great pleasure to write this Foreword, for a variety of reasons. First of all, John Rickford is a valued personal friend of long standing. Second, he is a colleague and scholar for whom I have always had the highest respect. Third, he is a native speaker of (some of) the varieties of Creole English that are documented in this book—something that is still relatively rare in creole studies. I must confess to having had some apprehension when he entered that field. All linguists who have worked on a language not their own must, if they are honest, admit to similar qualms; all of us have attended conferences at which some linguist has cited data from language X, only to have someone from the floor announce, "I am a native speaker of language X, and *you just can't say that in my language!*" Had I, too, managed to get Guyanese Creole all wrong somehow? Well, the reader of this volume will find many points about the language on which our agreement is something less than complete, but I am relieved to find that they involve questions of interpretation rather than questions of fact.

The book is, I think, unique of its kind; certainly no other creole language has been documented with this kind of depth and breadth. It is one thing to analyze the complex variation of Guyanese Creole with the aid of carefully handpicked examples, as a number of us, including Rickford, have done: it is quite another to confront the reader with the raw data themselves, in all their intractability, and still present analyses that will hold water. In any language, you can find native speakers who will disagree on a large number of marginal sentences; in Guyana, it is hard to find any two native speakers who will agree about any random selection of simple core sentences. It is unthinkable that anyone could ask a class of Italian or French or Dutch or German students for a translation of some everyday expression such as "I was sitting" and get thirteen different answers from twenty students; but that is exactly what happened to me in Guyana (and all the answers were right, too!). Even being a native speaker oneself provides no magic key to this laby-rinth. In such a situation, you need a wide range of texts, such as this book so amply provides, just to get your bearings, before you can begin to make any kind of sense of what native speakers tell you about their intuitions.

Countless linguistic issues await the reader in these texts, many of them illuminated by Rickford's detailed and insightful commentaries. He does not pretend to answer the biggest question of all, one apparent at least since the pioneering work of Reinecke in Hawaii and DeCamp in Jamaica, but largely ignored and certainly unanswered to date, namely, how the native speaker stores and handles this mass of variation while preserving its striking im-plicational regularities—regularities that make it impossible to dismiss ei-ther random mixing of dialects or some kind of performance phenomenon. But at least this book amasses the data and grounds the issues that any an-swer will have to take into account.

Of course one answer is simply to deny that there is a linguistic con-tinuum—in other words, to return to the simplistic model of two dialects with random switching and mixing that held sway in the 1950's, before Richard Allsopp first ventured into the slums of Albouystown with tape re-corder in hand. One of the best of the many good things in this book is the section in which Rickford defends the concept of the continuum against several of its recent critics. The defense is all the more impressive for its total lack of partisan animus, its absolute fairness, and its willingness to con-cede every point that could reasonably be conceded—for, when all is done, his conclusion that those critics are taking "a step backward" in the study of creole languages is inescapable.

But this book contains a great deal more than linguistic data and linguistic analysis. Let us hope that its linguistic orientation does not scare off the nonspecialist reader, for many people could derive both pleasure and knowl-edge from it—anyone interested in the history, folklore, and sociology of Guyana, or of the region in general, for that matter, since so much in Guya-nese language and culture is pan-Caribbean. The book is a mine of informa-tion on the beliefs and attitudes of the Guyanese people and on their rich and varied heritage. But it achieves something much more rare and valuable than the mere conveyance of information. In these texts, carefully and lov-ingly selected, Rickford has somehow managed to capture the true spirit of the Guyanese—their quick and lively wit, their mixture of credulity and skepticism, their pungent repertoire of oratorical styles, their sturdy sense of independence, and their extraordinary directness, openness, and lack of pretension—hatred of affectation, in many cases—which is, to me at least, their most endearing feature. At their best, and their best is by no means uncommon, these texts show a natural talent for the dramatic that might be the envy of many a sophisticated writer. I defy anyone to read Irene's tale of the coconut jumbie without a tremor of gooseflesh, or Lohtan's story of his daughter's death without being moved beyond pity to a deeper realization of what it means to be part of human society—"wi kyaan ombog di wedin, yu onstan?"

This is a book, then, that contains not just the bare bones of language, but the living flesh itself. For people who don't know Guyana or countries like it or for whom the concept "creole continuum" is just a dry abstraction, the book should be a mind-opening experience. For those already familiar with such things, it will remain an invaluable source of both linguistic data and analyses of those data. I do not by any means agree with all the analysis—I certainly do not buy Bonnette's "historical present," for instance—but few people know as much about Guyanese Creole as Rickford does, so even when you do not agree with him you cannot afford to ignore him.

This book, in short, is one that should be read not just by students of creole languages and language variation—that *they* should read it goes without saying—but by anyone who sincerely cares about language and about the quirky, unpredictable species that somehow, against all evolutionary odds, produced it.

Derek Bickerton

Dimensions of a Creole Continuum

Introduction

This book is devoted to the discussion of central theoretical and socio-historical linguistic issues concerning a creole continuum—that of Guyana, South America, to the presentation of texts exemplifying its various levels, and to their analysis in terms of a broad set of dimensions: phonology, morphology, syntax, lexico-semantics, discourse structure, and sociolinguistic significance.

People who have never heard of creole languages or Guyana might well ask why one should devote a whole book to this subject. Those who have grown up in creole-continuum communities and acquired a disdain for vernaculars short of the official standard might ask the same question.[1] Several answers to this question are possible, but the most important is that the theoretical and practical significance of pidgins and creoles is being increasingly recognized, that the analysis of data from the Guyanese creole continuum has figured fairly prominently in this recognition, and that further analysis and data from this source promise to be equally enlightening. Let me elaborate on these points before proceeding.

Definitions in pidgin-creole studies rarely meet with universal agreement, but Hymes's (1971a: 84) definitions of pidgins and creoles are widely cited, and provide a convenient frame of reference:[2]

Pidginization is that complex process of sociolinguistic change comprising reduction in inner form [the conceptual resources of a language reflected in its semantic and syntactic structure], with convergence [language mixture], in the context of restriction in use. A *pidgin* is a result of such a process that has achieved autonomy as a norm. . . .

Creolization is that complex process of sociolinguistic change comprising expansion in inner form, with convergence, in the context of extension in use. A creole is the result of such a process that has achieved autonomy as a norm. . . .

Pidginization is usually associated with simplification in outer form [the phonological and morphological structure of a language], creolization with complication in outer form.

To these definitions we might add the more recent characterization of pidginization and creolization as acquisition processes under conditions of restricted input (Bickerton 1977a: 49; Andersen 1983: 8–9). In pidginization, the restricted input occurs in the course of second-language learning by substrate speakers who have limited access to native speakers of the superstrate language. In creolization, the restricted input occurs in the course of first-language acquisition and derives from the rudimentary nature of the pidgin or pre-pidgin language that serves as a model. Bickerton hypothesizes (1981, 1984a) that children are forced to draw on an innate bioprogram to expand and develop this pidgin into a functionally adequate first language. Linguistic similarities among creole languages of different lexical bases and in widely separated areas provide part of the justification for this hypothesis.

The very concept of a creole continuum has become a source of controversy in recent times, but as originally defined by DeCamp (1971b), it refers to a situation where a continuum of intermediate varieties develops between creole and standard poles as creole speakers experience increased motivation and opportunity to modify their speech in the direction of the standard language.

The study of pidgins and creoles has come to be recognized as important for four primary areas of linguistic theory:*

1. *Language contact and change.* For historical linguists and students of multilingualism, pidgins and creoles are important as extreme examples of interlingual mixture and substratal influence, and of rapid, contact-induced linguistic change. For the same reasons, they constitute significant test cases for assessing, first, the validity of the assumptions underlying comparative reconstruction, the family-tree model, and glottochronology (Hall 1966: 105–25; Traugott 1977) and, second, the controversial issue of the creole origin of American Vernacular Black English (B. Bailey 1965; Stewart 1967; Dillard 1971; Rickford 1977a). More recently, Bickerton (1983a; 1984a) has suggested that creoles hold the key to puzzles about the origin and early development of human language that have remained locked for years.

2. *Sociolinguistic variation.* As Hymes (1971b: 5) notes: "The processes of pidginization and creolization . . . seem to represent the extreme to which social factors can go in shaping the transmission and use of language." This consideration, together with the extensive variability that pidgin-creole communities often display, has led pidgins and creoles to occupy a central place in sociolinguistics and variation theory. Implicational scaling was introduced to linguistics by DeCamp (1971b) with data from the Jamaican continuum, and Le Page's sociopsychological model has been developed al-

---

*See, most recently, Mühlhäusler's (1986) Chapter 6: "The Relevance of Pidgin and Creole Studies to Linguistic Theory."

most entirely with creole data from Belize and St. Lucia (see Le Page and Tabouret-Keller 1985).

3. *Language acquisition and processing.* The potential significance of pidgins and creoles for our understanding of first- and second-language acquisition has been emphasized by two recent works: Bickerton (1981), with its proposal that creoles provide a clear view of an innate linguistic bioprogram common to all humans, but apart from creoles evident only in child language; and Andersen (1983), which demonstrates the value of considering pidginization, creolization, and decreolization in the development of models of second-language learning, and vice versa.[3] Slobin (1979: 43–46, 188–94), too, emphasizes the value of pidginization and creolization for our understanding of linguistic processing strategies and the basic requirements of human language.

4. *Grammatical theory.* Less developed than the preceding areas, but no less important, is the recognition that pidgins and creoles have a role to play in grammatical theory, in the identification of language universals (Kay and Sankoff 1974; Muysken and Smith 1986), and in the choice between alternative descriptions and models of grammar (Muysken 1981). To Craig (1980), the simultaneous processing by creole-continuum speakers of overlapping systems of syntax and lexis highlights the need for a more abstract, conceptually based model of grammar; and he has suggested what features such a model might have.

In addition to their importance for linguistic theory, pidgins and creoles are often centrally involved in problems of social, economic, and political development in the communities where they are spoken: in attempts to reform and upgrade the educational systems, and in efforts to establish a new cultural identity or forge new means of artistic expression. It is because of the essential value of Pidgin English as an instrument of communication between speakers of many different languages that it was officially encouraged in New Guinea at the turn of the century, under German control (Hall 1966: 135), and it is because Haitian Creole was recognized as *the* native language of the vast majority of Haitians that, despite the prestige and entrenchment of standard French, Creole was experimentally introduced in the schools there in 1979. Linguists working in these applied areas of pidgin-creole studies have drawn on existing methods and models in bilingual education and language planning, and they have also contributed to the existing literature in these subfields (see Craig 1980; Samarin 1980; Wurm 1980).

But only a handful of these languages have been well enough studied to feature in the literature on these theoretical and applied issues. Guyanese Creole (GC) is one; others are Belizean, Haitian, Hawaiian, Jamaican, New Guinea Tok Pisin, Papiamentu (Netherlands Antilles), and Suriname's Croles, especially Sranan and Saramaccan.[4] Grammatical and lexical descriptions of GC began to appear in the early 1900's (Van Sertima 1905; Cruickshank 1916), but it was only after the Second World War that scholars began studying GC in a broader context, and with the tools of modern linguistics. Allsopp's master's and doctoral theses (1958a, 1962)—dealing with the pronominal and tense-aspect systems of Georgetown Creole—employed sociolinguistic field methods and quantitative analytic techniques before the Labovian model (1963, 1966) became established. Bickerton's books (1975, 1981), in providing many descriptive details about GC, brought them to bear on such larger theoretical issues as the notion of "system" and the nature of polylectal competence (1975), and led to his hypothesis of an innate linguistic bioprogram and its relation to language origin and acquisition (1981). Other theses, books, and papers have utilized GC data to exemplify or compare alternative variation models and sociolinguistic theories, including Bickerton (1971, 1973a, 1973b), Haynes (1973), W. Edwards (1975, 1983), Rickford (1979, 1980b, 1981), and Gibson (1982). The central comparative studies of Atlantic English creoles—Hancock (1969; n.d.*a*) and Alleyne (1980)—all include GC data; and such data have also contributed to our understanding of the creole continuum and the decreolization process (Bickerton 1975; Rickford 1983b; and Robertson n.d., which also draws on Guyanese Dutch Creole). The relevance of GC data to synchronic and diachronic issues concerning Vernacular Black English (VBE) has been demonstrated by Rickford (1974, 1977a, 1986), Bickerton (1975), W. Edwards (1979), R. Rodney (1981), and Mufwene (1983).

With respect to educational and other applied issues, Allsopp (see 1978 for discussion) is compiling a massive *Dictionary of Caribbean English Usage* that should be enormously helpful to teachers, testmakers, students, and administrators in Guyana and throughout the Caribbean; Ramdat (1978) and C. Thompson (1980) are lexical studies by students who have contributed to that project. An earlier work, Yansen (1975), is an independent lexical compilation by an educator whose interest in "Creolese" delighted and informed generations of Guyanese students. Guyana is one of the four West Indian territories Le Page (1968) saw as critically in need of educational programs that would take the local creole vernaculars into account; and Tyndall (1965), Cave (1971), Craig (1971), Haynes (1978), and Rickford and Greaves (1978) are some of the studies on language use in Guyanese schools that have actually been done. More recently, planning problems involved in the use of GC as an official language—including variety selection and standardization— have been extensively explored by Devonish (1978, 1983).

Although the importance of pidgins and creoles is being increasingly recognized, and work on GC has been done on almost every major theoretical and applied front in linguistics, this book is the first to present extensive textual data on GC drawn from a variety of points in geographical and social space and time. This spectrum of texts, together with their individual introductions and glosses and the subject and line indexes, is intended as a classroom and research resource for linguists, teachers, and the general public. It should be useful to those engaged in the analysis of individual linguistic features in other creoles and Vernacular Black English, to those interested in verifying, challenging, or extending previous analyses of GC, to those interested in the comparative and diachronic study of Atlantic and other creoles, to those interested in general linguistic theory, and to those interested in the educational and other applied issues in which pidgins and creoles often figure. I also hope that the texts themselves may be useful to scholars in other fields, such as oral history and folklore.

A certain amount of subjectivity is unavoidable when one comes to choose texts for analysis. So far as possible, however, I have tried to select each text and each feature with an eye to its relevance to descriptive and theoretical issues in the analysis of GC or other creoles. Spoken texts were selected from corpora recorded by myself or other Guyanese, and the written texts were selected from a wide variety of sources representing two hundred years of usage. In deciding which features of each text to discuss, I selected those that seemed most significant from one or more of the following perspectives:

1. They represented salient characteristics of GC or other creoles (for instance, the unrounding and lowering of back vowels known locally as "broadin yuh mout," discussed in the introduction to Reefer's texts in Chapter 4).

2. Their patterning or use illustrated, corroborated, extended, or challenged prior analyses of similar features in the literature on GC or other creoles, particularly where those analyses constituted the basis of larger claims about variation theory, universal properties of creole languages, or the like (for instance, Bickerton's well-known but disputed analyses of the Main Stative Rule and anterior marking in GC, discussed in the introductions to Derek's and Irene's texts in Chapter 4).

3. They were significant for theories of the historical development of GC, the genesis of creoles, or decreolization (for instance, the features that suggest the existence of early acculturation or pidginlike varieties in the Guiana colonies, discussed in Chapter 3).

4. Their patterning illustrated more general processes of language use or change (for instance, transitive markers arising out of third-person forms, discussed in the introduction to Cruickshank's texts in Chapter 3, or the nonreciprocal use of address forms between social unequals, discussed in the introduction to the selections from Carew's novel in Chapter 6).

I have avoided post-text linear notes, which seem to me better suited to simple glosses and very brief grammatical comments. The prose introductions preceding each text set allowed me more space and flexibility for substantive discussions of key features, including their treatment in the literature to date and their patterning across several texts.

Overall, tape-recordings of natural speech account for 22 of the 32 text-sets in this volume, and if the number and length of the texts from each source are taken into account, the numerical preponderance of oral samples is even more evident. The decision to include more samples of speech than writing to represent recent Guyanese usage—we of course have little choice for earlier periods—was guided by several considerations. First, the recorded samples permit us to make phonemic transcripts, which preserve more information about the phonological features of Guyanese speech than the written samples do, and can help us to interpret the orthographic conventions in the latter. Second, modern synchronic linguistics tends to concentrate on speech rather than writing, for the variety of reasons catalogued in introductory textbooks, such as the fact that speech occurs earlier and more universally than writing. This remains true despite the recent blossoming of interest in written discourse and its comparison with spoken discourse (see Tannen 1981). Third, recorded speech samples are particularly relevant for sociolinguists, one of the primary potential audiences for this book. Sociolinguistic theory and analysis have been based primarily to date on observations and recordings of spoken usage that have helped us to appreciate the orderly heterogeneity of normal speech communities, the organization of everyday discourse, and the structure of social and stylistic differentiation. Finally, pedagogical decisions about the teaching of English and other subjects in Guyanese and Caribbean schools need to be informed by an understanding of spoken usage in the students' homes and communities, so it is as important to provide samples of modern spoken GC for potential educational applications as it is for theoretical reasons.

All of this is not to say that the value of written texts should go unrecognized. Written samples are indispensable for historical work, and invaluable too for stylistic analysis, English-language instruction, and an understanding of a community's diverse linguistic repertoire. But they are also more readily available from literary works and newspapers than spoken texts, and this is one final justification for giving them somewhat less coverage in this volume.

One of the issues that occupied me considerably in preparing this work was the choice of an appropriate orthography or spelling system for the spoken texts. The written texts were of course no problem; even though these varied in their orthographic conventions, my duty was simply to reprint them as I found them. But in representing the tape-recorded samples, I had a choice between using a phonemic orthography and using a system closer to the conventions of ordinary English spelling. Initially, concerned that the book remain accessible to the nonlinguist, I represented all the texts in English spelling with only slight modifications, using a system comparable to that in Jan Carew's novel *Black Midas* (see Text set 27 in Chapter 6). However, besides losing valuable phonological detail, this system failed to convey the character and expressiveness of the speakers, and the feel and atmosphere of their interactions. Accordingly I decided to follow the lead of other scholars working on the Caribbean English-based creoles and use a modified form of the phonemic orthography originally devised by Cassidy (1961) for Jamaican Creole. The values of the characters in this system—which is more consistent and accurate than conventional English spelling—are explained below. Some of the resultant spellings may be unusual and distracting to those unaccustomed to them, but as Holm (1983: 23) points out, "The system is easier to learn and more convenient to write than the symbols of the International Phonetic Alphabet (IPA)," since it is restricted to the letters of the ordinary English alphabet. At the same time Standard English glosses have been prepared for each phonemically transcribed text so that it can be understood and enjoyed by members of the general public.

In the list below, phonemic characters are italicized and followed by their primary IPA equivalents in square brackets, along with articulatory descriptions, phonemically transcribed examples, and glosses (in single quotation marks). The italicizing and single quotation–mark conventions are followed in the text-set introductions throughout this volume. When citing or discussing nonphonemic forms, I use double quotation marks. The ordering of characters follows Cassidy and Le Page (1980: xxxix–xl). Stress, tone, and intonation are not indicated, not because they are unimportant, but because representing them is prohibitively complex. The interested reader is referred to Allsopp (1972), Holder (1972, 1984), Berry (1976), Wells (1982: vol. 3), Lawton (1984), and Carter (1983, 1984, n.d.) for discussions of these prosodic features.

Consonants

b   [b] voiced bilabial stop, as in *biit* 'beat,' *bobl* 'bubble'
p   [p] voiceless bilabial stop, as in *put* 'put,' *tap* 'top'
d   [d] voiced alveolar stop, as in *dash* 'dash,' *said* 'side'
t   [t] voiceless alveolar stop, as in *tek* 'take,' *staat* 'start'
g   [g] voiced velar stop, as in *gu* 'go,' *bag* 'bag'
k   [k] voiceless velar stop, as in *kooknot* 'coconut,' *laik* 'like'
gy [ɟ] voiced palatal stop, as in *gyal* 'girl,' *gyardn* 'garden'
ky [c] voiceless palatal stop, as in *kyaan* 'can't,' *kyar* 'carry'
m   [m] bilabial nasal, as in *miit* 'meet,' *jrom* 'drum'; [m̩] (syllabic) when no vowel is in syllable, as in *ribm* 'ribbon'
n   [n] alveolar nasal, as in *nais* 'nice,' *wen* 'when'; [n̩] (syllabic) when no vowel is in syllable, as in *botn* 'button'
ng [ŋ] velar nasal, as in *geng* 'gang,' *bangk* 'bank'; occasionally [ŋ̩] (syllabic) when no vowel is in syllable, as in *brookng* 'broken'

ny   [ɲ] palatal nasal, as in *nyuuzpeepo* 'newspaper,' *nyam* 'eat'
v   [v] voiced labio-dental fricative, as in *veri* 'very,' *sheev* 'shave'
f   [f] voiceless labio-dental fricative, as in *fain* 'find,' *if* 'if'
dh   [ð] voiced interdental fricative, as in *dhen* 'then,' *beedh* 'bathe' (SE pronunciation)
th   [Θ] voiceless interdental fricative, as in *thin* 'thin,' *bath* 'bath' (SE pronunciation)
z   [z] voiced alveolar fricative, as in *reezo* 'razor,' *bikaaz* 'because'
s   [s] voiceless alveolar fricative, as in *sing* 'sing,' *yes* 'yes'
zh   [ʒ] voiced alveopalatal fricative, as in *mezho* 'measure,' *okeezhn* 'occasion'
sh   [ʃ] voiceless alveopalatal fricative, as in *shi* 'she,' *mashiin* 'machine'
j   [ʤ] voiced alveopalatal affricate, as in *jomp* 'jump,' *brij* 'bridge'
ch   [tʃ] voiceless alveopalatal affricate, as in *chail* 'child,' *bench* 'bench'
l   [l] alveolar lateral, as in *lait* 'light,' *piil* 'peel'; [l̩] (syllabic) when no vowel is in syllable, as in *piipl* 'people'
w   [w] labio-velar approximant/semi-vowel, as in *wel* 'well,' *owee* 'away'
r   [r] alveolar approximant/semi-vowel, as in *red* 'red,' *kyar* 'car'
        [r̩] (syllabic) when no vowel is in syllable, as in *kovr* 'cover'
y   [j] palatal approximant/semi-vowel, as in *yu* 'you,' *yuuztu* 'used to'
h   [h] voiceless glottal fricative, as in *hoom* 'home,' *haid* 'hide'

The symbols ʔ [ʔ] (glottal stop) and *D* [ɾ] (alveolar flap) are used occasionally to represent phonetic, subphonemic distinctions of potential interest, for instance in *ʔa* 'that, the' (Text 16d, line 1082) and *eksaiDing* 'exciting' (Text 32a, line 1545). Instances of assimilation, deletion, and other phonological processes are noted in the introductions to the texts and listed in the subject index. Discussion of consonants like *th* and *dh* (and vowels like *O* and *oh*), which are found primarily or exclusively at one end of the continuum, is included in the introductions to the texts.

Vowels

ii   [i] high, tense, front unrounded, as in *piil* 'peel,' *iit* 'eat'; usually but not always longer than *i*
i   [ɪ] lower-high, lax, front unrounded, as in *bit* 'bit,' *ting* 'thing'
ee   [e] mid, tense, front unrounded, as in *beet* 'bait,' *eebl* 'able'; usually but not always longer than *e*
e   [ɛ] lower-mid, lax, front unrounded, as in *bet* 'bet,' *wenevo* 'whenever'
a   [a] low/open, short, central unrounded, as in *bak* 'back,' *chap* 'chap'
aa   [a:], low/open, long, central unrounded, as in *gaan* 'gone,' *shaap* 'sharp'
ai   [aɪ] falling diphthong (i.e., stress on *a*), as in *taim* 'time,' *waif* 'wife'

oh	[ɔ:] lower-mid, long, back rounded, as in *tohk* 'talk,' *thoht* 'thought'
O	[ɔ] lower-mid, short, back rounded as in *pOt* 'pot,' *pOsibl* 'possible'
Oi	[ɔɪ] falling diphthong (i.e., stress on *O*), as in *Oil* 'oil,' *enjOi* 'enjoy'
o	[ə] short, central unrounded, unstressed, or [ʌ] short, back unrounded, frequently (but not always) stressed, as in *fado* 'father,' *bot* 'but'
ou	[ʌʊ] falling diphthong (i.e., stress on *o*), as in *hous* 'house,' *widout* 'without'
oo	[o] long, mid, back rounded as in *stoorii* 'story,' *boot* 'boat'
u	[ʊ] lax, lower-high, back rounded, as in *put* 'put,' *kuk* 'cook'
uu	[u] tense, high, back rounded, as in *buut* 'boot,' *skuul* 'school'; usually but not always longer than *u*

Note that this system is phonemic, not phonetic or morphemic. This means, on the one hand, that it generally does not represent subphonemic detail, and on the other, that it does not attempt to provide a consistent representation for every morpheme without regard to its actual pronunciation, as some spelling systems do. I have tried to be as faithful to the representation of morphophonemic variation as possible, transcribing unstressed 'me' as *mii* (with a long, tense vowel instead of a short, lax one), and 'position' as *puzizhan* (with a voiced alveopalatal fricative instead of a voiceless one) when these words are pronounced as such, ignoring the fact that these are not their most common pronunciations in everyday speech or their conventional representations in the academic literature.

Transcription conventions and abbreviations

( )	in phonemic transcripts mark optional elements; thus *(h)ii* represents both *hii* and *ii*.
[ ]	in transcripts and translations mark my interpolations, usually enclosing words not actually said but inserted to aid understanding, sometimes indicating an action or reaction of a speaker (e.g. "points," "nervous laugh").
—	is used to mark hesitations, pauses, or changes of direction in the flow of speech. Usually frames fillers or hesitation vocalizations like "—uh—uh—" or "—am—am—", which have been retained in the transcripts because of their potential relevance for discourse analysis.
e−e	and other sequences of short vowels (*i, o, u*) separated by a dash represent instances in which the short vowel is protracted without changing to the tenser quality of *ee, ii, oo* or *uu* (see above).
. . .	represent material omitted, either because it was inaudible or because it was edited out for considerations of space.

Creole when capped always refers to the specific varieties of the country under discussion. In the transcripts of recorded speech, the author is identified by J (John) and the speaker by the first letter of his or her name. Abbreviations for other participants are explained in the concluding paragraphs of the introductions. Other abbreviations used are:

GC   Guyanese Creole (English)
IPA   International Phonetic Alphabet
NP   Noun Phrase
SE   Standard English
V   Verb
VBE   Vernacular Black English, that is, as used in casual, intimate speech in U.S. inner cities (Labov 1972c: xiii)
WH-   Question construction

Finally, a word about the organization of the book. Part One consists of two chapters that explore theoretical issues in the study of GC and other creoles and provide a context for the materials in Part Two:

Chapter 1, "The Concept of a Creole Continuum," explores the viability and usefulness of the continuum model in the face of the many criticisms it has recently received. The dimensions considered in this chapter include the discreteness or continuousness of the boundary between standard and creole, the uni- or multidimensionality of linguistic variation in the community, the extent to which social and stylistic constraints are considered, and the validity of the model's assumptions about past and ongoing linguistic change.

Chapter 2, "Historical and Sociolinguistic Background," begins with the first substantial Dutch settlements on the Guiana Coast in the seventeenth century and traces the major demographic and other historical developments that followed. Implications for theories of pidgin-creole genesis are indicated throughout, as are issues requiring further research. The chapter closes with a discussion of the role of education, social class, urbanization, and ethnicity in the recent and contemporary sociolinguistic situation.

Each of the chapters in Part Two, Chapters 3–6, contains eight text sets (79 texts all told). Each text set (text or texts from a single source) is preceded by an introduction describing its provenance and discussing selected linguistic features.

Chapter 3, "Early Written Texts," presents 19 written extracts dating from 1797 to 1905 that together document some of the earliest varieties of GC on which we have evidence, and attest a number of features that are either rare or nonexistent in modern times.

Chapter 4, "Recordings of Natural Speech: Cane Walk," contains 28 texts from eight speakers in Cane Walk, a pseudonym for a village just outside the capital city of Georgetown. These speakers represent a third of the sample that I used in my dissertation (1979), and include members of both sexes and the community's major social class and age groups. The point of selecting a stratified subsample of this type is to provide interested readers with the data base for a mini-analysis of the sociolinguistic variation in a cohesive local community. In keeping with this aim, and with the fact that the Cane Walk corpus from which they are drawn includes over one hundred hours of recorded speech, the text sets in this chapter are twice as long as those in any other. Their individual introductions are correspondingly longer and more detailed as well; many of the corroborations and proposed revisions of earlier analyses of GC occur in this chapter. Like all the spoken texts in this volume, the text sets in this chapter were selected to include a mix of different discourse types, such as narrative, exposition, and conversation.

Chapter 5, "Recordings of Natural Speech: Other Areas," also provides texts drawn from modern recordings of speakers, but over a broad geographic and ethnic range. Together, the 13 texts in this chapter—which take in the counties of Essequibo, Demerara, and Berbice; the capital city as well as rural areas; both the working and the lower-middle class; and Guyana's two main ethnic groups, Indo- and Afro-Guyanese[5]—represent some of the major internal distinctions within the Guyanese speech community.

Chapter 6, "Modern Texts from Diverse Domains," contains 19 texts from domains that creolists and sociolinguists rarely consider, but that are essential to our understanding of language variation and use within the speech community. Folk material, for instance, often preserves older forms, as shown by the first of the Guyanese folksongs in this section. The extracts from a novel, a newspaper column, and letters to a radio station offer three very different perspectives on the relations between oral and written channels and the incorporation of Creole in writing. The radio announcer conducting an interview, the lawyer in court, the teacher in her classroom, the overseas Guyanese broadcasting traditional "Christmas messages"—these represent the Standard English, or acrolectal, end of the continuum, but they are "live" performances, revealing the impeccable acrolect or standard as fictitious territory in which virtually no one functions in practice.

In addition to the usual subject and personal names indexes, a line index of selected morphosyntactic features has been included. This computer-prepared index lists the number of every line in the texts containing features likely to interest potential users, including (but not limited to) complementizers, copulas, relative clauses, tense-aspect markers, and instances of topicalization.

Part I
Background

1

The Concept of a
Creole Continuum

The characterization of Caribbean English-speaking communities in terms
of a continuum of varieties between creole and standard poles is over a
quarter of a century old. In the 1960's and early 1970's, linguists generally
agreed on the appropriateness and usefulness of such a characterization;
but over the past decade, disagreements and objections have increasingly
been voiced.[1] What of the continuum model, then? Is it still appropriate as a
description of Guyana or Jamaica? Is it still useful as a general theoretical
construct?

As the title of this book suggests, my answer to these questions is basically
affirmative. This does not mean that I accept *all* the assumptions that have
come to be associated with the continuum, that I am irrevocably committed
to its defense, or that I do not share some of its critics' concerns. However, I
find the continuum model—when reduced to its essentials—descriptively
accurate and theoretically convenient. In these respects it seems to me supe-
rior to most existing alternatives and worth continued consideration and
use. The discussion in this chapter provides the basis for these conclusions.

Scholars on either side of the continuum debate frequently raise questions about whether the linguistic variation in particular communities is
unidimensional or multidimensional, constrained by external factors or related to ongoing or prior change, without indicating precisely how these
questions relate to the continuum model itself, and whether they are fundamental or peripheral. In this chapter I will attempt to remedy this weakness.
The viability of the continuum model is usually addressed in terms of one or
more of the following five questions, the first three synchronic, the fourth
and fifth diachronic.

1. Do creole and standard represent discrete and sharply separated categories, or do they represent polar varieties between which there is continuous variation?

2. Is variation in the speech community unidimensional or multidimensional? That is, can all or most variants and varieties be linearly ordered in terms of a single dimension such as "creoleness" or "standardness"?

3. Does the continuum model do justice to the social and stylistic dimensions of linguistic variation?

4. Is it valid to maintain DeCamp's (1971b) view of the continuum as an extension of Bloomfield's (1933) life-cycle model—first a pidgin, then a creole, then a (post-) creole continuum?

5. Does linguistic variation in putative continuum speech communities (such as Guyana, Jamaica, and Hawaii) represent decreolizing change in progress, that is, movement away from creole norms and toward the norms of lexically related standard languages?

I will discuss each of these questions in detail, but it should be noted at the outset that only the first two are fundamental to the concept of a continuum. The others are interesting and important in their own right, but are relatively extraneous, involving ways in which scholars have used the model, or additional assumptions they have chosen to make, rather than inherent features or necessary implications of what it means to have a continuum.

Discreteness

The question of whether creole and standard constitute discrete categories in putative continuum communities may be fruitfully explored in terms of the property-item matrices that Labov (1973) uses to model alternative boundary relations between linguistic categories. Table 1.1 depicts a boundary between two clearly discrete categories, X and Y, which may be, for instance, different grammatical categories or language varieties. Items $a-h$

TABLE 1.1
Property-Item Matrix for a Discrete Boundary Between Categories

Item	Property							
	1	2	3	4	5	6	7	
a	+	+	+	+	+	+	+	CATEGORY X
b	+	+	+	+	+	+	+	
c	+	+	+	+	+	+	+	
d	+	+	+	+	+	+	+	
e	−	−	−	−	−	−	−	
f	−	−	−	−	−	−	−	
g	−	−	−	−	−	−	−	
h	−	−	−	−	−	−	−	CATEGORY Y

SOURCE: Adapted from Labov (1973: 344).

TABLE 1.2
Property-Item Matrix for Continuous Transition Between Categories

Item	\multicolumn{7}{c}{Property}	
	1	2	3	4	5	6	7	
a	+	+	+	+	+	+	+	CATEGORY X
b	+	+	+	+	+	+	−	
c	+	+	+	+	+	−	−	
d	+	+	+	+	−	−	−	
e	+	+	+	−	−	−	−	
f	+	+	−	−	−	−	−	
g	+	−	−	−	−	−	−	
h	−	−	−	−	−	−	−	CATEGORY Y

SOURCE: Same as Table 1.1.

may be, correspondingly, individual lexical items or speech samples, each of which either exhibits or does not exhibit properties 1–7. As Labov notes (p. 343) of this matrix: "It is plain that items a–d are X's and e–h are Y's. Though it is possible to select a single property as the distinctive, or criterial, or essential one, we feel much more confident about categories which are defined by the co-occurrence of a large number of items. Thus it is clear that French and English are different systems, and we use these terms without misgivings."

Table 1.2 illustrates continuous transition, or a nondiscrete boundary, between Categories X and Y. Item *a* may be unambiguously classified as an X and item *h* as a Y, but items *b–g* contain properties of both categories, in varying proportions. As Labov notes, the implicational relations in this matrix (*a+* implies +'s to the left, *a−* implies −'s to the right) constrain at least half the possible permutations of items and properties, but "any decision to locate the boundary between categories X and Y would obviously be an arbitrary one. . . . The transition between X and Y occupies the entire property-item space."

Traditionally, grammatical categories (noun, verb, and so on) were treated as dividing discrete fields, but Ross's (1973) "fake NP squish" demonstrated that different types of Noun Phrase—ranging from animate nouns like "Harpo" at one end to idiomatic elements like "tabs" at the other—formed a cline with respect to syntactic properties characteristic of "nouniness."[2] Traditionally, Creole and SE in Guyana and Jamaica were also regarded as relatively discrete phenomena, but a more continuous transition between these polar categories could often be discerned in the data, and was sometimes acknowledged. Thus, for instance, Van Sertima (1905) attempted to describe *The Creole Tongue of British Guiana*, but his texts are closer to the standard language than those of McTurk (1889) or Cruickshank (1905), as can be seen from the samples I reproduce in Chapter 3. For Jamaica, B. Bailey (1966) provided an idealized analysis of "the English based Creole spoken throughout the island . . . alongside the officially recognized English." But she admitted that there was "extensive cross interference" between these "interwoven co-structures"; and in an earlier work (1964: 105), she had acknowledged the existence of a continuum even more explicitly, siding, in this respect, with other linguists working on Jamaican speech at the time: "The situation has generally been described as a continuum, with Standard English at one end, and at the other Jamaican Creole. . . . Between these two poles lies a range of vernaculars representing the fusion and interaction of varying subsystems, *which exhibits no clear lines of demarcation.*" (Emphasis added.)

DeCamp's (1971b: 350) rejection of a discrete diglossic model and adoption of a continuum model for Jamaica was equally explicit:

There is no sharp cleavage between creole and standard. Rather there is a linguistic continuum, a continuous spectrum of speech varieties ranging from . . . "bush talk" or "broken language" . . . to the [most] educated standard. . . . Many Jamaicans persist in the myth that there are only two varieties: the patois and the standard. But one speaker's attempt at the broad patois may be closer to the standard end of the continuum than is another's attempt at the standard.

DeCamp went on (p. 354) to explain that though the variation in Jamaica was not literally a continuum, since the number of speakers was finite and the number of variable linguistic features limited, "By calling it a continuum I mean that given two samples of Jamaican speech which differ substantially from one another, it is usually possible to find a third intermediate level in an additional sample. Thus it is not practicable to describe the system in terms of two or three or six or any other manageable number of discrete social dialects."

DeCamp's remarks apply equally well to Guyana. The primary justification for characterizing the Guyanese speech community as a creole–standard continuum, rather than a bilingual or diglossic community whose members speak either creole or standard, is that this most accurately fits the synchronic facts. Over a quarter of a century ago, for instance, Allsopp (1958b) pointed out that there were not merely two discrete ways of saying "I told him" in Guyana, but at least nine, ranging from the most standard or acrolectal *ai tOuld him*, through intermediate or mesolectal versions like *a tel im* and *a tel ii*, to the most basilectal or distinctively creole version, *mi tel am.*[3]

That the samples of Guyanese speech in this book do not simply represent two (or more) discrete varieties, but a continuous transition between creole and standard poles, can be seen by considering the following four texts: Dhanish's 20, Anna's 21b, Bonnette's 15c, and Teacher's 30. Table 1.3 shows

TABLE 1.3

Linguistic Features of Four Texts in This Book Representing a Continuum-Like Transition Between Creole and Standard Poles

Text	gy	d	a V	V+∅	aa	dem	na V	wan
20	1	1	1	1	1	1	1	1
21b	1	1	1	1	1	1	1,2	2
15c	2	1,2	2,3	1,2	1,2	2	2,3	2
30	1,2	1,2	2,3	2	2	—	3	2

INDEX: *gy*: 1 = a palatized velar consonant in words like "car" and "girl"; 2 = a nonpalatized velar. *d*: 1 = initial stop in words like "this"; 2 = initial interdental fricative. *a* V: 1 = continuative aspect marked by preverbal *a*; 2 = continuative aspect marked by verb + "-ing"; 3 = continuative aspect marked by "be" plus verb + "-ing." V+∅: 1 = bare verb-stem used to mark past tense with nonstative verbs; 2 = "-ed" suffix or stem change used to mark past tense with nonstative verbs. *aa*: 1 = a low unrounded *aa* in words like "all"; 2 = a rounded *oh*. *dem*: 1 = *dem* is third-person plural subject pronoun; 2 = *dee* is third-person plural subject pronoun. *na* V: 1 = preverbal *na* or *no* as negator; 2 = preverbal *en* as negator; 3 = inflected form of "do" plus "not" as negator. *wan*: 1 = *wan* as indefinite article; 2 = "a" as indefinite article.

how these four texts line up in relation to several sociolinguistic variables. A numerical index of 1 represents a basilectal variant, and 2 an acrolectal one where there are only two variants (columns 1–2, 4–6, and 8), but 2 represents a mesolectal variant, and 3 the acrolectal one in the three-variant columns (3 and 7).

Dhanish's text 20 is clearly the most basilectal or creole in this group, registering invariant basilectal values on all eight variables. Teacher's text 30, recorded in a formal classroom setting, is the closest to the acrolect, although it contains some creole features. Anna's text 21b is intermediate between these two, but closer to Dhanish's basilectal sample, while Bonnette's text 15c is intermediate too, but closer to Teacher's. Other texts in this volume could be placed between those in Table 1.3 to round out the continuum depicted there.[4]

Now one could attempt to maintain a discrete interpretation of the situation by classifying intermediate varieties as "standard with incursions from the creole," or "creole with incursions from the standard' (B. Bailey 1971: 342). But as Bickerton (1973a: 641) notes, this has the defect of suggesting that "the continuum is simply produced by the random mutual interference of two discrete and self-consistent grammars."[5] DeCamp (1971b) shows instead that the kinds of implicational relations evident in the continuous property-item matrix of Table 1.2 are also present in Jamaican speech samples like those shown in Table 1.4,[6] reducing the amount of random variation significantly and simplifying the task of linguistic description. This potential for constraining and pinpointing the range of possible variation has made implicational scaling a popular method for the description of creole continua since 1971.[7]

Despite the documentable continuity of Tables 1.3 and 1.4, a continuum

TABLE 1.4

Implicational Scale for Six Jamaican Variables

Speaker number	Variable					
	a	b	c	d	e	f
i	1	1	1	1	1	1
ii	1	1	1	1	1	2
iii	1	1	1	1	2	2
iv	1	1	1	2	2	2
v	1	1	2	2	2	2
vi	1	2	2	2	2	2
vii	2	2	2	2	2	2

SOURCE: Based on DeCamp (1971b: 355–57). The variables and speaker numbers have been reordered. Speaker i corresponds to DeCamp's 4, ii to 3, iii to 7, iv to 2, v to 6, vi to 1, and vii to 5. Variable a corresponds to DeCamp's feature D, b to C, c to A, d to F, e to E, and f to B.

INDEX: a: $1 = d$; $2 = d\sim dh$. b: $1 = t$; $2 = t\sim th$. c: $1 = pikni$; $2 =$ "child." d: $1 = no\ ben$; $2 =$ "didn't." e: $1 =$ "nanny"; $2 =$ "granny." f: $1 = nyam$; $2 =$ "eat."

analysis might be resisted and a discrete co-systems analysis defended on various grounds. One is that some linguists who are native members of continuum communities (for instance, Tsuzaki 1971, Lawton 1978, and Gibson 1982) perceive variation there in discrete terms, and have argued for two- or three-system analyses. But there are other linguists from the same or similar communities (for instance, Cassidy 1961, Craig 1971, 1980, and myself) who have endorsed the continuum model in one form or another. In view of this variability, as well as the fact that the intuitions of theorists are difficult to separate from their theoretical backgrounds and orientations, it seems inadvisable to attach too much significance to linguists' perceptions on this point. It may be possible to draw on the perceptual judgments of "naïve" native speakers in addressing some aspects of this issue (as I suggest in discussing multidimensionality below, and as Lefebvre 1974: 67–69 has already done to some extent), but this is a different matter.

A second basis for resisting a continuum analysis would be to suggest, as Labov (1980: 384) does, that linguistic knowledge might not be evenly spread out across the continuum. For instance, more people might have vernacular control of the polar lects than of the intermediate varieties, making the polar lects quantitatively more significant. However, Guyanese and Jamaican speech samples examined to date appear to be fairly well distributed across the continuum (DeCamp 1971b: 358; Bickerton 1973a: 665; Rickford 1979: 392). The proportion of *speakers* at each level varies from one area to another (Bush Lot, Guyana, for instance, has more basilectal outputs than Cane Walk), but the claim that a continuum exists does not require that all lects exist with equal frequency, only that they be realized at least some of the time or be theoretically realizable.

A third basis for analyzing the continuum in terms of discrete categories would be the discovery that there were significant co-occurrence restrictions between features in different subsystems despite the general prevalence of variation (see Labov 1973: 345).[8] Sutcliffe (1982: 126–27) argues that this is the case in a sample of 17 texts of British Black speech from Bedford, England; although these texts show a relatively continuous decline in the relative frequencies of JC phonological features they contain (from 99.5 percent to 48.4 percent), there is a midpoint on the range (around 74.7 percent) below which certain accompanying JC grammatical features (continuative *a* and subject pronoun *mi*) disappear almost completely, constituting a relatively sharp dialect boundary. Sutcliffe himself notes, however, that "some other important aspects of the grammar such as past tense marking do not show sudden cut-off points, but evolve towards English along the continuum" (p. 127); in short, that the softness of the boundary between creole and standard varies according to the features that one chooses for consideration (on this point, see Craig 1983: 545). As long as some variables do not shift in lockstep with the others, and the samples under consideration are long enough to provide contexts for their occurrence, the continuousness of the transition between creole and standard will remain.

A final defense of discreteness might be to argue that there is a fundamental difference between the acrolect and all other varieties in the continuum, and minimal differences between the basilectal and mesolectal varieties. This position—forcefully argued by Gibson (1982)—is made plausible by the fact that the local term Creolese can refer to all varieties short of the acrolect, by the fact that schools regard both mesolectal and basilectal features as "nonstandard," and by the fact that in many cases different mesolectal and basilectal surface forms do represent common underlying syntactic/semantic categories.

But it is stretching matters to claim, as Gibson does, that the differences between the basilect and mesolect are purely lexical and not grammatical, except in a highly expanded conception of what counts as lexical and a sharply restricted conception of what counts as grammatical. Although I agree with Gibson that positing shared underlying categories makes it easier to account for communication across the various nonstandard levels of the continuum, and that there is more overlap between basilectal and mesolectal subcategories than Bickerton (1975) had suggested (see my discussion of the similarity between Bonnette's and Irene's tense marking in Chapter 4), there are undeniably some differences between basilectal and mesolectal varieties that cannot be reduced to alternative realizations of common underlying subcategories. Bickerton (1980) shows this is so in relation to some simple lexical items, and Alleyne (1980: 196–97) does the same in relation to a syntactic variable, arguing that "it is only when one reaches the intermediate zones of the continuum that English-like passives occur: *di trii get kot*." The distinction between the third-person pronominal subsystem in the Guyanese basilect and mesolect provides a second grammatical case in point: syntactic case (object *am*/nonobject *ii*) but not gender being distinguished in the former, gender (*ii*/*shii*/*it*) but not case being distinguished in the latter (see Bickerton 1973a; Rickford 1979).[9]

A related consideration is that even though the potential reference of a folk term like Creolese may appear to be very broad, what people mean by it is often much narrower. For instance, Georgetown speakers sometimes decry the use of "Creolese" while themselves using mesolectal forms; when this apparent contradiction is pointed out, it becomes evident that they consider their mesolectal forms a variant of "English," and by "Creolese" intend the basilectal forms. Conversely, when Katherine offered mesolectal Creole translations for acrolectal stimulus sentences in the controlled interview, her mother laughingly commented that Katherine did not know the real Creolese, meaning by this the basilect. Finally, even if it were possible to postulate shared underlying subcategories throughout the grammar and to assign their possible realizations unambiguously to basilectal, mesolectal, or acrolectal co-systems, there would be difficulties in accounting for the fact that some variants from different levels co-occur while others do not, as Bickerton (1975: 12–14) shows by trying to manipulate Allsopp's (1958b) possible realizations of "I told him" into discrete co-systems.

In the light of the preceding arguments and counterarguments, the continuum model of Table 1.2 appears to be the better representation of the gradient creole–standard relation in places such as Guyana and Jamaica, whereas a discrete co-systems model like that of Table 1.1 is more appropriately reserved for the sharper creole–standard boundary in places such as Martinique and Haiti.[10] Very few of the texts in this book are "pure" Creole or "pure" standard. The concept of a creole continuum does justice to the variability between extreme types that these texts exhibit, and that is the fundamental reason why the concept is retained in the title and exploited as a general framework in this work.

Unidimensionality

Thus far we have assumed that if the boundary between creole and standard (or basilect and acrolect) could be shown to be variable rather than sharply defined, then the appropriateness of a continuum model would be self-evident. However, a continuum model assumes that the variables can be ordered in terms of a single dimension. The hues on the normal solar spectrum, for instance, vary continuously from blue to red, but in terms of a single dimension only, wavelength. Similarly, the variants and varieties in a speech community would have to be linearly orderable in terms of a single dimension—"creoleness" or "standardness"—to fit a continuum model. If, by contrast, the variables cannot be clearly discriminated or ordered in terms of a single dimension, then a linear continuum model becomes less appropriate. Colors on the color solid, for instance, are represented by the intersection of values on three dimensions: hue, saturation, and lightness. And if the discrimination of variants and varieties in a speech community required other dimensions instead of or in addition to "creoleness"—as illustrated in Figure 1.1—then a multidimensional model would be required. Note that it is not enough for an urban-rural dimension to be recognized in addition to a creole-standard dimension. If urban variants were characteristically standard, and rural variants characteristically creole, that is, if urban-rural differentiation took place along the continuum rather than orthogonal to it, then a unidimensional continuum interpretation would remain feasible. The implication of the multidimensional model shown in Figure 1.1 is that v2, v2', and v2" are equally creole and differentiable only in terms of features that are distinctively urban or rural.

The question of the dimensionality of variation in Jamaica and Guyana was raised in the earliest descriptions of these communities as creole continua (DeCamp 1971b; Bickerton 1973b),[11] but it was not pursued at any length, and its relation to implicational scaling was not made clear. G. Sankoff (1974: 42–43) raised some theoretical concerns about the unidimensional implications of scaling, but it was Washabaugh (1977) and Le Page (1980a, 1984) who expressed the gravest reservations about a linear continuum model, arguing on the basis of usage data from San Andres and Belize/St. Lucia that a multidimensional model was required. Some of the

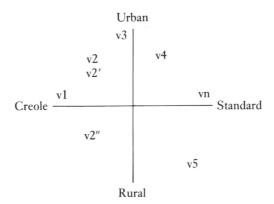

Fig. 1.1. Positioning of creole-standard varieties in a hypothetical multidimensional space

data needed to address this issue adequately (e.g. perceptual data) are still not available, but I will address it with what information is available and indicate directions for future research.

Guttman scaling (1944), of which DeCamp's (1971b) implicational scaling technique is a variant, is appropriate only for variables that can be uni-dimensionally or linearly ordered (Dunn-Rankin 1983: 102–3). DeCamp's technique ordered both speech varieties (vertically) and variants (horizontally) in terms of a single dimension, "creoleness." In Table 1.4, for instance, speech varieties or idiolects higher up are more distinctively creole than those lower down, and creole variants to the right are more distinctively creole than those to the left. The reason this approach is inappropriate for variables that are not unidimensionally ordered is that the implicational relations would then break down: one could not say that the use of variant i implies the use of less distinctively creole variant j, or predict that the difference between idiolects 1 and 2 would involve the prevalence of more creole variants in the former. Nor would the tight constraining of variation types provided by an implicational scale exist. As Dunn-Rankin (ibid.) notes, a Guttman scale involving five variables, each with possible values of 0 and 1, limits the range of possible scale types to six. If linear-scaling relations did not hold, the possible arrangements of 1's and 0's for five variables would be 32.

DeCamp did not spell this out explicitly, but he did note (1971b: 353–54) that a linear unidimensional continuum would simplify the task of grammatical description and multidimensionality would complicate it. He also expressed the view (p. 357), however, that *most* of the variation in Jamaica *was* located along the continuum, and that the variables that were not were easy to sort out:

Of all the variables which cannot be clearly located on the continuum—by this method [scaling], most are geographically determined. The amount of linguistic variation in Jamaica which is neither a part of the continuum nor a matter of simple word geography is surprisingly small. That is, relatively few features vary with age, sex, occupation, ethnic group, etc., except to the extent that these co-variables are themselves a part of the continuum; e.g., the very old and the very young tend more towards the creole end of the continuum than do young adults. . . . The true localisms and regionalisms are indeed incompatible with the linear continuum, but they are not difficult to sort out. They are almost entirely lexical. There are indeed a few western and north-coast characteristics in intonation; "h-dropping" is slightly more frequent in the vicinity of Kingston; there is a western preference for *de* rather than *a* as the continuative aspect particle; but generally the regional variables of Jamaican English would be adequately described by a word geography, and they do not seriously interfere with the analysis of the linear continuum by the methods which I propose.

DeCamp's argument, although valid, would have been strengthened by a systematic tabulation of all the major phonological and grammatical variables in his study, showing that few involved variants that were not classifiable as more or less creole. To date, no one has come close to doing this for any creole-speaking community.

Bickerton (1973b: 20) raised the question of whether a unidimensional scale was adequate to convey the complexity of a dialect continuum, and answered by suggesting that it appeared to provide a reasonable first approximation, especially if one allowed for contingent rule changes that "happen by historical accident to have diffused at roughly consistent rates in roughly consistent order." [12] Contingent implications, he suggested, "may (within narrow limits) be randomly ordered in the grammar," allowing us to "legitimately ignore many apparent breaches of strict implicational series." Again, these remarks hint at a relatedness between scalability, unidimensionality, and the notion of a continuum without making the point fully explicit.

Washabaugh (1977) was the first to suggest that the unidimensional continuum model might not be adequate for a Caribbean creole-speaking community. He argued that variation on Providence Island, Colombia, was not only "vertical" (e.g. between basilectal *fi* and acrolectal *tu* as complementizers) but also "horizontal" (e.g. between careful *fi* and casual *fə*, both equally basilectal). See Figure 1.2.

In reaction, Bickerton (1977b: 354) argued that since Washabaugh's horizontal dimension seems to involve, in the main, universal reduction or Stampean natural processes, it therefore "cannot constitute a separate axis of variation characterizing any particular language or dialect system." [13] However, though some phonological weakening and reduction processes in creole-speaking communities do represent nothing more than universal rapid-speech rules, some phonological processes in such communities affect vertical continuum levels. Pronominal forms with lax rather than tense final vowels are associated with creole rather than standard speech throughout the Caribbean, and mid-mesolectal speakers phonologically reduce mesolectal creole forms like the habitual tense-aspect marker "does" more often than their lower mesolectal counterparts (Rickford 1980a). The point is that at least some of the putative horizontal casual speech variants might lie along the vertical basilect–acrolect dimension; pursuing the point from the opposite direction, it is most unlikely that the careful/casual contrast does not involve elements of the acrolectal/basilectal opposition. Significantly enough, Abrahams (1983: 57) recognizes a West Indies–wide distinction between broad talk and sweet talk that appears to reduce the two dimensions in Figure 1.2 to one:

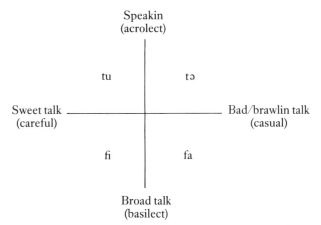

Fig. 1.2. Vertical and horizontal variation on Providence Island. The dimensions are labeled in local terms, after Washabaugh (1977).

There tends to be something of a separation made between two kinds of artful word use: one emphasizes joking and license, the other decorum and formality. The former emphasizes bringing the vernacular creole into stylized use, in the form of wit, repartee, and directed slander. The latter is a demonstration of the speaker's abilities in Standard English, but strictly on the elaborate oratorical level. From this distinction two types of man-of-words have been posited: the *broad talker*, who using license, brings creole into stylized form; and the *sweet talker*, who emphasizes eloquence and manners through the use of formal Standard English.

No one would deny that there are some variants that do not lie along the continuum; but from the available evidence, it appears that the number that have no association with continuum levels may, as DeCamp (1971b) suggests, be relatively small.

   Le Page's critiques of the unidimensional continuum are more far-reaching than Washabaugh's, partly because they involve variants and varieties (Spanish, French, Carib) that are more obviously off the creole–standard continuum, partly because Le Page documents the multidimensional pressures in more detail, and partly because his rejection of scaling and linearity is more radical. Whereas Washabaugh continues to use implicational scaling in the analysis of variants that are clearly on the vertical continuum (*fi*, *tu*), Le Page (1980a: 127–28) emphatically rejects this approach in analyzing the language use of three informants from Cayo District, Belize:

Neither the linguistic description of such speakers, nor of the collective corpus of texts culled from their utterances, is scaleable in the way Bickerton has claimed for his Guyanese verb-phrases, because there is no two-dimensional [i.e., unidimensional] linear progression from basilect to acrolect. One can only characterise their behaviour in terms of coordinates referring in a relational way to neighbouring cultures or internal models. The neighbouring cultures, such as Guatemalan Spanish or Coastal Carib or Belize City Creole or teacher's English are again in their turn related to other cultural models such as Castilian Spanish or Island Carib or West Indian Creoles or West Indian Educated Standards, or Standard British or American or written English.

Le Page (pp. 126–27) observes of these three informants (MP and GM, both schoolgirls, and an old lady whom we will identify as OL) that each regards herself as a Creole speaker, but that their Creole is not exactly that of Belize City, nor is it alike in all three cases: "It is supposed that each of the three in their linguistic behaviour exhibits the effects of both individual and communal acts of identity, and in doing so they position themselves in that multidimensional space I have referred to above." On the basis of the speech samples and descriptions provided, we may represent their positions in multidimensional space as in Figure 1.3.[14]

In the same paper, Le Page argues for the multidimensionality of linguistic variation in another setting, St. Lucia, on the basis of summed data from 100 schoolchildren on nine features, each of which is associated with one or more of the relevant linguistic models there: Educated Standard English, Barbadian Creole, and Creole French Patois. Cluster analysis, attending to similarities and differences in the children's usage of these nine features, places them in four groups (AI–IV) in the formal interview, and four others (BI–IV) in the informal interview. As Le Page concludes (1980a: 135): "We see from the Tables that we are indeed confronted with a *multidimensional* continuum. All the children make some use of nearly all the features—thus they share the same repertoire. . . . Nevertheless they can also

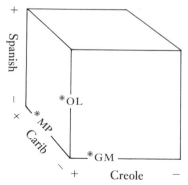

Fig. 1.3. Locations of three Belizean speakers in multidimensional space. The speakers shown are informants discussed in Le Page (1980a).

be clustered into groups of similar behaviour according to the *extent* to which they use each component of the repertoire." (Emphasis in original.)

In the face of Le Page's arguments and data, is the concept of the creole continuum still viable? In its past and present state, St. Lucia may be more obviously multilingual and hence multidimensional than Guyana or Jamaica, and Belize even more so, but any attempt to use this as a basis for "excusing" the unidimensional model's performance would certainly limit its usefulness. Furthermore, one could undoubtedly locate subsets of the Guyanese and Jamaican speech communities that are as linguistically complex as Cayo District, Belize. In Guyana, speakers who know Berbice Dutch, Bhojpuri, and an Amerindian language may draw on elements of these systems, as well as varieties along the Creole–English continuum, in their daily interactions; in Jamaica, Rastafarian language (or Dread Talk) includes many Creole elements, but contains orthogonal lexical and phonological innovations that stamp it as distinctive (Pollard 1983). It is clear that one must appeal to other considerations besides geography to reconcile the concepts of continuum and multidimensionality.

One could follow Le Page's own lead and refer to a "multidimensional continuum," meaning by this that idiolects or individual outputs could be located by coordinate points on two or more simultaneously applicable unidimensional continua, as in Figure 1.3. This would be in line with De-Camp's (1971b: 354) suggestion that even though multidimensional variation would complicate analysis of the continuum in scalar terms, it would not invalidate it ("Two or more simultaneous sets of index features would be required, and both the rules and every derivation based on them would be correspondingly complicated"). It would be in line, too, with Dunn-Rankin's more general observation (1983: 53) that "it is theoretically just as advantageous to create three separate unidimensional scales as it is to derive three dimensions from one multidimensional analysis. In fact, one methodology can serve as a check on the other."

Le Page's multidimensional approach is certainly similar in spirit to De-Camp's unidimensional continuum in recognizing the essential continuity and non-discreteness of the linguistic variability in the Caribbean communities in which English-based creoles and standards coexist. Linguists who interpret critiques of the unidimensional continuum as justifying a return to a simpler dichotomous analysis will find little comfort in Le Page's approach. Precisely because it is more complex and all-encompassing, it is more likely to accommodate all variants and varieties than unidimensional approaches, and less likely to result in categorizations (or exclusions) of individual usages as extraordinary or "deviant."

At the same time, the multidimensional approach may be too all-encompassing or unnecessarily complex, and it is theoretically useful for us to attempt to constrain it as far as possible, holding out the unidimensional model as an ideal. As Dunn-Rankin (1983: 53) notes: "Despite recent advances in multidimensional scaling, unidimensional methods have value because of their simplicity and versatility." Another reason for seeking to reduce the number of dimensions wherever feasible is that it provides a more plausible model of acquisition, production, and perception within the continuum. The problem is similar to the challenge of restricting the class of possible grammars so as to minimize the number of candidates for an explanatorily adequate theory.

Once we accept the theoretical usefulness of trying to work toward unidimensionality (rather than accepting evidence of multidimensionality at face value, or making it an *a priori* part of the model), there are several ways we can approach it. One is to ask the same kind of question we asked above in relation to the unidimensional model—about the extent to which the broad range of varieties possible in *n*-dimensional space is realized in practice. The three idiolects in Figure 1.3 occupy only a fraction of the three-dimensional space represented there, and it may well be that some of the theoretically possible points in that space (for instance, outputs that are simultaneously −Creole, +Carib, and +Spanish) are not realized in practice.[15] Another way is to ask how many and what kinds of variables lie along each of the unidimensional continua that together make up the multidimensional space. It may be, as DeCamp suggests for Jamaica, that the variables not on the central creole–standard continuum are relatively few and insignificant, so that while the situation may be more accurately portrayed by a multidimensional model, scaling along a unidimensional track still captures the essential features of the variability.

Two examples—one from the linguistic, one from the social sciences literature—are instructive. Sankoff and Cedergren (1976: 171) show that though it is possible to use multidimensional scaling to produce a two-dimensional scale of Ross's fake NP classes, the ordering of the NP classes on the two-dimensional analysis is essentially the same as on the unidimensional analysis, data from the second dimension being treated as "largely superfluous." Britton (1983) reports on a study measuring to what degree certain student disabilities might permit mainstreaming in regular classrooms. Eleven disabilities were studied for 23 respondents. The disabilities formed a unidimensional scale with respect to suitability for mainstreaming, with Learning Disability at the top and Autism at the bottom (scaled scores of 90.00 and 9.13, respectively). Further analysis revealed that two primary dimensions underlay the respondents' judgments—a Severe–Mild dimension, and a Physical–Mental dimension. However, the ordering of disabilities on the Severe–Mild dimension was similar to their ordering on the unidimensional suitability scale, and not surprisingly so, since this factor accounted for 60 percent of the variance in the data, as against only 15 percent for the Physical–Mental factor.

To see whether there are parallels to this in St. Lucia and Belize, we might consider not only usage data, as is usually done in linguistics, but also perceptual judgments of the type usually exploited in psychology and sociology. Using brief samples representative of the range of everyday speech in these communities, one could ask informants which two in every triad seemed most similar to each other, and subject the responses to multidimensional scaling to see whether the resultant orderings were more nearly unidimensional or multidimensional. One could also ask subjects to judge which one in every pair of samples seemed more like Creole, SE, or Spanish to see whether speakers identify these dimensions as readily as linguists do, and which features are most salient in the identification.

Although multidimensional approaches have scarcely begun to be used in creole-speaking communities, present indications are that they may not represent as fundamental a challenge to the notion of the creole continuum as critics have suggested. They clearly represent a challenge to traditional bilingual approaches, may be decomposable into combinations of two, three, or four unidimensional continua, and on theoretical as well as empirical grounds, may be open to reinterpretation in terms of a smaller number of dimensions or even one dimension. The recent work of Le Page and Tabouret-Keller (1985) represents a significant advance in the use of multidimensional approaches to the analysis of anglophone Caribbean data, but considerable room remains for the reconsideration of unidimensional alternatives along the lines sketched in the preceding paragraph.

Social and Stylistic Considerations

The final synchronic issue to be considered in relation to the continuum model is the extent to which it takes into account the social and stylistic dimensions of linguistic variation in continuum communities. Some continuum analysts are criticized for concentrating primarily on internal linguistic constraints (the implicational relations between different environments of an innovating feature, for instance), and downgrading or ignoring the sociopsychological context. Commenting on Bickerton's approach to the description of the GC continuum, Le Page (1978: 6) notes that "a continuum of lects is described, but not how a speaker is motivated to move across the continuum." Similarly, W. Edwards (1984b: 3) has commented:

Where social factors are mentioned by continuumists, these factors are relegated to a subordinate role in the descriptive framework. (See the appendix to Bickerton 1975.) Continuumists are generally concerned with showing that the linguistic output of speakers can be analyzed in such a way that orderly patterns of diachronic change can be characterized and that synchronic patterns reflect these diachronic changes.

The key point to note about these criticisms is that they apply to the way the continuum model has been used by some researchers to date, not to the continuum model itself. As it turns out, some scholars who subscribe to the concept of a continuum—such as Bickerton (1973a, 1975), Day (1973), Washabaugh (1974), and Akers (1981)—treat social factors or forces as secondary or relatively unimportant in their linguistic analyses and explanations, whereas others—including J. Edwards (1970), Winford (1972), Nichols (1976), and Rickford (1979)—treat them as significant. The continuum is merely a conceptual/analytical tool, which forces one neither to attend to nor to neglect sociopsychological considerations. The "asocial" criticism may derive in part from the tendency of continuum scholars to work outward from linguistic patterns to the social characteristics of their speakers (DeCamp 1971b: 355; Bickerton 1971) rather than vice versa; but this is also true of noncontinuum scholars like Le Page (1980a). Whether social characteristics are considered first or last does not in itself reflect their importance in the analysis.

The other speaker-oriented issue to surface in discussions of the continuum is whether individual productive competence is restricted to a narrow range (as DeCamp 1971b suggests) or is broader, offering speakers a wide range of choices in performance (as Le Page 1980a implies). Notwithstanding Bickerton's (1975: 203) reminder that it is not the speakers themselves, but their outputs on particular occasions that are located on implicational scales, earlier continuum studies do tend to suggest a more limited individual productive competence than later ones do (as noted by Rickford 1979: 483; Escure 1981: 32). To some extent this is an empirical matter, but the empirical findings have theoretical consequences. A community in which every speaker is equally capable of producing every variety would hardly conform to the assumption of some continuum supporters that synchronic variability reflects the different stages that individuals have reached in moving from the basilect to the acrolect (see point 5 below). So far, evidence from sociolinguistic interviews, combined with evidence from formal sentence translation tasks, has revealed that the competence of individual Guyanese speakers is broader than we might have assumed; but there are also limits to this competence, which in some cases occur precisely where a decreolizing continuum model would have predicted (Rickford 1979: 475–500; 1987). Although the empirical investigation of this issue continues, current indications are that neither the extremely narrow nor the limitless conception of individual competence in creole continuum communities is justified.

The Life-Cycle Theory

In arguing that linguistic variation in Jamaica is synchronically continuous and unidimensional or linear (therefore amenable to implicational scaling), DeCamp (1971b) was addressing essential features of the continuum model. But DeCamp—and Bickerton after him—also made some diachronic assumptions that, though neither presupposed nor affected by the concept of a continuum, are frequently debated by continuum critics. Since the postulation of a creole continuum does not *require* us to speculate about its evolution, we might simply ignore these diachronic assumptions. But because they add to the theoretical interest of the continuum model and have generated so much controversy we will consider them in some detail.

The first such assumption is that creole continua evolve from originally bilingual situations in which only creole-like and standard-like varieties coexist.[16] Under this assumption, the continuum is a simple extension of Hall's (1966) "life-cycle" theory of the way in which creole languages evolve: *first* a pidgin comes into being (this is a lingua franca arising from interlingual contact and showing reduction and admixture relative to its "input" languages), *then* it evolves into a creole (an expanded version of the pidgin that develops with its use as native or primary language), *then* it evolves into a creole continuum (if and when the creole continues to coexist with its lexically related standard, and creole speakers have increased opportunity and motivation to modify their speech in the direction of the standard). On this view, intermediate varieties or mesolects are younger or more recent than either of the polar lects, representing a filling in of the linguistic space between creole and standard language that parallels the filling in of the social space between the lowest and highest castes of colonial society after Emancipation.[17]

Some support for this evolutionary life-cycle theory in the Guyanese case comes from Pinckard's texts (Chapter 3, below). These texts, from the end of the eighteenth century, depict an early acculturation or pidginlike variety, whereas McTurk's and Kirke's texts, nearly a century later, reveal a robust creole, existing in basilectal as well as mesolectal varieties.

Against this near life-cycle theory of the origin of the creole continuum, however, Alleyne (1971, 1980) has suggested that the full spectrum of continuum varieties along the Atlantic seaboard may have existed from the earliest days of African-European contact, given the differences in the extent and nature of such contact (African house slaves having closer contact than field slaves with English-speaking masters, for instance).[18] And some scholars who initially adopted the assumption that an early invariant basilectal creole predated the modern continuum have been won around to Alleyne's position. As Bickerton (1983b: 9) notes: "Alleyne was right in supposing that acrolectal and mesolectal varieties of creole had existed from the beginning, and DeCamp (and I in following him) wrong in supposing that creole continua were relatively recent inventions (*NB*: this fact does *not* affect *synchronic* analyses of continua)."[19] Insofar as the textual evidence in this volume sheds light on the matter, Alleyne's contention is supported. Texts from Bolingbroke (1807) and St. Clair (1834) show that basilectal and mesolectal features were in use among the slave and free colored population at approximately the same period as the pidginlike varieties attested in Pinckard (1806). (Again, see Chapter 3 below.)

Clearly the situation was more complex than DeCamp had suggested, and it was so right from the very beginnings of the Africans' presence in the New World. And as we will see in Chapter 2, it was more complex right from the beginning of African/European contact in the Old World too.

Interestingly enough, however, Alleyne himself (1980: 192) ends up with an interpretation of the Jamaican continuum that is remarkably similar to DeCamp's, recognizing "a gradual shading off from one end of this spectrum to another" in which "forms and structures which can plausibly be shown to have West African historical origins are progressively replaced by English-like forms and structures." One reason why the early existence of intermediate varieties does not materially affect the diachronic course of events postulated by DeCamp is the numerical predominance of the field slaves, for whom it remains valid to hypothesize (Alleyne 1980: 194) that their creole grammar "preserved a high degree of homogeneity," since they "were involved in societal relationships almost exclusively with themselves," and "there was no pressure or motivation to adopt speech behaviors typical of other groups." Alleyne (ibid.) assumes that decreolization for this group came about only after Emancipation and subsequent social reforms "brought the first opportunities for mobility and the first really strong pressures for speech modification toward the prestige norm." In his view:

This speech modification was not so much a mixing of creole forms with standard forms as it was: (1) the rejection of a number of features perceived as being of greatest deviancy from English, and (2) the general adoption by each sector of the population of some of the speech characteristics of the social group above it. This meant first of all a constant erosion of features like vowel final syllables, a genderless pronominal system, and nasalized vowels . . . until they became obsolete, residual, or extinct. Secondarily, it meant that the most deviant forms of speech would be represented by fewer and fewer persons, while the intermediate varieties, of highly restricted demographic importance during slavery, now become prominent. The extreme variability of contemporary Jamaican speech is the result of the disappearance of forms that constituted a relatively well-stratified and homogeneous dialect via disappearance of speakers who used these forms in a consistent way. There have been few phonological or syntactic innovations in the modern period; rather, there have been shifts in the frequency of intermediate forms and a great deal of variability.

The only significant difference between this account of the development of the continuum and the account of DeCamp (1971b) and Bickerton (1975) is that post-Emancipation decreolization is portrayed as an increase in the adoption of already existing intermediate varieties rather than their creation. Alleyne's portrayal, moreover, gives explicit recognition to two other issues that I have emphasized elsewhere (Rickford 1983b): that what is really at issue in decreolization is the differential competence of successive generations of *speakers*, not just the existence of basilectal or other lects, and that decreolization may involve *quantitative* as well as qualitative phases. In some continua, between some points in time, only quantitative decreolization is evident, and some variables may show no movement at all or even an apparent reversal.

There are two other reasons why the existence of early intermediate varieties does not completely invalidate the diachronic, developmental interpretation of the continuum proposed by DeCamp. The first is that even those Africans who had frequent contact with speakers of English (for instance, house slaves) must have acquired this new language gradually (rather than instantaneously),[20] and via an interlanguage continuum (Selinker 1972). Their initial interlanguage or basilang (Schumann and Stauble 1983) may have been comparable in at least some respects to the basilect of the field slaves who had less contact with English speakers, and their progression through subsequent intermediate varieties may have been structurally similar to the kind of process that the field slaves went through more gradually and at a later date. Given that field slaves had less exposure to and interaction with native English speakers than house slaves did, the structural stages by which these groups acquired English probably differed in some respects. But we cannot assume *a priori* that such differences were significant, and to the extent that they were not, a conception of the continuum as having been produced by processes resembling decreolization would remain tenable.[21]

The other reason centers on the issue of what I have elsewhere (1979: 411–13) distinguished as "monogenetic" and "polygenetic" models of decreolization. Implicit in all discussions to date is the assumption that the only appropriate model is a monogenetic one, in which the varieties intermediate between the creole basilect and the standard acrolect are created at one point in time—the point at which the first slaves or immigrants with sufficient opportunity and motivation extended their competence from basilect to acrolect via an interlanguage continuum. In this model, once the continuum has been delimited in this way, subsequent speakers decreolize by adopting the available intermediate varieties in a relatively passive fashion rather than by actively creating them anew as they in turn reach out toward the acrolect.[22]

Alleyne (1980), DeCamp (1971b), and Bickerton (1975) all appear to agree in postulating a monogenetic model of decreolization, the primary difference between them being that Alleyne dates the existence of the continuum from an earlier period. I have suggested, however (Rickford 1979: 412), that a "polygenetic" view of decreolization is also possible:

In this view, the restructurings which produced the continuum in the past would be seen as actively continuing in the present. In decreolizing, speakers of the present generations would be seen not merely as the passive recipients of intermediate varieties marked out by their predecessors, but as active reshapers and restructurers themselves, affected by the same kinds of extralinguistic factors which operated in the past.

The issue is whether in going from basilectal starting point to acrolectal target, a speaker *adopts* already existing intermediate varieties (monogenetic) or essentially *creates* them anew (polygenetic). The fact that the intermediate varieties of successive generations appear to be basically similar does not require the monogenetic view, since recent research indicates that people acquiring English as a second language, independently of each other and without exposure to preexisting intermediate varieties, nevertheless tend to acquire forms and structures in a regular order (Duley, Burt, and Krashen 1982: 229). When their first-language starting points are similar, as they would be for successive generations of basilectal creole speakers embarking on the acquisition of varieties closer to the standard, even greater similarities in their interlanguage routes might be expected. These considerations heighten the plausibility of the "polygenetic" model of decreolization and reduce the significance of the question of *when* intermediate continuum varieties first came into being.

Variation and Change

The second diachronic assumption made by some continuum scholars— for instance, Bickerton (1975: 16–17)—is that linguistic variation in continuum communities always reflects ongoing change, and that such change is invariably unilinear, that is, in the direction of the standard language. Critics of this assumption do not always address the change issue itself, but are concerned rather with the negative orientation toward the creole and the positive orientation toward the standard that it seems to imply. Haynes (1973: 1), for instance, indicts the continuum as "an abstract construct which places people in the Caribbean on their hillsides, rolling the stones of phonological, syntactic and lexical mastery to a European summit, getting there, but never quite."

The impression that Caribbean populations have nothing but loathing for their native creole and nothing but longing for the Queen's English is certainly a mistaken one, as several recent studies have made clear. One finds creole varieties proudly embraced as a symbol of local identity or national unity, or both (Le Page 1978); as a marker of working-class membership and opposition to the dominant social order (Rickford 1983a); as an expression of one's preference for rural over urban life-styles and values (W. Edwards 1983); and as an indicator of peer solidarity or informal style (Escure 1984a). With the achievement of political independence, the exodus of European expatriates, and the rise of nationalism over the past few decades, British and other European accents no longer command the respect they once did, at least not in the mouths of native Guyanese, Jamaicans, or Surinamese,[23] and younger Caribbean authors appear to be using more creole dialogue in their works (Haynes 1984). Other evidence of positive orientations toward local creole varieties comes from reports that the Dread Talk of the Rastafarians is increasing in popularity throughout the Caribbean (Pollard 1983), that Creole is being increasingly used in the Jamaican mass media (Alleyne 1980: 221–22), and that many Garifuna-speaking Black Caribs in Belize aim their second-language acquisition efforts at Creole rather than SE targets (Escure 1984a).

The argument that positive creole attitudes like these work against the continuum theory can be met in two ways. In the first place, negative attitudes toward the local creole are not usually expressed by continuum supporters themselves, but by local newspaper columnists, political leaders, and the professional elite (see Rickford and Traugott 1985 for examples). And in the second place, despite the many signs that creole varieties are vibrant and positively evaluated, it remains true that SE continues to command considerable respect among Caribbean populations. If it is wrong to assert that attitudes toward the creole are always negative and attitudes to the standard always positive, it is equally wrong to assert the opposite. The actual situation, as Reisman (1970) and others have emphasized, is more complex. Caribbean speakers engage in style-shifting both up and down the continuum in everyday life, and although some people may be trying to increase their mastery or use of creole varieties, others are trying to do the same with SE.

As for the relationship between variation and change proper, it is clear that variation is not always a reflection of change in progress, and that ongoing changes are not always in the direction of the acrolect. In creole continuum communities, as in others (Labov 1966), some of the linguistic variation is stable, perhaps representing the effects of changes begun some time ago, but since arrested or reversed (C.-J. Bailey 1973; Fasold 1973). But determining what has happened in a specific situation requires attending to reference points in real or apparent time (age distributions), a step often omitted by creolists on both sides of the continuum debate (Labov 1982: 39). The available evidence indicates that no single trend is evident for all continua or for all variables.

At the moment we have only one longitudinal real-time study, Le Page (1980b: 335–36), which draws on reinterviews with Belizean informants interviewed as children eight to 12 years earlier. In it, some of the conservative Creole speakers appeared to be using more SE now that they were older and upwardly mobile, and this of course accords with the predictions of DeCamp's decreolization model. But the fit is not perfect because others "who had settled down as agricultural labourers or forestry workers had changed far less," and "young people in Spanish areas [were] turning more to Creole." Although it is perhaps significant that Le Page reported no movement *away* from SE toward Creole, the Creole end of the spectrum remained vibrant, continuing to be occupied by the no-change speakers, and newly occupied by speakers who had formerly used more Spanish.

The turn-of-the-century basilectal GC texts from McTurk (1889) and Cruickshank (1905) also offer us some real-time depth. Following Mufwene's (1985) suggestion that we look for evidence of decreolization in comparisons of the current basilect with the basilect of earlier stages, we note that though several turn-of-the-century basilectal features are still current, some have been lost, including the initial voiced stop in nonpunctual *(d)a* and the use of *um* or *am* as a transitivizing or object-agreement marker. So far, no clear instances have turned up in which today's basilect is farther from the standard than the turn-of-the-century basilect, and the evidence is therefore consistent (or at least not inconsistent) with decreolization.

As for changes in apparent time (based on data from different age groups), virtually every possibility has been documented: no change between generations for vowel laxing in casual style in Cane Walk, Guyana (Rickford 1979: 246); change toward the acrolect in some morphological pronoun subcategories in the same community (ibid., p. 370) and in the use of pronominal forms in the South Carolina Sea Islands (Nichols 1983); and change toward the basilect in the use of the copula among the youngest generation in Placencia, Belize (Escure 1984b). Inferences about change in apparent time are not always reliable, and need to be qualified in relation to the social class and style of the informants whose speech is used as evidence, but the indications that we have are similar to those of Le Page's real-time data: variation is not always indicative of change, nor is change always away from the basilect toward the acrolect.

But the reverse (and currently more popular) assumption—that nothing is changing, or that everyone is discovering their roots and furiously destandardizing—is equally unsupported. Speaking for Guyana and the South Carolina Sea Islands, the cases I know best, I have encountered many cases of grandparents controlling basilectal features that their grandchildren do not control, but none in which parents control upper-mesolectal varieties while the children are *restricted*, in terms of competence, to the basilect. And in at least some of the cases reported above, in which the youngest generations are using more creole features in casual speech, this is a performance display; in terms of competence, the young people's repertoires are broader and include more of the standard language than those of their elders (Rickford 1979: 249). On this point, note Escure's (1984b: 8) comment: "Of course, stating that the younger generation shows greater allegiance to the creole does not imply that their ability to speak English is lesser. On the contrary, the lowest age group has the widest repertoire, the best control of all varieties ranging over the continuum." This suggests that decreolization—proceeding by the addition of more standard varieties to the repertoire without the simultaneous loss of more creole varieties (see Rickford 1983b)—may be occurring even where surface indications are to the contrary.

Conclusion

In sum, it is clear that considerable work remains to be done in the analysis of synchronic and diachronic aspects of the creole-continuum issue. The diachronic assumptions of the early continuum model are the ones most weakened by recent research, but the non-discrete character of creole–standard variation in communities such as Guyana, Jamaica, and Hawaii provides the fundamental rationale for their characterization as continua. The gradient creole–standard relation in such communities needs to be distinguished from the sharper creole–standard boundary in such communities as Haiti;[24] and also requires that mainstream methods of analysis be combined with variationist models. The suggestion in some of the recent literature that a simple co-systems model—with (random?) switching between discrete systems—might be adequate for Guyana and Jamaica strikes me as a step backward, and I believe existing quantitative and implicational studies of the continuous variation in these communities represent advances commensurate with their complexity that we should be reluctant to sacrifice.

Whether we need to move even farther away from the co-systems model, to the multidimensional model for which Le Page has become the primary advocate, remains to be determined. As suggested above, it is theoretically desirable to attempt to restate multidimensional analyses in unidimensional terms, and to the extent that this is possible in practice, without sacrificing accuracy, the unidimensional continuum model will remain useful.

In any case, debate about the best ways to conceptualize and analyze Guyanese, Jamaican, and similar speech communities will undoubtedly continue. The texts and analyses presented in this book, along with those in such other recent publications as Bickerton (1977c), Holm (1983), Lalla and D'Costa (1984), and Le Page and Tabouret-Keller (1985), will hopefully inform that debate and contribute to its resolution.

Fig. 2.1. Modern Guyana

Historical and
Sociolinguistic Developments

Guyana (officially, the Cooperative Republic of Guyana) has an area of 83,000 square miles and lies on the northeast shoulder of South America, surrounded by the Atlantic Ocean to the north, Suriname to the east, Brazil to the south, and Venezuela to the west (see Fig. 2.1). Its history as a former British colony has set it off from its Spanish- and Portuguese-speaking neighbors. Linguistically and culturally, it is closer to former British colonies in the Caribbean like Jamaica than it is to continental neighbors like Venezuela. In Guyana, as in Jamaica, the official language is English. In both countries, however, the everyday language of most people is not Standard English, but a spectrum of creolized varieties of English. Alleyne (1980), in an insightful comparative survey of these varieties in the Caribbean and West Africa, refers to them collectively as "Afro-American" to emphasize the West African linguistic influences on their formation.

In 1980 Guyana had an estimated population of 758,000 (Baber and Jeffrey 1986: 47). Most Guyanese live along the coast and in rural areas. Most of the 314,000 people living in urban areas in 1980 were concentrated in or near the capital city, Georgetown. East Indians, most of whom are descendants of indentured servants brought from India between 1838 and 1917, are the country's largest ethnic group, 50.2 percent in 1980. The rest of the population is largely composed of Africans and Colored or Mixed peoples (most partly African), who together accounted for 43.2 percent in 1980 (30.0 percent and 13.2 percent, respectively). The Africans are descendants of people imported as slaves (between 1650 and 1820) or as indentured immigrants after Emancipation and the end of apprenticeship in 1838. The remaining 6.6 percent of the population is composed of several smaller groups: Amerindians (4.6 percent), the descendants of various tribes who migrated to this area from 900 A.D. or earlier (see Rouse 1953; R. Smith 1962: 11); Portuguese (1.0 percent) and Chinese (0.6 percent), most of whose forebears came to Guyana as indentured immigrants in the nineteenth century; and Europeans (0.4 percent),[1] among whom the English represent the most direct links with Guyana's recent colonial past.

English planters and colonizers were invited into "the Guiana colonies" (Essequibo, Demerara, and Berbice) by the Dutch in the middle of the eighteenth century, primarily to help in the establishment of the colony of Demerara; the Dutch had been in Essequibo and Berbice from the early seventeenth century. But within a few decades the English had succeeded in wresting control of the area from their Dutch counterparts. The colonies of Essequibo, Demerara, and Berbice—named after the rivers around which they were established—were formally ceded to the British by the Dutch in 1814. They were united as a single colony, British Guiana, in 1831. The British remained in continuous control until 1966, when the country became independent and assumed its present name, Guyana.

In the following pages, I shall review the historical and social developments in some detail, concentrating on information that seems to have particular sociolinguistic significance.

The Seventeenth Century

Little is known about the history of the Guiana colonies before 1600, beyond the fact that Amerindians had established themselves there several centuries earlier. By the Papal Bull of 1493 and the Treaty of Tordesillas in 1494, the Spanish and the Portuguese had divided the New World between them, and at the end of the sixteenth century, both had thriving New World colonies and plantations using African slave labor in Cuba, Brazil, and elsewhere. But they were soon to have competitors, for by then other European nations had become interested in the New World, their appetite for exploration and colonization whetted by reports of its riches in silver and gold. Two of the earliest non-Iberians to reach the Guiana region and record their experiences were Sir Walter Raleigh, the English explorer, and A. Cabeliau, a Dutch supercargo or ship's clerk, both of whom sailed through the Caribbean and along the "Wild Coast" of northern South America in the 1590's in search of Manoa, El Dorado's mythical city of gold (Goslinga 1971: 56–57). By the first quarter of the seventeenth century the Dutch, the English, and the French had established trading posts and colonies in what are now the countries of Guyana, Suriname, and French Guiana.

The date of the earliest Dutch settlements in the Guiana colonies is uncertain. The Dutch West India Company (established in 1621) was operating in Essequibo sometime before 1627, and in that year authorized the establishment of a new colony in Berbice, promising to supply it with "as many blacks as possible" (Daly 1966: 39). Initially, the Dutch were primarily interested in trade with the Amerindians, but after the middle of the 1650's they turned increasingly to sugar cultivation supported by African slave labor. This transition may have been fueled in part by the arrival in Pomeroon and Berbice of the inhabitants of the Dutch colony in Brazil—many of them experienced planters—who had fled after the colony was recaptured by the Portuguese in 1654 (Oppenheim 1907: 97, 105; Goslinga 1971: 421; Devonish 1978: 6–7). This group included Portuguese Jews who wanted to avoid the religious persecution that had driven them away from the Iberian peninsula in the first place. The Zeeland Chamber of the Dutch West India Company (WIC) had also specifically invited Dutch emigration to the Essequibo region in the mid-1650's, and people from Middleburg, Vlissengen, and Veere responded favorably. The second half of the seventeenth century therefore saw the increasing establishment of a plantation economy based on slave labor in the Guiana colonies.

This development was aided by the fact that the Dutch had assumed control of most of the Portuguese slaving factories on the West African coast by the mid 1640's[2] and were actively involved in the slave trade. The Dutch entered the slave trade on a regular basis in the 1630's, when they captured parts of Brazil (including the town of Pernambuco, modern Recife) from the Portuguese, and the WIC undertook to supply the Dutch colonists there with African labor. After the Portuguese recaptured these territories, the WIC found new outlets in its plantation colonies in the West Indies and the Guianas and in the New World colonies of other European countries. Among its most important customers were the Spanish, who signed a formal contract with the WIC in 1662 for the supply of 2,000 African slaves annually, a figure later (1675) increased to 4,000 (Postma 1970: 14–21). Developing the island of Curaçao as a New World transshipment point,[3] the Dutch became, in the last decades of the seventeenth century, the leading slaving nation in the world.

As Postma (1970: 97, 181) notes, the volume of the WIC slave trade is particularly difficult to assess for the period before 1700, and determining exactly where the slaves came from is even more difficult. A trading ship's port of departure gives no indication of what part of the interior its slaves were drawn from; moreover, ships sometimes stopped to take on slaves at other coastal ports before heading for the open seas.[4] Nevertheless, drawing on records of slaving voyages and other archival data in the Netherlands, Postma (p. 181) has identified "the relative significance of coastal areas and specific slave export ports used extensively by Dutch traders," and the information is of value to us as we attempt to uncover the roots of Guyanese Creole.

In Postma's Appendix A, for instance (pp. 231–32), we find two recorded WIC slaving voyages to Essequibo in the seventeenth century, one by the ship *Tholen* in 1675, transporting 344 slaves from Cabo Verde (presumably Cape Verde itself and its surroundings on the Senegambian mainland), and another by the *Brandenburg* in 1699, transporting 450 slaves from Ouidah (Whydah) on the Slave Coast, in what is now Benin. (See Fig. 2.2.) Since we know of at least two earlier movements of slaves—one in 1626, when the Zeeland Chamber of the WIC agreed to provide a ship to transport Angolan slaves to its colonies on the Amazon and the Wild Coast, including the Guianas (Goslinga 1971: 342), and one in 1665, when the Dutch colonists in Pomeroon moved to Kykoveral in Essequibo and took some 1,200 slaves with them (Daly 1966: 45)—these shipments obviously do not represent the sources of all slaves brought to the Guiana colonies. But they do provide a concrete backdrop against which the approximate sources of the Dutch trade in the seventeenth and eighteenth centuries can be assessed, and the range of linguistic repertoires estimated.

The Cabo Verde shipment is probably atypical, both of the importation of slaves to Essequibo and of the Dutch slave trade as a whole; it is the only

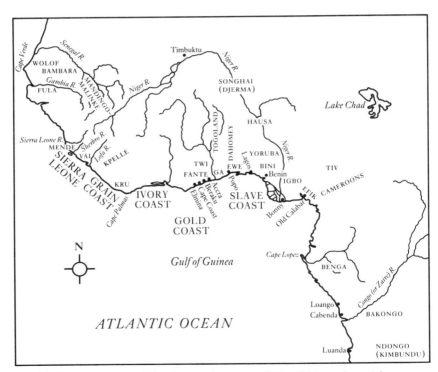

Fig. 2.2. Language map of the slave trade coasts of West Africa; adapted from Le Page (1960: 38–39).

shipment from this source among the 241 New World shipments Postma records for the years 1675–1737. Although a WIC document of 1679 refers to a lodge or factory at the Gambia River, Postma found no significant references to this area after that date and believes (1970: 220) that "the Dutch never acquired substantial numbers of slaves from either Senegambia or the Niger Delta region." [5]

The Ouidah shipment *is* typical, however, in that initially most of the Dutch slaves (two-thirds, according to Postma, p. 220) came from the Slave Coast. With respect to other sources, Postma has noted that the Dutch consistently acquired approximately one-third or less of their slaves from the Loango-Angola region, that they increased the supply of their slaves from the Gold Coast (modern Ghana) until this became the primary source of their slaves in the 1720's, and that after the breakup of the WIC monopoly in 1730, relatively few slaves were brought from the Slave Coast, and more (one-third of all those brought by the Dutch free-traders) from the Windward Coast (modern Liberia and the Ivory Coast).

Devonish (1978: 11–14), in an analysis of Postma's list of 16 Dutch slaving voyages to the Guiana colonies between 1675 and 1737,[6] observes that half were from the Gold Coast, undoubtedly including speakers of Twi, and three from the Slave Coast region, including speakers of Yoruba or Ewe. One of the ships, the *Duynvliet*, sailed from Angola, and Devonish speculates that the other three voyages made by this ship—their port of departure unspecified—may also have originated in the Angolan region. We cannot be entirely sure about this, for Postma's data show that the *Duynvliet* also sailed from Elmina and Appa in the same period. In any case, slaves from Angola, as Devonish (ibid.) notes, would probably have included speakers of the Lunda and Kongo groups of Bantu languages.

The Cabo Verdean slaves from the Senegambian area might have included speakers of Wolof, Fula, and Bambara. Since Postma documents only one voyage from this area, these languages may have played only a minimal role in the emerging linguistic mixtures on Guyanese plantations, though as the speech of slaves who arrived in the Guiana colonies more than 20 years before the next recorded WIC arrivals (1675 versus 1699) possibly a more influential role than we would expect. Robertson (personal communication), for example, has found a few Bambara items in modern Berbice Dutch Creole. On the other hand, it is well to keep in mind that there were already slaves of unknown origin in Essequibo and Berbice when these Cabo Verdean people came.

The linguistic influence of slaves from the Akan-speaking (Twi and Fante) Gold Coast region, documented by Cassidy and Le Page (1980) for Jamaica, appears to have been pervasive in the Guiana colonies as well, judging from the existence in modern Guyanese Creole of Twi-derived items like *kongkongsa* 'gossip' and the sentence complementizer *se*. Although Akan-speakers were less well represented in Jamaica's slave population than in Guyana's, their linguistic influence seems to have been equally strong in both places. This may be due in part to the relative linguistic homogeneity of the slaves from this region compared with slaves from other regions (Le Page 1960: 75–76), and in part to the fact that Twi served as a lingua franca in West Africa (Devonish 1978: 13, citing Heine 1970: 141–43).

In this respect, it is instructive to note an observation of Adriaan Van Berkel's. "Of the Negroes and Slaves" he saw on his travels in Berbice and Essequibo in the 1670's, he noted (1941: 133), "These are mostly brought from Guinea in Africa, and sold like dogs: [The Negro] is a mixture of all sorts of Nations, who are always living in contention and strife with one another." Van Berkel's opinions are not always reliable or fair-minded, but he appears to have been right about the heterogeneity of the slave population. Recent research on the origins of slaves brought to trial after the Berbice Slave Revolt of 1763 has revealed that they were a very diverse group (Ian Robertson personal communication, citing the work of Ineke Velzing). Contrary to what is frequently asserted, says Devonish (1978: 15), this heterogeneity "does not seem to have been the result of any deliberate policy on the part of the planters. . . . The mixing of Africans of different nationalities on the same plantations seem to be the result of the laws of supply and demand rather than some deliberate policy for preventing rebellion." Stewart (1974: 22) similarly denies that linguistic heterogeneity was an aim of the slave traders.

One last issue, and a much-debated one, must be considered before we move on to later developments. Did the slaves who arrived in the Guiana colonies in the seventeenth century speak a pidgin variety of some European language, as monogenetic theories of pidgin origin might lead us to expect? (See R. Thompson 1961; Taylor 1961; Stewart 1962; Whinnom 1965; DeCamp 1971a: 18–25; Todd 1974: 33–42.) A prime candidate would be Pidgin Portuguese, since Portuguese traders and settlers had been active on the Guinea Coast since the fifteenth century, and "for the 17th and 18th centuries, the existence of a Portuguese-based pidgin used in linguistic contact around the world is very securely documented" (Naro 1978: 315).

According to the monogenetic/relexification theory, this Portuguese pidgin was used by other European nations who entered the slave trade and may have undergone subsequent relexification:

When the French, Spanish, English, and Dutch entered into the trade, it is probable that this [Portuguese] pidgin served as their first language of wider communication, both with the Portuguese and with the West Africans. Subsequent relexification of the pidgin could have taken place both at the slave factories on the African Coast and, in some cases, later within the Caribbean itself. . . . These new French, Spanish, English, and Dutch pidgins were then used as the primary means of master-slave communication in the new plantation life in the Caribbean settlements, and were the immediate ancestors of the modern creoles (Stewart 1962: 47).

As we have seen, the Dutch took over many of the Portuguese lodges and strongholds on the Gold and Slave coasts in the 1640's, and (Pidgin) Portuguese might well have remained in the area, perhaps exploited by the Dutch and other European nations as a medium of trade. This much is suggested by the report of the seventeenth-century observer John Barbot that in 1679 the Portuguese lingua franca was still known "by the greater part of the population" at Axim on the Gold Coast, even though the Dutch had evicted the Portuguese 37 years earlier (Hancock 1969: 18).

However, in describing the life and trade on the Gold, Slave and Ivory coasts in the last decade of the seventeenth century, William Bosman (1814: 543) referred only once to a Portuguese/English lingua franca in use: "Here [at Buffoe] a Negro came on board, who called himself James and pretended to be Captain of Buffoe; he spoke a confused set of languages, being a mixed jargon of English and Portuguese." Much more frequent are his references to Africans who spoke only their native languages and with whom communication was either impossible or possible only through interpreters. On reaching the village of Sino, near Buffoe, he found that he "could not come at any farther information, for the Negroes speak such a barbarous language that they are not to be understood without difficulty" (Snoek addendum to Bosman 1814: 543). At Fort Vredenburgh (Komenda?) near Elmina, he had to rely on a Dutch soldier, who "called out to the Negroes from the breast work in their own language, telling them that he would present them with something to eat" (p. 351). Sometimes, when all else failed, gesture was resorted to: "I could not speak one word with one of them: my guide [an African from Corra], who should have been interpreter, was so ignorant of tongues that it was not without difficulty that I made him understand me with words and signs" (p. 541).

Since Bosman was the Chief Factor of the WIC on the Guinea Coast (Port of Guinea) at this time and was reporting on conditions in the lodges and ports from which the Dutch slave ships were sailing to the Guiana colonies,* these remarks must be considered particularly significant. In making no mention of a Dutch lingua franca in use on the West African coast[7] and minimizing the role of a Portuguese or any other European-based lingua franca in use among the Africans, they strongly suggest that most of the slaves knew only African languages when they set sail for the Americas. In this they agree both with what Hancock says with respect to Suriname and

---

*Seven of the WIC voyages to Essequibo and Berbice between 1700 and 1737 documented by Postma (1970) departed from Elmina, the lodge at which Bosman himself was principally stationed.

with what Alleyne has concluded more generally. In Suriname, Hancock concludes (n.d.*a*: 14), "speakers familiar with Guinea Coast Creole English were outnumbered by those who spoke only African languages." And Alleyne (1971: 179) finds the evidence very strong "that the majority of slaves in the English and French factories, on ships, and on plantations early in their existence, were speakers of African languages only."

Of course, Bosman's account of life in the WIC trading areas, although highly relevant, is only one source, and a definitive statement about the linguistic competence of these seventeenth-century slaves must await further research using documents in the Dutch archives and elsewhere.[8] In the meantime, however, we can go beyond Bosman and infer from a combination of known facts and sociolinguistic/language-learning principles that even if a Portuguese-, Dutch-, or English-based lingua franca was used in the areas in which the Dutch traded, it was unlikely to have been known by any significant number of exported slaves.[9] In those cases in which the existence of Portuguese pidgin speakers in West Africa is documented, they are invariably either Portuguese seamen, traders, or settlers (*lançados*), or Africans linked to them as castle slaves, hired hands (*grumettoes*), or middlemen (see W. Rodney 1970: 74–94, 200–222).* Thus, for example, the mulattoes who served as independent traders or as liaisons between Africans and Europeans were sometimes referred to by the Dutch as Portuguese because "this was frequently their origin and because they helped to perpetuate Portuguese as the commercial lingua franca of the West African coast" (Postma 1970: 48). Moreover, these middlemen were proud of this designation and cultivated their cultural resemblance to the Portuguese:

Most mulattoes clung to certain peculiarities of language, dress and religion to identify themselves outwardly as a community with a different heritage and a different social purpose from the mass of the Africans. The language was "Creole Portuguese," which was useful both as a link with the Portuguese patrimony and because of its function in matters of trade. The Afro-Portuguese acted as interpreters, and carried out all the tasks of middlemen in coastal trade, from acting as pilots on the rivers to serving as commercial advisers to the local ruling class (W. Rodney 1970: 203).

In general, Africans employed by or trading with the Europeans were the primary (if not the only) ones who would have had sufficient opportunity and motivation to acquire some form of European language in the Old

* According to Rodney (pp. 266–67), "In the forts and factories of the Royal African Company, a distinction was made between 'sale slaves' and 'castle slaves' (or 'factory slaves'). Both were acquired in the same way, but while the former were destined to face the Middle Passage, the latter were permanently retained around the forts and factories to help in the conduct of trade."

World. And they were the primary ones to whom Naro's (1978: 334) speculation that "given the socioeconomic force of the colonists and traders, Africans tried to learn the reconnaissance language [i.e. pidginized or destruc-
tured Portuguese]," might have applied.

Among the masses of slaves who did not enjoy these "privileged" relationships with the Portuguese—the "sale slaves" who remained victims
rather than facilitators of the slave trade, those who arrived at the African
seaports still suffering from the trauma of their capture or sale, those who
survived death and disease in putrid "dungeons" while awaiting transshipment, and those who survived the ordeals of the arduous middle passage—few are likely to have had either the opportunity or the motivation to
acquire a Portuguese lingua franca.

Goodman, in a detailed study of the Portuguese element in the American
creoles (forthcoming), has independently reached a similar conclusion, although we differ in our emphasis. For Goodman, three facts support this
view: that slaves came from the hinterland rather than the coastal areas in
which Pidgin Portuguese was known; that African languages rather than
Pidgin Portuguese would have been used for African interethnic communication; and that limited contact with Europeans while awaiting transshipment or on shipboard would have given slaves little opportunity to acquire
Pidgin Portuguese. I agree with him on the importance of these factors. It is
difficult to see how a significant proportion of a contingent of three hundred
or four hundred manacled slaves could successfully acquire the lingua franca
of guards and sailors who were physically separated from them most of the
time by dungeon walls or ship decks. But I wish to focus attention as well on
the sale slaves' likely preoccupation with physical survival and especially
their emotional tenor and abhorrence of their enslavers.* After all, consider
who the speakers of the Portuguese lingua franca were from the sale slaves'
point of view: the European officials who were branding, examining, and
manhandling them, the African kings and middlemen who were trading in
them, and the grumettoes and castle slaves who were helping to ensure that
they did not escape. Accounts of slave-trading on the West African coast
uniformly agree that the relationship between the sale slaves and the castle
slaves/free Africans (not to mention the Europeans) was brutally negative.
The following quote from Postma (1970: 210) is part of a longer section
(pp. 200–210) that is most revealing on this issue:

The chances for a slave to escape from a ship were very small, for even if he managed
to get ashore, he would most likely *be enslaved again by the free Africans*. In the case of
the *Neptunis* slave revolt, *some eighty Negroes were helping with their canoes to recapture*

---

*As Mervyn Alleyne (personal communication) reminds us, and as the extract on p. 55
documents, many slaves thought that they were going to be eaten.

the slaves, and all eight surviving slaves were returned to the captain of the ship. The same was true with the *Agatha* mutiny. Here *both free Negroes and Castle Slaves helped to recapture slaves* who tried to get ashore and escape enslavement. [Emphasis added.]

That significant numbers of these sale slaves would have been learning varieties of any European-based lingua francas in use among sailors and traders and their satellites is, to say the least, unlikely, particularly since physical, social, and psychological distance from speakers of a target language is generally considered to result in minimal acquisition of it by speakers of other languages (Schumann 1978; Andersen 1981: 192). Physical separation and psychological aversion of the type that must have characterized relations between enslavers and enslaved on the West African coast would have impeded acquisition even more decisively.

All things considered, it seems most likely that the vast majority of the slaves who were transported to Essequibo and Berbice in the seventeenth and eighteenth centuries began to acquire a Dutch-based lingua franca in the New World, as part of their gradual acculturation to life and work on the plantation, and with the help of the seasoned slaves in residence who had walked that road before them. Documentation from this earliest period is difficult to come by, but the plausibility of the preceding scenario is increased by late-eighteenth- and early-nineteenth-century references to distinctive varieties of "Creole Dutch" in use among both Africans and Amerindians in the Guiana colonies (Robertson 1974, 1981), but none to "Creole Portuguese," and to newly arrived slaves who had little or no knowledge of English, Dutch, or any other European language (see below). The recent discovery of two extant but quite *different* varieties of Dutch Creole in Berbice and Essequibo (Robertson and Jaganauth 1976) also reduces the possibility that they represent derived forms of a single European lingua franca imported by the slaves.

A number of questions still remain to be answered about the early linguistic situation in the Guiana colonies. If the first African slaves were outnumbered by Dutch colonizers, did they acquire a metropolitan variety of Dutch fairly successfully, with pidginlike restructuring only coming about as new waves of Africans poured in and acquired their Dutch from them in turn (Bickerton 1984b; Hancock 1986)? What was the social status and linguistic influence of the small number of Africans who may have arrived speaking a Portuguese, Dutch, or English pidgin? Did the fact that "they were African and they knew some form of the language of the European" lead them to become models for the others, as Hancock (1980: 32, n.15) suggests, or were their numbers too limited for them to make a significant impact on the developing linguistic situation? And if a monogenetic/relexification origin is rejected for Guyanese varieties of Creole Dutch, do their similarities to each other and to other New World creoles come from West African substratal influence (Baudet 1981) or creole universals (Bickerton 1981), or both?[10] The answers to these questions will eventually come from a combination of empirical research on the early settlement period in the Guiana colonies and theoretical debate about the respective merits of the universal and substratal explanations, both of which are being actively pursued (Muysken n.d.).

The Eighteenth and Early Nineteenth Centuries

By the end of the eighteenth century, the number of African slaves in the Guiana colonies had increased astronomically, but this was due less to the Dutch than to the English—English planters began to settle in Essequibo and Demerara in the 1740's, and English military forces were in control of the colonies after 1796.[11] As the eighteenth century wore on, the Dutch were increasingly unable or unwilling to meet the colonies' needs for "rations, slaves, and means of defence" (Harris and de Villiers 1911, 1: 48), and after relinquishing control temporarily to the French (in 1782) and the English (in 1781 and 1796),* they finally capitulated in the face of an English invasion in 1803 and ceded the colonies to England in 1814. The place to begin, therefore, is with the single most important linguistic development in this period—the influx of English colonists and their slaves.

In 1738 the Dutch administrative center had been moved from Kykoveral to Flag Island, concomitant with a general shift from upriver settlement to the coast and from trade to sugar cultivation. By the early 1740's English planters from Barbados, Antigua, and St. Kitts were responding to an earlier invitation from the Dutch authorities in the Netherlands to come and settle in Essequibo. As Laurence Storm Van's Gravesande, the commander of the colony, wrote in 1744:

The state of the Colony grows more flourishing daily; several mills are in course of construction and it is evident that the yield of sugar will become extraordinarily large. The English who have already established themselves here spare neither trouble, industry nor cost, and most of the planters here are beginning to follow their example. Several who intend to settle here are still expected, for the grounds in Barbados and Antigua are completely exhausted and expenses are much heavier there than here (Harris and de Villiers 1911, 1: 211).

*After occupying the Guiana colonies in 1782, the French began building present-day Georgetown (so named by the British). The linguistic influence of the two-year French occupation is most marked in place-names like Plaisance, La Bonne Intention, and La Retraite on some of the estates in Demerara, many of them close to the capital.

A little later on in his dispatches (ibid., p. 213), he mentions the arrival of "Messrs J. Gibbs, W. Caddel and J. Panter,"

three of the principal inhabitants of Barbados, bringing with them fifty slaves, six carpenters, six masons and everything necessary for plantations. They are already constructing water mills on their plantations and intend, on the arrival of slaveships, to reinforce each plantation to the number of 300 slaves; such exceptional growth will bring this Colony exceptional profit. These gentlemen are being followed by Lieutenant-General Baxter, Colonel West and Mr. Husband, who likewise intend to lay out plantations here; I expect them every day.

By 1745 all land grants at the mouth of the Essequibo River had been filled, and Gravesande, having been granted permission to expand to Demerara, encouraged his country's open-door policy, stimulating increasing settlement of this newest Guiana colony by English planters and their slaves. In a dispatch of 1753 (Harris and de Villiers 1911, 1: 289, 293), noting the arrival of Edward Simons from Nevis, who came from St. Eustatius with 72 slaves, he was moved to comment: "Applicants for land are arriving daily with their slaves." In the year 1762, according to a census he prepared, 34 of the 93 plantations in Demerara were English-owned, compared with just 8 of 79 in Essequibo.

The beginning of a rapid increase in the number of slaves in the colonies is also evident from Gravesande's censuses of the African slaves in 1762 and 1769 (Harris and de Villiers 1911, 2: 398–400). Over the seven-year period Essequibo's slave population climbed from 2,571 to 3,986, and Demerara's almost quadrupled, from 1,648 to 5,967. Since the Dutch had supplied very few slaves during this period (or much of it),[12] most of the newcomers must have been brought in by the English, either as part of the English settlers' original entourage or as illegal purchases from Suriname or English slave ships, to which there are several references in Gravesande's dispatches (ibid., 2: 595, 640).

By 1782 the African population of Demerara stood at 18,000, and assuming again that this increase was due mainly to slaves brought in by the English, the extent to which the English were beginning to displace the Dutch—politically as well as linguistically—can be appreciated. This is even more evident in the leaps and bounds with which the African population grew in Berbice after 1762. At that time, according to figures from Clementi (1937: 75–79), Berbice had 3,833 African slaves. By 1790 there were 5,862, by 1795 8,232, and by 1802 fully 17,885.

In the years of greatest growth in Berbice, 1796 to 1802, the English were in control of the colonies and were busily building new plantations and importing slaves, fortifying their numerical, economic, and linguistic dominance in the country, and indirectly helping to ensure that what would remain in widespread use in Guyana a century and a half later was a spectrum of Creole English varieties rather than Creole Dutch. As the English traveler Henry Bolingbroke (1807: 64) observed at the time, "A weekly paper is published here, entitled the Essequebo and Demerary Gazette. The proclamations of government are inserted both in the Dutch and in the English language. Some diverting mixtures of dialect occur in the advertisements: but the English language is steadily gaining ground, as the new settlers all bring that dialect."

In trying to characterize the language of the slaves at the end of the eighteenth century, we need to distinguish between (1) new arrivals from Africa, (2) those who came as part of the entourage of English planters from Barbados and other West Indian islands, and (3) those who had been resident on Dutch plantations in Essequibo, Demerara, and Berbice for some time.

Language of slaves newly arrived from Africa

Hancock (1986: 96) argues persuasively that "a range of creolized varieties of English became established in settlements along the Upper Guinea Coast which originated in the early seventeenth century in the family situations growing out of the unions between English speakers and Africans, and later between their children and the Africans who joined these communities." His additional claim—that this Creole "was being spoken in Sierra Leone (and the Gambia) prior to the arrival of the Jamaicans in 1800"—is also convincing. Less so is his belief that "there is sufficient historiographical and linguistic evidence to indicate that African slaves awaiting shipment to the western hemisphere had ample time to acquire some knowledge of Creole from the grumettoes who tended them, and that this continued to serve them as a lingua franca even after their arrival in the Americas."

Two considerations in particular lead me to have reservations about the possibility that any significant number of slaves came to the New World speaking or at least understanding a variety of Guinea Coast pidgin or Guinea Coast Creole English (GCCE) acquired while awaiting transshipment or on shipboard. For one thing, the relationship between the slaves and the GCCE speakers in West Africa (English settlers and their Afro-European and African slaves and employees) was probably as inimical to the acquisition of GCCE by the slaves in the eighteenth century as the relationship between sale slaves and enslavers or facilitators was in the earlier Portuguese case. The other thing that gives me pause is the existence of documentary evidence that newly arrived slaves knew no English (or Dutch) when they came. Consider, for instance, two letters written by Dr. George Pinckard, physician to the British forces of occupation, describing slave auctions he saw in 1796 and 1797, one English, one Dutch. With slaves depicted as urgently attempting to communicate with their prospective buyers by means of gesture and sign language, there is little to suggest that they knew anything but African languages at the time. In the first case, an English auction held in Stabroek (later Georgetown), Pinckard saw

friends, relatives, and companions, praying to be sold to the same master using signs to signify that they would be content with slavery, might they but toil together. . . . I observed two negroes, who were standing together entwined in each other's arms, watch him [the buyer] with great anxiety. Presently he approached them, and after making his examination affixed the mark only to one of them. The other, with a look of unerring expression, and, with an impulse of marked disappointment, cast his eyes up to the purchaser seeming to say—"and will you not have me, too?"—then jumped, and danced, and stamped with his feet, and made other signs to denote that he, also, was sound and strong, and worthy his choice" (Pinckard 1806, 2: 218–21).

The Dutch sale took place in Berbice, where one slave, asked

to exhibit the activity of his limbs, and to display his person, . . . sunk his chin upon his breast, and hung down his head in positive refusal—then, looking at the woman, made signs expressive of great distress. Next he pointed to her, and then to the chair, evidently intimating that he desired to have her placed by his side. . . . He looked again at the woman,—again pointed to the chair,—held up two fingers to the auctioneer, and implored the multitude in anxious suppliant gestures (ibid., pp. 328–29).

Given the urgency of their message, these slaves would surely have drawn on any fragments of English or Dutch or Portuguese pidgin they knew in order to communicate with their prospective European buyers; there is no indication that they knew any such contact varieties whatsoever.

Pointing in the same direction are the following passages in St. Clair (1834). Thomas St. Clair was on military duty in Berbice in 1806 when an American slave ship arrived in port, one of the last to enter the Guiana colonies before the Anti-Slave Trade Act came into effect that year. Although like other contemporary accounts, St. Clair's description of the slaves on board this ship (see also the following extract) is framed in derisive and racist terms, it is nevertheless of potential linguistic significance: "Upwards of two hundred and fifty were crowded on the deck: many of them smiled at me as I passed, and jabbered like monkeys with unpleasant voices and in unintelligible language" (St. Clair 1834, 1: 195). Since St. Clair was familiar with Portuguese as well as English, the fact that he found the slaves' speech "unintelligible" suggests that they were speaking neither a Portuguese nor an English pidgin. Unless many of them happened to be from the same ethnic group, however, they might have been using a West African lingua franca (like Hausa)—a possibility that has not received as much attention as it should in discussions of creole genesis. The other relevant extract from St. Clair's work is this one, in which he describes the way he and Captain Yates went about teaching English to two young boys (eleven or twelve years old) who had arrived on the same slave ship (ibid., p. 227):

Yates began with Nero. "Nero, the mustard." Poor Nero knew nothing more than the sound of his name, and stood, staring at his master with his mouth open. . . .

These two boys, from being our constant companions in boating, fishing and shooting, soon became strongly attached to us; and it was wonderful to see their readiness in finding out our wishes and the rapidity with which they learned our language.

To be fair, there is also evidence from a contemporary English observer that at least some slaves arrived on the Guiana coast knowing a degree of English:

I once witnessed a curious debate between two negro boys, in a sale room where the cargo of an African ship was landed. . . . I was induced to draw nearer to them, when the eldest of the two explained to me, by signs and broken English (which he had acquired in some factories on the coast of Africa, and from the sailors in the course of his passage), that the other boy was afraid he was going to be sold to white men to be eaten; . . . I soon eased the boy's mind by taking him into the yard, where there were some carpenters at work, and putting a hammer into his hand, made him to understand that he was to learn to build houses and work with the carpenters; at which, he began hammering and knocking away to shew his willingness, then ran to me and hugged me, pointed to my mouth and then to himself, at which I shook my head with abhorrence (Bolingbroke 1807: 212–13).

Note, however, that the competence in "broken English" reported is minimal (particularly in the case of the younger boy), and that it is heavily supplemented by gestures, suggesting that both boys had a considerable way to go in the colony itself before they could be said to have command of the lingua franca. Furthermore, even if we were to accept this passage (and the other from Bolingbroke quoted in Chapter 3, below) as indicating that something akin to Hancock's GCCE was brought into the early plantations, it seems likely, from all the other arguments we have considered so far, and from the fact that Africans arriving elsewhere in the Americas in the seventeenth–nineteenth centuries were reported to know no English (Bridenbaugh and Bridenbaugh 1972: 352; Littlefield 1981: 117), that this was the exception rather than the norm.[13]

As for the areas of West Africa from which the slaves would have been drawn, we get a hint from the figures presented in Table 2.1. Given the nature of the slave-trade system, and the effect of the tribal wars and animosities that had been taking place simultaneously, we have to be cautious once again about the linguistic interpretation of such point-of-departure data (Robertson, personal communication). However, the figures do indicate quite clearly that the slaves brought into the Guiana colonies by the British differed substantially in their origin from those shipped from Africa by the British in the early 1800's. Most of those arriving in the Guianas (almost 70 percent) were from the Gold Coast and the Windward Coast, regions

TABLE 2.1

Origin of Slaves Brought into the Guiana Colonies Under British
Rule, and of All British Exports from Africa, Early 1800's

Place of origin	Slaves imported to Guianas, 1803–7	All British-exports, 1801–7
Windward Coast	31.7%	4.2%
Gold Coast	37.8	8.3
Bight of Benin	—	2.0
Bight of Biafra	8.6	41.5
Central Africa	11.1	40.1
Other or unknown	10.8	3.9
TOTAL	100.0%	100.0%

SOURCE: Herskovits (1958: 49), cited in Curtin (1969: 155).

that together supplied only 12.5 percent of the exports. In terms of origin, then, these new arrivals were similar to those brought in earlier by the Dutch, as described above.

Language of slaves arriving from the British West Indies

The slaves who came in from English plantations in Barbados and other West Indian islands, assuming they had been there for some time, would have spoken some variety of English when they came.[14] There is some debate about how nonstandard it would have been: Hancock (1980: 22) claims that "it was a local metropolitan, rather than creolized, variety of English that was spoken by both blacks and whites" in Barbados, but Cassidy (1980) claims that "present-day Barbadian popular English preserves what can hardly be explained otherwise than as a creole residue." Their positions can be reconciled by suggesting that while relatively good opportunities for black/white contact in the seventeenth century might have led to the acquisition by Africans of metropolitan (often dialectal) varieties of English spoken by whites, more radical restructuring and African substratal influence must have been evident in Barbadian speech by the end of the eighteenth century, when the proportion of blacks to whites had increased almost geometrically (Niles 1980: 151ff; Hancock 1986: 95; Rickford 1986: 249–51). Eighteenth- and nineteenth-century archival evidence in Morrow (1984) reveals that Barbadian English was certainly more distinctively Creole than it is now, containing, for instance, several of the well-known basilectal tense-aspect markers (anterior *bin*, nonpunctual *da*, and so on). And the earliest samples of English in the Guianas, found in Bolingbroke, Pinckard, and St. Clair (see Text sets 1–3 in Chapter 3), show features that are commonly associated with pidgins and creoles rather than metropolitan English. Either Barbados did not have as much influence on the development of English-based Creole varieties in Guyana as scholars have suggested (Cruickshank 1916; Hancock, n.d.*a*), or it did, and Barbadian English was more creolized than some scholars have suggested.

Language of slaves on Dutch plantations in the Guianas

The slaves on the Dutch plantations in the Guiana colonies, which were primarily in upriver, interior regions, would still have been speaking a Dutch creole at the end of the eighteenth century. However, Bolingbroke's (1807: 49) reference to mixtures of "broken English and Dutch" indicates a process of adjustment to the growing English presence. At the same time, the widespread use of Dutch Creole as late as the 1830's and 1850's, attested to in the following quotations, suggests that the direction of influence might not have been entirely one way, and that the adjustment was not all that rapid or complete:

The great and peculiar impediment to the dissemination of instruction in British Guiana is doubtless the prevalence of Dutch Language amongst the negroes on the plantation. It reigns amongst a considerable proportion of the population of Demerara and Berbice, and must continue for some years to retard the process of education even where schools exist (E. J La Trobe's 1838 report on education in British Guiana and Trinidad, cited in Robertson 1974: 12).

In European families, English is of course the general language of communication; not so among the coloured people and negroes who talk a mixture, one might almost say a real pidgin (Kauderwalsch) derived from almost all the idioms of Europe and Africa, the indigenous so-called "Creole Dutch": The Dutch language which was brought by the first owners of the colony constitutes its basis (Schomburgk 1847: 161, cited in Robertson 1974: 13).

The Nineteenth Century

The nineteenth-century developments of potential linguistic significance are best studied from the dividing line of true emancipation, 1838, when those technically freed in 1834 were allowed to leave the plantations. The years before 1838 were marked by a vast influx of African slaves, and those after 1838 by the immigration of huge numbers of indentured laborers, most of them from India.

1800–1838

After six years of rule the British returned the Guiana colonies to the Dutch in 1802. But they had too much invested by then to let them go; they reoccupied the colonies in the following year, and remained in control until the Dutch formally ceded them in 1814. The slave trade was ended in 1807, but as we have seen, not before the volume of African slaves reached dizzying heights. And plantation settlement and expansion kept pace, as Adamson (1972: 24) notes:

The British reconquest of Guyana in 1796 set off what was perhaps the most feverish decade of speculation and expansion in the country's history. . . . A flood of newcomers, looking for instant wealth, poured into the colony. Most were planters from the islands, and they brought their slaves with them. The result in Demerara was a demographic explosion, the population rising from 29,473 in 1795 to 39,232 in 1798. Slaves accounted for over 90 percent of the increase.

Earlier, we saw that the number of African slaves in Berbice doubled between 1796 and 1802, when the African population reached 17,885. By 1811 the figure had climbed to 25,169 (Clementi 1937: 80)—representing a threefold increase since 1796, and a nearly eightfold increase since 1764. Most of these new slaves were African-born. Between 1800 and 1802, Suriname and the Guiana colonies received two-thirds of all the African slaves carried to British colonies, and as late as 1823, almost half of the slaves in Essequibo and Demerara (34,462 of 74,418) were African-born instead of "creole" or locally born (R. Smith 1962: 28). This dramatic infusion of new blood after the colonies came under British control would of course have aided and accelerated the transition from a Dutch-based lingua franca to an English-based one.

After the abolition of the slave trade, the trend reversed. The number of slaves in the Guiana colonies in fact declined, as deaths began to exceed births and only a handful of new slaves were brought in from other colonies. According to Adamson (1972: 28, citing Farley 1956: 62), the slave population fell from 100,000 in 1812 to 82,824 in 1838 (the year in which the emancipated slaves were free to leave the estates). With all the personae having been introduced, and few new arrivals coming in, the stage was set in the early nineteenth century for the full development of an English-oriented plantation society and culture. As R. T. Smith (1962: 31) has suggested, this period saw "the consolidation of a remarkable social hierarchy in which things English and white were highly valued; things African and black were lowly valued." Not only was there a distinction between the whites at the top, the free-colored in the middle, and the African slaves at the bottom; there were also finer distinctions among the Africans:

One big distinction was between the Africans of recent importation and those who were either locally born (creole) or had become thoroughly integrated into their new environment. . . . Another distinction of major importance was between house-slaves and field-slaves. The former enjoyed much higher prestige within the plantation community and were the most assimilated to European ways of living and behaviour (R. Smith 1962: 28).

Some of these values and distinctions had been evolving in the plantation society for some time, witness this comment of Bolingbroke's (1807: 107), referring to the 1790's: "It is worthy of remark, that the old seasoned people look with a degree of scorn on the new negroes, because they cannot 'talk buckra' [talk like a white person], and are not so clever and so active as they are, or so familiarized with the customs and manners of their white masters."* Note again the suggestion that acculturation to the language and customs of the whites took place on a significant scale only after the Africans began life on the colonial plantation and had the models of the "higher-status" locally born, creole-speaking slaves around them. The larger linguistic significance of these developments and attitudes is that different processes must have been going on simultaneously: besides pidginization and creolization and the diffusion of already pidginized and creolized varieties, pressures for decreolization and standardization must have been present as creole slaves and the free-colored sought to increase their familiarity with the customs and manners of their white masters.[15]

But that was among people at the top of or above the slave hierarchy. Few of those at the very bottom are likely to have had either the opportunity or the motivation to acquire more standard varieties of English until some years after full emancipation. Indeed, some of the slaves, perhaps many, no doubt deliberately cultivated the use of basilectal Creole and resisted adopting varieties closer to English as a symbol of nonaccommodation to their oppressors and of their own solidarity with others of the oppressed.[16] The Berbice Slave Rebellion of 1763 and the Demerara Insurrection of 1823 were only two of many indications that the sociocultural order of the plantation was by no means universally or willingly accepted.[17]

1838 and after

After the end of "apprenticeship" in 1838, droves of former slaves left the plantations and established small peasant villages of their own (Farley 1954). A significant number continued to work on the estates (Devonish 1978: 26–27), but the planters needed masses of resident, fully coercible laborers and turned to indentured immigrants—chiefly from India—to fill the gap. Contract immigrants were also brought in to work the plantations of Ja-

*The situation was probably not as clear-cut as either Smith or Bolingbroke suggests, however, since African traits and competencies would have been highly valued in some areas—the conduct of postnatal, prenuptial, and funeral rites, for example—as they still are in many parts of Guyana today. It is probably more accurate to assume with Reisman (1970) that there was ambiguity about the evaluation of symbols and institutions of both English and African origin. English values probably held sway in domains directly controlled by the ruling classes (jobs, schools, the courts), while African and Creole values probably came into their own in non-official settings and on private occasions where the masses had greater jurisdiction (homes, peer-group events). See Rickford (1983a), and Rickford and Traugott (1985).

maica, Trinidad, and Suriname after emancipation. Table 2.2 shows the primary groups for British Guiana.

Africans were the smallest of these groups of contract immigrants, but they are a fascinating group for two reasons: (1) we have some documentation on the process by which they acquired the Creole English of the time, and (2) they are undoubtedly responsible for some of the Africanisms that survive in Guyana and parts of the Caribbean today (see M. Smith 1965; Mintz and Price 1976; Trotman 1976; Schuler 1980: 9). Most of the immigrant Africans came early in the contract-labor period, 1838 to 1865. Although more came to British Guiana than to Jamaica or Trinidad (which each received about 8,000), they have been studied less. Their principal port of departure was Sierra Leone, which served at the time as a refuge for slaves seized by the British navy in enforcement of the anti-slavery blockade imposed when the British slave trade was abolished in 1807.

As Schuler (1980) notes, many of the first indentured Africans migrating to the West Indies from Sierra Leone were well settled in "Liberated African" villages and came voluntarily in response to enticing but often misleading promises of high pay and a better life abroad. By the middle of the 1840's, however, the migration had become far less voluntary, often involving orphaned children captured from slave ships who were attending school in Freetown. Between 1843 and 1845 alone, 244 liberated African schoolchildren were transported to Demerara and Berbice (Schuler 1980: Table 3, p. 114). After 1845 it was almost impossible to persuade the liberated Africans to emigrate. Subsequent African indentures were drawn almost entirely from British recaptives still in the Queen's Yard (the reception depot in Freetown), a group on whom the pressures to indenture themselves could be brought heavily to bear.

The 1848 Freetown census indicates that 83.9 percent of these recaptives came from the Bights of Benin and Biafra, with Yorubas constituting more than half of the entire group (Curtin 1969: 243–64 and Table 7). Although Curtin believes these figures might underrepresent the recaptives from nearby areas of Sierra Leone and the region south of Cape Lopez (including

TABLE 2.2
Contract Immigrants to British Guiana by Place of Origin, 1835–1917

Place of origin	Number	Place of origin	Number
India	239,149	China	14,189
West Indies	40,783	Africa	13,355
Madeira, Azores, Cape Verde	31,668	TOTAL	339,144

SOURCES: R. Smith (1962: Table 3); Nath (1970: 219–20).

the Congo), they are probably correct in indicating a substantial Yoruba constituency. Warner-Lewis (1982) found a fairly significant degree of knowledge (although not active use) of Yoruba in Trinidad among the grandchildren of nineteenth-century African immigrants, and Cruickshank (1916: 13–16) identifies Yoruba as the language spoken by an Ondu woman and an Oku man who arrived in British Guiana in the 1840's. In some Afro-Guyanese villages in Berbice, distinctive Oku and Kongo traditions (wedding and funeral rites, for instance) are still followed, and the older people recall tribal histories and local settlement patterns (Robertson, personal communication). There is much scope here for additional research.

Warner-Lewis (1982) and Cruickshank (1916) both provide insights into the linguistic adjustment of African immigrants to creole society that may apply to other ethnic groups who immigrated in the nineteenth century, and to the African slaves who had preceded them in the seventeenth and eighteenth centuries as well. Warner-Lewis (pp. 72–90) movingly enumerates the factors that limited the immigrants' transmission of Yoruba to succeeding generations of "African Creoles" (Yorubas born in the New World); notably, floggings by masters if they used their native language; their fear that their locally born children might betray them if they taught them the ancestral language; and deprecatory attitudes toward the Yoruba language among these creole and European-oriented offspring, some of whom referred to it as "hog," "pig" and "coarse." And just as Yoruba and the other ancestral languages were left to fall into disuse, so Creole English and the other creolized languages of the New World were being learned. Cruickshank's (1916: 14–16) interviews with early-twentieth-century survivors in British Guiana shed some light on this process:

A Demerara planter said they had to teach the Negroes not only how to work but how to talk. I asked an old African once, did he know any English when he came to Demerara?

"Engreesh! Whi'side me go l'arn um?"

"You know no English at all when you come to Bakra country?"

"'T all 't all!"

"Who teach you when you come?"

"Who l'arn me? Eh-eh! No me matty!"

.   .   .

"What fashion you learn?"

"Da Uncle me a lib wit' he se'f l'arn me. Uncle a say, 'Bwoy, tekky this crabash (calabash)'—de crabash dey a he hand—'go dip watah. *Watah—watah* da t'ing inside da barrel O.' So Uncle do, sotay me a ketch wan-wan Engreesh."

"So all of you catch Bakra talk, little by little?"

"Ah! Same thing! Matty a l'arn matty, matty a l'arn matty. You no see da fashion pickny a l'arn fo' talk—when he papa a talk he a watch he papa mout'? Be'y well."

The dialogue may be glossed as follows:

> "English! Where would I have learned it?"
> "You knew no English at all when you came to the white man's country?"
> "None at all!"
> "Who taught you when you came?"
> "Who taught me? Why, my fellow slaves, of course!"
>
> .   .   .
>
> "How?"
> "The old man I was living with—he taught me himself. He would say, 'Boy, take this calabash'—the calabash was in his hand—'and go and fetch some water. Water—that's the thing inside the barrel.' That's how he taught me, helping me to pick up English a little at a time."
> "That's how all of you picked up the white man's tongue—a little at a time?"
> "Ah! That's it! We each taught the other; each taught the other. Haven't you ever seen the way a child learns to talk—when his father talks he watches his father's mouth? Very well—just like that."

One of the many noteworthy features of this extract is the immigrant's explicit statement that he knew no English when he came.[18] This agrees with the bulk of the evidence presented above on newly arrived slaves in the seventeenth and eighteenth centuries, and is also corroborated by the following remarks of G. William Des Voeux (1903: 91), a Demerara magistrate in the years 1865–70:

> At nearly every court there was required interpretation for two or three Indian languages and one or more varieties of Chinese; while barely a week passed without cases in which witnesses or "parties" spoke only Portuguese or *some dialect of savage Africa. In the latter case to get anything beyond the vaguest idea of what was said was sometimes, even with the employment of the utmost patience, impossible.* (Emphasis added.)

Given the fact that Des Voeux was referring to a period more than half a century after the abolition of the slave trade, the Africans he refers to were undoubtedly newly arrived indentured immigrants rather than former slaves.

About the linguistic and cultural adjustment of the other immigrant groups—with the exception of the (East) Indians—we have little information. The West Indians, who came primarily from Barbados, probably spoke a creolized or dialectal variety of English and found much that was already familiar to them. We do not know whether the Portuguese who came from Madeira, the Cape Verde Islands, and the Azores arrived with a knowledge of any variety of pidgin or creole,[19] no more than we know what went on in the case of the immigrant Chinese, but Mother's imitation of a Madeira Portuguese woman at Bartica in modern times (see Text 24b in Chapter 5) suggests that the Portuguese acquired local varieties of Creole English very well, with only a few distinctive characteristics of their own (the pronunciation of *ch* as *sh*, for instance, as in *shail*). Bronkhurst (1883: 220), writing only 40 years after Portuguese immigration to British Guiana had begun, observed that locally born Portuguese children "do not seem to care a jot about Madeira" and "do not seem to care for the language of their parents, and prefer rather to converse in English than in Portuguese." This is of course very similar to what happened among immigrant Africans (see above); in both cases, adaptation to the New World by the second generation involved a rejection of the language and culture that their parents had brought with them from the Old.

Neither the Portuguese nor the Chinese proved very successful as estate laborers, but they remained in the colony in other occupations, including commerce. The Portuguese, in particular, rapidly came to control the small shopkeeping business, and to be perceived as part of the colony's economic superstructure; their shops were the target of looting and burning by frustrated African and Indian workers in the "Angel Gabriel" Riots of 1856 (see Adamson 1972: 70ff).

The introduction of over 200,000 Indian indentured immigrants—most of whom were never repatriated (R. Smith 1962: 49)—was the event of greatest historical and potential linguistic significance in the post-Emancipation period. India rapidly became the mecca to which British planters in Mauritius and the West Indies now looked to fill their labor needs. According to Gambhir (1981: 5), the majority of these immigrants were East Indians "from the eastern regions of Uttar Pradesh (then the United Provinces) and the western regions of Bihar in India. They mainly spoke several Hindi and Bihari related dialects from contiguous areas that represented a linguistic continuum." (See Fig. 2.3.)

Gambhir provides a fascinating study of Guyanese Bhojpuri, locally referred to as "Hindi" or "Hindustani." This is a "koine which developed out of several related Hindi and Bihari dialects of India," but which is threatened with extinction now, because "the youngest generation (thirty-six and younger) is monolingual in Creole/English and can neither speak nor understand Guyanese Bohjpuri except for some lexicon of cultural content" (Gambhir 1981: 4, 6). But interesting as the Bhojpuri story is (see also Gambhir 1983), more significant for our purposes are questions about the extent to which the Indians acquired the existing Creole English vernacular when they arrived, the sociolinguistic mechanisms and motivations that facilitated or retarded this process, and the degree to which they influenced Creole English in the process.

There are references in nineteenth-century sources pointing to the difficulties of communicating with newly arrived Indians who spoke little or no English. For instance, Bronkhurst (1881: 50–51) speaks of the imperfect understanding that results from "the intervention of an interpreter, or the

Fig. 2.3. Language map of India and adjacent areas, showing Hindi, with its subgroups, and other major languages; adapted from Gambhir (1981: 206)

use of the English language which a coolie can so imperfectly pick up, and with such difficulty express his wants in." However, less than a decade later, Bronkhurst (1888: 56), could say:

From the intense desire evinced by the East Indian population as a whole for a knowledge of the English language to be able to converse in it, I hesitate not to say that, were it possible for immigration from India to come to an end or cease, that within the next twenty or twenty-five years all the East Indian languages will become things of the past, and English will be the only living spoken language of the Immigrants in the Colony.

At least one modern commentator (Bickerton 1970: 6–7, 1973a) has suggested that the Indians not only successfully acquired nineteenth-century

Afro-Guyanese Creole, but are also one of the best currently available sources on it.

How did the Indians' acculturation to the Creole language and culture take place? It is commonly asserted that the Indians gradually acquired the Creole English of the Africans with whom they worked on the sugar estates.* This is undoubtedly true in a general sense, but whether it represents the entire truth is a subject that requires further research; details about the sociolinguistic stages and forces in this process of language acquisition remain to be filled in. One factor that must have been important in the linguistic assimilation of the Indian immigrants, as it was for the African immigrants of the same period, was the emergence of Indian creoles, children born in the colony and acquiring the Creole English around them as a first language. As Bronkhurst (1888: 47) observes:

I have stated that a very large number of our East Indian population is composed of those whom we may call Hindo-Guyanians, having a claim to both countries; being in origin or descent Asiatics or Hindus, and in birth, training, and language Guyanians or "Creoles," whose native tongue is the English, which they speak freely and well, and in many instances much better than the natives of the colony of African descent.

However, waves of Indian-born immigrants, bringing their native languages with them, continued to come in until 1917, and their adjustment to and impact on the local linguistic situation have yet to be investigated. The extent to which the Indians as a group were responsible for any fresh pidginization of English (or of the existing Afro-Guyanese Creole) has not been conclusively determined. Bickerton (1975: 8) suggests that there was no significant repidginization of this sort; but the Creole English spoken by Indians in the late nineteenth and early twentieth centuries shows some evidence of linguistic transfer or interference (Weinreich 1953) from Indian languages, and of novel developments that might be regarded as pidginization, even if most of them did not have a widespread or long-lasting effect (Devonish 1978: 42).

Even assuming that the Indian immigrants essentially acquired Afro-Guyanese Creole English, the extent to which this was facilitated by a common identity with the Africans, or by a converse desire to compete more successfully with them (Gambhir 1981: 3), is not clear. The indentured immigrants certainly often shared the same kinds of oppression and suffering

---

*Bronkhurst (1881: 15) notes that "the newly imported coolies find it difficult for a time to make themselves understood, but they manage it somehow or other when they converse with black creole labourers on the different estates." He also observes (p. 53) that "all [the Indian immigrants] learn the creole patois or corrupted English, and seem fonder of talking it than their own beautiful and poetic language, the Tamil. In visiting, I have come upon some Indian families where the children could not speak their native languages, but only creole."

that their African predecessors had experienced as slaves. Indeed, it was ex-slaves themselves who described the treatment of the very first batches of indentured Indians in horrendous terms before a Commission of Enquiry in 1839. One of these witnesses was Rose, a laborer on plantation Vreed-en-Hoop, who testified: "They appeared to me as severely punished as my 'matties' were during apprenticeship; when flogged they were flogged with a cat, the same as was formerly in use; they brought all from the sickhouse together, and took them to the negro yard to be flogged; they were tied to a post" (quoted in Nath 1970: 15).

But common oppression was not necessarily sufficient to produce a common identity. African creoles at the turn of the twentieth century echoed their predecessors who had struggled to survive economically in the post-apprenticeship period in protesting the state-aided immigration of laborers, "identifying it as the phenomenon which reduced employment, lowered wages, and increased the cost of living through the incidence of taxation designed to meet the one-third of the immigration expenses borned by the colonial state. State assistance to indentured immigration was particularly galling because Creole taxpayers were subsidizing their own retrenchment" (W. Rodney 1981: 174–75). Planters and government officials in turn fomented and exploited the tensions between these groups to guarantee their own safety and profit (Adamson 1972: 157–58; W. Rodney 1981: 187–88). As J. E. Tinne testified before the West Indian Royal Commission in 1897, "The two peoples do not intermix. That is, of course, one of our great safeties in the colony when there has been any rioting. If the negroes were troublesome every coolie on the estate would stand by one. If the coolies attacked me, I could with confidence trust my negro friends for keeping me from injury" (quoted in W. Rodney 1981: 188).

The limited intermixing referred to here was probably aided by a division of labor among the races that saw African creoles employed almost exclusively in certain capacities, such as factory work (Mandle 1973: 63). Furthermore, each group was encouraged to share the planters' disparaging stereotypes of the other: the Indians as uncivilized "Sammy" who were being Christianized and civilized by the English, the Africans as "rascal neegah" who "been a starve" (would have starved) had not Indian immigrants come in to save the sugar industry and the colony (Bronkhurst 1888: 186, cited in W. Rodney 1981: 180).* At the same time, as W. Rodney

---

*A cartoon published in the local *Argosy* newspaper sometime between October 1895 and March 1896 (no. 947 in the *Argosy* Collection, National Archives, Georgetown), depicts an African woman with a hat and long, Western-style dress upbraiding a sari-attired East Indian woman for refusing to greet her before being greeted. The coolie woman says, "*You* no tell me 'marnin,' *me* no tell you 'marnin,'" to which the black lady responds: "Dem coolies is gettin' too upstarted. Befo' time, it was 'marnin missy'; now, dem want decent people to tell dem 'marnin.' Dat is de worst of cibilisationin' rubbish lika dem."

(1981: 179) notes, cultural interpenetration among the groups was clearly evident in the influence of African creole funerary customs on similar practices among the Indians; in the adoption of rice (originally an Indian staple) as a staple in the diet of African creoles and other groups by the 1890's; and in the fact that both groups "responded in like manner to certain aspects of the culture of the dominant Europeans: notably to the game of cricket and to the institution of the rum shop." There were thus centripetal as well as centrifugal processes at work in African creole/Indian immigrant relations.

In addition to the forces mentioned above, five other factors should be considered in studying the linguistic acculturation of the nineteenth-century Indian immigrant:

1. The distinction between those who were still indentured and those who were not. Devonish (1978: 43) suggests that the latter group, including Indians who had completed their periods of indenture, would have been primarily Creole English–speaking and would have served as a higher-status reference group for the indentured.

2. The indigenizing effect of the "creole" gang on the sugar estates in which young children of both races did "manuring and other light field tasks" (W. Rodney 1981: 178).

3. The role of the magistrates' courts, before which indentured servants were regularly hauled for putative infractions of the Immigration Ordinance, and in which they had "their first contacts with the society at large" (R. Smith 1962: 137).

4. The effects of Indians moving off the sugar estates after their indenture, sometimes into greater proximity and interaction with African creoles, sometimes not.[20]

5. The role that the existence of different Indian languages among the indentured immigrants played in increasing their need to acquire Creole English to communicate with each other, much as the existence of different African languages among newly arrived slaves had a century earlier. Compare Bronkhurst (1883: 229) on this point: "We may often find in the colony that Indian immigrants, not being able to understand the language of each other, adopt the English, which they soon pick up on the estates."

The linguistic acculturation of immigrant Indians is a topic on which much more research can and should be done. Many of their children and grandchildren (and some who came as immigrants themselves, no doubt) are alive today and can provide relevant oral history. Documentary evidence on the nineteenth century should be even more accessible than comparable evidence for earlier periods. Timely mining of both sets of resources should yield a rich set of information, not only on the Indians' linguistic acculturation, but by extension, on the acculturation of the other ethnic groups who preceded and accompanied them in time, and on the nature of language contact and change in general. Comparison with other New World areas that experienced indentured immigration (like Suriname, Trinidad and Tobago, and Jamaica) should also be fruitful.

A final question remains: what effect did this influx of Indians have on Guyanese Creole English? Gambhir (1981: 52–53) notes that Indic (i.e. Bhojpuri) influence today is most marked in the lexicon. These lexical items fall into two categories. The first comprises a relatively large set of items connected with religion, kinship, rice-planting, and food preparation but used primarily by Indo-Guyanese. Examples occur in Derek's and Irene's texts in Chapter 4; others are presented and discussed in Ramdat (1978), Rampaul (1978), and Fredericks (1978). The second, smaller set consists of items that, as Gambhir (1981: 52–53) notes, "have become a part of the general slang speech of all Creole speakers." Two of his examples are "cunuh munuh," which literally refers to 'a little baby' in Bhojpuri and is used locally to describe a man who is ignorant of or tolerant of his wife's extramarital affairs, and "doghla," which means 'of mixed parentage" in Bhojpuri and is used of ethnic mixtures (particularly Indo-African) in Guyana.

Phonologically, Gambhir (1981: 47–48) recognizes a possible Bhojpuri influence in several features of Creole pronunciation, for instance, the realization of English *v* as Creole *b* (*lib* 'live'), but concludes that it is difficult to establish, given the occurrence of similar features in Jamaica and other parts of the Caribbean that had fewer or no Indian immigrants. The occurrence of this particular feature in the *eighteenth*-century speech of African slaves (note the uses of *hab* and *ebery* in Text set 1, Chapter 3) also argues against an Indic source, although Bhojpuri may have provided some reinforcement for its retention in nineteenth-century Guyanese Creole.

Equally hard to establish is the case for Bhojpuri influence at the grammatical level, the one exception being the use of "ke" and other Bhojpuri postpositions in Creole English sentences. Gambhir's (1981: 51) example here is the abusive term "camar ke bai' 'son of a person of the low chamar caste' (lit., "camar of boy"), which occurs in a popular Indian "rhyming song." I have found other examples, such as "stove ke top" 'top of the stove', in Port Mourant, Corentyne. These were in the speech of Indo-Guyanese, however, and the feature appears to be restricted to members of that ethnic group and others in close contact with them.

Devonish (1978: 39–42) has suggested that at least two other features of nineteenth-century Indian Creole reveal Indic influence. One is the occurrence of object-verb word order. There are apparent examples of this in lines 198–99 of Text 8 in Chapter 3, but see the discussion of that text for an alternative analysis. The other is the use of what Devonish classifies as a transitive verb marker, but what could also be described as an object-agreement marker: the occurrence of *am* or *um* in postverbal position preceding a co-referential and fully specified noun-phrase object, as in *full um belly* (line

199, below). There is apparently no exact parallel in Indian Bhojpuri, but Devonish refers to work by Domingue (1971: 27) and Tiwari (1960: 161) indicating that Bhojpuri has other potentially relevant mechanisms for distinguishing transitive and intransitive verbs. In Chapter 3 I point out some of the differences between object agreement in Bhojpuri and nineteenth-century Indo-Guyanese Creole, drawing on Shukla (1981).

One interesting point about this transitivizing or object-agreement marker is that it also shows up in Guyanese Bhojpuri, as in this example from Gambhir (1981: 55): "larkhan hamar bari dal laik*am* kare" (these children my a lot lentils like), 'These children of mine like lentils a lot.'" Gambhir observes (ibid.) that the *am* suffix in this and similar cases "is redundant, but seems related to the Creole third-person pronominal accusative." He also notes that in Guyanese Bhojpuri combinations of verb + *am* are always part of a conjunct verb phrase consisting of a noun or adjective, the Creole verb + *am*, and the semantically general verb *kar* 'do,' and that a similar phenomenon has been reported for Trinidad Bhojpuri by Mohan (1978: 140). The relation of this feature in New World varieties of Bhojpuri to the use of conjunct verbs in Bihari languages in India is worth pursuing. Its use in the nineteenth-century Indian Creole English of Trinidad, as attested in the following example, is also noteworthy: "Gi *um* pitty mangy, me sabby do *um* all someting dis side" 'If you give me a little food, I can do all the work you want' (Collens 1888: 48, cited in Warner-Lewis 1982: 64). As with the use of possessive "ke," however, this feature does not appear to have spread significantly to other ethnic groups or to have become a general feature of Guyanese Creole English.

The Twentieth Century

With the closing of the doors to Indian laborers in 1917, immigration to British Guiana essentially ground to a halt.[21] The achievement of independence half a century later—in 1966—marked, if anything, a reversal of the earlier direction as British colonial administrators and bureaucrats took their leave. The transition to Republic status in 1970 and the nationalization of three-quarters of the productive sector between 1971 and 1976 (including British-owned sugar estates and North American bauxite plants) symbolically augmented the country's political and economic independence.[22]

When the British left, Guyanese took over in government and business administration. One linguistic/cultural effect of this development, noted in the Introduction, is the emergence of an endogenous norm of Standard English, in which British and North American accents in the mouths of the locally born are sources of derision rather than admiration. One reflection of this change is that when young Guyanese academics and professionals go to Britain or North America for further education, they do not attempt, as the older generation (over age fifty) did, to master and retain a foreign accent. It is also reflected in the government's financial support of the Dictionary of Caribbean English Usage project (Allsopp 1978: 185) and its encouragement of studies of Guyanese Creole English (Seymour 1978: 16) and Amerindian languages (W. Edwards 1977: iv).

At the same time there have been definite limits to this process of linguistic and cultural revaluation (see Baber and Jeffrey 1986: 46–47, 51).[23] Independence has produced no recreolization or hyper-creolization (Le Page 1980b: 341) at the national level, nor has it stimulated the experimental use of Creole as a medium of early education, as in Haiti. The only significant endorsement of nonstandard linguistic norms in the post-independence Caribbean occurs among the Rastafarian groups and their admirers (Pollard 1983); but in Guyana as elsewhere these represent a minority, often criticized by the respectable for their anti-establishment values, lifestyle, and "knotty dread" hair-styles.

Moreover, the vacuum left by the exodus of the British and North Americans has stimulated upward socioeconomic mobility and may have even accelerated the use of varieties closer to Standard English, at least among the middle-class sectors of the population fortunate enough to share substantially in the new benefits. But this is only part of a general process of educational, occupational, and social-class mobility in which the Guyanese people have been involved for the past century, and it is to this subject that we now turn.

Education

When the Reverend John Smith, the "Demerara Martyr," arrived in the colony as a missionary in 1817, he was explicitly enjoined by the governor from teaching the slaves to read (Wallbridge 1848: 22). But he could and did open a school for the free-colored (R. Smith 1962: 34); and by the middle of the nineteenth century a number of mission schools and Christian organizations were educating ex-slaves. The reports of stipendiary magistrates cited in Barrett (1848) indicate the tremendous interest in the education of their children among the African peasants of the time. The following extract from an 1848 report by John Macleod, stipendiary magistrate for Georgetown, is typical: "From the information I have received from different ministers of the gospel, I have every reason to believe that the attendance at places of worship, as well as at schools, is regular and satisfactory. Parents seem all desirous of affording to their children the advantages of education."

By 1876 education was compulsory at the elementary level, and although (East) Indians were at first hesitant to send their children (especially daughters) to school for religious and other reasons, and were encouraged in this by colonial officials (Daly 1967: 121), they became less so as time wore on. The expansion of education from 1876 to 1960 is shown in the tabulation below (adapted from Mandle 1973: Table 29, p. 96):

Category	1876	1920	1960
Enrollment	17,238	35,490	125,348
Average daily attendance	10,222	19,874	102,535
Enrollment as percent of the 0–14 age group	19.9%	37.2%	48.4%

Opportunities for secondary education also increased significantly in the twentieth century. It is now available free of charge (like primary education) in over 80 schools, although parents frequently voice concern about its quality, particularly as measured by the success of pupils at external examinations (London University and, more recently, the Caribbean Examinations Council). The country has a number of institutions of higher learning, including vocational, agricultural, and teacher-training schools, and since 1963, the University of Guyana, which supplements—and to some extent replaces—the traditional migration to overseas institutions for college education and professional training.

The effects of this general increase in educational opportunities have been manifold, but from our point of view its role in "the dissemination of the language and culture of 'civilization,' meaning in this context of England" (R. Smith 1962: 146), is of primary interest. Not all schools succeeded equally in providing adequate models of or instruction in Standard English usage (see Le Page 1968)—there were and still are urban/rural and other interschool differences in these respects—but increased education has generally resulted in increased stigmatization of Creole and increased pressure and opportunity for the acquisition of standard varieties (DeCamp 1971b: 351). This is shown very specifically in my (1979: 370, 403) data on 24 Cane Walk speakers; in both the laborer and non-laborer classes those who had no secondary education used more basilectal Creole pronominal variants than others of the same class. The results for the estate, or field-laborer, class are shown below (adapted from Rickford 1979: 369–70):

Age group	N	Mean educational level	Basilectal pronoun frequency	Total number of tokens
Over 55	3	Primary only	.78	1,381
18–55	6	Primary only	.78	2,595
Under 18	3	Secondary (3 yrs.)	.63	1,256

Education has thus provided part of the impetus for decreolization in Guyana (and other areas), manifesting itself primarily in the extension of speaker's repertoires at the upper-mesolectal levels, and in the diminishing frequency with which basilectal and lower-mesolectal varieties are spoken.[24] At the same time these figures show that secondary education and its linguistic correlates have spread only to the youngest generation of the estate class (that is, fieldworkers on the sugar estate). For the thousands of adults in sugar-estate areas and other rural areas who have no more than a primary education, we would expect a similar finding; there are virtually no systematic, country-wide data on this point at present.

Social class

The effect of increased education extended beyond decreolization. Education brought with it changes in values and increased opportunities for occupational and social mobility. As one writer noted at the beginning of the twentieth century, "The general effect of education is a desire to become clerks, office-boys and shopmen. Field work is beneath the notice of the rising generation of black and coloured; and even the creole East Indian follows suit" (Rodway 1912: 158–59, cited in W. Rodney 1981: 201). It was through the training and employment provided by churches and their schools, increasing from the nineteenth century onward, that many black and colored people passed through "the doorway from working-class to middle-class status" (W. Rodney 1981: 116), becoming local pastors, teachers, headmasters, and civil servants, and even going abroad to receive professional training as doctors and lawyers. Educational mobility and literacy in English at first came more slowly for Indians than Africans.[25] Although some Indians entered the professions early on (Nath 1970: 201–8), most made their way up the socioeconomic ladder in the beginning by steps that demanded and effected less immediate acculturation to English norms, such as promotion to the rank of driver or field foreman on a sugar estate, or success in "cattle-rearing, rural landlordship, retail shopkeeping, moneylending and commercial rice-farming" (W. Rodney 1981: 110). The income from these activities, however, was frequently invested in the schooling and professional training of children and grandchildren (R. Smith 1962: 51; Devonish 1978: 51), increasing their exposure to and adoption of European-oriented values and behaviors (Robinson 1970: 55). This process has continued to this day.

The study of social stratification in Guyana is still in its infancy, but a three-class model, based primarily on occupation (upper middle, lower middle, working), is commonly proposed (R. Smith 1962: 114–17; Robinson 1970: 58–59; Rickford 1979: 143).[26] The upper-middle class includes government ministers and department heads, managers, university professors, secondary-school headmasters, engineers, doctors, and magistrates—this nonexhaustive list shows those professions ranked highest in prestige by local respondents in Graham and Beckles (1968). Many of these positions were of course once held by the British and other Europeans. The working class includes sugar-estate laborers, truck and rice farmers, domestics, hucksters, and stevedores; and the intermediate lower middle class includes nonmanagerial insurance salesmen, bank clerks, junior civil servants, skilled machine operators, and owners of small groceries or shops (roughly, those in occupational blocks III–V in Graham and Beckles, Table 2, pp. 371–72). Not surprisingly, given the centrality of the sugar plantation in Guyanese socioeconomic history, this division parallels to a considerable extent the traditional sugar-estate division between senior staff, junior staff, and laborers (Jayawardena 1963: 28–52).

Although occupational type is central, and educational attainment closely related to it, social class or status in Guyana is buttressed by a number of other factors, including skin color (less important now than in the minutely shade-graded colonial society), place and kind of residence, material possessions, consumption patterns, dress, and language use. The last item, naturally, is the one that interests us most. By and large the higher people's position in the social hierarchy, the more they will be expected to show competence in Standard English and the less they will use basilectal or highly marked Creole forms on a daily basis. Teachers and middle-class parents reproaching children for the use of Creole in a formal context sometimes warn that "you are judged by the way you speak," and as R. T. Smith (1962: 115) notes, "Proper English rather than local dialect is another most important criterion of status." This general association between social class and language use shows up clearly in the Cane Walk data. The following tabulation (adapted from Rickford 1979: Table 9.6, p. 342) gives the relative frequency of basilectal Creole pronouns by class:

Social class	N	*mi* as 1st-person subject	Number of tokens	*am* as 3d-person masculine object	Number of tokens
Estate	12	.89	2,309	.53	328
Non-estate	12	.11	3,012	.03	305

As we see, Cane Walk estate or working-class speakers use basilectal Creole pronoun forms significantly more often than their non-estate or lower-middle-class counterparts. Estate-class members associate primarily with other basilect-speaking estate-class laborers in the village, whereas non-estate members tend to associate with people outside the village, including friends, teachers, schoolmates, and fellow workers from higher-status mesolect-speaking groups in Georgetown.[27]

Differences in education and social networks are two of the features that help to define competence and performance limits on the linguistic repertoires of social classes. Just as some members of the Cane Walk estate class appear to have limited knowledge of the appropriate English variants in certain pronoun subcategories, so some members of the non-estate class have a limited grasp of the basilectal Creole variants (Rickford 1979: 477–500; 1987). But even where competence can be demonstrated by experimental methods to extend beyond the range that speakers reveal in everyday life, its full exploitation is limited by performance constraints of a social (sometimes political) nature. Irene, for instance (Text set 10), uses fewer English forms than she is able to use, partly because of a fierce commitment to creole and working-class norms, and Sari, another member of the estate weeding-gang I interviewed (she is not represented in the texts in this volume), pointedly admitted that if she were to use "good English," she would be laughed to scorn for trying to be an "English duck."[28] To a certain extent, then, while the use of more standard varieties can be a factor in people's social class mobility, their social standing sets competence and performance constraints on their language use as well.

This dynamic interrelation was perceived to a certain extent by R. T. Smith (1962: 115) when he wrote that "although speech pattern can be altered with relative ease, it would be considered presumptuous of a lower-class person to speak good English, just as in England a lower-class person would be thought to be 'putting on airs' if he adopted an 'Oxford accent' without acquiring the appropriate occupational status." The point is also addressed to some extent by Devonish (1978: 98–105), who asserts that linguistic variation in the Guyanese continuum is related to people's social class and their relationship to the means of production, and that people's "acts of identity" are more firmly constrained by these factors than Le Page's (1978) "social psychological" model suggests.

While social mobility, so striking among the middle classes in the twentieth century, has, like education, provided part of the fuel for decreolization, upward mobility and its linguistic effects have been limited among the working classes. In part this is because the plantation economy, depending on "a pool of underpaid and underemployed labor," has not fundamentally changed (Hintzen 1983). Whatever its causes, restricted mobility has limited the working class's opportunities and motivation for moving in the direction of Standard English and has acted to maintain Creole English as a sociopolitical symbol. This is undoubtedly one of the reasons why the basilectal pole of the creole continuum—particularly in rural areas—has not changed significantly since the late nineteenth century (Rickford 1983b; Devonish 1978: 105).

Urbanization and ethnicity

One factor closely associated with occupation and social class—and language use—is urban residence, particularly residence in the capital city of Georgetown. The bulk of the country's upper middle class is concentrated in Georgetown and its fashionable suburbs, and the most prestigious schools are also located there. Any person attempting to rise educationally and socially will almost invariably come to Georgetown or one of the other urban centers. Indeed, some people may even measure their success by whether they have managed to move to the capital or not. For instance, Seymour, a prominent non-estate or lower-middle-class Cane Walker, denied that he was the success his fellow villagers made him out to be, citing as evidence the fact that he was still living in the village (Rickford 1979: 129). His assessment is probably correct, for there are no representatives of the upper middle class in Cane Walk, as is true of most rural areas.

The relationship between urbanization and linguistic variation in the Guyanese Creole continuum has been explored in most detail by Walter Edwards (1975; 1983). Table 2.3 summarizes some of his data. Although Edwards shows that the pattern varies somewhat from one variable to another, Table 2.3 illustrates his basic finding that urban speakers use the basilectal Creole variants *mi* and *gat* significantly less often than their rural counterparts. Particularly interesting is the evidence of the seemingly rapid linguistic adjustment toward Standard English norms made by the nonnative urban group members, who were apparently attempting to avoid the pejorative label "country" or "rustic."

The relationship between urbanization and ethnicity has become a controversial issue in the analysis of the Guyanese Creole continuum, beginning with the claim of Bickerton (1975: 211) that decreolization has proceeded

TABLE 2.3
Relative Frequency of Basilectal Forms by Urban-Rural Residence

Form	Urban	Rural	Non-native urban[a]
mi as 1st-person subject pronoun	00.44	43.76	27.26
gat as modal (vs. *hav*)	42.94	71.59	69.02

SOURCE: W. Edwards (1983: Tables 2, 5).

NOTE: Each of the groups had two lower-middle-class and six working-class respondents. Blacks and Indians were represented in all three groups.

[a]People from rural areas who had been living in Georgetown for about nine months while working on a construction site.

further among Afro-Guyanese than Indo-Guyanese because of a "rural-Indian/urban-African" polarization. The most revealing discussion of this issue I have seen to date is Devonish (1978: 46–56). He points out that the Indian informants cited in Bickerton (1973a, 1975) are exclusively rural and the African informants almost entirely urban, and that when ethnicity and urbanization are carefully controlled, as in W. Edwards (1975), urbanization appears to be the more significant co-variable of linguistic behavior. Devonish (1978, following the *Area Handbook for Guyana* [1969: 55]) also reminds us of the common misconception that the bulk of the African population is urban. As these figures from the 1960 census show, the majority of people in both major ethnic groups are rural:

Group	Urban	Rural
Indians	35,950 (13.4%)	231,890 (86.6%)
Africans	79,607 (43.3%)	104,348 (56.7%)

It is still true, however, as a glance at these figures shows, that Africans outnumber Indians by more than two to one in the urban areas, and that Indians outnumber Africans by the same ratio in the country. If urbanization is as closely correlated with decreolization and approximation to English norms as Edwards's work suggests, it would still be true, given these data, that a higher *proportion* of Africans than Indians would have moved away from the basilect. Bickerton himself has undoubtedly overstated the point by suggesting (1973a: 656–67) that the linguistic repertoire of Africans is limited by a mid-mesolectal floor that is only occasionally broken. The evidence of Anna and Basil (Text sets 21 and 22, Chapter 5)—neither of whom is an "isolated individual"—suggests otherwise. But even if the issue of ethnicity is linked entirely to urbanization, there might still be quantitative differences between Indians and Africans in those parts of the Creole continuum that they regularly exploit. Further research on this issue is warranted, particularly since the urban proportion of the Indian population may well have increased significantly since 1960.[29]

Decreolization in the twentieth century

There has been a proliferation of linguistic studies of Guyanese Creole English in the twentieth century, particularly in the past decade, but our ability to make precise statements about the extent to which decreolization has occurred remains limited. It is clear that apart from the loss or restriction of a few features prevalent in turn-of-the-century texts (such as the transitivizing or appositive-object pronoun *am/um*), the Guyanese basilect has not changed significantly. The proportion of people who speak it, and the frequency with which they do so, has undoubtedly decreased since the beginning of the twentieth century, given the forces of urbanization and educational/social class mobility discussed above. Correspondingly, the proportion of upper-mesolectal or more standard speech can be assumed to have increased. But, again, bear in mind that the bulk of the country's population still has a limited education, is still working class, and is still predominantly rural. The decreolizing trends that seem so pronounced among the middle classes might be weaker and more gradual—almost nonexistent in some cases—among the working classes. Although we do not now have at our disposal a body of systematic data gathered nationwide to flesh out these speculations and hypotheses, the quantitative linguistic studies of specific communities that have emerged in recent years should provide an excellent basis for research on the extent to which change in "real time" (Labov 1966, 1972c) has occurred. In the meantime, quantitative distributions by age group like those presented above (p. 71)—still underutilized in studies of creole continua—provide some empirical confirmation of change in "apparent time" (Labov ibid.). The contrast in linguistic competence between different generations—for instance, between Katherine and her parents (Chapter 4)—sometimes furnishes dramatic evidence of the decreolizing forces at work in the twentieth century.

Part II
Texts and Analysis

3

Early Written Texts

In order to resolve open questions about the genesis and development of GC and other creoles—many of them central to pidgin-creole studies (Alleyne 1980: 5)—documentary evidence from earlier periods is important, if not essential. It is commonly asserted, however, that such evidence does not exist. Handler and Lange (1974: 3) observe, for instance, that slaves in the Americas "produced little direct documentation for historical reconstruction," and Lawton (1984: 123) argues that the relative absence of diachronic work on the Caribbean English Creoles is due to the fact that these varieties derive from an oral vernacular tradition: "No creole speaker wrote anything down that is now in our possession and constitutes a direct record of usage."

While it is unfortunately true that we have virtually no early records or descriptions of creole languages from the slaves, indentured laborers, and other proletariats who were the native or primary speakers of such languages—Thomas (1869), written by the son of freed slaves, is a rare exception—we do have access to the observations and descriptions of local speech contained in travelers' accounts published by Europeans visiting or working in the Guiana colonies as soldiers, doctors, clerks, magistrates, and administrators. Many more such works were produced than is commonly known or acknowledged.[1] They are not all equally valuable, to be sure. Some have reams to say about the flora and fauna of the area, but barely mention the slaves and indentured laborers on whose backs this corner of the colonial empire was built, let alone their language. Others describe the non-white populations with a level of sociocultural naïveté and prejudice that is disconcerting.[2] But some, like the ones that are considered in this chapter, offer important insights into the nature of the English-based precursors of the modern Guyanese Creole continuum.

In using these and similar accounts (see Jeremiah 1977, Brasch 1981, Abrahams and Szwed 1983, and Lalla and D'Costa 1984, for others from the Caribbean and the United States), one must make allowances for mis-

hearings or misinterpretations of local speech by foreign ears, and also for
the limitations of amateur transcription systems (see Lalla 1979).[3] However,
internal evidence (Bloomfield 1933: 294–96), comparison with other speech
samples, both contemporary and modern, and information about the authors and the circumstances under which they recorded each citation (how
long after its occurrence, for instance) can help us to sift through the evidence and separate out material that is crucial to many controversial or
unresolved issues. To name just a few such issues, did eighteenth-century
slaves arrive speaking "Guinea Coast Creole English" or something similar (Hancock 1969)? Did a "pidgin" stage precede the development of a
"creole," and did mesolectal Creole English varieties exist from early on
(Alleyne 1971)? Did the indentured Indians who came in the nineteenth
century effect any significant repidginization of Guyanese speech (Bickerton
1975: 12)? Finally, did Georgetown Creole have "different linguistic inputs"
and develop in a "different sociocultural milieu" than the language varieties
in the rest of Guyana (W. Edwards 1984a: 91)? The texts and discussions
that follow are only a start on what I hope will be a long and fruitful line of
research leading to the resolution of these and other questions.

1. Pinckard (1797)

Since the British did not have effective control of Essequibo, Demerara,
and Berbice until their occupation of 1796, and the slaves in these colonies
would have been speaking creolized varieties of Dutch almost exclusively
until British planters began arriving with their slaves in the mid-eighteenth
century, Pinckard's letters, written between 1796 and 1797, constitute a
record of Guyanese Creole English from the end of its first half-century of
existence. The value of Pinckard's letters is increased by the fact that they
can be compared with two other sets of observations from approximately the
same period—Bolingbroke (1807), covering the period from 1799 to 1805,
and St. Clair (1834), reporting on his stay in the Guiana colonies between
1806 and 1808.[4] British interest in overseas exploration and colonial consolidation was generally high around this period, providing a favorable market
for travelers' accounts of this type. Mungo Park's *Travels in the Interior District of Africa*, published in 1797, had been a popular success; Bolingbroke
had a copy with him in Demerara (see Text 2b), and Pinckard (1806, 3:
202–3) referred to other expatriates who were keeping journals or trying to
write local histories, showing that the genre was salient at the time.

George Pinckard, a physician, was born in Northamptonshire, England.
He was twenty-six or twenty-seven when he departed from England with
Ralph Abercromby's expedition to the West Indies on December 31, 1795.

The account of his trip (Pinckard 1806) is based on letters that he wrote to an unidentified friend in England on a regular basis, usually every night; although they were "frequently, traced with a drowsy pen, or hurried over with a wearied and reluctant arm, . . . all the occurrences were noted, whilst they were still alive in the memory" (Preface, p. viii). Because each letter is dated, we can tell how long the author wrote it after his arrival in the colony; other things being equal, later letters are likely to be more accurate than earlier ones.

Traveling on board the *Grenada*, Pinckard accompanied the military detachment that left Barbados in April 1796 to invade the Guiana colonies, and his book includes an interesting account of the troops' landing and the Dutch capitulation. He remained in Demerara and Berbice as surgeon-general to the British army of occupation from April 1795 until May 1797, and it was during these months that he wrote the letters extracted here.[5]

In the first text, part of a letter Pinckard wrote in February 1797, toward the end of his visit, the author reports a conversation he had had with a female slave, probably a house slave. No further details are provided about her, but the conversation is said to be representative of ones he had had with "different negroes, both men and women, with a view of ascertaining what was the state of their intellects, and particularly what were their sentiments with regard to the subject of freedom and slavery" (Pinckard 1806, 3: 252). This unidentified slave woman may seem quite accommodating, but she is much less so than the "pretty little Black Venus" quoted in St. Clair's Text 3e; she makes plain her aversion to "backra country" and is unequivocal about wanting to be free (line 8). The preference she expresses for a "backra man" was apparently quite commonplace, based on a calculated assessment of the avenues for socioeconomic survival available to black women at the time. As Glasgow (1970: 44–45) has observed:

Free and unfree colored women would rather concubinage with white men than with free men of their own complexion, even when the latter enjoyed higher economic standing. This was due to the dominant position of the upper classes in the society, a position which was reflected in political influences and political power. It therefore meant an improvement in a status obsessed society to the free colored group. To the colored slave it might even bring manumission.

Text 1b reports an incident that occurred on January 13, 1797, some nine months after Pinckard had arrived in the colony, and about two to six weeks before he recorded it in his letters. Prince—probably a field slave while still in captivity—had obviously defied the system of slavery more openly than the woman in Text 1a, but he is still dependent on whites and freemen for employment and assistance, and still open to linguistic accommodation. The iron collar with projecting spikes that he had been wearing when the author first encountered him was a typical punishment for runaway slaves, intended to prevent recurrences by rendering it "impossible for any human being to make his escape through the thick underwood in this country" (St. Clair 1834, 1: 213). Despite this encumbrance, and the fact that his body had been "flogged into deep ulcers" (Pinckard 1806, 3: 267), he had run away again, following Pinckard to a fort, where the soldiers removed the collar.

These two texts illustrate a basilectal feature that has attracted considerable attention in the recent literature on English-based Caribbean creoles—the use of *fu* as infinitival complementizer (introducing nonfinite or infinitival complements of a verb). Pinckard renders this form as "for" (15, 32), but it was probably pronounced *fu*, as it usually is today. The most recent publications about *fi/fu* in Caribbean English creoles (Byrne 1984; Winford 1985a) present alternative analyses of its prepositional and verbal functions and reach different conclusions about its possible origins in English ("for") and West African languages (Twi *fi*, Ewe *fe*, Yoruba *fu*). The older and better-known controversy about this form (Bickerton 1971, 1977b; Washabaugh 1974, 1977) involves the analysis of variation between *fu*, *tu*, and Ø as infinitival complementizers in GC and Providence Island Creole. I do not intend to enter into either of these controversies here; the data bases on which the earlier analyses were based were sparse to begin with, and the data base in Pinckard's Guiana texts (a total of 14 infinitival-complementizer slots in Pinckard's 16 citations of slave speech) is insufficient to address the substantive issues. But it is enough to reveal that *fu* varied with *tu* (one occurrence each in lines 12 and 25,[6] another in a text not reprinted here) from the very earliest attestations of Creole English in the Guianas, at least if Pinckard's record can be trusted. Pinckard's evidence on this point runs contrary to Bickerton's (1971: 481) speculation that "there was a time, perhaps in the early years of last [nineteenth] century, when F [fu] was universal." Alleyne's earlier and more general suggestion (1971: 182) that there was probably linguistic variability in slave speech from the very beginning of black/white contact is better supported by these data.

However, Pinckard's texts do confirm Bickerton's (1981: 56) analysis of "the way that creoles handle articles": definite article "de" for presupposed-specific noun phrases ("de backra man," line 19), indefinite article "one" for asserted-specific noun phrases ("one great iron collar," line 31), and Ø for nonspecific noun phrases ("Neger," line 12). Bickerton argues that this distinction is characteristic of creoles in many different parts of the world, including Hawaiian Creole, Seychelles Creole, and Papiamentu, and Pinckard's texts suggest that it was present in GC from a very early stage. Stewart (1974) notes that it is found in Nigerian Pidgin English.

The word "backra" (5, 6, and elsewhere), meaning a European or white person, is one of the most widespread Africanisms in New World black speech, occurring—sometimes in variants such as "buckra" or "baka(r)a"—in Jamaica (Cassidy 1971: 155; Cassidy and Le Page 1980: 18), in Suriname and the Cameroons (Hancock 1969: 58–59), in the Bahamas (Holm and Shilling 1982: 30), and in the Gullah spoken on islands off the coast of South Carolina and Georgia (Turner 1974: 191). The accepted etymology, as given by Turner, is Ibo and Efik *mbakara* (tones omitted) 'white man,' literally "he who governs or surrounds." [7]

Another interesting feature is the occurrence of "him" as a possessive pronoun in "wash him linen" (20); late-nineteenth-century and modern-day samples of GC attest *(h)ii* '(h)e' as the regular possessive form. One might suppose this to be a mishearing or recording error were it not for other evidence indicating that "him" was indeed unmarked for case in some varieties of late-eighteenth- and early-nineteenth-century Guyanese speech, as *im* is in modern JC (B. Bailey 1966). Compare, for example, the use of "him" as a subject pronoun in Texts 3c and 3d (from 1806–8). Other texts indicate that "him" was sometimes extended to the third-person plural and the second-person singular as well, making it a good candidate for classification as a "pidgin" feature (cf. Tsuzaki 1971: 330).

The case-marked noun possessives in lines 26 and 32 may well be misrepresentations, however, because case-marked noun possessives are among the last features to be acquired in decreolization (Fasold 1981: 174; Rickford 1985a: 108), and such an upper-mesolectal feature is unlikely to have co-occurred with the basilectal Creole features in Prince's speech. Those features include the substitution of the bilabial plosive *b* for the labio-dental fricative *v* in "ebery" (25), the use of "no" as a universal negator (30), the use of the West African lexical item "(g)nyaam" ('eat' 32),[8] and the use of "one" as an indefinite article, mentioned earlier. On the other hand, Prince's speech does seem slightly less basilectal than that of the woman in Text 1a overall—recall his variable versus her categorical use of the "for" complementizer and note that her possessive nouns are all uninflected (5, 6)—and his inflected possessives might have been part of a general effort to impress Pinckard, from whom Prince is seeking employment.

Two phonological Creole features worth noting are the absence of initial unstressed syllables (cf. Vaughn-Cooke 1980), as in "'fraid" (12) and "'blige" (25), and the variable loss of the initial consonant in "dem": compare the full form in line 10 with the reduced forms in lines 6, 12, and 31. Although word-initial *d* and other voiced stops are variably absent in preverbal tense-aspect markers in modern GC (see Rickford 1980a), this is not usually the case with pronominal *dem*, which instead tends to undergo final-consonant assimilation and loss (*dem, den, de*).[9] The "'em" in line 31 looks suspiciously like an object-agreement marker or transitivizer, a use that would establish the occurrence of this feature in GC before the arrival of Indian indentured

immigrants. (See the introduction to Text 8 below.) However, on closer in-
spection, it appears to be a demonstrative adjective, similar to the demonstrative pronoun "dem" in line 10, and translatable as 'those' in both cases.*
This analysis is supported by the fact that the form of the object-agreement
marker in the clear nineteenth-century instances is always "um" or "am,"
coincident with the third-singular object pronoun (see Texts 6a and 8a), regardless of whether the noun-phrase object they precede has a singular or
plural referent.

The instances of "zero copula" in line 5 and elsewhere are of course common in modern GC, particularly since forms cognate with English adjectives function as verbs in the basilect (Bickerton 1973a: 648). However,
Pinckard's texts reveal the absence of preverbal tense-aspect markers where
they would be required or expected in modern basilectal GC: in lines 15 and
17, where the irrealis or future/conditional markers *sa* or *gu* would be used
to mark the conditional predicate in the apodosis or consequence clause,
and in lines 31 and 32, where *bin* might be used (before "tell" and "at") to
mark anterior tense.[10] That these instances are not simply to be dismissed as
errors on Pinckard's part is suggested by the fact that other instances occur
elsewhere in Pinckard's texts and also in some of the black speech samples in
St. Clair, as in this sentence: "Oh me Ø soon do dat, massa" (St. Clair 1834,
2: 208). This sentence, and the others just cited, may be characteristic of a
hitherto undiscovered Guyanese "pidgin" or early acculturation variety in
which the Creole tense-aspect markers had not yet evolved, much as *bin* and
wen were later developments in New Guinea Tok Pisin (Sankoff and Laberge
1974) and Hawaiian Creole (Labov 1971b). Alleyne (1980: 127ff) has suggested that there were no similar developments in Caribbean English creoles,
and, more generally, that there is "no clear evidence that modern Caribbean
creoles represent 'expansions' of some earlier 'pidgins.'" The varieties of
late-eighteenth- and early-nineteenth-century English spoken by some of
the slaves in Pinckard and St. Clair are potential counterexamples to these
claims.

Further research is needed to determine whether the absence of tense-
aspect markers is attested in other sources from the same period. Preverbal
"been" is never attested in the citations of black speech in Pinckard and St.
Clair, but it does show up in the speech of blacks in Bolingbroke (1807), as
shown by Text 2b, lines 50ff. It is possible that Bolingbroke included *bin* in
his Guiana citations under the influence of Suriname "talkee-talkee" or
"Negro English," an older and more developed Creole to which he had been
exposed, and with which he was quite fascinated (pp. 340–41, 400); or that
it was indeed present in the Guiana colonies at the time, but was missed or

---

*Alternatively, prenominal "dem" could simply be a plural determiner or definite article
(see Alleyne 1980: 100–101).

ignored by Pinckard and St. Clair for unknown reasons, along with other Creole features like complementizer *se* and serial verbs (Hancock, personal communication).[11] One would also want to know what other distinctive features these "pidgin" or early acculturation varieties might have had; enclitic final vowels as in "heree," and the generalized "him" pronoun discussed above are two obvious candidates; and whether the more "complex" varieties of GC attested in later nineteenth-century sources can be established as developments from or elaborations of these earlier varieties (the latter could merely be importations from West Africa or the West Indies that never gained much ground). This last question is particularly hard to research, on both methodological and empirical grounds.[12] But it is important enough to make us intensify our search for appropriate methodologies and new evidence.

Text 1a below is from Pinckard (1806, 3: 253–54); 1b is from pp. 266–67 of the same work.

1a. *From Letter XX, Demerara, Feb. 11, 1797*

I give you the following conversation, literally as it passed;	1
from which you will be able to form a more correct judgment of the	2
sentiments which dictated the replies.	3
Would you not like to go to England?	4
No! Backra country no good! In Neger country they	5
no flog 'em, and dat better dan Backra country.	6
Should you not wish to be free?	7
O yes! O yes!	8
And if you were free, where would you live, and what would you do?	9
Live wid dem dat buy me free.	10
Well! and would you not go with them to England?	11
No! me 'fraid to go where 'em all Backra. Me love for see Neger	12
here and dere; me 'fraid for see all Backra.	13
But if those, who bought you free, should go away and leave you?	14
Den me live wid one Backra man, and hab one slave for work for me.	15
And if this Backra man should die?	16
Den me live wid one other Backra man. . . .	17
It was a very common reply from many of them to the question,	18
—What would you do were you free?—Live wid de Backra man dat	19
buy me free, wash him linen, and keep him clean!	20

1b. *From Letter XXI, Demerara, February 1797*

On the morning of January 13th, a well-looking robust negro,	21
unexpectedly presented himself at my door, tendering his services, and	22
begging that he might be allowed to work for me. Upon my going out	23

to speak with him, his countenance gladdened with joy, and looking   24
animated and cheerful, he said he would "do ebery ting to 'blige Massa,   25
wait upon Massa, clean Massa's horse, and do all de work Massa tell   26
him."   27
   Not immediately recollecting his features, I asked who he was,   28
whence he came, and how it happened that he addressed himself to me?   29
When he replied—"Ah Massa, if you no remember Prince, Prince no forget   30
dat Massa tell 'em soldiers for break one great iron collar off   31
Prince's neck, and gave him for gnyaam when Massa at Mahaica!"   32
This brought him to my recollection, and I recognised an unhappy slave,   33
whom, in one of my walks at Mahaica, I had met wandering in a cotton-   34
field, bearing a heavy iron collar upon his neck, with three long iron spikes   35
projecting from it.   36

2. Bolingbroke (1799–1805)

   Henry Bolingbroke, born in Norwich, England, in February 1785, spent nearly seven years in Demerara (February 1799 to October 1805) as an articled clerk. In his work *A Voyage to the Demerary*, which was "copied from successive letters written by the author to his family" during his residence in the colony, he describes (p. 3) how he chanced to come to Demerara: "Accident determined my destiny. The partner of a house in Stabroek [Georgetown], who was at London in 1798, wished to engage an articled clerk on terms which my friends thought liberal. Fancy and ambition painted, at the termination of a West Indian voyage, new forms of pleasure and of gain; and I embarked with delight on board the *Comet*, Captain Barrow, at Liverpool, on the 25th December, 1798." Bolingbroke's book is regarded by many historians and linguists as an important source of information on the period, and it does provide us with some valuable linguistic leads; but bearing in mind that the author was only fourteen when he arrived in Demerara, we should be wary when his testimony is not supported by other contemporary sources.[13]

   Bolingbroke's texts are interesting from several linguistic perspectives. Text 2a, an account of a slave explaining why he chose an "ordinary" wife, is identical in content and almost identical in wording with St. Clair's account (Text 3a). Since both writers were in the colony around the same time, one is tempted to ask whether they were eyewitnesses to one and the same event. However, Bolingbroke's account is of an incident that took place at a Stabroek auction and involved two male slaves from the Reynestein estate on the Demerara River; St. Clair's is set at an auction in New Amsterdam, Berbice, and involves two male slaves from the coffee plantation of "Old Catz" on the Canje River. This suggests that St. Clair (whose book was published 27 years after Bolingbroke's) "borrowed" the account from Bolingbroke and added word-final enclitic vowels ("workee," "wifee") to make it seem authentic, or that both were reporting a legendary or stereotypical story popular in expatriate circles at the time. The only remaining possibility—that the events they report had indeed happened and independently involved virtually identical wording—is rather unlikely. In any case, Bolingbroke's version is like St. Clair's in attesting the verb-like use of "handsome," without the nonfinite copula that would be required before an adjective in many nonstandard dialects of English ("for *be* handsome").[14] As noted in the introduction to Pinckard's texts, forms cognate with English adjectives function as (copula-less) verbs in basilectal GC. The recorded speech of Irene, a sugar-cane worker (see Text set 10, Chapter 4, for more details), provides modern examples:

hou lang mi na bina wok, mi bin yuuz fu Ø sik stedii 'Whenever I wasn't working, I'd be sick, continually.'

halidee gun Ø tuu far from nou 'The holiday will be too far from now.'

wel sondi yu se yu doz Ø bizii 'Well, on Sundays, you say, you're usually busy.'

This feature is not characteristic of VBE or other metropolitan English dialects that display copula absence, and I have suggested elsewhere (Rickford 1980a, 1986) that this is one reason why invariant "be" does not emerge as an independent habitual marker in GC as it does in VBE. In Black American communities—the process is still not complete on the South Carolina Sea Islands—sentences like "he *does be* sick" have been entirely or almost entirely replaced by "he *be* sick," apparently through the assimilation and loss of habitual "does."

Text 2a contains one occurrence of "him" with clear feminine reference (39), suggesting that this pronoun might have lacked both case-marking and gender-marking at the end of the eighteenth century. It is possible that the form might actually have been *am* or *om*, and that Europeans used "him" as the closest semantic/phonetic correlate in English grammar. However, although pronominal *am/om* is unmarked for (natural) gender in modern GC, it is not caseless like early-eighteenth-century "him." In the basilect *am/om* is used only as an object. *Um* is sometimes used as a subject pronoun in mesolectal—particularly Georgetown—speech ("Um don' taste good"), but never as a possessive.

Text 2b includes two (originally) non-English lexical items: "sabbe" meaning 'know,' a Romance-derived form that occurs almost universally (often as "savvy") in the world's pidgins and creoles (Todd 1974: 35);[15] and "kie," a form that occurs also in JC and Gullah. Cassidy and Le Page (1980: 259) define "kie" as "an expression of surprise, amusement, satisfaction, etc." Turner (1949: 196) lists possible sources in Yoruba, Fon, Hausa, and Twi.

Dutch *kijk* 'look' is a potential, but less likely, etymology; see Schuchardt (1979: 97).

Text 2b includes a morphologically inflected noun-phrase possessive, "the moor's country" (54), that seems as out of harmony with the basilectal Creole features with which it co-occurs as the noun-phrase possessives did in Text 1b. The two other instances of a noun-phrase possessive in Bolingbroke's citations of slave speech ("Buckra country," twice, on pages 25 and 308 of the 1807 edition) are both uninflected, however, as they typically are in modern GC.

The most interesting feature in this text set is the "for me" possessive in line 52. Possessives of this type (for + pronoun + noun phrase) are not common in modern GC, but they are the norm in JC. This feature, together with the use of "him" and "kie," may represent the speech or influence of Jamaican slaves brought into the Guiana colonies by the English in the second half of the eighteenth century. Fewer slaves appear to have come in from Jamaica during this period than from Barbados, but their influence is obvious in other lexical resemblances between GC and JC (Goodman n.d.).[16] Bolingbroke and Pinckard may just have happened to record the speech of slaves who had come from Jamaica, or the features in question may have spread to other slaves without persisting for very long thereafter.

Apart from historical contact between JC and GC speakers, there are two other possible explanations for these JC/GC resemblances: they could represent independent but parallel developments, or they could be evidence of a more conservative variety of pidgin or creole that was ancestral to both GC and JC. Hancock (personal communication and 1985), noting that the slave of Text 2b was from the Mandingo-speaking Senegambian area in which "Guinea Coast Creole English" (GCCE) may have originated, and had been in Demerara only "about two years" (Bolingbroke 1807: 105), suggests that his speech represents the possible GCCE ancestor of both GC and JC. Of course, if the slave in Text 2b had picked up this Guinea Coast English while waiting on the West African coast for transshipment or enroute to the New World, he would have had less time to acquire the dialect, and less favorable language-learning conditions, than on a Demerara plantation. The possibility is nevertheless an interesting one, worth further consideration.

Text 2a is from Bolingbroke (1807: 102); 2b is from p. 105 of the same work.

2a. *Choice of wives by slaves at Stabroek "sale-room"*

Two chose pretty women, and the third an ordinary one. On my   37
asking him why he did not like a handsome wife, he replied, "No, massa,   38
me no want wife for handsome, me want him for do me good, and for work   39
for massa as well as me."   40

2b. Mandingo slave's claim to have seen Mungo Park in Africa

Mungo Park's [book of] Travels was among the number; in looking   41
over the vocabulary of the Mandingo tongue, I called Peter, a negro of   42
that nation, and asked him a question in his own language. "Kie!   43
massa, you sabbe talk me country," was the exclamation. I had now   44
an opportunity of proving Mungo Park's correctness, and desired   45
Peter to turn the question I had put to him into English, which   46
he did, with several others, and from their agreeing with the   47
translation, he convinced me that the travels in Africa deserved credit   48
and confidence. However, to prove further, I told Peter what I was   49
reading, when he replied with energy, "massa, me been see that white   50
man in me country, in de town where me live, he been come dere one   51
night for sleep, one blacksmith countryman for me been with him, me   52
been give him rice for he supper, and soon, soon in the morning   53
he been go towards the moor's country."   54

3. St. Clair (1806–1808)

Thomas Staunton St. Clair, a Scotsman, was a lieutenant-colonel in the 1st or Royals regiment of the British army, his initial commission having been secured through his father's personal friendship with the Duke of Kent, commander of the regiment. St. Clair was in the Guiana colonies with the 1st battalion of the regiment between January 1806 and June 1808, though the account of this sojourn was not published until 1834.

Vincent Roth (who provides the preceding biographical details in his introduction to the 1947 Guiana edition of this work) notes (p. ii) that St. Clair's "spelling of place-names may not in every case be exact" and "on occasion, he may confuse a jaguar with an ocelot and a labaria snake with a boa-constrictor." These lapses lead him to think that St. Clair may have written up his memoirs long after he actually experienced them. The fact that it took so long to publish them would support this possibility. On the other hand, there are references to specific times ("On the 2nd at 3 p.m.") and other details that suggest St. Clair did not depend entirely on his memory, but wrote his book with the help of notes he kept while he was in the Guiana colonies. St. Clair himself says (1834: 56) that his book is based on journal entries.

We need not linger over the word-final enclitic vowels in Text 3a, which were discussed in the introduction to the Bolingbroke texts, except to note that there are other examples in Texts 3c and 3d: "heree" and "Missee." Words with enclitic vowels like these are especially common in modern-day Krio and the Suriname Creoles (Hancock n.d.a), but are also occasionally seen in modern GC and JC. Their frequency in older texts like St. Clair's may represent a restructuring of English words to fit a consonant-vowel syllabic pattern common among the native West African languages of the earliest Caribbean slaves (Alleyne 1980: 62–69). However, similar examples show up in Chinese and Japanese Pidgin English, and the emergence of the unmarked consonant-vowel syllable in these and other contact varieties may be equally attributable to "universal" principles of simplification (see Mühlhäusler 1986: 140).

Miss Fanny in Text 3b does not conform to the usual stereotype of the obsequious and accommodating servant (cf. the "poor girl" in Text 3e), and she is therefore of considerable sociolinguistic interest. (The text is interesting also because it is a rare and vibrant instance of blacks talking to each other rather than to the white author.) Like the two friends she is addressing, Miss Fanny is a free black woman, living in the capital city (then named Stabroek). Bolingbroke (1807: 51) notes that many free women of color were wealthy hucksters, possessing "ten, fifteen, and twenty negroes," whom they employed in the retail trade. Miss Fanny appears to be a member of this class. As St. Clair (1834, 1: 116) comments, had Miss Fanny's riches "consisted only in what she had just stated, it was enough to make her a person of great consequence among her tawny neighbours." His description of her dress (ibid.) is fairly detailed, and worth reprinting to emphasize that her status was a cut above the ordinary:

Her dress was like that of most of the free black women of this country. A clean white handkerchief is tied round the head, something like a turban; on the top of this is placed a little black, red, or yellow hat, so exceedingly small, as if made for a little infant, which is stuck on in its place by means of a long pin, run through it and the turban. A short white bedgown, without any stays, was the only upper garment; a blue petticoat with bright coloured borders, black legs, and coloured shoes, of which they are as fond as the Spanish ladies, completed her equipment.

As might perhaps be expected of someone of her social status, Miss Fanny's speech reflects a frequent use of "-s"-marked plurals (six of eight occurrences) and a consistent use of case-marked first-person pronominal possessives ("my" occurs throughout). Her most distinctively creole features, in fact, are lexical and phonological, and this is also true, to some extent, of the middle class today.

Words in Miss Fanny's text that appear to be creole or are at least not characteristic of SE are "cra-cra," "kabba, kabba," and "tand." "Cra-cra" (69) occurs as an adjective in JC. Cassidy and Le Page (1980: 128) define it as 'Nervous; therefore erratic, clumsy, careless, etc.,' and link it to Twi *kra kra* 'restless, excited.' Their entry for the noun "craw-craw" (pronounced *kraa-kraa, kra-kra*) is also relevant, however (p. 129): "cf. *OED*: 'app. a Dutch Negro name, from Du. *kraauw* scratch, *kraauw-en* to scratch, to claw. A malignant species of postulous itch, prevalent on the African coast, especially about Sierra Leone'; . . . Cf. also Twi *kɔré*, a cutaneous eruption, a kind of itch in the skin." A "Dutch-Negro name" would probably have been even more widely known in Guyana than Jamaica, and the noun could have been used adjectivally to make a particularly derogatory insult of the type that Miss Fanny is obviously striving for in line 69.

The term "kabba, kabba" in the same line occurs in Jamaica too, defined by Cassidy and Le Page (1980: 255) as 'poorly done, worthless' (adjective) or 'Someone or something that is worthless' (noun). The authors relate it etymologically to Yoruba *kábakàba*, an adverb meaning 'confusedly, not smoothly.' Yansen (1975: 15) defines Guyanese "cabba-cabba" as a 'hybrid or any common breed of fowl,' which is well within the range of the Cassidy and Le Page definition. The verb "tand" (69) derives from "stand" by a process of initial sibilant + stop simplification that was more common in nineteenth-century GC than it is now. The word "(S)tan(d)" itself is still common, however, referring throughout the Caribbean to the way something or somebody is, looks, or feels.[17]

The word "chintz" (64) is not particularly creole. Of Hindi, ultimately Sanskrit and Indo-European origin, it is defined by the *OED* as "*orig.* a name for the painted or stained calicoes imported from India; *now* a name for cotton cloths fast-printed with designs of flowers, etc. in a number of colours, generally not less than five, and usually glazed." The word "joe" (65) may be less familiar. According to the *OED*, it is an "abbreviation of *Joannes* or JOHANNES, a Portuguese gold coin." An *OED* citation from Marryat (1834: xxxi) refers to "half a joe, or eight dollars." However, Cassidy and Le Page (1980: 248) define "joe" as 'sixpence,' and this may have been the monetary value to which Miss Fanny was referring.

Three features in the St. Clair samples are unusual and/or of doubtful origin. The first is the utterance, "Si, Massera" in line 57. The "Massera" is explainable by means of consonant-cluster simplification and vowel epenthesis from English "master," but what of "Si"? Does it represent a widespread Romance loanword, or just the influence of St. Clair's travels in Portugal and Spain, where he served in the military between 1810 and 1820? The nonfinite "be" in line 83 is also unusual. It does not seem to have a habitual force, unless the preceding "him" refers to the slave's real master rather than the author, and the slave is making the unlikely suggestion that, appearances notwithstanding, his master is usually good. More plausibly, the sentence means "You are a good man," but the use of "him" with second-person reference is otherwise unattested in the Caribbean English creoles.

The third item of interest, closely related to the second, is the use of "him" for a plural subject in lines 74 and 75. This suggests that, in addition to being caseless and genderless, early-nineteenth-century "him" might have been numberless as well, something that is quite unusual in English creoles, which typically show an even more faithful marking of number distinctions in the pronouns than SE does: compare "allyuh," "y'all," and

"'mong you" as second-person plural forms. The only comparable example
of "him" with plural reference I have come across is, significantly enough,
from an eighteenth-century sample of JC cited in Cassidy and Le Page
(1980: 225): "1790 Moreton 156, You no work him like a-me! *You don't make
them* [the hips] *move as I do* [in dancing]!"* Furthermore, if we accept the
interpretation of the "him" in line 83 as meaning "you," it would appear that
"him" was virtually personless as well, a semantically bleached pronoun that
could have almost any referent (except the speaker himself or herself).

This very broad range of meanings for a single form is more typical of
pidgins than creoles, and would provide additional evidence for the existence of a pidginlike variety in the Guianas at the beginning of the nineteenth century. But exactly how and when this form began to be restricted in
its scope of reference and replaced by other forms cannot be documented
from the texts in this volume. Our next text sets are from three-quarters of a
century later (the 1880's and 1890's), and by then "him" either fails to occur
("am/um" and "(h)e" being used instead for the third-person singular,
"dem" for the third-person plural, and "You" and "allyuh" for the second-
person singular and plural, respectively) or occurs more or less in its SE
function as a third-person masculine object pronoun. Some other pidginlike
features of early-nineteenth-century GC do persist until late into the nineteenth century, however, as we will see in connection with Kirke's texts
(4a–4c).

All the texts are from St. Clair (1834) as follows: 3a, 1: 222–23; 3b,
1: 115; 3c, 1: 129, 133; 3d, 1: 209; 3e, 2: 158.

3a. *Choice of wives by Old Catz's slaves*

Old Catz, turning round to his Negroes, pointed out two rather good-   55
looking girls, and said: "Will these do for you?" One of them   56
immediately replied: "Si Massera," and took hold of one of the girls'   57
hands. The other . . . answered his master thus: "No, no, Massa, me no   58
want wifee for handsome; me want him for workee for Massa and   59
workee for me."   60

3b. *Miss Fanny's views on "buckra"*

I was just in time to hear the last speech of Miss Fanny, who exclaimed,   61
and not in the most delicate manner: 62
"Ante Seri, me tell you true; Miss Fanny (this was herself)   63

---

*It is possible that Moreton heard "'em" or "um" and regarded it as a reduced form of
"him" rather than "dem." But if the Jamaican situation was anything like the Guyanese, reduced forms of "dem" would have been relatively rare. See the discussions preceding Pinckard's
texts above and McTurk's texts below.

no care for buckra. She hab my tree chintz gown, my four muslin gown, 64
my fine shawls, that cost me a joe apiece, my two nigger-wenches 65
(meaning slaves—she herself was as black as a coal) my house 66
in Tabrock, my two sows in pig, and my tree chests full of good 67
fine clothes. Buckra, me no care for you. Me, me, me,—Miss Fanny! 68
you tink me tand like dem cra-cra girls. Kabba, kabba, me Miss Fanny. 69

3c. Little Johnny's comments while hunting

I took aim at and killed the last of them [guinea-fowl]. Johnny 70
now returned to me, [and] exclaimed in rapture: "Buckra, him dam well 71
kill!" . . . I followed him down a straight road leading back to Mr. 72
Heathcot's house, when a loud and furious scream, from the top of one of 73
the trees, startled me, and induced me to stand still: "Him dam 74
macoco," said little Johnny. "Heree! heree, Massa! heree him run!" 75
I looked where he pointed, and saw nearly fifty large baboons, scouring, 76
from the tops of the fruit-trees across the road, towards the forest, 77
having taken the alarm from their sentinel, who had been perched on 78
the top of a high tree to keep a look-out. 79

3d. Words of a slave whose right hand has just been cut off at a public "execution" for the "abominable, rebellious, and horrid crime of striking a white man"

I walked up to him, disgusted with the severity of the Dutch law, 80
and, putting a golden joe into his left hand, I said to him: "I pity 81
you." The poor fellow looked at the joe, then at me; tears at length 82
started from his eyes, and he exclaimed: "Eh! massa!—Him be good man!" 83

3e. Comments of "one of the pretty little Black Venuses" about life in the white household

"Well," said I, "you all look very happy in this house." "Yes," 84
replied the poor girl, with an expression of joy in her countenance, 85
"him all good. Missee good, Missee Chatrine good, Missee Sopie 86
good, and Neger happy." 87

4. Kirke (1872–1897)

Henry Kirke, born in Derbyshire, England, was a magistrate in (then)
British Guiana for 25 years. His duties took him to several parts of the
colony besides Georgetown; he also served on many important commissions
and was frequently called on to act as a judge on the Supreme Court. His

account of his experiences was published in London in 1898. Vincent Roth, who wrote the introduction to the 1948 Guiana edition of that account, found two of Kirke's children resident in Guiana when he arrived there in the 1920's. In general, Kirke remained longer in Guyana and had better opportunities to familiarize himself with local conditions and cultures than most of the Englishmen who published accounts of their travels in the Caribbean. His samples of late-nineteenth-century Afro-Guyanese speech are valuable both for the linguistic forms and structures they exemplify and for what they reveal about the speech events and ways of speaking of the time.

Text 4a also appears in Abrahams (1970), who faults Kirke for mistakenly seeing this elaborate Afro-American speechmaking as a simple and inadequate imitation of white behavior. As Abrahams notes (p. 522), this "highly decorous eloquence" of Afro-Americans falls within the larger category of "talking good or sweet," which makes use of approximations to SE and "emphasizes order and the ability to make discretions and distinctions." "Talking good" contrasts with "talking broken or bad or broad," which makes use of everyday Creole and emphasizes "wit through word play, . . . contest punning and other ambiguities, and . . . rapid fire delivery." As Abrahams shows, with examples from other parts of the Caribbean, the wedding toast belongs in a subcategory of "talking good," along with speeches at baptismals, send-offs, thanksgivings, and the like. In these, "the conventional formalism of the language . . . underscores the ritualistic nature of the occasion."

A minor point about the elaborate speechmaking in Text 4a, especially when it involves a prepared script as in this instance, is that it depends on the speech-maker's being literate and reasonably well read. It is this attribute, together with a more or less deliberate training in the art of talking sweet (Abrahams 1972) and direct study of the dictionary (Allsopp 1980: 104), that allows the speech-maker in Text 4a to stack up a pile of subordinate qualifying clauses and phrases (as in lines 92–95) before finally introducing his main clause (in 95); to select the polysyllabic and unfamiliar word instead of the simple or ordinary one ("mirth and aggrandisement," in line 92, instead of "happiness"; "repair," line 93, instead of "return"; "heralding the consummation of their enterprise," lines 94–95, instead of "toasting their marriage"); and to spice his speech with Latinate expressions ("Ne quid nemus," line 97). This elaborate use of language is referred to as "fancy talk" by Dillard (1972) and as "display diction" by Allsopp (1980: 103).[18]

The second text is interesting for its humorous reference to the fact that the colony was once Dutch. This, after all, was 75 years after the colony had been ceded to the British. Robertson (1974) draws attention to reports made well into the nineteenth century of Dutch Creole being spoken in

Guyana. Text 4b provides no direct evidence of this, but the readiness of one man to suggest that the obscure motto is in Dutch might well have arisen from experiences with speakers of a "foreign tongue" who appeared to be linked to the earlier Dutch period in some way.

The speech of the three black men is itself interesting. On the one hand, it contains such SE features as subject-auxiliary inversion in yes/no questions ("Don't you see, . . . ?" 113) and a fairly consistent "is" copula, and on the other, it contains such creole features as focusing/clefting with "Is" (108), and nonpunctual, habitual "a" (114). Note in particular that although "belong" (111) is a stative verb, and one that would therefore be expected to require a preceding "bin" to signal past reference, it occurs without "bin." This suggests that some varieties of GC may have continued the absence of (some) tense-aspect markers right into the final quarter of the nineteenth century.

The third text is one of the rare examples we have of Afro-Guyanese women interacting. (There is of coure St. Clair's Text 3b.) Reams have been written about the speech events of black males in the New World, but very little about those of black females (Abrahams 1976: 59). The specific speech event involved in Text 4c is described as a "quarrel" (therefore a subset of "talking broad"), but it is more frequently referred to locally as "rowin" (Rickford 1979: 158). Although a row may begin with argument over a particular point, it frequently degenerates to the trading of insults unrelated to the matter at hand. When it descends even further, to the point where obscenities and slanderous remarks about the other party and his or her relatives are introduced, it is referred to as a "bus(e)ing" (see W. Edwards 1978), a term derived from English "abuse" by the loss of the weak initial syllable (Vaughn-Cooke 1980).

The grandiose self-titling of one of the "girls" in this text, "Diana de Goddess of Chaste," is similar to what occurs in St. Clair's Text 3b (less grandiosely) in the speech of "Miss Fanny," line 68. It might be seen as one example of the employment of words as magical devices, as a means of defying and shaping reality. As modern Afro-American examples, we can cite the grandiloquent titles that Marcus Garvey bestowed on himself and the officers in his Back-to-Africa movement, and the often misunderstood loquaciousness and boasting ("I'm the Greatest") of the onetime heavyweight champion Muhammad Ali.

As to the form and structure of these samples, the "for" possessives in lines 122 and 123 reinforce the evidence of Bolingbroke's considerably earlier text (2b) that this was indeed a feature of eighteenth- and nineteenth-century GC.[19] One of the two occurrences in line 123 is a possessive absolute: "for your own" (probably "for *you* own" as originally uttered, reported

by Hancock n.d.*a* in this form for St. Vincent and Tobago). Note that if the
"for" tokens in lines 122 and 123 are classified as part of the possessive or
genitive construction—and it seems that they must be—they cannot also be
conjunctions (equivalent to "because"), and the individual clauses in Diana's
final, long sentence have to be seen as connected by parataxis (juxtaposition) only. Is this another "pidgin" feature that has not survived in general
use?[20] And is the absence of an infinitival complementizer in line 120
(before "know") in the same category? The answers to these questions
must come in part from additional eighteenth- and nineteenth-century
attestations.

Texts 4a–4c are from Kirke (1898), pp. 257, 258, and 268, respectively.

4a. A "fancy talk" wedding toast

Their speeches are as wonderful as their letters. At a black wedding	88
one of the guests delivered an oration which he had carefully written down.	89
"My Friends, it is with feelings of no ordinary	90
nature which have actuated my inmost heart on this present occasion,	91
for on such festivities so full of mirth and aggrandisement, when the	92
Bridegroom and Bride in all their splendour repair to the house of	93
reception, and there we find familiar friends and neighbours heralding	94
the consummation of their enterprise, it fills me with that enthusiasm	95
which otherwise would fail to draw out our congratulations. * * * * * *	96
"And now I must close, and take the phrase *Ne quid nemus*—'too much of	97
one thing is good for nothing.' Trusting these few remarks may be found	98
multum in parvo, as I am now attacked with *cacoethes loquendi.*	99
I shall resort to my *ex cathedrâ* asking the ladies present	100
melodiously to sing for me a verse of the hymn—	101
How welcome was the call,	102
And sweet the festal day."	103

4b. Comments of three "black men" on the wording of the colony arms

I remember overhearing three black men talking together at a local	104
exhibition held in the Assembly Rooms in Georgetown, where the Colony	105
Arms, with the motto *Damus petimusque vicissim* were conspicuously	106
displayed.	107
First scholar: "Is what language is this?" (referring to the	108
motto). "It must be some of dem foreign tongue."	109
Second scholar: "Yes, bo, you is right, is Dutch. Before time,	110
you know, de Calony belang to de Dutch."	111
Third scholar: "Dutch who! it ain't no Dutch, is English.	112
Don't you see, D-A-M Dam, U-S us—Dam us. Is what	113
buckra always a do us poor people."	114

4c. "Wordy war" between two "black girls"

My old friend X. Beke told me a ridiculous story about two black girls   115
who were returning from work, and met on the road. They were wearing   116
but a scanty amount of clothes, but each had a baby in her arms, . . .   117
There was some quarrel between them, and a wordy war ensued. At the   118
close one damsel, turning away, said, "Well, I don want no more dis-   119
coorse with you, Miss Teraza." "Me make you know, marm," retorted the   120
other girl, "that for me name no Teraza but Tereesa." "Well, me dear,"   121
was the reply, "Teraza or Tereesa both de same, for me name a better   122
name than for your own, for me name Diana de Goddess of Chaste;" and   123
she strutted off with a swing of her ragged skirt.   124

5. McTurk (1881/1899)

Michael McTurk, known as Quow, was an Englishman (born in Liverpool in 1843) who spent most of his life in British Guiana. He owned a sugar estate ("Airy Hall") in the Essequibo region, and held a number of different administrative positions between 1872 and 1915, the year of his death. The source of his nickname is uncertain, but it may be related to the JC *quaw* (pronounced *kwa-o* or *kwa-u*), 'an albino negro' (Cassidy and Le Page 1980: 371, which gives such synonyms as 'White Eboe,' 'Norwegian,' and 'Whitey-Whitey').

Quow's grandfather—also named Michael McTurk—had participated in the 1823 trial of the Reverend John Smith, the Demerara Martyr (Wallbridge 1848), and some of Quow's grandchildren still reside in Guyana. Quow him-self was intimately acquainted with the interior regions of Guyana and was considered an authority on the Amerindians living there. His experiences as revenue officer, traveling magistrate, and surveyor—primarily in the Essequibo region—led him to acquire "the linguistical knowledge of the labouring classes of the time" (in the words of Vincent Roth, editor of the 1949 Guiana edition of McTurk's work). The contents of *Essays and Fables* . . . first appeared as separate pieces in the *Argosy* newspaper,[21] which subsequently published them in book form in 1881.

McTurk had a longer and closer acquaintance with nineteenth-century British Guiana and the local speech than any of the Englishmen whose writ-ings on the subject have come down to us, and his book is usually regarded as an excellent source of linguistic information on the period. Unlike the works that we have drawn on up to this point, McTurk's book is not a record of his experiences in the colony, but a collection of his own creative writings in a fairly basilectal variety of GC. It consists primarily of poems—mostly narrative verse—but includes such prose pieces as a sermon, some letters and mock encyclopedia entries, the (presumably fictional) proceedings of a court case, and the meeting report excerpted as Text 5a, below. This adds up to a considerable quantity of "dialect data"—more, in fact, than can be gleaned from all the relevant quotations in Pinckard, Bolingbroke, St. Clair, and Kirke combined. To be sure, the very fact that the book *is* essentially a creative/imaginative work makes the authenticity of its Creole suspect. Such suspicions can never be dispelled completely, but they are reduced by three considerations: McTurk clearly had been extensively exposed to local varieties of GC; his renditions of it are highly consistent; and his usage agrees in detail with contemporary as well as modern samples.

Bickerton (1981: 74, 308) praises McTurk's book as a literary source, but warns that his renderings of the speech of literate blacks (unlike his renderings of the speech of illiterate blacks) "are spoiled by facetiousness and condescension." This is certainly true of Text 5a, in which the town hall meeting of the "Kullad Gen'lmans" is heavily caricatured. However, exaggeration and caricature are also present in McTurk's depiction of the less-educated rural participants in "A Case in Court" (published in Rickford, ed., 1978: 197–204), and seem to be general characteristics of his "comic" style. It may be that the speech of the people who were likely to have been members of the "Aglicultulal and Debating Society" in the late nineteenth century contained fewer basilectal elements than are present in Text 5a, but the caricature appears to involve a selection from actually occurring levels rather than the invention of unattested features.

McTurk's detailed attempts to represent the pronunciations of his day by means of dialect spellings, dashes, hyphens, and apostrophes make his work difficult to read, but they hold a mine of information for the historical phonologist. For instance, the simplification of initial sibilant + stop clusters that is attested in St. Clair's texts is exemplified even more often in McTurk's, in forms such as " 'tart" (126), " 'tan' " (142), and " 'cattah" (= 'scatter').* The rendering of 'without' as "biout" in line 126 is significant not only for its initial stop (*b* instead of *w*), but also for the elision of the medial consonant; in modern GC the interdental fricative would be realized as an alveolar stop (wi*d*out), but would rarely be deleted. The realization of the half-open vowels in English "grog" and "duck" as a low, maximally open *a*, as in "grag," "dack" (126), is still one of the most salient phonological features of basilectal GC, described by some Guyanese as "broadin(g) yuh mout." Folk references to creole speech as "broad talk" on Providence Island apparently involve the same feature. "Speakers say that basilectal talk is 'broad' or 'wide open.' All examples of such 'broadness' include the very low central [a] vowel" (Washabaugh 1974: 100).

---

*The last form occurs in McTurk (1949: 34). It is cited because it shows that the simplification applied to *sk* as well as *st* clusters.

McTurk's texts provide further examples of the realization of SE *v* as Creole *b* found in Pinckard's texts ("hab" 15, "ebery" 25; cf. "Gubnah" 128), and reveal the parallel replacement of alveolar *z* (voiced, although spelled with an "s") by *d*, as in "bidness" (131). The replacement of voiced fricatives by stops is a consonant-strengthening process (Hooper 1973), and since consonant-strengthening processes tend to be favored in syllable-initial rather than syllable-final positions, it is interesting that both of McTurk's examples are syllable final. In syllable-initial position, we find instead a consonant-weakening process, the realization of the SE labio-dental fricative as a labio-velar glide or semivowel (*w*, as in "wituparashan" 136).²² Its complete elision in one syllable-final case ("gie" 151) is, however, in line with general expectations, as is the "strengthening" realization of SE *w* as *b* ("biout" 126) and as a bilabial fricative ([βεl] 'well'). Although the bilabial-fricative pronunciation is not attested in McTurk's texts—perhaps he found it too difficult to represent—it is common enough in modern GC.

Other features of modern GC pronunciation exemplified in Texts 5a and 5b are (1) the simplification of syllable-final clusters ending in *t* or *d* ("an'," "las'," 125, 129), (2) the absence of postvocalic, word-final *t* in pronominal particles (interrogative and relative "wa(')," demonstrative "da," 137, 142, 146), and (3) variable syllable-final *r* constriction ("haada," but "hear," 128, 136). The realization of word-initial alveolar *s* as alveopalatal *sh* ("Shitty" in the title of Text 5a, "sheketary" 135) is not attested in any of the modern texts in this volume; the realization of *ch* as *sh* (*shail* 'child,' Text 24b, line 1319) is the only instance that even comes close.* The most significant difference between the phonology of these texts and modern GC, however, is the alternation between "da" and "a" as continuative/habitual markers. This confirms the hypothesis advanced in Rickford (1980a) that the GC aspect marker, now "a," may have been "da" at an earlier stage, the initial *d* being removed by a general pan-creole rule deleting initial voiced stops in tense-aspect markers. The deletion of the initial stop in "da" was apparently conditioned by the nature of the preceding segment, more likely to occur after a consonant (as in line 129) than after a vowel or pause (132, 133, 137).²³

When we compare McTurk's texts with the early-nineteenth-century texts of Pinckard and St. Clair, three grammatical differences emerge. First, the early-nineteenth-century use of an all-purpose "him" is no longer attested. Second, instead of the "for" + noun phrase constructions of the early texts, we find possession being marked, fairly consistently, by juxtaposition without inflection ("he name," "Muddu Hubbard daag," 134, 149), as in modern GC. Third, the preverbal markers whose absence we noted in some of the

*However, Lalla (1979: 53) cites the occurrence in a Jamaican Anansi tale of the phrase "pity you fat washe" as an instance in which "an early English dialect feature, the replacement of [s] by [š], survives in Jamaican Creole."

early-nineteenth-century GC varieties are all present in McTurk's texts: continuative/habitual "(d)a," [24] anterior/past "bin" (138), completive "done" (149), [25] and future/irrealis "sa" (131). Furthermore, in connection with this last point, the "done" form occurs clause-finally, an archaic and markedly basilectal position (see Bickerton 1975: 40). This appears to have been done deliberately, to facilitate a rhyme with "none" in line 145; but poetic license in this case probably reflects the everyday speech patterns of the time. The anterior and irrealis markers also combine ("bin go," "bin sa," 148, 150) to yield a counterfactual conditional, equivalent to "would have" in SE and comparable to *ben sa* in Sranan, the Surinamese English-based Creole (Voorhoeve 1957: 383; Bickerton 1975: 52). The variety of GC attested in these texts is obviously a robust and complex one, capable of subtle grammatical and semantic distinctions. One very real possibility, however, is that McTurk's GC is richer than Pinckard's or St. Clair's, not because the language itself has developed in the intervening years, but because McTurk knew it more intimately and could demonstrate its resources more adequately.

One of the rare respects in which McTurk's texts parallel their early-nineteenth-century predecessors rather than modern GC is in the use of "um" as a third-person *plural* pronoun (126). As noted above in our discussion of Pinckard's texts, pronominal *dem* does not usually lose its initial consonant in modern GC, but the presence of plural "um" here suggests that this might still have been the case in the late nineteenth century ("dem" > "'em" > "um"). Even if the "um" of line 126 is really a reduced form of "dem," however, it is clearly an exceptional case, since there are more than a dozen other cases of unreduced "dem" in these texts. If the "um" is seen instead as a reduced form of "him," then what we have in line 126 is a morphological and semantic linkage of the singular and plural third-person categories similar to that represented by their common realization as "him" in St. Clair's texts above. Regardless of which analysis is finally agreed upon, plural "um" remains one potential link with earlier varieties of GC.

The copulative forms "was" (134) and "isn't" (141) are the most striking nonbasilectal items in McTurk's texts, although several of the phonological features referred to above are variable rather than categorical, and the infinitival complementizer varies between "fo'" (130) and "to" (138). These mesolectal elements are offset by a host of other basilectal elements in morphosyntax, including the use of "say" as a sentence complementizer (128) and the tense-aspect markers discussed above. In terms of the lexicon, there are several basilectal items in these texts, including reduplicative "nuff-nuff" (132), "matty" (132), "'tan" (152), "nyam" (148), and "make brigah" (145, glossed by McTurk 1949: 75 as 'make bounce or empty brag'). Bickerton (1975: 7–8) rightly interprets the constellation of basilectal elements in

McTurk's *Essays and Fables* as an accurate record of nineteenth-century working-class Afro-Guyanese vernacular.[26]

Texts 5a and 5b are from McTurk (1949), pp. 42–43 and 75, respectively.

5a. From "Repote ob de Meeting ob de Kullad Gen'lmans Aglicultulal and Debating Society, dat was hel' in de Town Hall of de Shitty ob Gaagetown on Saturday, de 29 day ob February in de presen' year"

Mr. Hugh: . . . Tomorrow Sunday, an' gen'lmans can' get	125
dem grag biout Pilice no' a 'tart behin' um like dack	126
behin' acourie. . . .	127
Mr. Isa Dore: . . . I hear say de Gubnah dem	128
discha'ge de las' hangman dem bin got, an' dem a pay good	129
money fo' hang people. . . . Dem pay fo' hang by de task	130
'an de bidness sa' pay well dis time, pa'ticlah sence dem	131
Berbice people a kill matty nuff-nuff fashion, an' backra	132
da hang dem like dem aunty da hang claat fo' dry.	133
Wan Uncle bin deh wan side, he name was not	134
know by de sheketary; de gen'lman say Haada. Gen'lmans	135
haada, no faada wituparashan.	136
Mr. Isa Dore: Da wa' dat?	137

Translation

. . . Tomorrow is Sunday, and gentlemen can't get	
their grog without Police starting behind them like ducks behind	
acourie [fruit].	
. . . I hear that the Governor and his administrators	
have discharged the last hangman they had, and they are paying good	
money to hang people. . . . They pay for hanging by the task,	130T
and the business should pay well at this time, particularly since those	
Berbice people are killing each other a lot, and the white man is	
hanging them like those old ladies hang clothes out to dry.	
An old man was sitting by the side. His name was not	
known by the secretary; the gentleman said, "Order. Gentlemen,	135T
order. No further vituperation."	
What is that?	

The first translation line is marked 125T.

5b. "Muddu Hubbard: A little song for the Electives"

Ol' Muddu Hubbard bin go to the cubbard to gi'e she	138
po' daag a bone,	139
But w'en she meet dere de cubbard was bare, an	140
so da daag isn't get none.	141

An' all dem adda daag wa bin 'tan' up one side, fo' fite   142
    an' take way de bone,   143
W'en dem see how t'ing t'an—come out empty han'   144
    an' make brigah, say, dem no want none   145
But if Muddu Hubbard bin fin' da piece bone, w'en   146
    she bin look in de cubbard, da day,   147
Dem tarrah daag dere bin go nyam am an cla'h, w'en   148
    dem lick Muddu Hubbard daag done.   149
Dem [sic] dem bin sa cack dem one yase, make knot in dem   150
    tail, an' gie couple wink wid dem yie,   151
An' say if you wan' fo' see man—come see how we 'tan   152
    an' Muddu Hubbard daag sit down an' cry.   153

Translation

Old Mother Hubbard went to the cupboard to give her
    poor dog a bone,
But when she got there, her cupboard was bare, and   140T
    so that dog got none.
And all those other dogs that had stood up on one side, to fight
    and take away the bone,
When they saw how things were, came out empty-handed,
    and bragged emptily that they didn't want any anyway.   145T
But if Mother Hubbard had found that piece of bone, when
    she looked in the cupboard, that day,
Those other dogs there would have eaten it and clashed, once
    they had licked [beaten] Mother Hubbard's dog.
Then they would have cocked their one ear, made a knot in their 150T
    tail, and given a couple winks with their eye,
And said "If you want to see a man, come and see how we are,"
    and Mother Hubbard's dog would have sat down and cried.

6. C. S. Argus (ca. 1891–1896)

"Argus" was the pen name of an anonymous cartoonist whose work appeared in the *Argosy* newspaper in British Guiana between 1885 and the end of the nineteenth century. One of the cartoons in the valuable but fragile collection in Guyana's National Archives bears the initials "C.S.," and I adopted the convention in Rickford (1978: 205) of referring to the cartoonist as "C. S. Argus," with the thought that even so small a clue would aid any future search for his real identity.[27]

Text 6a, "Every Man Has His Price," dates from about 1891. The two characters depicted in this cartoon stand in stark contrast with each other. The one, a well-dressed and self-righteous European woman, is probably

from England. The other, a turbanned, dhoti-clad beggar, is probably a recent immigrant whose period of indenture on the sugar estates has expired
without his returning (or being returned) to India. He is no doubt a Hindu—
hence the evangelical thrust of the woman's remarks. The disproportionate
social status of the artist's two subjects is conveyed by obvious verbal as well
as visual cues: he uses a respectful address term ("missy") and an accommodating discourse style, whereas she does not use an address term, and
her insistent interrogatives have the ring of imperatives. Without for a moment condoning it, we should note that it is her status as a charity-giver that,
added to the weight of her ethnicity and social status, makes her feel she has
the "right" to engage in this kind of questioning. And it is his status as a
recipient of her charity that, added to his ethnicity and social class, places
him under an "obligation" to answer. A refusal to answer would constitute
"dumb insolence," and an insulting answer, however justified as a strike for
his own self-respect, would at the very least result in the loss of her charity
(if indeed she decides to let it pass and not hand him over to the authorities).

The speech of the woman in Text 6a is perfectly standard. The suggestion
in line 155 that the beggar had not understood what she had been saying
could be interpreted as evidence that this immigrant had a limited receptive
competence in SE, especially the "Received Pronunciation" variety (see
Wells 1982, 1: 117) that this expatriate woman may have been using. But it
should be interpreted in part as evidence of his resort to the "feigned mis-
understanding" that those of lower status or authority frequently employ as
a defense mechanism against their "superiors."

The beggar's speech includes several nonstandard phonological features:
the enclitic final vowel in "meesy"; the tense or long medial vowel in the
same word; and the absence of affrication in "sappel" (initial "s" instead of
"ch").[28] Grammatical features of note are the use of "s'pose" as a conditional
marker, attested also in Bolingbroke (1807: 297, 308), which parallels the
use of "sapos" as the primary conditional connective in New Guinea Tok
Pisin (Mihalic 1971: 31); "sa" as an irrealis or future marker, said to be rare
in modern GC (Bickerton 1975: 42); and the object-agreement marker
"um" (discussed in more detail in the introduction to Cruickshank's text),
which virtually disappears from use after the 1920's. The use of a prepositional phrase ("for me") to mark the indirect object is quite unusual, and
appears to have been limited to sentences like this one, in which the appositive object pronoun, an indirect object, and the noun-phrase object all
co-occur. The fact that the preposition is "for" is also interesting, as is the
fact that this is the only preposition in the beggar's remarks; note the curious
absence of prepositional "a," which would be virtually required between
"go" and "sappel." Todd (1982: 66) observes that "for" may have been the
only preposition in early Cameroon Pidgin English, and its use here might

6a. *"Every Man Has His Price"* (ca. 1891)

Lady: (Who has given a penny to the beggar and
is conversing.) Don't you understand me? I mean,
are you a christian and do you go to chapel?

Beggar: No, me meesy, me no go sappel, but s'pose
you gie um for me one bit, me sa go sappel.
("No, my missy, I don't go to chapel, but if you
give me a bit [eight cents], I will go to chapel.")

154
155
156
157
158

indicate a certain degree of repidginization of GC by nineteenth-century Indian immigrants. The fact that the stem form "go" (157) does not have the past reference interpretation that a nonstative stem form would be expected to have in modern GC might also be interpreted as evidence that the beggar's speech is pidginlike; the habitual meaning intended here would normally require a preceding nonpunctual "a" in basilectal GC. It may be that this nonpunctual "a" marker was phonologically deleted following the vowel of the negator (that is, "na a" or "no a" becoming "no"); or that its absence is simply a slip on the part of the cartoonist (who was probably depicting, in any case, a likely rather than an actual event).

Text 6b, "Insult and Injury," dates from between 1895 and 1896. It is valuable as another rare example of women in verbal interaction, here in the form of a domestic servant who meets a friend and begins "bad talking" her former employer, whom she has "discharged."[29] In contrast to Text 6a, the social equality and solidarity between the participants here is signaled by their use of first names and terms of endearment ("Rebecca," "me dear"). They also face each other, unlike the participants in the first cartoon, who are shown standing at awkward right angles to each other—he presumably positioned at the edge of the path, she poised to continue on her way. The beauty of the cartoons as documents of an earlier time is the insights they give not just through words and dress, but through positioning, body gloss, gesture, facial expression, and the other myriad components of "body language" to which Birdwhistell (1970), Goffman (1972), Key (1975), and others have drawn our attention.

Notable linguistic features in Text 6b include the use of "dishoness" as a nominal, an example of the grammatical multifunctionality for which pidgins and creoles are famous;[30] the "becausin" conjunction, the additional syllable of which occurs occasionally in modern GC, and presumably reflects the preferred status of (consonant +) vowel + nasal, alongside (consonant +) vowel as a creole syllable type; the stem form "leff," derived, like the stem forms of a few other verbs ("loss," "bruck") from SE inflected-past forms (see Alleyne 1971: 173); the combination of "a" and "one" (162), with the "one" having the force of "single" here, although both are indefinite articles at mesolectal and basilectal levels of GC, respectively; and the occurrence of "womans" as a plural form, showing that the speaker has begun to acquire SE number-marking for regular or weak forms, but has not yet mastered the irregular or strong plurals.[31]

The speech of the Afro-Guyanese servant in Text 6b is closer to SE than the speech of the Indian beggar in Text 6a. She uses "I" as subject pronoun where he uses "me," and she does not use the object-agreement marker "um." This might be taken to suggest that decreolization, or linguistic acculturation toward English, was more advanced among Afro-

6b. "Insult and Injury" (1895 or 1896)

    Friend: Hi! Rebecca, you leff you' bus'ness?   159
    Rebecca: Yes, me dear, I leff. She abuse me fo'   160
dishoness, becausin' I borrow a pair o' she stockin' and   161
a one bare handkercher fo' me daughtah to wear at   162
Confummation, so I gi'e she discharge. Dem white   163
womans have a bad mind.   164

    "Hi, Rebecca, did you leave your business [job]?"
    "Yes, my dear, I left. She abused [quarreled with] me for dishonesty, because I
borrowed a pair of her stockings and one single handkerchief for my daughter to
wear at Confirmation, so I discharged her. Those white women are mean."

Guyanese than among Indo-Guyanese (having had more time), but the Afro-Guyanese domestic is probably a long-time resident of Georgetown, and we should be cautious about generalizing from her cartoon.

6a is no. 453 in the *Argosy* Collection, National Archives; 6b is no. 904.

7. Van Sertima (1905)

J. Van Sertima was a Guyanese who, in his own words, gave "some attention to the language (very quaint and puzzling to newcomers) spoken by 'mine own people.'" The following texts are from his book *The Creole Tongue of British Guiana*. Interestingly enough, the author was his own publisher (his printer was the Berbice Gazette Store, New Amsterdam, Berbice). One wonders whether he had tried to interest the *Argosy* publishers in his work, given their prior association with dialect material (including the newspaper cartoons by Argus and several editions of McTurk's book), and why, if he had, they did not agree to publish it. Was it because he was a local author rather than an expatriate? We may never know the facts of this particular case, but in general native Guyanese writers have not been as well received at the established publishing houses as foreign visitors have, and much of their work has been self-published and marketed. This is true, for instance, of the voluminous output of the distinguished mathematician and author Norman E. Cameron, and it is also true of Yansen's (1975) slim but valuable lexicon of GC. As a result of this limited access to local and foreign publishing houses, many of the ideas and perspectives of native Guyanese have never found their way into print (Basil Armstrong's work on GC is one example); and even when publishers accepted such works, they were brought out in locally printed, small editions that are extremely difficult to obtain. In this respect, Van Sertima's self-published book reflects a general—and still largely existing—state of affairs.

The fact that Van Sertima was a native Guyanese did not prevent him from accepting and propagating slanderously racist stereotypes about the African contribution to Guyanese Creole. In his introductory chapter, for instance, he claims, on the one hand, that the African slaves essentially acquired their Creole speech from the English inhabitants of the colony, then claims, on the other, that its features reveal physical or mental defects in the slave population, thus absolving the English of all responsibility. That this paradox was characteristic of other early works on creole languages, such as Reed Smith (1926), may make Van Sertima's acceptance of it easier to understand, but the racist terms in which he frames the theory are no less chilling for all that: "The negro travelled along the line of least resistance. Readily, he who was half-devil and half-child, corresponded to his environment. He

adopted the language of his masters; and his descendants inherited it, carrying it wherever they journeyed, and, largely through hereditary causes, which
may connote physical defects of ear or tongue, damaging it in transit" (p. 5).

If one ignores this kind of claptrap, Van Sertima's book can be appreciated
as an interesting record of a decreolized or mesolectal variety of early-
twentieth-century GC, probably representative of the middle-class urban
variety with which he was most familiar. The introductory chapter is followed by a long chapter of "Philological Notes" (an alphabetical glossary of
GC lexical items, including copious references to parallels in English literature), a chapter on "Accidence" (notes on pronunciation and grammar), and
a brief chapter of "Translations," in which extracts from "The Pilgrim's
Progress," "The Parable of the Sower," and "The Aeneid" are translated
into GC, with a few accompanying notes. The texts given here are extracted
from his translations.

That Van Sertima's texts are closer to SE than those of McTurk and most
of the others in this chapter is evident from a number of features. The only
basilectal GC usage in the personal pronouns is the occurrence of "he" as
masculine possessive (168, 169)—this being, as both Bickerton (1973a) and
Rickford (1979) show, the singular-pronoun subcategory that is least frequently realized by an SE form in the speech of modern Guyanese speakers.
By contrast, the first-person-singular subject pronoun is consistently "I"
(165ff), and the third-person-plural subject and possessive pronouns are
consistently "dey" (185, 186). The "dem" tokens in lines 184, 186, and 187
are not personal pronouns, but occurrences of the Creole demonstrative/
deictic pronoun, equivalent to SE "those" (which occurs once, as "dose," in
184). This particular feature persists fairly high into the mesolect.[32]

Continuatives are expressed by "verb + ing" (168) instead of preverbal
"a", and past tense by "was" or "did" (167) instead of "bin." Preverbal "did"
is not attested in any of the earlier texts in this chapter, and occurrences of
"a" as indefinite article (instead of basilectal "one") are more profuse in Van
Sertima's texts than in any of the preceding ones. Semantically plural nouns
in these texts generally take the SE inflectional "-s" suffix ("buds," "t'ings,"
177, 182) except when preceded by a plural quantifier ("hundrid time" 181).
Negation is accomplished by the SE system of postverbal negative place-
ment ("wasn't," "shouldn't," 171, 186) rather than by the preverbal "no" or
"na" of basilectal Creole. The basilectal complementizer "say" does occur
(167), but in combination with nonbasilectal "dat"; like masculine object pronoun "he" (173; cf. basilectal *am/um*), this is characteristic of the mesolect,
which includes forms and combinations of forms found in neither the basilect
nor the acrolect.[33]

It is primarily in phonology that these two texts are most basilectal, notably
in consonant-cluster simplification ("han'" 169), the absence of unstressed
initial syllables ("'pon" 181), the replacement of interdental fricatives by

dental stops ("de," "t'o'ns" 'thorns,' 165, 180), and the realization of SE syllable-final *aun* as GC *ong* ("grung" instead of "ground" 181). There are also some morphosyntactic basilectal features, including the use of the non-stative verb-stem for past-marking ("come," "speak," 165, 175), the grammatically unmarked Creole passive in line 177,* and the consistent use of "fo'" as infinitival complementizer (166, 171, 183).

Van Sertima (p. 56) felt moved to add the following note about the last feature: "A common form of the Infinitive, meaning *for to*. The *to* is lost. 'And Miss Arabella wondered why he always said he was going *for to* do a thing.'—*The Sad Fortunes of the Rev. Amos Barton*." The *OED* lists several other attestations of "for to" = 'in order (to),' dating from 1175 to 1774; and suggests that its use in place of "to" spread from the purposive environments to nonpurposive ones (attestations are from 1225–1624). The purposive "for to" is classified by the *OED* as "archaic or vulgar," and its nonpurposive equivalent as "obsolete in educated use," but assuming that both uses persisted longer in speech than in writing, they might well have been present in the speech of the earliest English colonists in the Caribbean, and they might indeed have provided one model for the Creole infinitival complementizer, as suggested by Van Sertima.[34] However, other sources must plainly be considered, including Twi *fi* and Yoruba *fu* (J. Edwards 1974). What is most likely is that West African and English sources converged with or reinforced each other in the emergence of the Creole complementizer (Byrne 1984; Winford 1985a: 621).

According to Bickerton (1975: 8), Van Sertima's texts suggest that "the continuum of Guyanese speech, far from being a recent innovation, is at least the better part of a century old." The mesolectal features in some of St. Clair's early-nineteenth-century texts—possessive pronouns and inflected plurals in Text 3b, for instance—indicate that the variation may have been present from even earlier, as Alleyne (1971) suggests. Note, however, that tempting as it is to regard the mesolectal features in St. Clair's and Van Sertima's texts as characteristic of Georgetown, or of urban speech more generally, we should not ignore the intersecting role of social class and network. St. Clair's Miss Fanny speaks a Creole that is closer to SE than the speech of the other blacks he quotes, but this is probably to be attributed less to the fact that she is from Georgetown than to the fact that she is a free and relatively wealthy woman, associating with "buckra" and other SE speakers on a level that slaves seldom (if ever) did. Similarly, Van Sertima was probably a member of the Georgetown middle class, and his native variety of Creole—the one he seems to have drawn on for these translations—would have been less basilectal than the speech of the Georgetown working class.[35]

---

*The "it" in "it trod down" is interpretable as underlying object rather than subject because it is [−animate], referring to "seed," while the verb requires a [+animate] subject/agent. See Allsopp (1983).

We will see later that the speech of rural and urban middle-class people is marked by similar mesolectal features, and that there are always some Creole features at all social class levels that link the urban and rural speakers. These similarities suggest that urban and rural varieties of Creole in Guyana may indeed have developed from similar if not identical bases, and that it is only because of the greater prevalence of SE models and the more numerous opportunities for upward mobility in the city that mesolectal varieties are encountered more often in urban than in rural areas.[36]

Texts 7a and 7b are from Van Sertima (1905), pp. 55 and 57, respectively.

7a. From his translation of 'The Pilgrim's Progress'

As I bin walkin' troo de wildaness of dis wirl, I come to a   165
certain place whe' a den was, an' I lie down de' fo' sleep: an' as I   166
was sleepin' I dream a dream. I dream say dat I see a man—he did got   167
on rags an' he was stan'in' in a certain place wid he face tu'n from   168
he own house, wid' a book in he han' an' a big bundle 'pon he back. I   169
look an' I see he open de book an' read in it; an' as he bin readin',   170
he begin fo' cry an' trimble; an' when he wasn't able fo' keep in   171
he'self no longa, he bu's' out wid a big cry—mek you'   172
hawt (heart) feel fo' hear he—sayin' "Wha' I gwine do?"   173

7b. From his translation of "The Parable of the Sower" (Luke, 8:4–13)

An' when plenty people did gadda togedda, an' did come to he out a   174
every city, he speak in a parable: 175
    A sowa went out to sow he seed: an' as he was sowin', some a de   176
seed fall by de wayside; an' it trod down, an' de buds eat it   177
up. An' some fall 'pon a rock; an' as soon as it spring up, it widda   178
away 'cause it didn't got no moisture. An' some fall in between   179
t'o'ns; an' de t'o'ns spring up wid it an' choke it. An' de oddas   180
fall 'pon good grung, an' spring up an' bear fruit a hundird time.   181
An' when he done sayin' dese t'ings, he holla out   182
"Whoeva got e'as fo' hear, le' dem hear." . . . Now de parable is   183
dis: de seed is de wo'd of God. Dose by de wayside is dem dat   184
hear; den de devil come an' tek away de wo'd out a dey   185
hawts, so dat dey shouldn't believe an' be save'. Dem 'pon de rock   186
is dem who, when dey hear, tek in de wo'd wid j'y.   187

8. Cruickshank (1905)

J. Graham Cruickshank, the most important chronicler of early-twentieth-century GC, was a close and accurate observer of the language and culture of the "ordinary people." His observations and notes are preserved in a number of books and articles, including *Negro Humour: Being Sketches in the Market, on the Road, and at my Back Door* (1905), *Black Talk, Being Notes on Negro Dialect in British Guiana, with (inevitably) a Chapter on Barbados* (1916), and "The Wreckage of an Industry" (in *The West India Committee Circular*, March 6, 1930). The ethnographic techniques he used, as conveyed in the following extract, could still be recommended to students of field methods in linguistics or anthropology:

Do you want to know how the other half of the City lives—what it eats, how much it pays for it? Do you want to pick up rough diamonds in the way of wit and humour? Stroll through the market on Saturday night—eyes and ears open, forgetting you are somebody, remembering you are nobody, shedding for awhile any little dignity that may be yours or thought to be. Listen to the talk, the badinage, the "greetings in the marketplace," the shrill abuse which falls on the Portugee like rain on a duck's back. Go the round of the stalls, note the infinite variety of wares, the coolness and re-source of stall-owners. You will assuredly find food for interest, for amusement (1905: 21).

From the journal *Timehri* (27 [1944]: 150–51) we learn that Cruickshank was born in British Guiana in 1877, apparently of European parents. Edu-cated in Scotland, he lived and worked in British Guiana for nearly five de-cades, from 1896 until his death in 1944. *Black Talk*, consisting primarily of notes on words and phrases that he had encountered in the colony, was published in 1916 but was actually begun around 1895. In his Foreword, Cruickshank tells us that he was impelled to take these notes when he was interrupted one day in "the framing of a judgmatic Audit Report" by an old black man who had come to his back door to beg. Cruickshank, who laments the fact that earlier writers on British Guiana and Barbados had neglected "the human element" and failed to record the undoctored dialogue of the local black population, reproduces the entire conversation (p. i):

"Massa, I beg a copper!"
"Old man," I said, "have you no family to support you? Have you no children?"
He played deaf. "Sah?"
"Have you no family?" I repeated.
"Massa, my family them all dead out."
"How do you live?"
"Sah?"
"How do you make out?"
"How me mek out?" He pointed upwards to the black rafters of the kitchen. "Tatta Fadda a mek provide-ance. He-self a gi'e me nyam."
This was well but vague.
"Do you get poor relief: you does get poor money?"
"Wan s'illing a week"—he held up one finger. "Da, no more."

"Are you hungry?"
"But look me trial!" said he apostrophising the coal-pot. He put his hand before an open mouth. "Hungry! Youse'f too!"

The very fact that Cruickshank was able to understand the basilectal dialogue of this "old-time Negro" (note the habitual aspect marker and benefactive serial-verb construction in "He-self a gi'e me nyam"), and even use a few mesolectal Creole forms himself (habitual "does," for instance), is noteworthy, but it is because of his impulse to jot down the old man's words and phrases and vow to keep notes on all the conversations he heard thereafter that the historical linguist has such a treasure trove of material. He had some faults—he was somewhat sentimental about the attributes of the "old-time Negroes"; and in extolling the "benefits" of slavery (1905: 72), he is as much an apologist for that iniquitous institution as Bolingbroke and other nineteenth-century writers were. At the same time, he was probably more conscious than any of his contemporaries that the "Negro Talk" of his day was in flux (1916: ii) and wanted to put it on record before it disappeared "with the last of the old people." He lost no opportunity to do this, as is evident in his newspaper article (1930) on the decline of the sugar industry on Wakenaam Island, Essequibo, in which he devotes considerable space to the recollections—in dialect—of two "old-time Negroes" from the island.

Whatever his earlier occupations might have been (his reference to his work on an audit report suggests that he had been trained as an accountant), Cruickshank was serving as the superintendent of Government Archives by the mid-1930's, when John E. Reinecke, then at work on his Ph.D. dissertation (1937), corresponded with him about the "Negro English" and "Negro Dutch" of British Guiana.[37] In this capacity, he wrote the Foreword to the first of the Guiana Edition volumes, the 1941 reprint of Bolingbroke (1807), and published a review in the *Daily Chronicle* newspaper (July 1941) of the second volume, Walter E. Roth's translation of Adriann Van Berkel's *Amerikaanische Voyagien* (1695). In sum, Cruickshank was not only a meticulous chronicler of the speech of his time, but also a scholar who pursued his interest, through correspondence and commentary, with other observers and scholars of Guyanese speech and culture, past and present.

Black Talk is well known among students of Creole for its first-person account—recorded from an old immigrant—of how the indentured Africans acquired English in the New World. (See pp. 61–62, above for the full quotation.) Bickerton (1975: 9) commends Cruickshank for his readiness, "long before Herskovits and Herskovits 1934, . . . to give the contributions of African languages their due," and it is hard to dispute this assessment, since Cruickshank was as sensitive to those languages' direct loans as to their influence in the form of loan translations.[38] "Part of the survival of the African tongue," he wrote (1916: ii–iii), "takes the shape of genuine African words. Part of it takes the shape of English words—altered and done up again in a characteristically African way. The most subtle survival of African is the survival of African idiom—*in Negro English*! The last phase is of peculiar difficulty, and is therefore of peculiar interest."

However valuable *Black Talk* is, and it is valuable indeed for its description of GC (including historical notes as well as a glossary), Cruickshank's earlier book, *Negro Humour*, is more valuable still for its lengthy GC texts, and it is from this source that we draw the last text in this chapter.

Text 8, "A Gill Seasonin'," provides superb material for the ethnographer of communication (Hymes 1964, 1968), especially for one attempting a "reconstructive ethnography of speaking" (Zenk 1984). The dialogue it contains is realistic in tone, and it is also similar in grammar and discourse convention to what one might overhear in a Guyanese market today. Shoppers of all social classes are expected to engage in bargaining and banter of the type exemplified in this text, and to do it in some variety of Creole; the use of Creole is an important element in indicating that one is familiar with local prices and produce and custom, and therefore not easily fooled. Another element in successful bargaining is a relaxing of the politeness maxim (Grice 1975) that applies in other speech situations. Note, for instance, that the huckster's remarks are impatiently interrupted by both the author (lines 191, 194) and the second customer (201); that the author does not attempt to conceal his disbelief that the huckster is poor (192); that the second customer quickly takes umbrage (202) when the huckster jokes that seasoning is not to be used as a main dish; and that the "slatternly girl" deprecates the merchandise (207) and expresses indignation when her request for a free pepper is denied. The verbal strategies of the retail customer come as no surprise to the huckster, for they are the very ones he himself employs when buying his produce wholesale from the producers and middlemen. Cruickshank outlines these strategies on an earlier page (p. 8):

When buying oranges, for instance (and this is a tip I got from my friend of the red scarf), assert that they are thin-skinned and sour as a lime, small and dry, also that the "white peoples dem" don't eat oranges now as they used to, even though none of these statements may, strictly speaking, be correct. For thereby you will get the fruit for less perhaps, and greater profit will accrue. "You must wo'k dese people wid a system," said Red Scarf, confidentially to me, "fo' dey is got a lot a sma't mans among dem."

In the role of seller, however, the huckster's strategies are quite different. They include respectful address ("sahib," "muma"), joking with and conciliation of the customer (199, 203), and hyperbolic praise of the merchandise (208–9). The verbal routines of the huckster in this passage resemble those of the Jamaican candy seller in Bennett (1966); they are typical of hucksters throughout the Caribbean, perhaps of hucksters everywhere.

In terms of phonology, lexicon, and syntax, Text 8 contains several of the basilectal features discussed in connection with the earlier texts, including vowel epenthesis and the substitution of a labial stop for a fricative in "bekis" ('vexed' 203); infinitival "fo'" (201); conditional "sup-pose" (189, 198); and the multifunctional use of a word, represented here by verbal "full" (201). But there are a few features worth noting that we have either not seen or not commented on before, such as the nasalization of the labial stop in "tomacco" (189). Also to be noted is the variation between the basilectal speech of the seller and the mesolectal speech of the customers (who hold the upper hand in these interactions), marked among other features by his use of pronominal subject "me" and object "um" and their use of "I," "A," and "it."

The real value of this text lies elsewhere, however: it is one of the best records we have of turn-of-the-century Indo-Guyanese speech, and with it we can extend the analysis we began in Chapter 2 of the distinctive elements of that variety. In particular, Text 8 affords the opportunity to examine the two features—object-verb word order and the use of "um" as transitivizing or object-agreement marker—that Devonish (1978: 39–42) singles out as distinctive of Indo-Guyanese Creole.

Devonish's thesis that object-verb word order is a distinctive trait of turn-of-the-century Indo-Guyanese Creole, and one reflecting Indic, specifically Bhojpuri influence, at first appears to be supported by the following usages in Text 8: "bittle buy" (198), "tomacco s-moke" (199), "two peppa gi'e um" (214–15). However, four considerations suggest that these merely represent reversals of normal verb-object word order to achieve object topicalization, a process common enough in other varieties of GC as well as in SE. First of all, the transitivizing "um," which occurs in lines 214–15 and in other examples of object-verb word order in Kirke (1898: 239) cited by Devonish, such as "no money hav um" ('I have no money'), is normally inserted only where an object noun phrase follows the verb in surface structure; or where it can be assumed to have followed the verb in underlying structure prior to the operation of *WH*-question formation, topicalization, or some other movement rule. Second, the common Bhojpuri subject-object-verb word order is not attested in Cruickshank's texts or any of the other available sources, which is what we would expect if Bhojpuri word order had been transferred to Indo-Guyanese Creole intact. Instead, the sentences illustrating object-verb word order all lack overt subjects. The unexpressed subjects in each case refer to the speaker or hearer, and there are other examples in nineteenth-century Indo-Guyanese Creole, as well as modern GC, of first- and second-person-singular pronouns being deleted more often than any others because of their facile recoverability from the discourse context (see below and Rickford 1979, 1981). Third, the vegetable seller in Cruickshank's text uses verb-object word order (e.g., "mus gi'e um peppa" 214) more frequently than he does object-verb word order, suggesting that object-verb word order, if in fact transferred from Bhojpuri, has been limited both syntactically and quantitatively in the process. Finally, the equative noun phrase in line 191 ("Poor coolie man, me—") clearly has been fronted by topicalization, even though the sentence is incomplete, so we have independent evidence that this movement transformation was alive and well in the market-seller's speech.

On the other hand, transitivizing or object agreement "um" was indeed a unique feature of (East) Indian speech; no examples occur in the speech of any of the Africans or Afro-Guyanese represented in Argus's or Cruickshank's texts.[39] On the basis of the nine examples in Text 8—three in lines 198–200, two in 214, and one each in 205, 208, 212, and 215—plus 21 examples that I culled from other texts in Cruickshank (1905) and elsewhere,[40] we can now make several generalizations about this important syntactic feature:

1. The canonical form of the sentences in which object agreement "um" occurs is

X	subject noun phrase	transitive verb	um	object noun phrase	Y,

where X and Y are free variables and the subject noun phrase may be a pronoun (not so the object noun phrase, which must include a full noun). Unlike the "um" that occurs in lines 188 and 189 ("Coolie call um cheelum"), the object agreement "um" in line 198 is not simply the pronominal creole equivalent of SE "it," and cannot be translated as such (*'sell it everything'). It is weakly stressed and morphologically linked to the verb as a clitic, serving as the object-marking equivalent of the subject-agreement or appositive subject forms that are prevalent in pidgins and creoles worldwide, as in Tok Pisin "ol *i* sindaun" ('all he sit-down' = 'they sat down') and GC "di piipl dem *di* tiifin tuu baad" ('the people them they are stealing too much' = 'the people are stealing too much').

As Givón (1976: 185) notes, grammatical (subject and object) agreement occurs in a wide variety of languages worldwide, usually arising "from anaphoric pronominalization in topical discourse contexts."[41] Object agreement, on this analysis, represents a reanalysis of "marked" topic shift (TS) and afterthought topic shift (AT) as neutral (ibid., p. 157):

TS ("marked")	AT ("semi-marked")	Neutral ("demarked")
the man, I saw *him* ⇒	I saw *him*, *the man* ⇒	I saw-*him* the man

Although it is important to differentiate the object-marking "um" from the simple pronominal "um," Devonish (1978: 41) perhaps overstates the point when he says that "*um* here has nothing to do with the 3rd person singular Creole marker *am/um*." Givón (1976: 180) claims that "verb agreement paradigms *always* arise from anaphoric pronoun paradigms," and in addition to the examples from Bantu and other languages that Givón cites, Joseph Greenberg (personal communication) has drawn my attention to the suffixed "-m" of Salish and the prefixed "i-" of Gilyak as examples of the general tendency for transitive (object-marking) forms to derive from third-person markers, which in turn have evolved from demonstrative markers.

2. The subject or agent of the verb is rarely expressed in overt form (only in five of 30 cases), and whether overtly expressed or "understood," most frequently refers either to the speaker or the hearer (21 of 30 cases), although this may be due to the predominance of conversational dialogue over narrative in the sources. The absence of overt subject forms may reflect the diachronic (if not synchronic) relation of object marking to object topicalization or focusing.

3. Modals (like "can" and "mus'") and negative particles ("no," "na") may precede the verb, but tense-aspect markers like "bin" and "sa" never do. Since these forms are rarely evidenced elsewhere in the speech of object-marking "um" users, such speech may represent a pidgin or early acculturation variety for indentured Indians.

4. Where no object noun phrase immediately follows the verb, the underlying object typically occurs in sentence-initial position, suggesting (a) that it has been fronted from postverbal position in underlying structure by means of *WH*-question formation (as in lines 200 and 212) or conventional topicalization (line 215 and elsewhere), and (b) that "um" insertion must precede these and other movement rules. But sentences like "tomacco s-moke Ø" (line 199) and "Wha' mo' want Ø?" (in Cruickshank 1905: 18) show that object-agreement marking with "um" is not obligatory.

5. Indirect objects and the transitivizing/object agreement "um" can only co-occur if the indirect objects are specially marked by a preposition, and follow the "um" as in the example in Text 6a (line 158): "gie um *for me* one bit." Whenever an indirect object, particularly a pronoun, follows the verb without any prepositional marking, the transitivizing "um" is omitted, even if an object noun phrase follows, as in line 211: "gi'e Ø me a pepper!" This may correspond to Givón's (1976: 160) observation that datives stand above accusatives and humans above nonhumans in the topicality hierarchy.

6. The verbs that take object-marking "um" form a rather restricted set: "buy," "sell," "want," "gi(v)e," "got," "gat," "get," "hav(e)," "do," "drink," "eat," "take," "pay," "plant," and "make." Note that the list includes possessive verbs ("got") and result verbs ("make") but excludes perception verbs like "see" (cf. Simpson 1983: 25). The objects themselves are all nonhuman and inanimate, and most frequently generic in reference.

These syntactic details should facilitate further research into this object-agreement marker, and should also enable us to track down its sources and parallels in other languages. Given that it is restricted to the speech of Indo-Guyanese, it is natural to attribute it to interference or transfer from Bhojpuri, the native language of most Indian indentured immigrants. Bhojpuri does contain an object-marking postposition *ke*, as in the following example from Shukla (1981: 98): "ham laiki: (*ke*) moha:-b" = 'I girl (object marker) love" (first-person, singular, future) = 'I will love the girl.'[42] But Shukla's analysis reveals that *ke* differs from object-marking "um" in turn-of-the-century Indian GC in almost every respect: *ke* follows the noun, is never used with nonhuman object nouns and direct objects, and marks the indirect rather than the direct object when both occur in a sentence.

Devonish (1978: 42) has noted the parallel between GC "um" and the transitivizing *im* of New Guinea Tok Pisin (as in *har-im* 'hear' and *bruk-im* 'break'). The parallel may turn out to be a revealing one for our understanding of the universals of pidginization, for the Tok Pisin construction appears to have few immediate sources in the surrounding Melanesian or Austronesian languages (Gillian Sankoff personal communication). However, there are differences between the Tok Pisin and GC cases. In Tok Pisin, the *im* is obligatory for many transitive verbs, the transitive verbs take *im* regardless of whether the object is a pronoun or a full noun phrase, and the transitive verbs allow co-occurrences of direct and indirect pronominal objects (see Wurm 1971: 22–38), all unlike Indo-Guyanese Creole.

The text is from Cruickshank (1905), pp. 17–19.

8. *"A Gill Seasonin'"*

"Coolie call um *cheelum*," said the vegetable seller, affably.	188
"Englis' man call um pipe. Sup-pose tomacco dey, s-moke	189
—ah, same lika fire." He waved his hand to the galvanised roof.	190
"Sahib, me beg you li'l' tomacco! Poor coolie man, me—"	191
"Poor?" I pointed to the tomatoes, etc., parcelled out on the sacking.	192
"'Ow much, sahib? No mo' gill-gill	193
—salat, tomatee, ceeleri—"	194
"I know. How much you sell in a day?"	195
"Wan day!" He held up one finger. "Sometime two-bit,	196
s'illin', bit-'n'alf, five	197
cent. Sup-pose white people buy, sell um every'ing: bittle buy,	198
full um belly, tomacco s-moke. H-a." He grinned affably. . . .	199
"Ow much want um, muma? Seasonin'	200
no' fo' full belly—"	201
"A know all about seasonin'. Tek it back!"	202
"A'right muma, no bekis—". . .	203

Approaches . . . a slatternly girl with straw hat giving way at the crown.   204
"Babu, got um any lime?"   205
"H-a. Good lime, cent, cent."   206
Slatternly girl (shaking her head dubiously). "N-o, dey is too dry up."   207
Babu: "Good lime, muma. Prappa sweet. Can' get um   208
betta lime whole ma'kit." . . .   209
Slatternly girl (doubtfully): "Well, a dunno. Leh me see. Babu—ol'   210
man, gi'e me a pepper!"   211
"H-a. Wha' somet'ing buy um?"   212
Slatternly girl: "Gaad! An' it is only a pepper a askin' you fo'!"   213
"Sup-pose buy um anyt'ing—*mus'* gi'e um peppa—two   214
peppa gi'e um."   215

Translation

"East Indians call it cheelum," said the vegetable seller, affably.
"The Englishman calls it a pipe. If tobacco was available, I'd smoke
—ah, just like fire." He waved his hand to the galvanised roof.   190T
"Sahib, I beg you for a little tobacco! I'm a poor coolie man, I—"
"Poor?" I pointed to the tomatoes, etc., parcelled out on the sacking.
"How much, sahib? No more than a gill [penny] here, a penny there
—salad [lettuce], tomato, celery—"
"I know. How much do you sell in a day?"   195T
"One day!" He held up one finger. "Sometimes two bits [sixteen cents],
a shilling [twenty-four cents], a bit and a half [twelve cents], five
cents. If white people were buying, I'd sell everything: buy
food, fill my belly, smoke tobacco. Ha." He grinned affably. . . .
"How much do you want, Muma [address term]. Seasoning [eschallot]   200T
isn't to fill your belly—"
"I know all about seasoning. Take it back!"
"All right, muma, don't be vexed—." . . .
Approaches . . . a slatternly girl with straw hat giving way at the crown.
"Babu, do you have any limes?"   205T
"H-a. Good limes, a cent, a cent."
"N-o, they are too dried up."
"Good limes, muma. They are proper sweet. You can't get
better limes in the whole market." . . .
"Well, I don't know. Let me see. Babu—old   210T
man, give me a pepper!"
"H-a. What did you buy?"
"God! And it is only a pepper I'm asking you for!"
"If you buy something, I'll give you a pepper for sure—two
peppers I'll give you."

Recordings of Natural Speech: Cane Walk

In this chapter we turn from the written texts of earlier periods to recordings of natural speech made more recently.[1] Before I go into the details of
these texts, let me say a word about the sense in which they can be considered "natural." Many of the tape recordings from which they are drawn involve interaction between close friends, relatives, and peer-group members,
and in all the recordings I drew on techniques designed to minimize the constraints of the recording context (Labov 1972a). As a result, a large proportion of the material consists of excited, emotionally charged, and spontaneous or casual speech. Now, I do not wish to claim that casual speech is
more natural—in an absolute sense—than any other variety.[2] By natural I
simply mean that the spoken samples in this and subsequent chapters are
characteristic of everyday speech in an everyday setting. Unlike some of the
written samples in Chapters 3 and 6, they are not reconstructed from memory, conventionalized, or fictionally created.

All the texts in this chapter were recorded in Cane Walk, a pseudonym for
a sugar-estate community on the East Coast Demerara, located within half
an hour's drive of the capital, Georgetown. Most of its residents are Indo-
Guyanese (East Indians). The history and social structure of the community
and an analysis of pronominal variation therein are provided in Rickford
(1979). From the sample of 24 speakers studied in that earlier work, eight
were selected for this chapter. Together they represent the major sociolinguistic divisions in the community, notably its two social classes, both
sexes, and the three main age groups, as indicated in Table 4.1.

For Cane Walk's two social classes, I use the designations "estate class"
and "non-estate class," which are equivalent to working class and lower-
middle class, respectively. Estate-class members have less prestigious occupations, earn less money, and in general have had less formal schooling,

TABLE 4.1
Cane-Walk Speakers in This Chapter by Class, Age, and Sex

Text set number and name	Social class	Age	Sex
9. Derek	Estate class	14	Male
10. Irene	Estate class	42	Female
11. Reefer	Estate class	35	Male
12. Granny	Estate class	58	Female
13. Katherine	Non-estate class	14	Female
14. Sheik	Non-estate class	35	Male
15. Bonnette	Non-estate class	29	Female
16. Ustad	Non-estate class	62	Male

often no more than "third standard" or grade 3, than the others. But the distinction between them is primarily ethnographic and community-based. Estate class identifies those who work in laboring positions on the sugar estate, such as cane-cutting and weeding, essentially continuing the traditional role of their Indian forefathers who came to Guyana between 1838 and 1917. Members of this class are often referred to as "estate people" or "fieldworkers" in local usage. Non-estate class refers to those people who have managed to break away from field labor on the sugar estate and from the estate "culture." They (or their parents, in the case of the young speakers) work as shopkeepers, contractors, bookkeepers, and clerks, and enjoy a more regular salary, better working conditions, and the promise of higher socioeconomic status.

Estate-class members tend to have social networks almost exclusively within Cane Walk, to speak basilectal and lower-mesolectal varieties of GC that, like their occupations, are similar to those of their forefathers, and to express some skepticism about the value of speaking "proper English." Non-estate members tend to have extensive social networks outside of Cane Walk, some of them with higher-status groups in Georgetown, to speak mid-mesolectal to acrolectal varieties, and to agree much more strongly that speaking "proper English" helps one to "get a better job and get ahead" (Rickford 1983a).[3]

The three age groups represented in Table 4.1—"young," "middle," and "old"—reflect distinctions that are ethnographically significant. The cutoff age for the young group is seventeen—eighteen being the age at which one is eligible to vote and is considered a "big man" or woman. The old group includes everyone above fifty-five, the age at which many sugar workers retire. The middle group consists of the adults in between these two major transition points, many of whom work and socialize together without significant age differentiation.

9. Derek (1975–1976)

Derek is the youngest person in this sample—fourteen years old when he was recorded in 1975 and 1976. He was at the time in form IV, at the secondary school level, making him also one of the most highly educated persons in the sample. His father is a cane cutter, and neither he nor Derek's mother had gone beyond the fourth grade. Although Derek had already gone farther in school than the average estate-class child, he remained very close to his estate roots. From his grandmother, an accomplished storyteller, he had learned a rich repertoire of folktales, and he narrated these with aplomb, complete with the basilectal wording in which they had originally been framed. His social network did not extend significantly beyond Cane Walk—four of his five best friends came from there—and even though he demonstrated in Creole-to-English Correction tests that he had a good control of SE forms and structures, his overall performance in the recordings made him one of the most basilectal speakers in the sample. He was, for instance, one of only six speakers who never used morphologically marked possessive pronouns in the first-person and third-masculine subcategories—always *mi(i)*, *(h)ii*, never *mai*, *hiz*, over a total of 66 and 30 occurrences of each subcategory, respectively.

The formulaic opening (*dis bina won maan*) and closing (*stoorii don!*) in Text 9a are characteristic of folktales in many parts of the world. More elaborate closings are sometimes used in Guyana (*di bokit ben, an di stoorii en*), similar to those reported for other parts of the Caribbean (Parsons 1918; Beckwith 1929). This text contains several other morphosyntactic features of note. The use of *naso* as a negative conditional connective (223 and elsewhere), translatable as 'if not' or 'or else,' has not previously been reported for Guyana or any other Creole, but Ian Hancock (personal communication) reports that it occurs in Sierra Leone Krio and (as *daso*) in Cameroonian. I recorded other instances in an interview with a group of youths at Port Mourant, Corentyne, but the occurrences in this narrative are the only ones I encountered in Cane Walk.[4] Its etymology is uncertain—reduction from English "(if) not so" is conceivable in phonological terms, but the phrase strikes me as too stilted to have served as an actual model. Other features of interest in Text 9a are the emphatic or rhetorical *positive* in line 239, expressed by *na*, plus rising intonation (see B. Bailey 1966: 93–94; Christie 1979), and the unmarked relative clause in line 226 (*a mek ail*), which has no surface relative pronoun.

Texts 9b–9d contain other morphosyntactic features of interest. Line 256 (M.'s speech) contains one example of an *it a* ('It have') existential. This structure is more typical of Trinidad, the usual GC existential being *ii ga(t)* or *de(e) ga(t)*. Line 263 contains a morphologically complex *WH*-formative (*wisaid*, 'where'), of a type that is found throughout the Caribbean. Compare *wa mek?* ('why?'), in Irene's texts below (381; see also Bickerton 1980: 118), and *wa paat* ('where') in Antiguan Creole (Reisman 1970).[5] The occurrence of finite *mos* instead of infinitival *tu* or *fu* in lines 282 and 283—*shi waan yu* mos *du om* instead of *shi waan yu* tu *du om*—is characteristically basilectal and illustrates what is apparently a pan-creole preference for finite verbal complements over nonfinite ones (Bickerton 1980: 117). The use of *bin* preceding *gat* in 264 is problematic because in combination with a stative verb like this, *bin* should mean—according to Bickerton (1975: 35)— that the state no longer exists, but it is clear that Derek's family still has the machine. The problem here may be due to the fact that the speaker used stative *gat* instead of a nonstative/dynamic predicate like *get* 'obtain'[6] or *bai* (the predicate used in 266). Alternatively, the problem may lie in the analysis of *bin* itself. In the introduction to Irene's texts, Bickerton's analysis of *bin* will be considered in detail. Text 9d includes virtually the full set of habitual markers in the continuum—*a* or *o* (267, 271), *doz* (290), *gu* (292) and Ø (295)—and illustrates also the use of *stedii* (281) to express a persistent, repeated, or continuative action. "Steady" is commonly used in a similar way in VBE, as in "And you know we be *steady* jammin all the Crips" (Baugh 1983: 85–87, 1984). This usage may reflect VBE's prior creole ancestry.

Derek's texts also contain four occurrences of preverbal *don* (221, 228, 235, 241), and they all occur in *wen* clauses. The two occurrences of "done" in Chapter 3 (149, 182) also occur in "when" clauses, and so do all the five *don* sentences in Bickerton's (1975: 40) discussion of the role of this preverbal marker in the basilect. Bickerton does not note this fact in discussing the examples, but in the chapter dealing with the mesolect (pp. 85–87), the occurrence of *don* (or *finish*) in the subordinate *wen* or *afta* clause of a complex sentence is presented almost as a precondition for the use of the form, and given a reasonable interpretation: "the first of two actions has to be completed before the second can be begun." Bickerton goes on to note that when *don* does not occur in a subordinate temporal phrase, its completive function is still evident, and it is translatable as 'completely' or 'definitely.' In a similar vein, Labov et al. (1968: 265–66) suggest that VBE *done* carries intensive meaning. A completive/intensive interpretation (and adverbial glosses like 'already,' 'definitely,' or 'really'; cf. Labov 1972c: 56) will generally apply also to GC occurrences of *don* outside of subordinate *wen* clauses. There are five such occurrences in this volume:[7] three from basilectal speakers (Irene 383; Lohtan 1082; and Dhanish 1122, one from a mesolectal speaker Ali 983, and one in the newspaper extract in Chapter 6 (1362).

However, with stative predicates, *don* signals, not the completion of a state, but its inception and continuing existence or relevance. In GC *ii don marid*, as in VBE "He *bin* [stressed] married," for example, the referent is to be understood as still married at the moment of speaking or at a reference point in the past established by other elements in the sentence or discourse context. This point is made in relation to GC *don* both by Bickerton (1975: 41–42) and by Gibson (1982: 166–71). Although Gibson attempts to spell out the interaction with stativity explicitly, her analysis is not helped by the fact that she gives *don* two different and virtually opposed definitions with stative and nonstative predicates. With statives, *don* is said to refer to a "*temporally restricted but non-punctual situation*"; with nonstatives, she describes it as a "*punctual aspect marker*," meaning that the situation is "not conceived of as lasting in time."

On the other hand, the description of *don* as a "completive" marker is potentially misleading with respect to stative predicates. To avoid the difficulties of both definitions, we could follow Comrie (1976: 16ff) and describe it instead as a perfective marker, indicating a view of the situation as "a single whole, without distinction of the various separate phases that make up the situation." One virtue of this definition is that the elements of completion and punctuality would be implied, although not strictly so, and the ingressive meaning of *don* with statives would fit in with Comrie's general observation that in many languages, "the perfective forms of some verbs, in particular of some stative verbs, can in fact be used to indicate the beginning of a situation." However, a better way of achieving a unified analysis—better because it more closely approximates what seems to be the real semantic force and function of this form—would be to describe *don* instead as an emphatic perfect; whether we are dealing with processes (nonstatives) conceived of as having been *completed* in the past, or with states (statives) *initiated* in the past, *don* might be seen as an emphatic indicator of the "continuing present relevance of a past situation" (Comrie 1976: 52). The frequent occurrence of *don* in complex sentences with *wen* would fit in with this analysis, for in these sentences two actions or states are juxtaposed, and *don* explicitly signals the relevance of the completed action/continuing state in the *wen* clause to the action/state referred to in the main clause. Note finally that although *don* can sometimes be replaced by zero (in the case of nonstative verbs; see Alleyne 1980: 82; Gibson 1982: 168) or by *hav* (in lects closer to English; see Bickerton 1975: 86), these alternatives are not available in all situations (see Bickerton 1975: 42, Gibson 1982: 168), and they lack the emphatic force of *don*.

One interesting but little-known fact about *don* is that it can be used before noun phrases in equative sentences with human subjects, as in *na blod don?* 'Isn't she blood (i.e. related by blood) already?,' and *(shi) don o chainii wumon oredii do* 'She's already a Chinese, though.' This usage occurs both prenominally and clause-finally, like its basilectal pre- and postverbal equivalent. Unlike the latter, however, it can occur with an inflected form of the English copula ("be") and persists well into the mesolect.[8] This prenominal/ postnominal *don* has not been discussed before, either in Bickerton (1975) or elsewhere in the literature on pidgins and creoles. There are no examples in the texts in this volume, but this may be due in part to the fact that these occurrences of *don* seem to occur primarily in agitated discussions (rare in recordings), where one participant vigorously asserts the prior membership of a person in a more general class (an ethnic group, a blood relation, a particular nationality or occupation) as a means of clinching an argument about that person's conduct.

Derek's texts also allow us to test Bickerton's (1975: 30–33) claim that nonpunctual aspect markers like *a* and *doz*—which are used to describe events as continuative/progressive or iterative/habitual processes rather than occurrences at a single point in time—do not occur with stative predicates. The claim, expressed as the "Main Stative Rule," is that these iterative and continuative markers are deleted or nongenerated in the derivation of stative predicates even where they are semantically appropriate and would otherwise (with a nonstative predicate) be required. The stative predicates in question include stative verbs like *waan*, *hav/gat*, and *noo*; modals (*mos*); passives; and clauses beginning with conditional *if* or temporal *wen*.

Walter Edwards (1983: 299–300) challenges this claim with respect to *wen* clauses. I am sympathetic to the attempt, since I have observed counterexamples to Bickerton's claim in my own data and find Bickerton's eclectic explanations of counterexamples in his own data (1975: 35, 38–39) unconvincing. But Edwards's challenge is based on a hypothetical rather than a factual counterexample ("When she *doz* come here, she *doz* get on bad"), and one that seems questionable to me and other Guyanese whose intuitions I elicited (they all prefer "When she Ø come here, she *doz* get on bad," with the aspect marker absent from the *wen* clause). Furthermore, the effect of temporal clauses on aspect-marker "absence" in my data is pretty much in line with the predictions of Bickerton's claim. For instance, in Derek's Text 9c, both he and his friend use habitual *a/o* (267, 270, 271, 277) in describing the teacher's actions; but in the very first *wen* clause (279), the *a* is not generated, and the verbs in the main clause are also unmarked (*kom*, *lash*). The same systematic effect is observed in the nongeneration of habitual *doz* in the *wen* clause in Text 9d, line 292, and in the *if* clauses in lines 294 and 295. Furthermore, not a single *wen* clause containing habitual *a* or *doz* turned up in a computer run that I did of all the lines (101 in all) containing *wen* in the texts in this volume. Four of these clauses did contain continuative *a*, however (561, 1127, 1152, and 1216), establishing that the Main Stative Rule is by no means watertight. Since two of the *wen*-clause violations occur in Dhanish's Text 20, Chapter 5), I will say more about them in the introduction to that text.

Derek's texts do reveal other violations of Bickerton's Main Stative Rule, however. One is the co-occurrence of habitual *doz* (sometimes reduced to an enclitic *z* attached to the preceding word) with modal *gat* (280 as *gO*, 287, and elsewhere), paralleled by its co-occurrence with *hav* in the speech of Katherine and Bonnette (664, 812). If it is claimed that these are upper-mesolectal speakers, among whom the Main Stative Rule might have weakened, note the occurrence of *bina* with the stative adjective *lil* in line 1151 of Dhanish's text, an indisputably basilectal speaker. Gibson (1982: 57–59), drawing on data collected by Walter Edwards (and separately analyzed in Edwards 1975), has found several other counterexamples to the Main Stative Rule, cases in which habitual *a* or *doz* appears with stative verbs like *biliiv* and *waant* or with modal *gat*. In her own analysis of habitual and progressive aspect markers in GC (pp. 127–33), she permits habitual *a*, *doz*, and *yuuz tu* before both statives and nonstatives. Given the violations of the Main Stative Rule that we have just noted, this seems reasonable enough, but what of those cases where the rule does seem to apply, and *a* and *doz* are absent just where the rule would predict: in the *wen* clauses in lines 279 and 292–93, before *waan* in line 283, and before *ha* in line 292 (where Derek shifts from *doz* to modal *gu* to mark the habitual)?

One solution to this dilemma would be to say that the absence of the aspect markers in these cases is due, not to the Main Stative Rule, but to a more general provision for optional marking of iterativity or habituality where the "context" minimizes or eliminates ambiguity. This would be a generalization of Gibson's (1982: 130) observation that unmarked nonstative verbs can have habitual meaning depending on the context (the context being important because "out of context, uninflected non-stative verbs have past meaning"). However, we need to specify contextual constraints on this optionality, even if their effect is variable rather than categorical; for instance, the absence of habitual marking on *kom* and *lash* seems to be sanctioned by the occurrence of habitual *a* and *doz* in preceding sentences of the same discourse, and it may be generally true that subsequent aspect markers in a series can be omitted once preceding predicates have been marked.

In commenting on an earlier version of this discussion, Bickerton (personal communication) suggests that, taking the perspective of the philosophy of science, we should not expect rules or laws of grammar "to predict every occurrence in performance of every morpheme." Expanding on the point, he says:

It should be obvious that omission of like constituents under identity is a performance feature which may undergo certain constraints but is probably not open to specific prediction any more than Newton's first law is supposed to tell you which apple will drop next. . . . Note further that NO analysis based on "missing constituents" usurps an alternative analysis *as long as that alternative correctly specifies what they shall mean when they are there.* . . . Showing that it [a form] *was* there when it shouldn't be would be, of course, a different story, provided that (a) this could be done in a significant number of cases, and (b) there was an alternative, nonvacuous analysis that fitted the facts better [emphasis in the original].

Although one might grant the general point, and agree also with Bickerton's (1975) specific analyses of the meaning of *doz* and *a* when they do occur, the cases in which these forms occur when they should not—according to the Main Stative Rule—are too numerous to dismiss as performance error. Unless we are willing to accept unrestrained free variation in this area of the grammar, we cannot abandon attempts to establish alternative constraints on the occurrence of these forms. The intuitive nongrammaticality of * "When she *doz* come, she *doz* get on bad" (for those Guyanese who share my intuitions about this sentence), suggests that in addition to any general provisions for deleting identical constituents of the type suggested above, specific syntactic, lexical, or semantic constraints are involved, including some of those originally proposed by Bickerton.

Derek's texts also illustrate several salient phonological features of GC. In order to avoid redundancy, we will discuss only a few of the relevant features here, considering the remaining ones as they come up in the samples of other speakers.

In listening to Derek and other basilectal speakers, one is struck particularly by the speed of the delivery and the related frequency of morphophonemic condensation or reduction. Many dialects of English allow variable deletion of final *t* or *d* after consonants (consonant-cluster simplification; see Guy 1980), but the variable absence of these and other consonants after *vowels*, as attested in Derek's texts and in Creole speech more generally, is rarer. The final consonants affected include *t* (*abou* 248, *bot* 297), *d* (*wi* 216; cf. *wid* 305 and the devoiced variant in *wit* 226), *v* (*gi* 229, *ha* 292), *n* (*ogi* 302), and *ch* (*mo* 303). Of these consonants, the absence of postvocalic *t* is the most frequent, particularly in short, high-frequency forms ending in *a* or *o* (*ga* 217, *da* 266). For some of these forms—*da/do* and *wa/wo* are good candidates (cf. occurrences in the newspaper column and the teacher's speech in Chapter 6)—there is little reason to postulate underlying lexical entries with the final consonant, and a variable insertion rule seems most appropriate. Reduction processes also involve the absence of initial *d*, *t*, and *h* (as in *at* 218, *em* 251, *o* 293, *ou* 240), but at a lower frequency than the final-consonant-deletion processes, and more obviously restricted to a few function words. Words like *dat* and *doz* vary between consonant absence in initial position (*at* 218, *oz* 288) and consonant absence in final position (*da* 266, *do* 302). Cases in which the consonant is absent in both positions are also possible, but rarer and more markedly basilectal; the single example in Derek's texts is *a* (264), equivalent to *dat*. This particular form, which varies in function between a demonstrative adjective and a definite article, and is distinguishable from the indefinite article *a* in always receiving some stress and never reducing to *o*, occurs also in the speech of Reefer and even more frequently in the speech of Lohtan and Dhanish (Chapter 5, Text 11c, *a maan* 465).

These and other reduction processes make for a rich array of stylistic variation (Labov 1971b) and for smooth transitions between different lects on the continuum in both synchronic and diachronic terms. These processes are, in a sense, the phonological equivalents of the morphosyntactic and semantic adjustments that have taken place in the Kupwar varieties of Kannada, Marathi, and Urdu over several hundred years of contact, facilitating translatability and code-switching between them (Gumperz and Wilson 1971). For instance, the mesolectal third-person non-object pronoun *de* can be produced as easily from vowel laxing of acrolectal *dee* as from assimilation/deletion of the final nasal in basilectal *dem*; and *do*, as a nonpunctual marker, although more plausibly related synchronically to mesolectal *doz*, also relates to its synchronic basilectal equivalent *a*, and both of these to their diachronic antecedent *da* (see line 133 in McTurk's Text 5a, Chapter 3). The relationship between these accordion-like phonological processes and grammatical variation and change in creole languages is a fertile area for research, but it has scarcely been explored.[9]

Reduction also involves the absence of retroflexion, which is virtually obligatory in weakly stressed word-final position (*reezo* 223, *pardno* 296). Postvocalic "r-lessness" is much rarer in stressed preconsonantal position (*shaap* 217, but *shaarp* 221 and *yeerz*, *baarn* 264, 266, respectively). Vowel-laxing/shortening in open syllables—not generally possible in SE—occurs regularly in GC and other English-based creoles, particularly in pronominal forms (*yu* 219, *mi* 223, *di* 235, *we* 260) and certain high-frequency lexical items (*se* 218). Although many scholars and popular writers represent the pronouns of Caribbean creoles as having invariant lax or short vowels, there is almost always some variation with tense or long vowels.[10]

Furthermore, vowel-laxing in forms consisting of a consonant and vowel seems to be mutually exclusive with processes for removing the preceding consonant. There is, for example, no **i* for *mi*, and *hee* and *hii* are reduced, respectively, to *ee* 240 and *ii* 227, not **he* and **hi*. The function of this inverse symbiotic relationship between consonantal and vocalic strength is to preserve the forms from total obliteration at the hands of successive reduction processes.[11] The occurrences of *i* in 245 (and in Reefer, Text 11b, 430) are rare instances in which both *h*-deletion and vowel-laxing have occurred, and the combined effect is to leave just a bare vestige of the form, subject to total disappearance if further reduction should occur. The occurrence of *ho* in 229 and elsewhere is an interesting example of the operation of reduction processes to conflate whole syllables: here just the consonant of *hee(r)* and the reduced vowel of *wa(t)* remain. Compare intermediate *hee wo* (222).

Finally, two minor phonological features are worth noting. One is the pronunciation of "cutlass" as *kotlish* (220), which alternates in the basilect with *kotlaas* (305). The other is the one-time occurrence of an intrusive *p* at the end of *jrom* 'drum' (*jromp* 243). Although this is rare, the parallel occurrence of *dongk* 'down' in Irene's speech (line 365) shows that it is not idiosyncratic, but systematic, involving the addition of a homorganic voiceless stop in words ending in nasal consonants. Whether this process is more general in Bhojpuri or Indic languages is not known, but since Derek and Irene are both Indo-Guyanese, it may well be of Indic origin.

Texts 9a, 9b, and 9c are from Tape SI56, tape counter nos. 558–80, 034–37, and 116–19, respectively; 9d is from Tape CW52, nos. 334–70. The speakers F. (Texts 9a and 9c) and M. (Text 9b) are friends of Derek's.

9a. The story of the monkey and his razor

D: dis bina won maan. wel ii a piil kookno—wan kookno—wi	216
wan dol kotlaas. wel dis bina mongkii—hii ga wan shaap reezaa.	217
an ii se at ou—hii a paas a rood an dis—ii se at ou,	218
"ongkl! yu waan dis reezo fu piil yu kooknot?" wel di man	219
glaad, bikaaz hii noo dat ou hii kooknot na—hii kotlish	220
na shaarp. wel ii—wen di mongkii len om, wen ii don	221
piil am, di reezo brok. hee wo di mongkii se,	222
"pam-paa[m]! gi mi bak mi reezo naso gi mii yu kooknot! gi	223
mii bak mi reezo naso gi mii yu kooknot!" wel di man giyam	224
ii kooknot.	225
ii a gu, ii a waak. ii miit wit wan leedii a mek ail.	226
ii se, "antii, yu waan dis kookno fu mek ail?"	227
dis leedi se, "ye-es!" wel wen dis leedii don mek di	228
ail, ho [= hee wo] ii se, "pam-pam! gi mi bak mii kooknot naso gi	229
mii yu ail! gi mi bak mi kooknot naso gi mii yu ail!"	230
wel di leedi giyam ii ail.	231
wen ii guwin, . . . ii miit op tu—tu won leedii a mek laktoo.	232
ii se, "antii, yu waan dis ail fu mek laktoo?"	233
di leedi se, "ye-es!"	234
wen di leedi don mek laktoo, ho ii se, "gi	235
mii bak mi ail naso gi mii yu laktoo! gi mi bak mi ail	236
naso gi mi yu laktoo!" wel di leedi giyam ii laktoo. wen	237
ii a gu nou, ii miit op tu—wedin. wel dis	238

weding—dem—dem a gu bariiyaat. wel di na a   239
gu? ii se at ou, "ee bai! ayu waan mii kook—aa—mi   240
laktoo fu iit? dem bai se, "ye-es!" wen di don iit,   241
ho ii se, "pam-pam! gi mi bak mi laktoo naso gi mi yu   242
jromp! gi mi bak mi laktoo naso gi mi yu jrom!" wel dem   243
bai giyam ii jrom.   244
wen ii don, ii gu a striit an hee i halo, "kudungkuu-kudungkuu!   245
mi nak am aal about! reezo bring kooknot;   246
kooknot bring ail; ail bring laktoo; laktoo bring jrom!   247
kudungkuu-kudungkuu! mi nak am aal abou!"   248
    F: [simultaneously joining in] "kudungkuu-kudungkuu! mi nak am   249
aal abou!"   250
    D: wel ii bin ga nof mongkii pan aal em chrii. an aal de heerin,   251
de jomp fu ge dis jrom. wel, dis big mongkii, hii   252
tek som(pn) ou dis jrom, an dash om in di riva. wel   253
aal o dem a jomp forom. an di bobl, an dem ded.   254
    F: stoorii don!   255

Translation

    There was this man. Well he was peeling coconuts—a coconut—with
a dull cutlass [machete]. Well, there was also this monkey—he had a sharp razor.
And he said that [how]—he was passing on the road and this—he said,
"Uncle, do you want this razor to peel your coconut?" Well the man
was glad, because he knew that [how] his coconut wasn't—his machete   220T
wasn't sharp. Well he—when the monkey lent him, and he had finished
peeling it, the razor broke. Hear what the monkey said,
"Pam-pam! Give me back my razor or else give me your coconut! Give
me back my razor or else give me your coconut!" Well the man gave him
his coconut.   225T
    He [the monkey] went on walking. He met a lady who was making oil.
He said, "Aunty, do you want this coconut to make oil?"
The lady said, "Yes!" Well when the lady had finished making the
oil, hear what he said, "Pam-pam! Give me back my coconut or else give
me your oil! Give me back my coconut or else give me your oil!"   230T
Well the lady gave him his oil.
    As he was going along, . . . he met—a lady who was making laktho.*
He said, "Aunty, do you want this oil to make laktho?"
The lady said, "Yes!"
    When the lady had finished making laktho, hear what he said, "Give   235T
me back my oil or else give me your laktho! Give me back my oil

---

*"Laktho" is an Indian sweetmeat (Ramdat 1978: 127) or *mithai* (cf. Hindi *mi:tha:* 'sweetmeat'; Chaturvedi and Tiwari 1975: 600–601). The "bariat" (see following paragraph) is the
name for the groom's wedding party when it marches in procession to the bride's house (cf.
Hindi *bara:t*; Chaturvedi and Tiwari 1975: 502–3; and for a description, Rauf 1974: 85).

or else give me your laktho!" Well the lady gave him his laktho. While going along
now, he ran into a—wedding procession. Well this wedding—they—they were
going to a bariat. Well they were going along. He said to them, "Hey, fellas! Do you
want my coconut—ah—my   240T
laktho to eat? The guys said, "Yes!" When they had finished eating, hear what he
said, "Pam-pam! Give me back my laktho or else give me your drum! Give me back
my laktho or else give me your drum!" Well the guys gave him his drum.

    After this, he went into the street, hollering, "Kudungku-kudungku!   245T
I knocked it all about! My razor brought a coconut; the
coconut brought oil; the oil brought laktho; the laktho brought a drum!
kudungku-kudungku! I knocked it all about!

    Kudungku-kudungku! I knocked it
all about!   250T

    Well, there were many monkeys in the trees. And when they heard this,
they all jumped to get this drum. Well, this big monkey, he
took something out of this drum, and threw it into the river. Well
all of them jumped in for it. Bubbles came up from them, and they died.

    The story is done!   255T

9b. Sewing machines

M: it a wan naif, o smaal won tu do wudo fit di	256
hool, bot—	257
D: ayu na ga non wo doz oopn mashiin	258
an so?	259
M: wel iz do wo O tek an me-en no we ii—we	260
ii teek it.	261
D: wii ga wo—wen wii bai wi mash—wii mashiin, wii get	262
o hool set. wel mii no noo wisaid den de. yu noo ou	263
laang wii bin gat a mashiin? mi tingk fiftiin yeerz.	264
M: m-hm?	265
D: sins wen mii na bin baarn yeet, mamii in bai da mashiin.	266

Translation

    There's a knife, one smaller than that, which would have fit the
hole, but—

    Don't you guys have the kind that are used to open [sewing] machines
and so on?

    Well, that is the one that O. took, and I don't know where he—where   260T
he took it.

    We have one—when we bought our mach—our [sewing] machine, we got
a whole set. Well I don't know where they are now. Do you know how
long we've had that machine? I think it's about fifteen years now.

    Mm-hm?   265T

    Even before I was born Mummy had bought that machine.

9c. Floggings in school

F: noo, shi a biit mi aal oovo mi skin!   267
D: aalvo yu hed an ting.   268
J: e-he?   269
F: aal mi hed an so shi a biit mi.   270
D: shi o paas rong wi yi wail keen an o laash yu.   271
J: shiz hit yu pon yu hed n ohl do? shii—shi kyaan duu   272
do, doo.   273
  F: e?   274
J: shi sopooz tu biit yu pon yu hed?   275
D: noo.   276
F: aal oova shi a biit. aal oovo yu skin. shi a bench dem   277
gyal aal.   278
  D: wen shi—wen shi sii yu—yu na a du yu wok, shi kom in   279
i di wail keen, kyan lash yu in yu bak. yuz gO fu du   280
su stedii stedii.   281
  F: shii waan yuu—shi in waan yu mos—stodii an du yu wok.   282
shi waan yu mos du om seemtaim.   283
  D: an wontaim shi di raidin o mooto baik, an it—wen shi lef di 284
moot baik, dem bai pongcho shi wiil!   285

Translation

No, she would beat me all over my body!
All over your head and so on.
Oh yes?
All over my head and so on she would beat me.   270T
She would pass around with the wild cane and lash you.
Does she hit you on your head too? She—she can't do
that, though.
Eh?
Is she supposed to beat you on your head?   275T
No.
All over she beats you. All over your body. She benches [spanks] the
girls and all.
When she—when she sees you—you're not doing your work, she comes in
with the wild cane and lashes you on your back. You have to do   280T
so [i.e. put up your hands for protection] constantly.
She wants you—she doesn't want you to deliberate over your work.
She wants you to do it hastily.
And once she was riding a motorbike, and it—when she left the
motorbike (parked), the boys punctured her wheel [tire].   285T

9d. The game of "Salt"

J: hou yuz plee da?   286
D: yuz gatu pik o said. tuu—tuu said yuz gatu geeta.   287
. . . huu win, doz getu ron in, an huu luuz, oz gatu fiil.   288
J: an hou yu doz du dis ron in an so?   289
D: wel—ii doz got s—lain soo. an waan laang schreek lain. an   290
yuz gat won big haarts hed. wel ii—huu da ruul   291
dis lang lain gu ha tu ron an halo "saal!" an wen ii   292
halo "sa!" evribadi ga o chrai fu paas. huu a   293
ron in, gatu chrai fu ge fu paas. an if de nak yu, yu out.   294
an if yu ron out til outsaid an yu kom bak an halo   295
"saal out!," do miin yu pardno no—wo ge out—hii   296
kon kom in bak di geem. bot if yu o wan kyaptin   297
an yu ge nak, di hool said out.   298
J: an wee alyu yuuztu plee dis? in di schriit? wo—hou   299
juz jraa di lain?   300
D: laik kraas. waan laang lain so, an den hee   301
so, den hee ogi. yu do gOtu mek pen,   302
plentii pen. ho mo pen yu waan mek, yu o mek.   303
J: yu, yu jraa om wid wo—charkool? wid kool?   304
D: noo, yu doz kot it—di graas—wid kotlaas.   305

Translation

How do you play that?
You have to pick a side [team]. Two—two sides you have to get.
. . . Whoever wins gets to run in, and whoever loses has to field.
And how do you do this running in and so on?
Well—there are lines like this. And a long straight line. And   290T
there's usually a big heart-shaped head. Well he—whoever is ruling
this long line has to run and holler "Salt!" And when he
hollers "Salt!," everybody has to try to pass. Those who are
running in have to try to get past. And if they knock you, you're out.
And if you run all the way out and come back and holler   295T
"Salt out!," that means your partner isn't—the one who'd been out—he
can come back in the game. But if you're a captain
and you're knocked, the whole side is out.
And where did you guys play this? In the street? What—how
do you draw the lines?   300T
Like crosses. A long line so [demonstrating], and then here
so, then here again. You have to make pens [squares],
many pens. You make as many pens as you want.
Do you draw them with charcoal? With coal?
No, you cut it—the grass—with a cutlass (machete).   305T

10. Irene (1975–1976)

In her early forties when she was recorded, Irene is a weeder on the sugar estate, a strong and articulate woman, and a vigorous exemplar of estate-class language and culture. The forcefulness of her speech, which is quite evident in the tape-recorded samples, is completely in character. As a child, she did not have the opportunity to go beyond fourth standard in primary school, but she has a sharp wit and a capacity for concise reasoning that recalls the examples of vernacular logic Labov presents in his 1970 article, "The Logic of Non-Standard English." Irene is well aware of the physical hardships and low prestige of estate work, but neither bothers her unduly. As she observes:

som piipl prifor work wi di—am—yu noo, a wok in afis an ting, ka den fiil da moo iizi. bika nof piipl se, "fiil wok! da a jakaas wok!" de na eebl wid am. nait, reen an son, aal yu gatu dee in. bot huu akostom turam, da na notin tu dem.

Some people prefer a job with the—um—you know, a job in an office or something like that because they feel that's easier. Because many people say, "Field work! That's jackass work!" They can't hack it. Night, rain and sun, all you have to put up with! But if you're used to it, it's nothing.

Irene's entire network of friends is in Cane Walk, and most of them are female co-workers in the weeding gang. She describes herself as speaking "Creolese—the same patois taak—me na got no more kind talk," and in more general terms, expresses the view that real (basilectal) Creole speakers vary little: "wel huu akostom fu taak so, de na gat non taim! deng kan iivn gu i—biifoo di praim minista—iz di seem taakin deng gat!" (Well for those who're accustomed to talking like that [i.e., in basilectal Creole], there's no time for them [to use SE]! Even if they went before the prime minister, they'd still talk the same way!)

Like Derek, Irene used only the basilectal variants for the first-person possessive and third-person-masculine possessive pronouns—*mi(i)*, *(h)ii*—in her recorded spontaneous speech. But she was also invariant in her use of the first-person subject pronoun, saying *mi(i)* in all 395 occurrences of this subcategory. At the same time, she was almost as successful as Derek in producing the required acrolectal features (including *ai* as first-person subject pronoun) in the Creole-to-English Correction tests, which is particularly remarkable considering how little formal schooling she has had. Moreover, one would not have thought—on the basis of her recorded natural speech— that the acrolectal variants were within the range of her productive competence. Clearly, her basilectal output, like that of several others in the estate class, is more a matter of linguistic choice than limitation, a way of expressing the fact that she feels most comfortable with and committed to estate/ Creole culture and life-style.

The four extracts from Irene's recordings presented below demonstrate the kind of historical and cultural insights that scholars can gain from stepping outside of the library and into the field. The first documents the economic difficulties that often took children out of school to work, and the eager—even irresponsible—way the sugar estate, thirsty for cheap labor, accepted them. The second describes a Hindu wedding, one of the primary institutions through which Indic culture is being maintained in Guyana, although not without its changes (see Rauf 1974). The third and fourth deal with two central figures in Guyanese folk mythology and superstition: the "Ole Higue" (a folk spirit reputed to suck the blood of babies) and the "jumbie" (ghost).

Irene's texts contain a number of interesting grammatical features. One is the occurrence of *gu* as a serial verb indicating direction (*kyarii am gu* 331, *ron gu* 367)[12] and as an infinitival complementizer for realized complements (*getawee gu wee a wok* 318). Roberts (1980) and Bickerton (1981: 32–33, 59–61) discuss the use of *go/gu* to mark realized complements; but in Irene's line 335, as also in Reefer's 421, the complement is generic rather than specific, not limited to any one occasion and not referrable to an already realized action. Bickerton (personal communication) points out that both of these examples carry the strong implication that the action will be realized, and so are only apparent counterexamples. This is particularly so in the case of *gu berin am* in line 335, which is followed by the observation that until this action is finished, the wedding cannot end. The point that *go/gu* as a complementizer covers both actually realized and likely-to-be realized cases is not explicitly made in the literature, however. One final observation in relation to complementizer *gu* is that its complementizer function is closely related to and sometimes difficult to distinguish from its "directional" serial-verb function. The relation is all the more striking in view of the fact that *kom* 'come'—common as a directional serial verb—is also used as a preverbal complementizer (see line 386).

The use of *na mos* in lines 385 and 395 is relatively rare, for modals are the first verb forms in decreolization to appear with postverbal negation (*mosn*) instead of with basilectal preverbal *na* (Bickerton 1975: 43; Rickford 1983b). Further, these two occurrences of *na mos* demonstrate another respect in which the GC basilect differs from SE: GC imperatives can contain modals without explicit specification of subject 'you'; contrast with lines 385 and 395, the ungrammaticality of *"Must not go there by yourself!" in English.

The form *batam* in line 362, although derived from the corresponding

English noun "bottom," has full prepositional status and does not need to be embedded in a prepositional phrase; compare GC *kana* ('corner') in *hous kana wan romshap* 'house corner (= next *to*) a rumshop,' and contrast English "*at* the bottom *of*." Note also the morphological structure of the pronominal reflexive in line 385 (*yuu waan* 'by yourself,' literally "you one") and the pronominal dual in 388 (*abii tuu* 'the two of us,' literally "we two")—still other features of GC morphosyntax that have not previously received attention in the literature.

Irene's preverbal tense-aspect markers are noteworthy in a number of respects. The perfect-aspect marker *dom* (< *don*, with the final nasal assimilating the bilabial articulation of the following *m*) displays co-occurrence possibilities in line 383—preceding two modals—not noted in earlier discussions of GC or other creoles, and in line 393 there is a reduplicated *de* as locative copula that is quite unusual. The second feature is not just a performance error, for Irene uses reduplicated *de* elsewhere in her recordings. Her use of *a* is typical of other basilectal speakers, however, and allows us to note the multifaceted functions of this auxiliary/copula form.[13] In line 356 it functions as a prenominal copula, equivalent to English "be." The form *iz* in line 398 is one of the rare examples of the SE copula in Irene's speech; interestingly enough, it occurs in a syntactic position (prenominal) that researchers working on creoles and VBE have found to be very "copula-demanding"; it also occurs in a phonological environment—preceded and followed by *a(a)*—in which basilectal *a* would have been avoided. In lines 338 and 360, *a* occurs not as copula, but as a nonpunctual-aspect marker, again unmarked for tense, but denoting a habitual process in the former and a continuative or progressive one in the latter. Note that in line 338 continuative *a* precedes the stative locative copula *de*,[14] as well as *stedii*, the form whose continuative function is mentioned in the introduction to Granny's texts. In *a koonot* (372) and *a somting* (389), *a* occurs as a subjectless prenominal copula—that is, without dummy *ii* or *da* as subject. The case of *a da wa mii se* (351) is more complex, involving the use of copulative *a* and pseudo-clefting from *mii se da* to focus or topicalize the object.[15]

Irene's fine "coconut jumbie" narrative (Text 10d) affords us a good opportunity to introduce and examine the anterior/non-anterior distinction that has come to be regarded as fundamental to creole tense-modality-aspect systems around the world, although we need to be cautious about generalizing from narrative to all kinds of discourse, and to bear in mind that tense-aspect markers may not be as neatly partitioned in practice as "rational" linguistic descriptions of them might suggest (Sankoff and Labov 1985). Bickerton (1981: 306) notes that the anterior/non-anterior distinction is often difficult for the non-creole speaker to understand and recommends that readers refer to his detailed account of the distinction in GC (1975: chap. 2). In what follows, we will therefore draw most directly on this account, modifying and extending it where necessary.[16]

"Anterior" is defined in Webster's Third New International Dictionary as meaning "before in time: antecedent" (sense 2a). In the GC basilect it is marked by *bin*, either alone or in combination with nonpunctual *a* (*bina*). Non-anterior is marked by the occurrence of the verb stem or other predicate without *bin*, which we will represent hereafter as $\emptyset$. The interpretation of anterior *bin* and non-anterior $\emptyset$ is affected by the stative/nonstative distinction, so we will consider stative and nonstative predicates separately.

Anterior bin *and non-anterior* $\emptyset$ *with statives.* With stative predicates—verbs like "know," "want," and "have," most adjectives, passives, modals, and other predicates that refer to a state rather than an action—non-anterior $\emptyset$ is defined by Bickerton (1975: 46) as referring to "'now,' i.e. that the state of liking, knowing, wanting, or whatever, though it might have commenced in the past, would still be in existence at the present moment." Since non-anterior $\emptyset$ with statives refers to "now," anterior *bin* would, with the same class of predicates, refer to "'not now, no longer,' i.e. a terminated state" (ibid.). Thus we could have a contrast between anterior *mi bin no* 'I knew,' referring to a state of knowing that existed before the moment of speech but no longer exists, and non-anterior *mi $\emptyset$ noo* 'I know,' referring to a state that is still in existence at the moment of speaking. From these glosses, it would appear that anterior and non-anterior with stative predicates are equivalent to past and nonpast, respectively, and this is precisely how Bickerton (1975: 28–29, 35) describes them.

Let us look at the past-reference stative predicates in Irene's Text 10d to see whether this distinction in fact operates as Bickerton's analysis would lead us to expect. The list is short enough to give in full (see Table 4.2). Note, first of all, that this one text yields seven stative *bin* tokens, as against a mean and a mode of four for each of Bickerton's basilectal speakers (1975: 36, Table 2.4). It is therefore an adequate data base for comparison, particu-

TABLE 4.2
Past-Reference Stative Predicates in Text 10d by Line Number

Statives with *bin*		Statives with $\emptyset$ (no *bin*)			
bin gat	352, 359	$\emptyset$ smaal	354	$\emptyset$ a kooknot	372
bin ga	361	$\emptyset$ a mii plees	356	na $\emptyset$ de de	385
bin ton dong	361–62	$\emptyset$ a mii antii	359	na $\emptyset$ noo	386
bin de	362	$\emptyset$ a waan eej	359	$\emptyset$ kyan kom	386
bin ga	363, 368	$\emptyset$ taiyord	364	$\emptyset$ a somting	389
		$\emptyset$ berin dong	370	na $\emptyset$ waan tel mii	389

larly because it allows us to see the use of *bin* and *Ø* in a discourse context rather than in isolated sentences.

The text itself gives us no basis for determining whether the stative predicates with *bin* refer to states that no longer exist; but from real-world knowledge and experience (e.g., we know that the incident in question had happened about 30 years before, and that Felicity Village had been almost completely taken over by sugar-cane cultivation), it is probable that they do not. If we had access to Irene at the moment (unfortunately, we do not), we could ask her directly, "Is your grandfather still alive?," "Does he still own a place at Felicity Village, with a mango tree by the side of the building and a coconut tree by the side-line canal?," and so on. If she told us clearly that the states were no longer in existence, the use of *bin* in this text would conform perfectly to Bickerton's analysis. If she told us clearly that the states were still in existence—that her grandfather still owned the place and so on—either the analysis or her usage of *bin* would have to be erroneous.

Interestingly enough, however, there is one other situation in which Irene's usage of *bin* would be justified—if she were to tell us that she did not know (or care) whether the states in question were still in existence. Intuitively, this is what is crucial for the reader or listener to infer from her narrative—that whether or not the states in question are still in existence at the time the narrative is being told, they were in existence at the point in the past when the events referred to in the narrative were taking place.

This suggests that it might be useful to treat the "no longer" component that Bickerton associates with stative *bin* as an implicature rather than a strict implication (Grice 1975; Comrie 1976: 29). If a semantic feature is a strict criterion for or implication of the use of a form, a conjoined sentence with "but" that contains the form in the first clause and a variant expression of the semantic feature in the second clause should strike us as semantically odd (indicated by * in the sentences below), since it presents information as new that has already been given, as in *"It's a chair but you can sit in it" (Labov 1973: 348) and *"He used to be, and has at some time been a member of a subversive organisation" (Comrie 1976: 29).

Applying this test to stative *bin*, however, we find that the following sentence is *not* semantically odd, but perfectly natural: *ii bin noo di ansa, bot ii na noo am nou* ('He knew [used to know] the answer, but he doesn't know it now'). Contrast this with the oddness of the following sentence with *don*, which includes the strict implication that the speaker knows the answer now:[17] *ii don noo di ansa, bot ii noo am nou*. Furthermore, as is generally true of implicatures (as against strict implications), the normal implicature of *bin* that the state is no longer in effect can be denied:[18] *ii bin noo di ansa, an mi tingk i stil noo am* ('He knew [used to know] the answer, and I think he still

does'). Contrast, once again, the impossibility of denying the strict implication of *don* that the speaker knows it now: * *ii don noo di ansa, an ii na noo am
nou*. In the light of the preceding, we might redefine anterior *bin* with
statives as referring to a time before the moment of speaking while neither
specifying nor excluding continuing truth, and non-anterior Ø with statives
as including the moment of speech while neither specifying nor excluding
preceding truth.[19] We can continue to think of the basic meaning of non-
anterior with statives as "true now," but we need to modify Bickerton's
(1975: 46) description of anterior with statives as "not now, no longer
(true)" to read "true before now." Normally this would carry the implicature
that the state in question is no longer true, but unlike a strict implication, it
would not absolutely exclude it. In addition to facilitating the intuitively correct interpretation of the *bin* statives in Irene's text, this reformulation would
also account for the following example in Bickerton (1975: 36), in which *bin*
is used for a state that is still in effect at the moment of speech: "(2.53) *dis
fut bin swel he si di tu a saiz* 'This foot has swelled up, compare the size of the
two.'" It would also cover this additional example (p. 41), in which the continuity of the past state into the present appears to be left open: "(2.73) *mi bin
gat wan dag* 'I had a dog' (but some time ago, and I may not still have one)."
Without modification, Bickerton's claim that *bin* with statives means "not
now" would not square with these examples from his own data.

The interpretation of the unmarked statives in Irene's narrative as non-
anterior, or "true now," is not problematic in the case of *a mi antii* and *a
waan eej* (59), since these propositions appear to be true both in narrative
time (when the narrator was a young girl) and in real time (at the moment of
speech). The unmarked statives that occur in direct speech (370, 372, 385,
386, and 389) also pose no problem for Bickerton's analysis, since they obviously refer to states in effect at the time that the events referred to in the
narrative occurred.

The absence of *bin* with *smaal* (354) and *taiyord* (364) *is* problematic,
however, since the speaker could not possibly be asserting the current truth
of either of these propositions. However, in the case of *taiyord*, the "missing"
form is more likely habitual *a* or *doz* (unmarked for tense in the basilect, as
shown by past-reference tokens in lines 356 and 363) than anterior *bin*, and
we can account for this case by appealing to the GC rule permitting the deletion of aspect markers in temporal clauses (Bickerton 1975: 31–33). The
smaal is more difficult, since the "missing" form in this case is clearly the
tense marker *bin*, which Bickerton explicitly excludes (p. 32) from the temporal clause deletion rule, citing in support of its exclusion, "(2.30) *wen mi
bin yong, yu know hau awi yuus tu wok* 'You know how we used to work when I
was young'" and ruling out the omission of *bin* as ungrammatical in "(2.31)
* *wen mi Ø yong, yu no hau awi yuus tu wok*."

Given the virtual identity of Irene's *wen* clause in line 354 (*wen mi smaal*) with this sentence, we would be forced to classify it, too, as ungrammatical. However, both cases seem intuitively grammatical,[20] primarily because the presence of *nyuustu* in the main clause provides a past or anterior frame of reference for the entire sentence, making specification with *bin* optional.

The predicate *a mii plees* (in which the *a* is a nominal copula) poses the biggest problem of interpretation. The speaker clearly could not be asserting that it is currently her (favorite) place, and the reference is obviously anterior, theoretically requiring *bin*. That the absence of the anterior form here is not due to any inherent difficulty of combining it with copulative (as against habitual or continuative)*a* is shown by the occurrence of past copula *bina* elsewhere, as in Derek's opening narrative sentence, *dis bina won maan* ('This was a man' 216), and in this example from Bickerton (1975: 51): "(2.96) *wan bina goolsmit an wan bina kaumaina* 'One was a goldsmith and one was a cowherd.'" We will therefore have to treat *a mii plees* either as a violation of Bickerton's analysis, as a mistake on the speaker's part, or as something akin to the English "historical present"—a description of a past event as if it were present to make it more vivid or dramatic. I am most inclined to give it this last interpretation, which links up well with the interpretation of unmarked predicates in Bonnette's Text 15c, which we will discuss below.

Anterior bin *and non-anterior Ø with nonstatives.* With nonstative predicates—verbs like "kiss," "tell," and "come" that refer to actions rather than states—it is commonly suggested that *bin* simply means "past." But we would then be hard put to explain why certain past actions in a narrative are referred to with *bin* whereas others are not. Bickerton's (1975: 47) explanation is that although an action might be "past" simply because it occurs prior to the moment of speech, it must also be "anterior" to another action or actions to take *bin*. Given two events that are sequentially ordered in real life as E_1 and E_2, only E_1 would be "anterior" and thus eligible for marking with *bin*. There is an additional qualification, however. As Bickerton (p. 109) notes, a nonstative predicate only requires marking as anterior "when the speaker inverts normal narrative order (i.e., refers to an earlier event after a later one)." Elsewhere (p. 53), he makes the point even more explicitly: "even where one [past event] occurred prior to another, both can be handled by the English simple past, but (*unless the actions are sequent ones in a narrative*) creole will normally give the [− anterior] one the stem form and the [+ anterior] one the marked-past form" (emphasis added).

The "unless" case—in which the actions described are sequential in a narrative—provides for the use of the *unmarked* stem form with an anterior nonstative predicate. Givón (1982: 121) makes the same point: "It [*bin*] marks *out-of-sequence* clauses in the narrative, specifically those which 'look back' and relate events that occurred *earlier than the preceding clause in the narrative.*" As an example, note the following hypothetical sentence, in which the temporally prior E_1 occurs after E_2 in narrative sequence and thus requires marking with *bin*: *ii Ø gu* (E_2) *tu di spat we ii bin plant* (E_1) *dis siid* ('He went (back) to the spot where he *had planted* this seed'). In this system nonstative stem forms without *bin* would thus be either those that are the last of two or more events in real time (like E_2 above and below), or those that, even if anterior to some other action in an adjacent clause, are presented in a narrative order that is iconic with the actual order, like E_1 in this hypothetical example: *ii Ø plant* (E_1) *dis siid an ii Ø gu* (E_2) *hoom* ('He planted this seed and he went home').

Turning now to Irene's text to see whether the past-reference nonstative predicates conform to this analysis, we notice, first of all, that the vast majority of them occur without *bin*. In general these zero stems conform to the above analysis, since the narrative sequence of actions follows the sequence of events in real time, as the following narrative sequence of nonstative verbs indicates:

Ø go bak 370	Ø faal 371	Ø ron gu 372
Ø lai dong bak 370–71	Ø git op 371	Ø se 372

The relative rarity of *bin* with nonstatives in this text supports Bickerton's observation (1975: 35) that the form is commoner with statives than nonstatives. However, the few cases in which we do get *bin* or *bina* with nonstatives contain some problems for his analysis. One such case is *bina lai dong* (365–66), in which the lying down had begun prior to the hearing and the other events that subsequently occur, but since it is in its appropriate narrative sequence, it might be expected to occur without *bin*.[21] Contrast the very next sentence (*wails mi a lai dong* 366), which repeats the *lai dong* predicate, but without *bin*—correctly so, according to Bickerton's analysis.

A different kind of problem is posed by the occurrence of *bin lai dong* in line 379. Since a nonstative verb-stem by itself refers to a + punctual or "single, non-extended" action (Bickerton 1975: 46), and since the speaker seems to be describing the lying down as an extended process, she should have used either *bina lai dong* or *a lai dong*, the alternatives she had employed earlier in lines 365 and 366. Of these alternatives, *bina lai dong* would have been required according to the above analysis because the speaker's preceding sentence refers to temporally subsequent actions (*kooknot faal . . . na sii non* 376).[22] The omission of the *a* after *bin* in this example may be simply due to its elision in fast speech.

The final problem case is *bin heng* in line 391. The use of *bin* in this example could be justified on the grounds that *bin heng* comes after *noo a waa* in narrative sequence but before it in real life. But since the knowledge is a state, and since it is queried (rhetorically) rather than asserted or stated, the concept of two sequentially ordered *events* is rather strained here. The hanging seems more firmly linked to the grandfather's subsequent account of the similar experiences he had had at the same spot (*dis ting hapn tu mii tuu, chrii taim*), but the narrative sequencing here is iconic with real-time sequence, and if *bin* were only allowed for out-of-sequence anterior events, its use in this clause would be unjustified.[23]

The solution to these "problem" cases is to revise Bickerton's analysis to provide for *optional* marking with *bin* when anterior E_1 precedes E_2 in narrative sequence, as against the *obligatory* marking when anterior E_1 follows E_2 in narrative sequence. *Bin* marking on non-anterior E_2 would still be excluded.[24] The possibilities are these:

E_1 (*bin* or Ø) . . . E_2 (Ø only)

E_2 (Ø only) . . . E_1 (*bin* only, out-of-sequence anterior event)

We might think of the optional inclusion of *bin* when E_1 and E_2 are iconically sequenced as a reflection of the redundancy that creole systems, like other full-fledged languages, contain (see Mühlhäusler 1980: 23).[25]

With respect to phonological features, Irene's texts illustrate several striking consonantal processes in basilectal GC. The first is the variable deletion of the initial stop in the tense marker *bin(a)* (*bin* 322, *in* 306, *mina* < *mi bina* 325). This is characteristic of the speech of the most basilectal speakers (cf. Lohtan, Text 19, 1074) and is significant for two reasons. For one thing, the analyst who is unaware of this variation may miss instances of this important tense marker. For another, the deletion of initial voiced stops in tense-aspect markers like *bin* and *gu* is more common than the deletion of initial consonants in other forms, and represents a subtle and systematic pan-creole rule (attested in Sranan, Jamaican, Antiguan, Gullah, Hawaiian Creole, and VBE) that provides a vehicle for morphosyntactic variation and change.[26]

Another interesting feature is the susceptibility of final nasals to assimilation (*dom mos*) and loss. Irene's uses of pronominal *de* are undoubtedly from *dem* rather than *dee* because they all occur before nasals, as in *de na* (342). The use of *ting* for *taim* in line 307 is interesting because of the velarization of the final nasal and the monopthongization of the vowel. Monopthongization is attested also in *sailin* ('sideline' 367) once again before a final nasal.

The palatalization of velar stops (*g, k*) before *a* is illustrated in *gyal* (333), *kyari* (322), and *kyaan* (345); note that it does not usually occur in words containing *a* historically derived from *O*, so that 'got to' is *gafu* (322), not **gyafu*.[27] This palatalization is common among Caribbean English creole varieties (see Alleyne 1980: 58–59; Cassidy and Le Page 1980: lviii; and Wells 1982, 3: 569), and occurs in many of the spoken texts in this book. The fact that it does not show up in any of the written texts illustrates the selective and conventional character of popular dialect spellings and their limited usefulness for phonological analysis.

Another consonantal feature that is illustrated in Irene's speech but not in the written texts is the realization of the initial labio-velar semivowel/glide (*w*) as a bilabial stop (*b*, as in *bel* 331 and *bilid* 352—note too the loss of the fricative element in the final consonant of the latter word). It is even more frequently realized as a voiced bilabial fricative (the *wel* in 333 is of this type), but this is not a phonemic distinction and is not represented in my orthography. However, the realization of SE labio-velar fricatives as bilabial stops, represented by *greeb* (360), is fairly common in written texts; see the introductions to the Pinckard and McTurk texts, above.

One final consonantal feature of interest is the palatal nasal in *nyuustu* ('used to' 354). Alleyne (1980: 52) glosses Saramaccan *ñusu* as 'accustomed' and gives other variants, but does not discuss the initial palatal nasal. However, Turner (1974: 243) reports that several English words beginning with a palatal glide/semivowel (such as "use," "young," "united," and "new") begin with a palatal nasal in Gullah, and he observes that the palatal nasal occurs in Yoruba, Twi, Ewe, and "many other West African languages, . . . especially in initial and medial position."

We will postpone discussion of the very distinctive lowering of *O*, *oh*, and *o* until we come to Granny's texts, but the raising of *a* before final velar nasals—represented by Irene's *geeng* (329) and *heng* (391)—is rarer and worth mentioning here. This process appears to be restricted to a few lexical items; it may have been more productive in earlier times, but the written texts are again silent on this phonological detail. The laxing of final vowels in open syllables is even more widespread in Irene's than in Derek's speech, affecting more items outside of the pronominal set, including *mosi* 317, *kontinyu* 339, *mondi* 339, and *kriyool* 325 (the last case valuable for revealing that the relevant environment is syllable-final rather than word-final).

Text 10a is from Tape SI37, tape counter nos. 008–020; 10b, 10c, and 10d are from the same tape, nos. 124–30, 295–99, and 303–36, respectively. In Text 10c, M. is a friend of Irene's, A. is the local dispenser.

10a. Starting to work in the cane fields

I: mii bn smaal, bot mi in staat wok aredi wen di skiim	306
kom—lang ting. mii staat wok fan twelv yeer.	307
J: twelv?	308
I: ye-es.	309
J: hou yu start so yong?	310
I: wel, akardinlii tu, yu noo lang ting, praiveeshan. yu	311

sii, mi modo an faado bin separeet. den mii staatu—em—aftor   312
mi sii ponishment staat, mii staat fu wok. . . . mi goo op tu   313
foot standod.   314
     J: foot standod?   315
     I: mi paas fu goo oova a fif, an mi lef skuul. mi le—op tu nou   316
mi buk an evriting mosi lef in di skuul. mi lef skuul   317
an get awee. go—getawee gu wee a wok. . . .   318
     J: wel—am—iz su di esteet tek yu aan widout di noowin yu—   319
if yu modo noo, ar yu tiicho? bo di na aas dem   320
pomishon?   321
     I: noo, noobadii, noo. yu sii, at dem taim de, yu na bin gafu kyari   322
bort sortifikeet fu wok. jos hou—if van—if yu fiil   323
fo wok, yu gu an yu wok. mii staat wok a twenti   324
foor sens a dee. . . . mina wok a kriyool.   325
     J: kriiyool. wen yu fos—wo yu hafu du in kriiyool?   326
     I: m—yu a chroo manyoor, yu a beel pont, yu noo,   327
aal difren taip a wok. . . . afta mi groo an mi get lil mo big,   328
mi—mi gu wee a wiiding dee—fam di wiiding geeng gu wok.   329

Translation

     I was small, but I had started to work already when the Housing Scheme
came, a long time ago. I started to work at twelve years of age.
     Twelve?
     Yes.
     How did you start so young?   310T
     Well, according to, you know how it was long ago, deprivation—You
see, my mother and father had separated. Then I started—em—after I
saw punishment starting, I started to work. . . . I went up to
fourth standard [fourth grade].
     Fourth standard?   315T
     I passed to go over into fifth, and I left school. I left—up to now
my books and everything must be left in the school. I left school
and got away. I went, got away, went away and worked. . . .
     Well—am—is that how the estate took you on, without knowing if your—
if your mother knew, or your teacher? But they didn't ask their   320T
permission?
     No, nobody, no. You see, in those times, you did not have to carry
a birth certificate to work. Just so—if you wanted—if you felt
like working, you went and you worked. I started to work for twenty-
four cents a day. . . . I was working in creole [gang].   325T
     Creole [gang]. When you first—what did you have to do in creole [gang]?
     I—you would manure the field, you would bail the punts, you know,
all different types of work. . . . After I grew and got a little bigger
I—I went away to the weeding gang—to the weeding gang to work.

10b. *From a description of a Hindu wedding*

I: wel, da til mondi maanin dem gu luus da an dem gu   330
kyarii am gu an, beriiyon am in di chrench. bel if a wan bai said,   331
de gu pik op di mour, an gu an beriyin da tu. bot   332
if a wan gyal said, wel, di gyal said na ga da.   333
bot ii stil ga fu tek dis sim kanggan—aal dis ting wo   334
ii gat an kyar am gu berin am. hou lang da na don,   335
di wedn na don.   336
  J: piipl de—piipl de aal di taim?   337
  I: piipl a de stedii. from fraidi nait yu a ge piipl stedii,   338
kontinyu, antil mondi nait. wel wen aal dis ting kom   339
out mondi maarning, den den—yu si den staat kilin—am—miit.   340
hou lang dem ting dis na kom out   341
fan di hous, de na a kil. hou lang de na gu an beryin aal   342
den ting dis, de na a kil notn.   343

Translation

Well, it is not until Monday morning that they will loosen that [kangan] and   330T
carry it and bury it in the canal. Well, if it's the groom's side,
they will pick up the mowhr and go and bury that too. But
if it's the bride's side, well, the bride's side doesn't have that.
But they still have to take this same kangan—all these things that
she has—and carry them and bury them. As long as that is not done,   335T
the wedding is not finished.*
  People are—people are there all the time?
  People are there continually. From Friday night, people are continuing
to pour in, until Monday night. Well, when all these things come
out Monday morning, then they—you see them start killing—am—animals.   340T
As long as these things I just mentioned have not come out
of the house, they don't kill. Until they have gone and buried all
these things, they don't kill anything.

10c. *Ole Higues as "living people"*

I: mii—ga waan oopinyan, dat, az dem se hool aig a livn   344
piipl, wai shud piipl kyaan set op an kech waan?!   345
  M: yee.   346
  A: gud pOint. veri gud pOint.   347
  I: set ap an kech waan!   348

*The "mowhr" is the elaborate headdress the bridegroom wears in an Indian wedding cere-
mony (cf. Hindi *maur*; Chaturvedi and Tiwari 1975: 623). Irene describes the "kangan" (cf.
Hindi *kāṅgān* or *kāṅkan* 'bracelet'; ibid., p. 109) as a piece of cloth containing a "supari" (in
standard Hindi 'betel nut'; ibid., p. 822) that had been used in the wedding ceremony the previous day. (Cf. Rauf 1974: 88 on *kakan*.)

M: kyar if—?i hool aig soo greet, kyan kom in yu hous   349
an sok piknii, wai den kyaan gu in di bangk an jraa monii?   350
   I: wel a da! a da wa mii se!   351

Translation

I have one opinion, that, since they say Old Higues are living
people, why shouldn't people be able to set up and catch one?   345T
Yeah.
Good point. Very good point.
Set up and catch one.
Because if Old Higues are so great that they can come in your house
and suck children, why can't they go in the bank and withdraw money?   350T
Well that's it! That's what I say!

10d. The coconut jumbie at Felicity Village

   I: mii granfaada bin gat plees a filisiti bilid.   352
   J: e-he.   353
   I: an mii nyuustu gu wen mi smaal, wid hii evriitaim.   354
   M: mm-hm. chruut!   355
   I: an neva, mii—mii doz gu an plee pan da greev, da a mii plees.   356
   J: yu plee pon di greev self?   357
   I: evriidee! fu gu op—klaim pan da greev an plee. mii an di—ii   358
bin gat wan o ii daata, wich a mii antii, bot abii tu a waan eej,   359
waan groo maach. evriidee abi a gu plee pan da greeb.   360
an abi neva sii notn. bo mi granfaada bin ga wan ool boot, bin ton   361
dong batam wan big manggoo chrii bin de rait a hed a   362
di biling. jos de ii doz tai dii boot. bel ii bin ga wan   363
ool boot an ii ton an dong so wen ii taiyord   364
ii doz gu an lai dongk an res fan dis boot. wel wan dee mii bina   365
lai dong pan dis boot. wails mi a lai dong mi heer somting   366
faal—baazhai—in dis chrench. mi git op an mi ron gu a di sailin.   367
jos de ii bin ga wan kookno chrii. wel mi se, "kooknot faal."   368
mi ron gu. mi na sii non kooknot. mi se, "e-e, we di   369
kooknot? di kooknot berin dong." mi go bak, mi lai   370
dong bak pan dis boot. ogeen somting faal. mi git op ageen an   371
mi ron gu. mi se, "a kooknot." mi se, "dis k—na gu berin—   372
mi mos ge dis waan." wen mi gu, mi na sii non kooknot ageen. an   373
naido noo waato in dis chrench na a sheek. wel mi muuv nou.   374
mi na gu bak a di boot. mi goo in insaid nou an mi a tel   375
mi granfaada. mi se, "naanaa, tuu taim kooknot faal an mi na   376
sii non."   377
   ii se, "we yu biin?"   378
   mi se, "mi bin lai dong batam di—di manggo chrii pan di boot."   379
   ii se, "na staan de dis ouwa. staan wid mii in ya."   380

mi se, "wa mek?"   381
ii se, "na notn."   382
mi se, "ii dom mos gatu bii somting mek yu tel mi na gu   383
de."   384
    ii se, "notn na de de. bot na mos gu de yuu waan. 385
yu na noo eniibadii kyan kom kom nak yu dong de. wen   386
den heer kooknot faal, dem an aal gu ron gu."   387
    wel wails abii tuu o kom nou wi dis boot, mi tel 388
am, mi se, "naanaa, a somting an yu na waan tel mii.   389
tel mii a waa!"   390
    ii se, "yu noo a waa? wan maan bin heng iiself pan da 391
chrii." se, "dis ting hapn tu mii tuu, chrii taim,   392
dat eniitaim mii waan de de de, mi a heer somting a faal,   393
an wen mi gu, mi na a sii notn." se   394
"yuu waan na mos gu anda de—em—manggu chrii, no moo,   395
wen ii miit twelv a klak."   396
    J: twelv o klak a deetaim an—?   397
    I: deetaim. da iz aal, bot mii neva sii notn in dat bilin, 398
neva, neva. mi neva sii notn in dat bilin.   399

Translation

My grandfather had a place at Felicity Village.
Eh-heh.
And I used to go, when I was small, with him everytime.
Mm-hm. That's true!   355T
And never—I used to go and play on that grave, that was my place.
You played on the grave itself?
Everyday! I used to go up—climb on that grave and play. I and the—he
had a daughter who is my aunt, but the two of us are the same age,
the same grow-match. Everyday we used to go and play on that grave.   360T
And we never saw anything. But my grandfather had an old boat turned
down underneath a big mango tree that was right in front of
the building. Just there he used to tie the boat. Well, he had this
old boat, which he had turned down so that when he was tired
he would go and lie down and rest on this boat. Well, one day I was   365T
lying down on this boat. While I was lying down I heard something
fall—baajai—in this canal. I got up and ran to the sideline canal.
Just there there was a coconut tree. Well, I said, "A coconut fell."
I ran over. I didn't see any coconut. I said, "Eh-eh, where is the
coconut? [Probably] the coconut is submerged." I went back. I lay   370T
down again on this boat. Again something fell. I got up again and
ran over. I said, "It's a coconut." I said, "This one won't sink—
I must get this one." When I got there, again I saw no coconut, and
the water in the trench wasn't moving either. Well, I moved away now.
I didn't go back to the boat. I went inside now and started to teli   375T

my grandfather. I said, "Nana, twice coconuts fell, and I didn't
see any."

He said, "Where were you?"

I said, "I was lying down under the—the mango tree, on the boat."

He said, "Don't hang around there at this hour. Stay with me in here."   380T

I said, "Why?"

He said, "Nothing."

I said, "It must be something to make you tell me not to go
there."

He said, "Nothing is there. But you mustn't go there by yourself.   385T
You never know—anybody can come and knock you down there. When
they hear that coconuts have fallen, they themselves will run there."

Well, while the two of us were coming along now in this boat, I told
him, I said, "Nana, something is wrong, and you don't want to tell me.
Tell me what it is!"
                                                                              390T
He said, "Do you know what it is? A man hanged himself on that
tree." He said, "The same thing happened to me two or three times,
that whenever I was there by myself, I would hear something falling,
and when I went (to check it out), I didn't see anything." He said,
"You mustn't go alone under that—em—mango tree, anymore,   395T
once it gets to be twelve o'clock."

Twelve o'clock in the day, or—?

In the day. That is all, but I never saw anything in that building,
never, never. I never saw anything in that building.

11. Reefer (1975–1976)

In his mid-thirties when recorded (four times in 1975 and 1976), Reefer was
a leader among the Cane Walk cane-cutters, representing them in industrial
disputes with the sugar-estate management, and serving as a nucleus for
discussion and socializing among them. After work, small groups of cane-
cutters would meet on the grass dam outside his home to play cards, read the
newspapers, and *gyaaf* ('shoot the bull,' 'exchange small talk'). Circumstances had permitted him to go only as far as fourth standard in primary
school, but he was literate, articulate, and well informed on political matters,
both locally and worldwide. The first two texts demonstrate the vigor and
eloquence with which he spoke on working conditions in the sugar industry,
revealing why he was at once a spokesman for the sugar workers and a threat
to the estate management.

This solidarity with the workers and with estate-class culture, coupled
with opposition to the status quo, was reflected in Reefer's performance in
his interviews: of all the Cane Walk speakers, he was the most consistently
basilectal. In five of nine singular-pronoun subcategories, he used the bas-

ilectal Creole variant exclusively. This was apparently by design, for he subsequently revealed that he knew the acrolectal or English variants in Creole-
to-English Correction tests and reinterviews that I arranged with three
expatriates, two Englishmen and an American.[28] He also articulated more
clearly than anyone else the need to get away from exogenous English norms
as a means of political-cultural liberation:

Abi na waan dem ingglish maan tiichin an ting da no moo, maan. dem ting da mos
don. yu sii, dem a rait de hoon buk fu suut de hoon self, an abi mos laan from dem,
on *sobjuu* ondo dem! (SI44)

We don't want the English people's teaching and so on any more, man. Those things
must come to an end. You see, they write their books to suit themselves, and we must
learn from them, and be *subdued* under them!

Reefer's texts are a rich source of information on basilectal and lower-
mesolectal GC, particularly with respect to relative-clause marking. His
most common relative pronoun is basilectal *wa* or *wo*, which can be used for
inanimate as well as animate—and human—subjects, as illustrated in lines
414, 460, and 463.[29] But we can also see traces of the SE relative-pronoun
system here too: in line 423, where *huu* is used for a human subject (note
that *badi* = 'person'), and in line 430 (*wok dat wa ii wok*), where English *dat*
and Creole *wa* are combined. We have already encountered a similar combining of basilectal and nonbasilectal forms in Derek's *at ou* complementizers (218, 240), which are intermediate between Creole *(h)ou*—a form
middle-class Georgetown parents sometimes correct by saying "how bow-
wow"—and English *dhat*. J. Edwards (1974: 14) reports another such decreolizing form for Providence Island—*unuaal*, which is intermediate between the basilectal African-English-derived second-person plural pronoun
unu and mesolectal English-derived *yohl* 'y'all.'

In Text 11c, lines 457–58, there is an unmarked relative clause, that is, a
relative clause without a relative pronoun, consisting entirely of the word
swiit; compare *kozn wo swiit* (463). Normally, when *swiit* means 'intoxicated,'
as it does here, it is used only in predicative and not in attributive position,
thus ruling out ** ii swiit kozn*. One reason for the absence of a relative pronoun here might be the fact that the prepositional phrase *from di rom shap*
intervenes between the head-noun (*kozn*) and the relative clause (*swiit*),
creating possible confusion about the subject had *wa* been inserted. In any
case, lines 458 and 460 show us that relative-pronoun deletion interacts
with other constructions and processes in complex sentences, and that the
phenomenon goes beyond the conditions set out in Bickerton (1981: 62):
"In GC, for instance, this [i.e. deletion or noninsertion of subject pronouns]
can happen when the head-noun of the relative clause is the object of the

higher sentence and when the main verb of that sentence is an equivalent of *have* or *be*: . . . *wan a dem a di man bin get di bam* 'One of them was the man who had the bomb.'"

Reefer's texts also allow us to go beyond Bickerton (1975: 43) and Rickford (1983b) in the analysis of negative *na*, incorporating the functional perspective advocated in the latter work. *Na* or *no* is the form of the negative particle when it functions as a preverbal negator (400, 448) and when it signals an emphatic affirmative (466, uttered with the rising intonation that distinguishes such sentences from the usual negative sentences, uttered with a falling, declarative intonation). When the negative serves as a prenominal quantifier, however, as in line 455 (*noo ada riisoors*), it is usually *noo*, with a long vowel. When used as an isolated particle—in answer to a question, for instance—it frequently takes this form too (484). This distinction does not appear to have been made in earlier varieties of GC; note the occurrence of "no" in both functions in lines 5 and 6 of Pinckard's (1806) Text 1a (although we have the usual difficulty of interpreting the spelling). Nor does it appear to be made in modern JC (see B. Bailey 1966: 54).

Reefer's texts offer three neat contrasts between basilectal GC and SE. The first involves the use of personal pronouns in line 417 (*aal yu fuud*) and line 453 (*foor chilren, an ii waif*), where SE would employ a definite and indefinite article, respectively. The second is in line 486, where F., Reefer's friend, does not apply the particle-movement rule that would be obligatory in adult SE before a pronoun (yielding "carry them in" instead of *kerii in dem*).[30] The final contrast is in line 482, where SE would normally delete the subject pronoun or noun phrase in the second of two conjoined sentences when it is referentially identical with the subject of the first (which would have yielded, had Reefer followed a similar rule, *mi sidong de an Ø witnis da*). This final example lends some support to Stewart's (1970: 372–73) contention that the conditions for conjunction reduction in Gullah and VBE are different from those in SE (VBE: "We was eatin—an' *we* drinkin', too"; SE: "We were eating—and drinking too"). Note, however, that in other cases Reefer does apply the deletion rule (*an Ø kyar dem* 488), suggesting that the use of *mi* in line 486 may have been for effect.

With respect to the phonology of these texts, a salient feature once again is the speed of the delivery. At times Reefer speaks even faster and more animatedly than Derek, leading to a frequent incidence of eroded final consonants (*fai* 448 vs. *faiv* 449, *somi* 'sometime' 417) and unstressed syllables (*wee* 'away' 439). Initial consonants are also affected, including the labiovelar glide of *(w)ee* 'way'; its realization as *i* in 406 is the cumulative result of vowel-laxing and initial-consonant deletion.[31] Initial *h* is also subject to deletion, most frequently in pronominal *(h)ii* (407), but occasionally elsewhere (*hou* 463 vs. *ou* 468, *hool* 461 vs. *ool* 464). Under primary or emphatic stress, however (as in *hii* 411), the initial *h* is invariably realized, suggesting that it is present in underlying form. Note that the variation between tense and lax vowels in the open-syllable pronominal forms is almost identical; under primary stress (*yuu* 414), the tense variant is usually obligatory.

One of the most salient features of Reefer's speech, and of GC phonology in general, is the realization of SE *O* and *oh* as *a* and *aa*, respectively, as in *shap* (458), *kwalifai* (436), *faal* (474) and *aadineri* (458), to cite only a few examples. These open, unrounded vowels, as noted in the discussion of McTurk's texts in Chapter 3, are one of the most distinctive characteristics of Creole speech, and have led to its being described by some as "broadin' yuh mouth" or "broad talk." Note that words with *o* (covering both the central schwa vowel and the backer caret vowel) are affected too, as shown by *piiryad* (429) and *pasent* (438), but the vowel opening in these cases is rarer (cf. *aveelobl* 445, *shigo* 456 with *o* instead of *a*). There is only one instance of *O* or *oh* in Reefer's texts—in the form *Or* in 415—and there are other morphological indications in the same sentence (possessive *yoor* and plural *tingz*) that Reefer is here making an unusual upward shift in the direction of SE.

Text 11a is from Tape SI44, tape counter nos. 271–78, 303–5; 11b and 11c are from the same tape, 392–407 and 061–69, respectively. The F. in the texts is a friend of Reefer's; he too is a cane-cutter.

11a. *Getting cramp working in the cane fields*

R: swet plenti. yu ge kramp. yu badi na a muuv. somtaim	400
yu ge mosl bong. somtaim yu sii k mi de ya nou,	401
mi ge mosl bong, mi lef sim i so.	402
F: ii ge haard.	403
R: dis kyaa kom out. dis na a kom out.	404
F: yu gadu naint it.	405
R: dis lef sim i so ou ii de if mi ge mosl bong. somain	406
mi de a wok, an mi fut lef in dis puzizhan. ii ge	407
mosl bong, wid big ting swel out ya so.	408
F: ii ge—ii get o maan—	409
R: aal di veen kom an tai tugeda, an kom fat so! sodaim—	410
sodaim if hii a mi pardno, ii a wok, sotai ii	411
kom, ii gu rob, ii gu rob, ii gu rob, ii gu chrai pul, ii gu pul,	412
ii gu pul, yu noo? pul an rob an pul. no le mi tel yu	413
wo yuu ga tu duu—wo gat di mosl bong. yu stomik	414
Or yoor livo waan bos out, wid peen, yu noo, wails hii gu	415
duu dis kain o tingz.	416
F: somi yu vamit out aal yu fuud wo yu iit—wen yu ii—wen	417
aal do—stoori hapn wid yu.	418
R: wen yu ge kramp, yu ga fu lee dong op—o lee—lee dong o di	419

keen—ai—a—in di fiil. yes! . . . wel das wai wen yu waan   420
da tablit yu gatu ron gu gu sarch fu di maan. or yu ge won   421
kot, yu gatu ron gu n luk fu di maan. yu noo, if yu get   422
ful taim piipl, di—di badi huu gu du di wok gu   423
kom rong in di fiil. bika da a hii wok—ii   424
na go notn els fu du!   425

Translation

You sweat a lot. You get cramp. Your body does not move. Sometimes   400T
you get muscle-bound. Sometimes, you see like how I am here now,
if I got muscle-bound, I'd be left just like this.
It [the muscle] gets hard.
This [pointing] can't come out. This doesn't come out.
You have to anoint it [with oil].   405T
This would be left just as it is if I got muscle-bound. Sometimes
I am working and my foot is left in this position. It becomes
muscle-bound, all swollen here.
There is—there is a man—
All the veins become tied together, and get fat! Sometimes—   410T
sometimes if he is my partner, he would work, sometimes he would
come over, and rub, and rub, and rub, and try to pull it, and pull,
and pull, you know? Pull and rub and pull. Don't let me tell you
what you have to do—whoever is muscle-bound. Your stomach
or your liver wants to burst out, with pain, you know, while he is   415T
doing these kinds of things.
Sometimes you vomit all the food you ate when you—when
all those things happen to you.
When you get cramp, you have to lie down in—in—lie down in the
cane—in—in the field! Yes! . . . Well, that's why when you want   420T
the tablets you have to run and search for the man. Or if you get a
cut, you have to run and look for the man. You know, if you had
full-time people, the—the person who is doing that job would
come around in the fields. Because that would be his job—he
wouldn't have anything else to do!   425T

11b. Out-of-season pay for sugar workers

R: yu sii, waan di beesik ting in C ripoort, i—ii moos   426
hart-rendin, yu noo, fu noo dat—am—misa jostis C se dat   427
a woka in di shigo indoschri, a non—outa grainin   428
piiryad, ii mos orn twenti daalo fu sevnti-faiv posent a di   429
wok dat wa ii wok. an i mos orn tweni fai daala fu nainti   430
posent, yu noo? a maan, bai iiself, kaan liv pon twenti daala   431
a wiik. wat obout o man wid ii waif an chilrin? hou den kan   432
mek out wid twenti an twenti fai daala?   433

J: ai miself kyaan duu it. yuu kaan gu in dii—stoor   434
an bai notn!   435
    R: an yu sii, di esteet—wi yuustu kwalifai fu sevnto-faiv posen   436
tu get a bak pee, an eeti eet pasent fu get o prodokshan   437
boonas. nou hii bring am nainti pasent—in odo wordz, hii   438
bring moo sleevri pan awi. awi a chrai fu get wee from   439
sleevrii, hii ad mo pan abi. ii ad nainti pasent bifoo   440
yu intaitl a twenti-faiv daala a wiik wok. an ii   441
ad sevnti faiv posent bifoor yu intaitl a twenti daala   442
a wiik wok.   443
    J: wo—nainti posent o wo?   444
    R: nainti pasent a di amongt a deez aveelobl. 445
    F: a di dee!   446
    J: oo, o sii wo yu miin.   447
    R: den yu o ge tweni-fai daala wenevo di esteet na a fain   448
wok fu yu. an sevnti-faiv posent a di deez aveelobl yu   449
gatu wok biifoo yu get twenti daala—a wiik—wenevo di   450
esteet na a fain wok fu yu. o woko—waan maan bai   451
iisef kaant liv pon twenti daalo nou. wot obout o man wid,   452
lawii se foor chilren, an ii waif? wo dem gu du wid   453
twenti daala monii? dem ga wan—dem ga fu tek am n wach   454
am so. yu sii? an wii na ga noo ada riisoors, yu noo,   455
ar noo ada ingkom, eedo dan di shigo indoschri.   456

Translation

You see, one of the basic things in C.'s Report, it—it is most
heart-rending, you know, to know that—am—Mr. Justice C. said that
a worker in the sugar industry, in the non—the out-of-grinding
period, must earn twenty dollars for seventy-five percent of the
work that he does. And he must earn twenty-five dollars for ninety   430T
percent, you know? A man, by himself, can't live on twenty dollars
a week. What about a man with his wife and children. How can they
make out with twenty or twenty-five dollars?

    I myself can't do it. You can't go in the—store
and buy anything!   435T

    And you see, the estate—we used to qualify at seventy-five percent
to get back pay, and eighty-eight percent to get a production
bonus. Now he has brought it to ninety percent—in other words, he
has brought more slavery on us. We are trying to get away from
slavery; he has added more on us. He added ninety percent before   440T
you are entitled to twenty-five dollars a week for work, and he
added seventy-five percent before you are entitled to twenty dollars
a week for work.

    What—ninety percent of what?
    Ninety percent of the amount of "days available."   445T
    Of the days!

Oh, I see what you mean.

Then you get twenty-five dollars, whenever the estate doesn't find
work for you. And seventy-five percent of the "days available," you
have to work before you get twenty dollars a week whenever the   450T
estate is unable to find work for you. A worker—one man by
himself cannot live on twenty dollars now. What about a man, with,
let's say, four children and a wife? What would they do with
twenty dollars? They have one—they would have to take it and watch
it so [in amazement]. You see? And we have no other resource, you know,   455T
or no other income, other than the sugar industry.

11c. *A police incident at a rum shop*

R: waan maan a tek out waan o ii kozn   457
from di romshap swiit. an chrii—tuu puliismaan wid a aadineri   458
konstobl, yu noo—a kom in di shap. an mii si dong   459
rai de, mi witnis da wid mi ai wo gaad gi   460
mi. di tuu puliisman kom in, su di bai a hool ii kozn   461
an a kya am. wel di bai—dis maan na waan fu gu,   462
yu noo hou, di jentlma—dii kozn wo swiit   463
na waan fu gu, so ii a ool a—so di puliismaan kom,   464
an a hool di bai—a maan—ya su.   465
wel di maan na ton bak fu gu in di bar? i hool di maan   466
ya so. wel di maan a se, "luus mi!" yu noo   467
ou? wel di man no noo dat i wan puliismaan hool ii a   468
ii bak.   469
   J: ye, ii jos—ii swiit.   470
   R: so afta di maan a pul ou di—di puliismaan grabl di   471
maan ya, an ii giyam waan chok bak so, yu   472
noo hou? an di maan a—yu noo, di maan swiit, ii   473
akshulii o faal dong. so ii ada kozn gu tu di puliiman   474
se, "man, wo yo chok di maan fa?" di puliismaan hool   475
ii—di ada bai—joosii—nen nee teer dong, teer op di maan   476
hool shot. yu noo, lil ting kuda   477
don—   478
   J: ye-es.   479
   R: yu noo, an ii—de mek am big; teer op di bai hool shot,   480
bos op aal dis ting ya—in di presen—mi wit—   481
mi sidong de an mi witnis da.   482
   J: wee da? B?   483
   R: noo. rait a di romshap de. wi gat o . . . o romshap de.   484
   F: da—de na don! di kech dem a rood,   485
den kerii in dem.   486
   R: an di puliismaan, wen di poor piipl dem gu we, di puliismaan dem   487
kech di maan dem a rood, an kyar dem   488
gu lak dem op.   489

Translation

A man was helping his cousin, who was sweet [intoxicated],
from the rum shop. And three—two policemen, together with an ordinary
constable, you know—came into the shop. And I sat down
right there, I witnessed that with my own eyes which God gave   460T
me. The two policemen came in, so the guy was holding his cousin
and carrying him. Well, the guy—this man did not want to go,
you know how, the gentleman—the cousin who was intoxicated
did not want to go, so he was holding him. So the policeman came
and was holding the guy—that man—here so [indicating the place].   465T
Well, the man turned to go back into the bar. He held the man right
here like this. Well, the man kept saying, "Let me loose!" You know
how? Well, the man didn't know it was a policeman holding him from
behind.
     Yeah, he just—he was tipsy.   470T
     So after the man was pulling away the—the policeman grabbed the
man here [indicating the spot] and he gave him one push backwards, you
know how? And the man—ah—you know, the man was drunk, he
actually was falling down. So his other cousin went to the policeman
and said, "Man, why did you push the man?" The policeman held   475T
him—the other guy, Josie—and they tore down, tore up the man's
whole shirt. You know it was a little thing; it could have
been finished—
     Yes.
     You know, and he—they made it big; tore up the guy's whole shirt,   480T
broke up all these things here—in the presence—I wit—
I sat down there and I witnessed that.
     Where was that?—B.'s?
     No. Right at the rum shop there. We have a . . . a rum shop there.
     They—they weren't finished. They caught up with them on the road,   485T
and they carried them in [to the police station].
     And the policemen, when the poor people had dispersed, the policemen caught
up with the guys on the road, and carried them [to the jail] to lock them up.

12. Granny (1974)

Granny, a retired sugar estate weeder, was fifty-eight when I first interviewed her in 1974. Although she had no formal schooling as a child, she is
rich in experiences and lessons learned from life. That she possesses the
gift of dramatic, effective self-expression is clear from all of the texts presented here, but particularly Text 12b, in which she eloquently conveys the
unrelenting drudgery of estate labor, and the weariness that it etches on the
bodies and minds of its practitioners.
     Granny's account of the activities of a legendary Ole Higue in Text 12a

and her report of her own sighting of a jumbie in Text 12c are both studded with graphic, persuasive detail. Apart from their folkloric value, Granny's three texts exemplify several of the classic features of basilectal GC. For instance, prepositional *a* covers a broad range of semantic functions, indicating the source or starting point of movement (*a mi aan* 561–62 = 'from'), the target or destination of movement (*a dongsteez* 552 = 'to'), possession or location with respect to an object (*a ii nek* 501 = 'of'), location with respect to time (*a di nait* 497 = 'on'), and location with respect to place (*a manchroos* 566 = 'in'). Sometimes prepositions are absent where they would be required in SE or even mesolectal GC, as in *luk Ø di plees* 507, 'looked at the place,' and *de Ø bakdam* 556, 'are at the backdam.' A detailed analysis of this phenomenon is needed, but these instances of apparent preposition absence seem to depend as much on the governing verb (*luk* equivalent to 'look at,' *de* equivalent to 'be located in') as on the kinds of objects they govern (both represent static locations). The basilectal use of pronominal *ii* for female as well as male referents is exemplified in the shift from *shi* to *ii* in lines 495 and 541–53, where it is the Old Higue woman who sucks the blood and vomits it out as she leaves.

Lexical items of interest include the Creole intransitive use of *ponish* ('suffer' 558) and the use of *ton bak* 'turn back,' followed by a conjunction and verb (*ton bak an sok i* 529), to express a retaliatory action, one carried out in revenge. Note too that the locative verb *de* is used for age expressions (*ii bin de bou ten yeer* 493–94), and, apropos of the point made in the preceding paragraph, that it sometimes co-occurs with *in*, as in *hou moch yee(r)z yu de in?* 'How old are you?' The basilectal indefinite article—*wan*—is also exemplified in lines 556 and 567, although this varies with nonbasilectal *a/o* in 566 and elsewhere. Note too that *ded* in lines 557 and 559 is the verb-stem (*dai* does not occur in basilectal GC), showing that English past participles can serve as the model for creole verb-stems—*brok* 'break,' *laas* 'lose,' and *lef* 'leave' are other examples—even though the commoner model is the English infinitive or present (e.g. *tel* 495). On this point, compare Alleyne (1971: 173) and Bickerton (1975: 28).

Granny's Text 12b contains two occurrences of adverbial *somtaim* (556 and, as *ontai*, 559), contradicting Bickerton's (1975: 33, n7) claim that "basilectal creole lacks adverbs of indefinite time such as 'sometimes,' 'often,' 'usually,' etc." Compare the occurrences of *somtaim* in Reefer's Text 11a (400, 401) and *evriitaim* (354) and *evriidee* (358) in Irene's Text 10d. Moreover, since these examples show clearly that the basilect has time adverbials, they also weaken Bickerton's argument (ibid.) that the absence of such adverbs accounts for apparent exceptions to his Main Stative Rule. (For discussion of exceptions to this rule, see the introduction to Derek's texts.)

Granny's texts are particularly valuable for what they reveal about GC sentence structure. One example is the special kind of serial-verb construction seen in line 546 (*di blod a wash a kom dong* 'The blood was coming down in a wash') and lines 549–50 (*ii a chro ou di blod a kom out* 'she was throwing up the blood as she came out'). These resemble the "directional" serial-verb constructions found in a number of English creoles, as well as in Niger-Congo and some Asian languages; compare the Sranan sentence *a tyari den fisi kon* 'He brought the fish,' literally, "He carried the fish come" (Huttar 1981: 294; see also Alleyne 1980: 92, 171). In both these constructions and Granny's the final verb is a verb of motion, but in Granny's case this motion verb is modified by adverbs (*dong, out*), establishing that the *kom* she uses retains a strong verbal identity and has not become a simple directional adverb. Furthermore, in Granny's examples the first verb provides further specification or elaboration about the process referred to in the second, whereas in the directional type the specification is usually the other way around (contrast *tyari kom* 'bring' with *tyari go* 'take'), as it is also in corresponding SE constructions (note the order of verbal elements in the translations for lines 546 and 549–50). These "elaborative" serial-verb constructions (to coin a term for them) resemble the "instrumental" serial-verb constructions more closely in this respect; note that in *ii tek naif kot am* the instrumental specification comes before the basic action, in contrast to its SE translation 'He cut it with a knife.'

One final wrinkle in the analysis of these elaborative serial-verb constructions is provided by the example in line 532 (*iina ben an waak* 'she used to walk bent over'). This is similar to the preceding examples in providing the elaboration in the first rather than the second verb, but differs from them, since its final verb is not one of the common directional verbs and is conjoined with *an*. However, Givón (1975) includes conjoined verbs among his stock of serial-verb constructions, and it seems advisable to consider *ben an waak* in this category too.

Just as this example invites further analysis, so do the examples with *fu* in lines 551, 552, and 555. Like the *fu* in line 567, they occur in a locative environment, but they are harder to translate or classify. The examples in lines 551 and 552 have elements of the modal obligation that *fu* has elsewhere (see Bickerton 1981: 109) and are translatable as 'the place where one has to walk in,' but they might also be classified as complementizers, translatable by 'to' + verb or verb"-ing" (e.g. 'coming down the step'). In either case there is a strong locative force in all these examples that extends beyond the complementizer/modal auxiliary analyses provided for *fu/fi* in the literature preceding Winford (1985a).

The "causal" constructions with *hou* in 559 and 560 are also worth noting. In contrast to causal constructions with *mek* (in which the order of the conjoined sentences is always iconic, cause preceding effect), constructions with *hou* show greater syntactic freedom; since the cause sentence is always marked with *hou*, it can come either first (560) or second (559). In general, Granny's texts are rich in the complex sentence structures that we associate with a mature creole language and a fluent creole speaker. Note the long, complex sentence running from line 541 to line 546.

In phonological terms, Granny is one of the "broadest" Creole speakers in Cane Walk, and her texts include almost all the distinctive features of GC phonology discussed in the introductions to the texts of Derek, Irene, and Reefer. We find, among other things, the "broad mouth" pronunciation of SE *oh, O,* and *Oi* as *aa, a,* and *ai*, respectively (*smaal* 526, *spat* 538, *bai* 496) and the variable deletion of initial *b* in the tense-marker *bin* (*in* 567, with *min* in line 571 revealing nasal assimilation as an intermediate stage, and *iina* in line 532—reduced from *ii bina*—revealing subsequent absorption of the vowel of the tense marker). Other examples are the deletion of initial *w* (*id* 'with' 506) and *h* (*aan* 562, *ool aig* 519),[32] and the variable absence of postvocalic final *t* (*bou* 493) and *f* (*haa* 563).

One phonological feature found in the preceding texts we have not discussed is the absence of postvocalic *r* in stressed syllable-final position. This is quite regular in Granny's texts, as examples like *pyoo* ('pure' 505) and *bifoo* ('before' 562) show, but the fact that the *r* is retained before a following vowel (*poor out* 'pour out' 511–12, *beerii* 'barely' 538) suggests that it is present in the underlying form.[33]

There are two other consonantal processes that we have not commented on before. One is the realization of *p* as *f* (*fan* 'pon' 565—here plausibly representing partial assimilation to the immediately preceding *v*, but compare *flatfohrm* in Sheik's Text 14c, line 756, where there is no preceding *f* or *v*. The other process is the variable devoicing of word-final *z* (*bikaas* 'because' 492, *monchroos* 'Montrose' 566). Both of these are more characteristic of Indo-Guyanese than Afro-Guyanese speech; Bickerton (1975: 61) ascribes the frequency with which the mesolectal habitual marker is realized as *das* rather than *doz* among Indo-Guyanese to the absence of a voiced sibilant (and low back vowel) in Hindi. This seems to be the case also in Bhojpuri, which is a more likely candidate than Hindi for the ancestral language of Indo-Guyanese (Gambhir 1981).

One minor feature that should be mentioned before we leave the subject of consonantal processes is the existence of alternate routes for the simplification of the word-final cluster in *vraidz*, the first element in the village name "Vryheid's Lust"; I simplify it in line 522 by deleting the final sibilant (*vraid*), but Granny, like other villagers in the area, deletes the preceding stop instead (*vraiz* 521). "Simplification" of final clusters ending in *t* or *d* (as in the second element of this village name: *los* 'Lust' 522) is of course so widespread and frequent in all but the most nearly acrolectal levels of

Guyanese speech that there is little basis for positing the clusters in underlying structure.

In terms of vowels, one interesting feature of Granny's speech is her tendency to prolong occurrences of lax *e* without converting them to tense *ee*,
represented by the dash in *ye-es* (492) and *e-evribadii* (519). Related, too, is
her expressive use of reduplication in 'leak' (*lii—iik* 545) and 'hard' (*ha—
haard* 560) to achieve an iconic representation of the leaking of the blood
and the hardness of the work. The final *o* in *kuk-o* (565) is yet another by-
product of her energetic and vigorous delivery; like the final *a* in Derek's
geeta (287), it appears to be a by-product of the explosive release of the preceding voiceless (fortis) stop.[34]

Text 12a is from Tape SI13, tape counter nos. 360–406; 12b and 12c are
from the same tape, nos. 325–31 and 550–78, respectively. The U. in Text
12c is Ustad; see Text set 16.

12a. *The Old Higue who sucked Granny's brother's neck*

J: wo bo ting laik ool haig an so, yu biliiv in dem	490
ting? yu evo heer bo dem tingz?	491
G: wel ye-es. mi biliiv in am, bikaas—mi brodo wo—am—bina	492
chrobl o—a ool aig wuman. mi brodo bin smaal, ii bin de bou	493
ten yeer. . . . hii bina chrobl o—a—o—a ool leedii, an shi bin—	494
shi tel am se ii gu sok am. an ii bigin fu sok dis	495
bai, an dis bai ge sik, an den kyar ii tin aaspital in	496
esteet. mi fado kyar ii tu aaspital. an wel, a di nait	497
wen—wen di—wen dis hool aig kom an a sok dis bai,	498
sok om bihain ii nek hee, bak o ii nek.	499
J: yu sii o mark?	500
G: ye-es. ii sok am bak a ii nek so. dis bai	501
a sii ii an ii a halo fu—mi fado bina sliip wid ii	502
in di aaspital, pon di bed. an ii se—am—am—"paa! paa!	503
luk! luk! luk wo—luk o dis wuman a sok mi nek!" an wen	504
ii oo—wen ii wach so, ii sii pyoo blod, a ron out ii nek. an	505
aal di bed in pyoo blod, mes op id blod. bot noo	506
skrach an noo kot, wen dem luk di plees.	507
J: iz jos di blod kom out?	508
G: jos di blod poor out, an mes op a . . .	509
J: bo di blod bin de, doo? soo o—it reelii hapn?	510
G: mi te?u?e-evribadi sii di blod, an sii dii wee o ii poor	511
out bak ii nek.	512
J: soo wo hapn den? dee di tek ii tu aspitol, an wo—	513
di dakto di noo wi tu duu?	514
G: yes. wel dem chrai wid ii—an ii—an ii get oova. ii	515
na ded. so das wai mi biliiv dat ii ga hool aig.	516

J: so dis leedii hee, so wo shii yuuztu duu? shii yuuztu wok
ool aig? yuaal di noo shi wuz o ool aig leedii?
    G: yes, e-evriibadii noo shiiz a ool aig in di esteet.
    J: wee wuz dis? in—am—at manchrooz?
    G: noo—da—a in liv in vraiz los—di ool leedii.
    J: da in vraid los. yuu wuz bout hou ool den?
    G: mii bin mosii—a—mii bin big. mi mosi bo—de
bou—footiin, fiftiin yeer i di taim.
    J: oo, bo hii di smaalo?
    G: hii bin smaal.
    J: oo, obout hou ool? siks? sevn?
    G: bo ten yeer. . . . ii a kaal shii hool aig an faiya raas,
an di—leedii ton bak an sok i.
    J: hou ool shii wuz?
    G: do leedi bin hool! mi no noo hou ho—bot ii bin ool—
iina ben an waak, hou ii ool.
    J: so afto dis ting hapm ee, so nobadii in tel shi noting
ar so?
    G: no, noobodii in tel shi notn.
    J: di fraikn?
    G: na tel shi notn. de na kech ii—de na
kech ii a di spat, yu noo. de beerii—di—oo—an di bai
sii ii wid ii—ee—ii ai.
    J: ii sii shii?
    G: ii sii shi, bot mi no noo ou ii disapeer! bot ou
ii waak dong from di aaspital—from til o opsteez,
bin tuu stoori aaspital—hou ii waak dong
fran oopsteez kom til a dongsteez, a so di blod
lii—iik til ii ton out, an gaan
a di rood! di blod a wash a kom dong! shi—ii a—
vamit out di blod, rait chru di aaspital.
    J: afto ii kom out?
    G: afto ii kom out, di blod—ii a chro ou di blod a
kom out. laik ii kyaan stomik di blod. aal di step, di
aaspital step, aal o—fu waak in di gya—am—a di—a di—di
gyalorii—aal in blod! fu kom dong di step a dongsteez
aal! . . . dee falo di blod, di blod an hii aal. hou—di
a chrees di blod an sii hou shi gaan. so ii vamit
di blod fu kom ou til a di rood.

517
518
519
520
521
522
523
524
525
526
527
528
529
530
531
532
533
534
535
536
537
538
539
540
541
542
543
544
545
546
547
548
549
550
551
552
553
554
555

Translation

    What about things like Ole Higue and so? Do you believe in those
things? Have you ever heard about those things?
    Well, yes. I believe in it, because my brother who—am—he used to
tease an Ole Higue woman. My brother was small, he was about ten

490T

years old. . . . He used to trouble a—an old lady and she was—
she told him she would suck his blood. And she began to suck this   495T
boy, and the boy got sick, and they carried him to the hospital on the
estate. My father carried him to the hospital. And well, in the night
when—when the—when this Ole Higue came and was sucking this boy,
she sucked him behind his neck here, at the back of his neck.
　　Did you see a mark?   500T
　　Yes. She sucked him at the back of his neck here. This boy
saw her and hollered for—my father was sleeping with him
in the hospital on the bed. And he said —am—am— "Pa, Pa! Look! Look! Look at
this woman sucking my neck!" And when he—when he looked, he saw a lot of
blood running out of his neck, and   505T
all the bed drenched in blood, messed up with blood. But there was
no scratch and no cut, when they looked at the place.
　　It's just that the blood came out?
　　Just the blood poured out, and messed up a . . .
　　But the blood was there, though? So it—it really happened?   510T
　　I tell you everybody saw the blood, and saw the way it poured out of the back of
his neck.
　　So what happened then? Did they take him to the hospital, and what—
did the doctor know what to do?
　　Yes. Well, they tried with him—and he—and he got over it. He   515T
did not die. So that is why I believe in the Ole Higue.
　　So this lady here, so what did she do? She used to do the work of
an Ole Higue? Did everyone know that she was the Ole Higue lady?
　　Yes. Everybody on the estate knows she is an Ole Higue.
　　Where was this? In—am—at Montrose?   520T
　　No. That—I lived in Vryheid's Lust—the old lady.
　　That was in Vryheid's Lust. About how old were you then?
　　I was, I must have been—am—I was big. I must have been about—
about fourteen or fifteen years old at the time.
　　Oh, but he was smaller?   525T
　　He was small.
　　Oh, about how old? Six? Seven?
　　About ten years old. . . . He used to call her Ole Higue and Fire-Rass,
and the lady, in retaliation, sucked his blood.
　　How old was she?   530T
　　That lady was old! I don't know how old—but she was old.
She used to walk bent over, she was so old.
　　So after this thing happened here, didn't anybody say anything to her or
something?
　　No. Nobody said anything to her.   535T
　　Were they frightened?
　　They didn't say anything to her. They didn't catch—they didn't
catch her on the spot, you know. They barely—the—only the boy saw her with
his—his eyes.

He saw her?
He saw her, but I don't know how she disappeared! But along the   540T
route that she walked down from the hospital—from upstairs,
it was a two-story hospital—along the route that she walked coming downstairs
from upstairs, all along there the blood had
le-eaked, until the point at which she had turned out and gone   545T
down the road! The blood was coming down in a wash! She—she was—
she vomited the blood throughout the hospital.
After she came out?
After she came out, the blood—she was throwing up the blood as she
came out. Like she couldn't stomach the blood. All the steps, the   550T
hospital steps, the place to walk in the—ga—am—at the—at the—the
gallery—all in blood! Coming down the steps leading downstairs and
all! . . . They followed the blood, the blood and her too. The way—they
traced the blood and saw the way that she left. She had vomited
the blood all the way to the road.   555T

12b. The rigors of field work on the sugar estate

G: somtaim yu fiil wan fiilinz, ar yu get—yu de bakdam,   556
yu faal dong, yu se, gaad! i beto yu ded,   557
hou haad yu a wok, hou yu gatu ponish. "i beto   558
mi ded!" ontai yu wok, wok, hou di wok   559
ha—haard ya. hou di wok soo haad, yuz chro dong yuself a di   560
bangk an yu se, "laad, a wen dis kotlis a gu kom out a mi   561
aan? i beto mi ded, bifoo mi a liv!"   562

Translation

Sometimes you get a feeling or you get—you are at the backdam,*
and you fall down and say, God, it's better you were dead,
how hard you have to work, how you have to suffer. "Better that
I were dead!" Sometimes you work and work, because the work
is ha-a-ard here. The work is so hard you throw yourself down on the   560T
ground and say, "Lord, when will this cutlass [machete] come out of my
hand? It's better for me to die than live [like this]!"

12c. The jumbie she saw

G: iz foo—obou haa paas faiv in di maanin.   563
U: haa paas faiv?   564
G: ye-es, in di maanin! mi a kuk-o! mi a liv fan ma—a—mi did   565

*The backdam marks the limit of cane-field cultivation as one moves inland from the Atlan-
tic coastline or from a river. The term is often generalized (as it is here) to refer to the entire
cane field or cultivated area behind a village.

liv a manchroos. an, awii liv fan o daam, an da di   566
pasijee fu piipl paas. so wan maan in ded de, an,   567
dii maanin mi git op n mi o kuk, rong haa   568
paas faiv. mi sii is. dem jres ii—   569
    U: wo di maan bin neem?   570
    G: J! di maan bin neem J! an dis man, dem min jres ii wid—   571
am—a koorta, an wid dootii. . . . an wen mi oopn di windo so,   572
mi sii di man a paas in front o mii so!   573
    J: di-iz afto ii ded?   574
    G: o-he! afto ii ded! da ii chrii dee ii   575
go reez. an den mi—aam—mi bin yong gyorl. mi na in   576
marid yet. an mii kaal fu mi moda, mi se, "modo!"—   577
am—se, "kom! sii J a paas!" asunaz mi mek so fu   578
kaal fu mi modo, mi mek bak so, di man miit   579
bout o—twenti faiv raad. oonii mek so an mek so.   580
wel mii kom out a di dam, an mi a wach fu sii,   581
bika ii ga sevn roo waiya, we di kou dem, di   582
kou fens. ii gatu do—an ii dok—a—ii   583
na dok di waiya, ii paas jis so.   584

Translation

It was four—about half-past five in the morning.
Half-past five?
Yes, in the morning! I was cooking! I was living on Mon—I was   565T
living at Montrose. And we were living on a dam, and the
passageway for people to pass was there. So a man had died there and on
the morning in question I got up and I was cooking, around half-
past five. I saw this. They had dressed him—
    What was the man's name?   570T
    J.! The man's name was J.! And this man, they had dressed him with—
am—a koortah* and his dhoti. . . . And when I opened the window like this,
I saw the man passing in front of me like this!
    This is after he had died?
    Yes! After he had died! That was three days after, when he was   575T
due to rise. And then I—am—I was a young girl. I hadn't gotten
married yet. And I called out for my mother. I said, "Mother!"—
am—I said, "Come, see J. passing!" As soon as I turned so to
call my mother, I turned back like this, but the man had gone
about twenty-five rods. I only turned around so and turned back.   580T
Well, I came out on the dam and I was watching to see [where he
went] because there were seven rows of wire, where the cows, the
cows were fenced in. He had to duck—and he ducked—ah—he
did not duck under the wire, he passed through just like that.

    *The "koortah" (cf. Hindi *kurta:*) is "a loose-fitting upper garment" (Chaturvedi and
Tiwari 1975: 141).

13. Katherine (1978)

In moving from Granny to Katherine, we move from estate to non-estate class, and to one of the most upwardly mobile persons—in social and linguistic terms—in the Cane Walk sample. Katherine was thirteen years old when she was first interviewed in 1976, and she was reinterviewed twice in 1978. The daughter of a building contractor, she was just completing form I at one of the most prestigious secondary schools in Georgetown. When asked to name her five best friends, she listed no one from Cane Walk; all were classmates from Georgetown. The four texts in this section are all taken from an animated interview with Katherine conducted in 1978 by Angela Rickford, who had taught at the same school the year before, and was able to talk with her on a number of school-related subjects as an insider.

Katherine says she normally speaks "Proper English"—"unless I'm with those people who speak Creolese," among whom she identifies cane-cutters. According to her, you should "try to bring down your language" in such contexts "so that they will understand and don't think that you're trying to play high and mighty on them." At the same time she admits that she does not mix much within Cane Walk, and that some of the Cane Walk children look at her "as if, well, you different from them. . . . You're going somewhere, right? That is what they take it to . . ."

Partly as the result of her association with acrolectal speakers outside the village, Katherine's control of the acrolect is extremely firm. For instance, she was the only person in the Cane Walk sample who never used a single creole morphological variant (basilectal or mesolectal) for singular personal pronouns.[35] To develop and explain this point, let me summarize the distinction between phonological and morphological pronoun variants that I first drew in Rickford (1979: 189–90). Variation between *mii* and *mi* as allomorphs of the first-person pronoun is classified as phonological because the forms vary in terms of a phonological feature (vowel-laxing) that is not unique to the forms in question and can be described by a general phonological rule. By contrast, the variation between *mi* and *ai* is suppletive and cannot be described by any general phonological rule. To distinguish this type of variation from the preceding phonological type, and because it invariably represents the incorporation or nonincorporation of higher-level grammatical/semantic distinctions (here, morphological encoding of the subject-object distinction), I refer to it as morphological. It could alternatively be classified as morpholexical.

The distinction is significant not just because different levels of the grammar are involved in each, but also because unlike phonological pronominal variation, which displays gradient social stratification, morphological pronominal variation displays sharp social stratification, as has been found to be true of phonological versus morphosyntactic variation more generally (Labov 1966: 253; Fasold 1970: 560–61). Whereas most of the phonological pronoun variants lie within the productive competence of every Guyanese (note Katherine's *hii* vs. *ii* 587–88), with social class and other social distinctions marked primarily in quantitative terms, this is not true of the morphological pronoun variants. There are fluent GC speakers who never use the morphological acrolectal variants in some pronoun subcategories (like *hor* for third-person feminine object), just as there are some fluent English speakers who never use the morphological basilectal Creole variants in some subcategories (like *am* for third-person feminine object) and who do not appear to "know" them in the productive sense of the term. Katherine falls within this latter category. Not only did she consistently use "English" morphological variants in her recorded speech, but in the English-to-Creole Correction test, in which she made an effort to display her best basilect, she did not appear to know what the basilectal variant was in six of those subcategories. As her mother jokingly commented in the background—for this was a source of pride rather than despair—"She can't . . ." (i.e. speak basilectal Creole).

The texts presented here provide further evidence that Katherine tends to use English rather than Creole variants insofar as morphology and syntax are concerned. For the first time in this chapter we see a wide range of morphologically inflected acrolectal variants, including forms of the English copula "be" (*iz* 585, *wuz* 587) and pluralizing "-s" (*peepoz* 616). We also find several examples of other upper-mesolectal/acrolectal features, such as negative attraction to the indefinite without negative concord (*noobodii wOntid* 602), "be" passives (*C . . . wuz noowi tu bii fongd* 606), and existentials marked with English "there + copula" (*di wu* 668) rather than Creole *ii + gat* (compare the basilectal equivalent of the existential in lines 668–69: *ii bin ga wan blak chap*). Katherine uses the English indefinite article *a(n)* 15 times in these texts; this is almost as much as the total for the preceding four estate-class Cane Walk speakers (18 tokens), who frequently employ instead the unstressed basilectal GC indefinite article *wan*.

As noted in the discussion of phonological pronoun variants above, nonstandard or Creole elements are found in the speech of upper-mesolectal/near-acrolectal speakers like Katherine primarily in the phonology, and we would expect increased vowel elision, *h*-deletion, consonant-cluster simplification, and the like to mark their excited, emotionally charged speech. As we shall see, Katherine's speech certainly displays these and other processes of morphophonemic condensation, but it also contains some nonstandard morphosyntactic features. Subject pronouns are sometimes absent (616), as are required forms of the English copula (636, 670). One of her examples of copula absence—between *im* and *aim* in 671—occurs in "exposed" clause-final position, where SE clearly does not permit contraction.[36] Katherine also uses two forms that are unique to the mesolect; both are used only once: *in* as preverbal negator in line 653 (cf. basilectal *na*, acrolectal *doont*) and *doz* as habitual marker (reduced to *z* in line 664; cf. basilectal *a* and acrolectal *yuuzhwulii* or present tense). Finally, note her use of *kom* in lines 587, 590, and 616, where it has the semantic force of indignation or surprise and the semi-auxiliary status (particularly in line 616) of VBE 'come' (Spears 1982), although the following verb is not continuative or progressive as it usually is in VBE.

The most striking area in which Katherine varies between standard and nonstandard forms, however, is in past-tense marking, where we find marked *rapt* and *pusht* (589, 591) alongside unmarked *rap* and *push* (588, 608). Overall, Katherine marks three of every four semantically past verbs (74/98, excluding indeterminate cases like *oopn di* 592, where a *t* or *d* follows a weak verb). Modals and other auxiliaries, including "do," are the most frequently marked verb forms (15/17, or 88 percent), with the English copula next in line (22/28, or 79 percent). These findings are in line with Bickerton's (1975: 104ff) statement that, in decreolization, "The first affirmative English past forms to be acquired are *had* and *waz*." After this, Bickerton (1975: 102ff, 142ff) finds past-marking acquired in the following order: syllabic weak verbs (like *start*, which end in *t* or *d* and add "-ed" to form the past tense in English); strong verbs (like *kom*, which undergo stem change in the past); and nonsyllabic weak verbs (like *rap*, which do not add an extra syllable when "-ed" is suffixed). This ordering is replicated in Katherine's data, with 80 percent (4/5) of her syllabics (e.g. *wOntid* 602), 70 percent (30/43) of her strong verbs, and 60 percent (3/5) of her weak nonsyllabics morphologically marked for past tense.

Within the category of weak nonsyllabics, however, the nature of the following phonological environment makes no difference, contra Bickerton (1975: 151) and studies of past "-ed" marking in other dialects (for instance, Labov et al. 1968). Two of Katherine's marked cases come before vowels (*rapt On* 589, *pusht* 591), but the two unmarked cases also come before vowels (*rap On* 588, *konform it* 602).

Finally, Bickerton's prime constraint—that past-marking should be most frequent with punctual verbs (referring to an event at one point in the past) and with verbs that do *not* occur in temporal clauses[37]—receives no support from Katherine's Text 13a, which was specifically examined for the possible operation of this constraint. In this text, past punctuals are in fact marked slightly less often (8/15 or 53 percent) than past nonpunctuals (9/13 or 69 percent). One constraint, which is rarely considered in the analysis of creole communities but seems to be operating here to some degree, is the deliberate coding of past actions as "historical presents" for dramatic narrative effect. The *siz* 'says' in line 595 and the *kyaan* 'can' in line 596 seem to be deliberate encodings of the present, not a nonmarking of the past, and lend some support to a "historical present" analysis. This possibility will be explored at greater length in connection with Bonnette's speech (Text 15c in particular).

I suggested above that the nonstandard or Creole elements in Katherine's speech are primarily phonological, and her texts bear this out. They share a whole range of phonological features with the texts of the basilectal estate-class speakers we have surveyed. Among these are variable *h*-deletion (*edmasto* 597, *adnt* 632, *iz* 591) and *r*-lessness (virtually obligatory in unstressed syllables like *peepo* 613; less frequent in stressed syllables: *hee* 620 vs. *heer* 668; *fohm* 619 vs. *sohrts* 661). Other such features are the palatalization of velars before *a(a)* (*kyaan* 652); consonant-cluster simplification (*tes* 637, *dozn* 599); vowel-laxing (*di* 'day' 587); variable absence of postvocalic *t* (*bo* 601) and initial *w* (*ud* 662); the use of stops rather than interdental fricatives in *mat* (610) and *den* (609); the use of alveolar rather than velar nasals in participial suffixes (*laiyin* 627, *pleeyin* 661, but cf. *biiting* 674); and the deletion of initial voiced stops in tense-aspect preverbal markers (*di doz* reduces to *diz* in Katherine's line 664 just as *yu doz* reduces to *yuz* in Granny's line 560).

Some of these features occur less frequently than in the estate-class texts, but the effects of morphophonemic condensation are sometimes even more drastic in Katherine's speech, making it extremely difficult to transcribe in places. For instance, the articles are completely eroded in *wu(z) (o) niigroo bOi* (668–69) and *bai(di) taim* (605), as is the preposition in *kep mii (in) hOspitol* (642). In general the qualitative class differences that we observe with morphosyntactic features—for instance, the fact that Katherine never uses anterior *bin*, habitual *a*, genderless pronominal *am*, or many other basilectal forms—are simply not visible in the phonology. This agrees with the evidence referred to above that phonological variables in the creole continuum show gradient rather than sharp stratification, and are therefore more amenable to unified analyses in which different classes within a community are assumed to share common underlying forms.

The one major phonological difference between Katherine and the estate-class speakers is a feature that frequently separates mesolectal and basilectal speakers: she uses *O*, *Oi*, and *oh* rather than the corresponding "broad-mouth" pronunciations *a*, *ai*, and *aa*; see *gOt* 621, *bOi* 669, and *ohl* 671. In terms of social stratification, this is the single most important phonological variable in the GC continuum.

Text 13a is from Tape SI94, tape counter nos. 072–080; 13b, 13c, and 13d are from the same tape, nos. 241–53, 110–22, and 369–85, respectively. The A. in all these texts is Angela Rickford.

13a. A "bad boy" in school

K: C iz verii baad op tu nou.   585
A: oo gohd, C, oo shoks! doon tohk bot C!   586
K: mis H wuz tiichin os hischrii wohn di, hii kom   587
n rap On di door. oparontlii ii laik som gyorl id klas.   588
di gyorl gu bai do neem S. ii rapt On di   589
door. shi din teek im On. shi noo it wuz C! ii kom   590
n pusht iz fees o di windoo. shi din teek im ohn. hii   591
oopn di door, keem rait in, sat On or desk!   592
A: yu kidin!   593
K: ye, hii keem in, sit On di desk. wol shi kun teek it On   594
eniimoor. shi siz—am—"C, pliiz liiv mai fohrm."   595
hii rifyuus tu liiv. wol shii kyaan diil wit him! su shii   596
si shii iz goowin tu di edmasto.   597
A: oo yi.   598
K: oparontlii shi dozn noo hiz neem.   599
A: oo-oo.   600
K: bo yu noo shi jos thoht ii wuz C. bo noobOdii   601
reelii konform it woz C. noobodii wOntid tu get im in   602
chrobl, bikoz yu noo wol iz bad bOi!   603
A: m-hm, rait, rait. koz yu siiz—rait, rait.   604
K: shi went tu di edmaso. baitaim shi—broht di hedmasto   605
bak, C kud noowi—wuz noowi tu bii fongd! hi disopeerd.   606

Translation

C. is very bad up to now.   585T
Oh God, C., oh shucks! Don't talk about C.!
Miss H. was teaching us history one day, he came
and rapped on the door. Apparently, he likes some girl in the class.
The girl goes by the name of S. He rapped on the
door. She didn't take him on. She knew it was C. He came   590T
and pushed his face against the window. She didn't take him on. He opened the
door, came right in, sat on her desk!
You're kidding!
Yeah, he came in, sat on the desk. Well, she couldn't take it
anymore. She says—am—"C., please leave my form."   595T
He refused to leave. Well, she couldn't deal with him! So she said she was going to
the headmaster.
Oh, yeah.
Apparently, she didn't know his name.
Oh.   600T
Well, you know, she just thought he was C. But nobody
really confirmed it was C. Nobody wanted to get him in
trouble, because, you know, well, he's a bad boy.

Mm-hm, right, right. Because you see he's—right, right.
She went to the headmaster. By the time she brought the headmaster   605¶
back, C. could nowhere—was nowhere to be found. He disappeared.

13b. School exams

K: wid ingglish, rait? ai fong maiself spenin tuu moch ov di taim   607
on mai esee. ai jos push mai esee Ondoniit n it kom—wen   608
ai wuz finish, den ai went bak tu mai esee. . . .   609
in di mat, ai defnaitlii kudn finish. noobOdii finish di   610
peepo. hii geev os haaf n ouwo ekschro, n wii kudn finish.   611
  A: reelii?   612
  K: ye, it o jii sii ii peepo ii tuk op, som yeer bak.   613
  A: oo-hoo.   614
  K: an ii geev os di egzam from di jii sii ii peepo, wit ohl inschrok— 615
w—ii tool os nOt o word. kom shee out diiz jii sii ii peepoz,   616
giv os chrii shiits ov peepo, an lef do ruum.   617
  A: dis iz ot wich levl?   618
  K: tord fohm. giv os di jii sii ii peepo an left. . . . ye, ii giv 619
os di peepo an left. an op tu nou a hee sombodii gO   620
nainti tuu! ai wOnid tu heer huu gOt nainti tuu!   621

Translation

With English, right? I found myself spending too much of the time
on my essay. I just pushed my essay underneath and it came—when
I was finished, then I went back to my essay. . . .
In the math [exam], I definitely couldn't finish. Nobody finished the   610¶
paper. He gave us half an hour extra, and we couldn't finish.
  Really?
Yeah, it's a G.C.E. paper he took up, [from] some year back.
  Oh no.
And he gave us the exam from the G.C.E. paper, with all the instruc—   615¶
he told us not a word. Came and shared [handed] out these G.C.E. papers,
gave us three sheets of paper, and left the room.
  This is at which level?
Third form. Gave us the G.C.E. paper and left. . . . Yeah, he gave
us the paper and left. And up to now I hear somebody got   620¶
ninety-two! I wanted to know who got ninety-two!

13c. An attack of typhoid fever

K: wen ai wu bou eet, a had—am—taifOid.   622
A: reelii? taifOid fiivo?   623
K: ye. di dOkto geev mii op.   624
A: ye, kuz taifOid iz yuuzhulii—   625

K: ai wuz laiyin dong in deer. ai—dee neerlii geev mi op fu—hoom.   626
ai uz laiyin dong, momii keem tu as mi wo wohnt from di maarkit.   627
n ai startid twisin op mai aiz n den o gO stif oz o boord.   628
    A: oo gohd!   629
    K: n do reen wuz fohlin, dadii wuz in o aksdnt, ii brook iz   630
finggoz, so noobOdi wuz dee tu teek mi tu di rood tu get mi o   631
taks—wi adnt o kar den. baidai tun dOkto K, hii   632
see dot—am—i diipenz biikaim—ai wuz verii wiik. ai had ot bout   633
wiiks biifoor an dee kun fain wot wuz reelii rohng wit mii.   634
    A: yu jos had fiivo ohl di taim?   635
    K: rait, ohl di taim, rait? an dee—evtin dee teekin   636
blod tes n aik—parontlii dee kun fain wot uz rohng   637
wit mii, ontil dis meejo otak.   638
    A: an hou di fong out i wuz taifOid?   639
    K: on di seem dee ai went in, ii tuk onOdo blod tes. An oparontlii   640
evrituz geting wors. dhen dee fongd out. soo di   641
kep mii hOspitol obout o dee. . . . yu noo, dadii din wohn tu   642
liiv mii. n sins dOkto K iz o famolii frend, ii sed ookee   643
fu dem tu teek mii oom, bot—mos chek bak, evrii wiik.   644
    A: soo wo—wo—wo yu had tu—iit sortn tingz ohr ho—?   645
    K: jos iit sortn tingz laik jos likwidz. ai kun iit enii   646
sOlidz, fu bout o mont, or tuu. do iz aa—wen ai wuz raitin   647
kOmn enchrons, momii ad tu teek mai s—mai fuud tu skuul   648
n fiid mii. ai nevo yuustu gu bai maiself. . . .   649
    A: Onislii?   650
    K: ai kun iit. op tu nou somtai ai sidong o teebl n   651
sii do fuu—ai kyaan iit. if ai sii o lOt of fuud, ai kaan iit.   652
yu hafu—dish mai fuud an giv mii tu iit. ai in won   653
dish, op tu nou.   654

Translation

When I was about eight I had—am—typhoid.
Really? Typhoid fever?
Yeah. The doctor gave me up.
Yeah, because typhoid is usually—   625T
I was lying down in there. I—they nearly gave me up for—home.
I was lying down, mummy came to ask me what I wanted from the mar-
ket. And I started twisting up my eyes and then I got as stiff as a board.
Oh God!
And the rain was falling. Daddy was in an accident. He'd broken his   630T
fingers, so nobody was there to take me to the road to get me a
taxi—we hadn't a car then. By the time they took me to Dr. K., he
said that—am—it depends because I—I was very weak. I had had it
for weeks, and they couldn't find out what was really wrong with me.
You just had fever all the time?   635T
Right, all the time, right? And they—every time they would take

a blood test, and like—apparently they couldn't find out what was wrong
with me, until this major attack.

And how did they find out it was typhoid?

On the same day I went in, he took another blood test. And apparently   640T
everything was getting worse. Then they found out. So they
kept me in hospital for about a day. . . . You know, daddy didn't want to
leave me. And since Dr. K. is a family friend, he said it was okay
for them to take me home. But I must check back every week.

So wha—wha—what did you have to do—eat certain things or what?   645T

Just eat certain things, only liquids. I couldn't eat any
solids for about a month or two. That is all. When I was writing the
Common Entrance (exam), Mummy had to take my—my food to school,
and feed me. I never used to go by myself. . . .

Honestly?   650T

I couldn't eat. Up to now sometimes when I sit down at the table
and see the food—I can't eat. If I see a lot of food, I can't eat.
You have to—dish out my food and give it to me to eat. I don't like
dishing it out myself, up to now.

13d. *Driving out a jumbie at a Kali Mai ceremony*

K: laik diiz piipl, rait? dee fain dir sik, rait? . . .   655
deed see wel, dee teek yu tu dis leedi imself, rait?   656
di see dot shiiz di—am—di kalii mai, rait?   657
shiiz di modo ov di ooshon. . . . an oba—shii kud tel   658
yu wedo deez o spirit wur—am—chrobling yuu, rait?   659
an if yuu—if shii sez "yes," rait, yu mait iivenchlii   660
start pleeyin, rait? an jompin op an ohl sohrts o ting,   661
rait? an dee ud chai tu biit dis spirit out ov yuu.   662

A: litorolii biit yuu?   663

K: biichuu, yes! diz hav o big roop, ohr o wail keen.   664
dil biit it chout ov yuu!   665

A: reelii?   666

K: ye, bika ai went wohns wen dadii wuznt at oom, an wii went.   667
biikoz heer it wuz oopn dee, yu kud goo. n di wu niigroo   668
bOi, rait? o lit—o yong bOi—mosii bout, a shud see bout   669
twelv. an di had dis vail kin n biitin dis chail. n   670
ohl di chail kud kiip teln im, "aim from bokstn semichrii.   671
aim from bokstn semichrii." . . .   672

A: reelii?   673

K: an di had tu kiip biiting an ii see ot iiz nOt   674
komin out, iiz nOt komin, hii wuzn goon tu tel dem   675
eniiting. an di bii dis bOi, ntil iz hool skin iz oonii maarks.   676
an i rifyuuz tu tel dem eniiting. oonii tu tel, "aim   677
frm bokstn semichrii." ohl ii kep telin dem. an do wuz   678
di ochrakshn o di dee. evriibOdii sorongdid im.   679

Translation

Like these people, right? They find they're sick, right? . . .   655T
They'd say, well, they'd take you to this lady herself, right?
They say that she's the—am—Kali Mai, right?
She's the Mother of the Ocean. . . . And apparently—she can tell
you whether there's a spirit—am—troubling you, right?
And if you—if she says "Yes," right, you might eventually   660T
start playing, right? And jumping up and all sorts of things,
right? And they would try to beat this spirit out of you.*
    Literally beat you?
    Beat you, yes! They usually have a big rope, or a wild cane.
They'll beat it out of you.   665T
    Really?
    Yeah, because I went once, when Daddy wasn't at home, and we went.
Because here it was open day, you could go. And there was a Negro
boy, right? A litt—a young boy—he was about, I should say about
twelve. And they were beating this child with a wild cane. And   670T
all the child could keep telling them is, "I'm from Buxton cemetery.
I'm from Buxton cemetery." . . .
    Really!
    And they had to keep beating him. And he [the spirit] said he wasn't
coming out [of the boy], he wasn't coming, he wasn't going to tell them   675T
anything. And they beat this boy, until his skin had welts all
over. And he refused to tell them anything. He only told them, "I'm
from Buxton cemetery!" That was all he kept telling them. And that was
the attraction of the day. Everybody surrounded him.

14. Sheik (1976)

Thirty-five years of age when I first interviewed him in 1976, Sheik is the
quintessential example of the rags-to-riches story. As a young boy he had to
leave school in fifth standard for financial reasons, and his first occupation
was the one that has traditionally been the "manifest destiny" of male Cane
Walkers: cane-cutting. However, after working as a cane-cutter on the backdam for several years, he was offered a job as a shop assistant in a distant
town, and he grabbed at the opportunity. The friend who told him about the
job cautioned that it would initially bring in less money than cane-cutting,
but Sheik's response—a classic statement about the need to break away from
estate-class culture to advance socially and economically—was, "Man, I
wouldn't mind. I mean—anything to get out o' the backdam." Eventually,

---

*The ceremony Katherine is describing here—which typically involves animal sacrifice and
spirit possession—is more formally referred to as Kali Mai Puja (Hindu *pu:ja:* means 'worship';
cf. Chaturvedi and Tiwari 1975: 436).

Sheik returned to Cane Walk to open his own store, expanding it until it became one of the best stocked and most prosperous for miles around.

As a successful shopowner, not only did Sheik move away from the financial uncertainties of the estate class; he also moved away from such estate-class cultural accoutrements as the nansi story.* Text 14a reveals that although he apparently enjoyed such stories as a youth (note the warm texture of the memories in lines 686–99), he had come to consider them "nonsense" by the time he was recorded in the mid-1970's.[38]

However, unlike Katherine, who was never herself a part of the cane-cutting/estate-class milieu, Sheik started out in life in this milieu and is fully competent in the basilectal GC associated with it. As a result, although he has acquired more mesolectal varieties from his contacts with upper-mesolectal speakers, he can draw on the resources of basilectal features for stylistic switching when necessary, as in Texts 14b and 14c, where subject *mii* (747), habitual or continuative *a* (746), and negative *na* (772) all emerge as he becomes more excited. Overall he shows more morphosyntactic variation between English and Creole elements than Katherine does. This is particularly evident in his personal-pronoun usage: he was one of only three people in the Cane Walk sample (Ustad was another) who displayed morphological variation in every one of the nine singular-pronoun subcategories investigated (see Rickford 1979: 384).

Together, the three extracts from Sheik's recordings illustrate several aspects of GC—some unique to the mesolect, others true of virtually all levels short of the most acrolectal or standard speech. Note, for instance, that Sheik's mesolectal habitual marker, *doz*, retains the tenselessness of basilectal *a* (*doz* is past in 687, nonpast in 730). Katherine's *doz* tokens, by contrast, represent an upper-mesolectal level, in which *doz* is clearly nonpast, and *yuustu* marks past habituals. In Text 14c, Sheik uses preverbal *bin* once (in line 766, where it is realized as *bii*) to mark anteriority, but most of the time he uses *did* (sometimes reduced to *di*) to mark anterior events—the window that had been left open (752), the door that had been locked up (761, 770), and the other events that had occurred *before* the theft in question. This confirms Bickerton's (1975: 69ff) suggestion that mesolectal *did* at first assumes the functions of basilectal *bin* while appearing more English-like in outer form—a characteristic decreolization strategy.

The variation between *dem* and *diiz/dooz* as demonstrative modifiers in Sheik's Text 14a (701, 704, 717) is worth noting. In the idealized basilect only *dem* would be expected, with *de* or *da* (< 'there, that') postposed to the noun phrase to mark distal or "far" objects (*dem ekspreshn de* 737 and *dem tingz o* 701 are related uses, meaning 'the things we were talking about'), and

---

*(A)nansi is the spider-hero in a large number of Caribbean/New World trickster narratives. Cf. Twi *anànse* 'spider' (Cassidy and LePage 1980: 10). In the Caribbean the term "(a)nansi story" is often extended to folktales in general.

ya or *dis* postposed to the modified noun phrase to mark proximal or "near" objects. There are no examples of the proximal type in Sheik's texts; *dem ting ya*, an artificial example, would mean 'these things (here).' In short, English deictic expressions of the form "those noun + s" have Creole equivalents of the form *dem (noun) da/de*, and English deictics of the form "these noun + s" have Creole equivalents of the form *dem (noun) dis/ya*.

The verb particle *out* occurs, apparently redundantly, in lines 735, 740 and 747 (realized as *ou*). As Rickford and Greaves (1978: 43) have suggested with respect to other examples ("fry up," "rob off"), the "redundant" particles add intensity and vividness without affecting the referential meaning of the preceding verb. *See* functions as a sentence complementizer, equivalent to SE 'that,' in line 687 and elsewhere, but *sii* is used after *fain* with the same function (727, 730).[39]

Several important aspects of GC sentence structure are illustrated in Sheik's texts. The forms *bai* and *from*, which function as prepositions in modern English, serve as sentential conjunctions in lines 767 and 742–43, with the meanings of 'since' and 'after,' respectively. The *from* sentence also serves to support Bickerton's (1980: 117, 1981: 99ff) claim that GC, like other creoles, does not have nonfinite sentences (unmarked for tense and person/number), since it has a pronoun and tense auxiliary (*from ii gu jringk*), whereas the equivalent English nonfinite clause would contain neither ("After drinking . . ."). In English, of course, a finite equivalent could also be used ("After he drinks . . ."), but the difference is that no such choice exists in this area of the grammar in basilectal GC: only a finite subordinate clause is possible in line 743.

At the same time, the locative verb complements in lines 756, 771, and 772 are clearly nonfinite. In the case of line 772 (*wii dee in de—A JRINGK*, with the complement capitalized), deletion of the underlying subject of the second clause, by identity with the subject of the first clause, is obligatory (**wii dee in de WII A JRINGK* is ungrammatical).[40] And though the line contains an aspect (*not* tense) marker, this is merely the basilectal equivalent of the continuative "-ing" complementizer that English has in comparable constructions, the one that shows up in the mesolectal equivalents in lines 756 and 771 (*di ado res de pon di flatfohrm WEETIN*, and my sentence, *ayu de in hee JRINGKIN?*). The general form of the sentences that produce this important exception to Bickerton's claim that creoles lack nonfinite sentences is

$$\text{s}_1(\text{noun phrase } \textit{de(e)} \text{ location}) \; \text{s}_2(\text{verb [+ continuative]}).$$

Note that location could be expressed by a single adverb like *dongsteez* or a prepositional phrase like *in di hous*, and the continuative verb could be either basilectal *a* (verb) or mesolectal verb + "ing." However, the copula in the matrix sentence must be basilectal *de(e)*.

Interestingly enough, in an early article Bickerton (1973a: 650) explicitly claimed that one of the functions of GC *de* is "introducing non-finites." Even though this claim was made several years before his more general claim that creoles lack nonfinites, it is clearly the latter rather than the former claim that requires modification. It is also possible to relate this particular nonfinite construction to the durative *de a* constructions in GC and JC exemplified in Devonish (1978: 204)—*dem de a taak* 'They are busy talking'— and further discussed in Mufwene (1982). Bickerton (1973a: 650) had introduced an example of just this type to support his claim that *de* introduced nonfinites: *mi de a luk mi kau* 'I was (there) looking for my cow.' The gloss itself suggests one way of relating these examples to constructions of the above nonfinite type: by postulating an underlying locative adverbial *de*, deleted when redundant (as here) in surface structure. Alternatively, the nonfinite complements of *de* in all of these cases (*a luk mi kau*, etc.) could be analyzed as locative prepositional phrases, parallel to the capitalized portion of JC *Im de A TOUN* 'He is in town' (Mufwene's example 5b). This is the analysis that Mufwene suggests. My initial reaction is that although this analysis might reflect the diachronic development of this type of construction (if Mufwene is correct about this), the prepositional and nonfinite complements are different enough in their synchronic syntactic properties to require differentiation. Nevertheless, this and other aspects of these important creole constructions require further investigation.

Finally, in relation to sentence structure, Sheik's texts allow us to note three other features: that questions in GC are usually not inverted (there is no support *duu* to invert in auxiliary-less sentences like the one in line 711 anyway), that it is possible to topicalize constituents by fronting them without a preceding *a* or *iz* copula (*dee oon step di si dong* 694–95), as in English (see Perlmutter and Soames 1979: 229ff); and that existential constructions begin with a nonspecific impersonal pronoun (*di, yu(u), it*) in conjunction with a verb of possession (some form of *goht/gat* or *hav/had*, as in lines 722 and 735–76) instead of with English *dheer* plus some form of *bii*. The relationship between locatives and possessives, which has been noted elsewhere in human language (Clark 1978), is nicely revealed in these GC existentials. Note too, however, that the sentential modifiers of the noun phrase in the *di had* existentials in lines 714, 722, and 725 do not require relative pronouns, as equivalent structures would in SE ("There was a man there *who* had a radio"). In this respect they recall the unmarked relatives discussed in the introduction to Reefer's texts.

Sheik's checkered occupational and socioeconomic background reveals itself not only in his morphosyntax, but also in his phonology, which varies similarly between Creole and English norms. Nowhere is this more evident than in his use of both broad and nonbroad pronunciations in words like "got" (*gat* 745, *gOt* 685), and "one" (*waan* 714, *wohn* 754), unlike Granny, who uses only *a/aa*, and Katherine, who uses only *O/oh*. In several cases his actual pronunciation is intermediate between the two, and it was difficult to decide whether to transcribe it with *a/aa* or *O/oh*. The *waan* of lines 709 and 728, for instance, is not quite as open or unrounded as the *waan* of 739, but did not seem back or rounded enough to merit transcription as *wohn*. One is reminded of pronunciations like *de* before nasals, which can masquerade as either *dem* or *dee*—a characteristic mesolectal phenomenon.

Other phonological features show Sheik's acquaintance with both basilectal and acrolectal norms. His speech includes sporadic examples of some of the features that show up occasionally in estate-class speech but never in the speech of non-estate-class members like Katherine and Bonnette: monopthongization of *ai* to *i* (*tim* 'time' 760; cf. Irene's *sailin* 'sideline' 367); the addition of a homorganic voiceless stop after a word-final nasal (*sidongk* 'sit down' 686; cf. Irene's *lai dongk* 'lie down' 365, Derek's *jromp* 'drum' 243); and the devoicing of final *z* (*biikohs* 'because' 706; cf. Granny's *bikaas* 492).

At the same time he rather sharply constrains many of the Creole condensation/reduction processes. The presence of retroflexion in an unstressed syllable like the one in *ouor* (752) is rare in Cane Walk speech. Applications of consonant-cluster simplification, as in *didn* (764), alternate with nonapplications, as in *front* (685) and *ofekt* (751), in which the final *t* is weakly released but nevertheless there. Clear cases of the deletion of word-final postvocalic *t* (that is, not before a following dental, as in *da taim* 720) occur primarily in Text 14b, where he is agitatedly describing why and how he banned beer-drinking in his shop (*ga* 733, 745; *da* 746); even here, when the following word begins with a vowel, the final *t* is preserved (*get* 744, *gat* 745). This conditioning applies elsewhere in Sheik's texts (685, 707, 759), as it does also in the speech of Katherine (602). And although there are examples like *oparon* ('apparently' 776) and *bi* ('must be' 751) that show the loss of an entire syllable, phrases like *ohr wOtsooevo di kees mait bii* (707–8) reveal— both in their lexical selection and in their relative absence of morphophonemic reduction—that Sheik is speaking relatively carefully and approximating SE norms. Note, finally, his occasional use of an American-like flap for postretroflex *t*, as in *kwohrDo* ('quarter' 686) and *starDu* ('start to' 723), a feature that shows up also in the speech of Ali (Text 17b, line 990). These are the only two businessmen represented in the spoken texts, and the flap appears to be an Americanization that they have picked up in the course of their extensive contacts with speakers from Georgetown and other urban areas.

Text 14a is from Tape SI 72, tape counter nos. 115–32; 14b and 14c are from the same tape, nos. 200–211 and 260–83, respectively.

14a. Nansi story-telling in the old days

S: wel, mai fado yuuztu—izu—hii wuz o jenorol fu ron nansii.   680

J: yos ii yuuztu tel aalyu oloon, or ado chirin yuuztu   681
kom oovo?   682

S: noo, wel yu sii wen wir taakin nansi   683
nou, rait? yu fain   684
see yu gOt o reenj. wel aal di front step, yu noo,   685
aal—aal di piipl huu liv in di kwohrDo sidongk a di step nou.   686
n yu fain see yu doz si dong a di step an ii gun staat taak.   687
wel ii mout big. evribOdi heerin, n laafin, n yu no—   688

J: den piipl kom rong. . . .   689

S: nou wen hii finish o neks man mait pik ii op ogeen   690
an star taak ogeen. su yu fain si—   691

J: an ii wud gado dem den an startu taak moo stoorii   692
n so, ehe.   693

S: iz taakin rait pon yu step, yu noo. dee oon step   694
di si dong. bikO yu nOt faar.   695

J: wol ii mait see, "do rimain mii o sompn so," an hii—bring   696
out onado won.   697

S: m—m, an den hii staartu taak juk an yu noo, laaf an   698
taak an gyaaf.   699

J: rait, rait, rait. yu kyaan rimembo non o dem stoorii?   700

S: maan dem tingz o—[laughs] kyaan rimembo dem tin.   701

J: iz somtin o reeli laik tu get, bot it siim nouwodeez piipl   702
doon—am—geDit.   703

S: [sucks teeth] mnn, piipl doon reelii tingk obou dooz ting—   704
langtaim—yu noo. yu noo? mait—haardli yu mait fain sii—o   705
porsn mai tohk o nansi nou. biikohs, yu get—yuu get—ts—nohlij   706
nou tu noo wOt iz—wOt iz rait an wOt iz rohng, ohr wOtsooevo   707
di kees mait bii. an yuu torm dat az nOnsens. yu noo, yu   708
wun iivn tingk obou dem. moos yu mait, yuu waan tu hee   709
nou—jooks from di—di reejo. rait? dat iz moor [laughs]   710
edikeeshonol ohr wOtsoo as . . .yu ohnstan?   711

J: do o neks ting tu—yu din had reedyoo an so—tumoch   712
in di loojii?   713

S: noo, wel di had waan maan had o reejo deer an, evri sondii   714
ii dos—oopn di reedyo big,   715

J: an evriibadii kom rong—   716

S: an evribOdi o gu an dem gu staart, yu noo yu ge diiz—   717
am—saang komin oovo o sondi naits?   718

J: ehe. an yu dans an ting in front an so.   719

S: su yu gu lisn ohn di. kohz a da taim, yu noo, reejo   720
woz—no, noobOdii haardlii kud afoord tu bai o reejo an kyaar. an   721
di ad wohn maan yuusu ad o kyaar de tu. wen wii sii dii kyaar kom   722
in, wii starDu ron bihain di kyaar, maan [laughs], bika, yu no—   723

J: di kyaar—   724
S: di gyaar iz o gud achrakshon. [Laughs.] wel di ad bogii   725
yustu teek piipl dong ongtong. jreekyaat bogii.   726

Translation

Well, my father used to—he's a—was a general with nansi [stories].   680T
He just used to tell your family alone, or did other children
come over?
No, well you see, when we are talking nansi,
now, right? This takes place
in the range [logie or barracks].
Well, all of the front steps, you know,   685T
all—all the people who live in the quarter sit down on the steps now.
And you sit down on the step and he would start to talk.
Well, his mouth is big. Everybody is hearing and laughing, and, you know—
People come around. . . .
Now when he is finished, another man might pick up where he left off and start   690T
to talk again. So you find that—
And he would gather them then and start to tell more stories
and so on.
This talking is right on your step, you know. Right on their own step they sit   695T
down, because you're not far [from your neighbor].
Well, he might say, "That reminds me of something," and he'll bring
out another one [nansi story].
Mm-hm. And then he would start to tell jokes, and, and you know, laugh and
talk and chat.
Right, right, right. You can't remember any of these stories?   700T
Man, those things—[I] can't remember those things.
It's something I really like to get, but it seems nowadays people
don't—am—get it.
[Sucks teeth] Man, people don't really think about those things—[about]
long ago [things], you know. You know? Might—you might hardly find a   705T
person talking nansi now. Because, you've gotten—you have knowledge
now to know what is—what is right and what is wrong, or whatsoever
the case might be. And you term that as nonsense. You know, you
wouldn't even think about them. The most you might, you want to hear
now—is jokes from the radio. Right? That is more   710T
educational or whatso[ever]. You understand?
That's a next thing too—you didn't have many radios and so on
in the logies?
No, well, they had one guy who had a radio there and, every Sunday,
he used to turn on the radio loud.   715T
And everybody would come around—
And everybody would go and they would start, you know they have these—
am—songs coming over on Sunday nights?

Yes. And you dance and so on in front?
So you would listen there. Because at that time, you know, radio   720T
was—no, nobody could hardly afford to buy a radio and car. And
there was one man who had a car there too. When we saw the car come in, we
would start to run behind the car, man, because, you know—
    The car—
    The car is a good attraction. Well, there were buggies   725T
[that] used to take people downtown. Draycart buggies.

14b. Difficulties with youngsters in his shop

S: ai liv gud wid evribOdi, rait? yu mait fain sii nou diiz   727
yongsto, som o dem mait kom waan mek—kom in yu shap. di   728
mait waan kors op n ting, yu noo, an det—ai doon—o—tOloreet   729
it otaal. ai doz chees em out. su fain—yu fain sii di   730
yongo jeenoreesho doon laik mii otaal, bikohs—wo dee—wo   731
dee—wo ai stan for, aid—ai—ai doz chees dem out. da dii riizn   732
wai ai—ai yuustu had a beer gyardn hee, rait? an o had—yuuzu ga   733
skitl bOks. an di staartu yuuz op di langwij, an ai jos—   734
klooz dong di hool ting, an ai sel out di bOks. bikohz ai—yuu,   735
yuu gOt gyaal chirin, dem piipl jaal chirin, kostomo gyaal chirin   736
komin in in hee. yuu gu staartu yuuz ohl dem ekspreshn de?   737
    J: an dem ool piipl an so an so . . .   738
    S: ai jos chee dem, biga mii na waan noobOdii kom tel mi   739
notn, rait? soo ai jos don out wi da, an mii ron mi—if   740
o man kom in hee in mii shOp fu bai o beer an ai sii ii jrongk,   741
a wun sel im. ai o se ai—ai kyaan sel im, bikaaz—ai noo from   742
ii gu jringk—jringk wohn beer, ii gu staartu gu ohf ii—ii pin.   743
    J: ii gu jringk waan, ii gu ge moo—ii gun staatu get ohn moo baad.   744
    S: mi se, "maan, ii gat Odo shop ga juuk bOks n ting, ayu gu   745
da sai, rait? wii na a sel beer an ting." bikaaz, yu oonli   746
gono chees ou—mii—mii gu luuz moo kostomo, bikaaz if—if   747
tu or chrii gyor—yong gyorlz kom in an sii o jrongk man in ye,   748
de in gun kom in.   749

Translation

I live good with everybody, right? You might find now that these
youngsters, some of them want to make—come in your shop. They
might want to curse up and things, you know, and that—I don't tolerate
it at all. I chase them out. So you'll find that the   730T
younger generation doesn't like me at all, because of what they—what
they—what I stand for. I chase them out. That is the reason
why I—I used to have a beer garden here, right? And I used to have a
skittle game. And they started to use their bad language, and I just
closed down the whole thing, and sold the game. Because I—there   735T

are girls, people's daughters, customer's daughters
coming in here. How could you start to use all those bad words?
   And [in front of] the old people and so forth and so on.
   I just chased them away, because I didn't want anybody to come and
complain, right? So I just finished with that, and [now] I run my—if   740T
a man comes in here in my shop to buy a beer, and I see he's drunk,
I won't sell to him. I can't sell to him. Because, I know
after he drinks—drinks one beer, he'll start to go crazy.
   If he drinks one, he'll get more—he'll start to behave worse.
   I would say, "Man, there are other shops with a jukebox and so on. Go   745T
that side, right! We don't sell beers and so on." Because, you're only
going to chase away—I—I will lose more customers, because if—if
two or three girls—young girls come in and see a drunk man in here,
they won't come in.

14c. Experiences with thieves

   J: yuaal iz ge enii prabem wid tiif an so hee?   750
   S: ye-e man, wii i—do ting doz ofekt wi baad. a nait, bi obou   751
faiv o dem keem in ouor hous. parontlii, di windo did lef   752
oopn an di ool leedii wuz osliip in da ruum. an yu noo, wel,   753
di plee wu hOt, yu no. shii oopn di wino, an wohn—di   754
mosi sen op o lil wohn o dem. an shii—hii krohl in di ting an ii—   755
di ado res de pon di flatfohrm weetin fu ii oopn di door.   756
an wail ii wuz oopn di door, di cheen staartu rakl. shii—ii   757
jomp op. wen shi jomp op, sODo, wel ai ron out. an wen a   758
ron out, dee ron out, an di jomp oovo di ting an, get owee. . . .   759
den o neks tiim won—mii an tuu fren de in hee, tekin a lil   760
jringk. oh—wiiz park i kyaar ou de. wel di door an su did   761
lOk op n thing. wel wii lef dis—wii bin dongstee—wel di ool   762
leedii—wo aapn, a di ad—di seem—a di ru—o wuz ripeerin   763
dis ruf. an dim baiz didn kompliit it. su di reen doz faal,   764
an di—di bin had o valii, yu noo, di valii—di goto rOtn   765
wee an yu had tu—liik out, yu noo, su di bii ad tu set   766
o big beesn fu kech di wohto, yu no. . . . bai wii in hee, di   767
ool leedi lef di door oopn. and o blak felo mosi sii. iz o   768
blak felo. i musi sii di ting oopn, an ii jomp oovo di   769
yaar, bika wii di lOk dis geet.   770
   J: ayu de in hee jringkin?   771
   S: an wii dee in de—a jringk, an wii na noo notn, an ii   772
waak op schreet an ii gu bai . . . ii kyar wi won wOch, an—   773
   J: wo? do o deetaim?   774
   S: naitaim . . . an wel, de goo in di—ool leedi wohn. di seem   775
tai di ool leedii get op an, oparon hii ron get owee.   776
wen ii ron out, ii jomp oovo di fens an ii gaan.   777

Translation

Do you guys get any problem with thieves here?   750T
Yeah, man, we—that affects us badly. One night about
five of them came in our house. Apparently, the window had been left
open and the old lady was asleep in that room. And you know, well,
the place was hot, you know. She had opened the window and one—they
must have sent up a small guy. And she—he crawled in and he—   755T
the rest were waiting on the platform for him to open the door.
And while he was opening the door the chair started to rattle. She
jumped up. When she jumped up, sort of, well, I ran out. And when I
ran out, they ran out, and they jumped over the things, and got away. . . .
Then another time one—two friends and I were in here taking a little   760T
drink. Ah—we parked the car out there. Well, the door and so on were
locked up and everything. Well, we left this—we were downstairs—well, the
old lady, what happened, I had—the same—I was re—I was repairing
this roof. And the boys didn't complete it. So the rain usually falls,
and they—there was a valley, you know, the valley—the gutter had rotted   765T
away, and you had to—leak out, you know, so they had had to set
a big basin to catch the water, you know. . . . Since we were in here, the
old lady left the door open. And a black fellow must have seen. It's a
black fellow. He must have seen the thing open, and he jumped over the
yard [fence], because we had locked this gate.   770T
And you guys were in here drinking?
And we were in there—drinking. And we didn't know anything, and he
walked straight up and he went by . . . he carried away a watch and—
What? In the daytime?
Nighttime . . . And well, they went in the old lady's room. At the same   775T
time the old lady got up and apparently he ran off and got away.
When he ran out, he jumped over the fence and took off.

15. Bonnette (1976)

At the relatively young age of twenty-nine, Bonnette held one of the most
prestigious jobs in the Cane Walk sample—that of a senior civil servant in
Georgetown. She also had the highest level of education, having completed
form V in secondary school, and taken the British overseas G.C.E. Ordinary level exam. She had taught for one year at a secondary school before
assuming her present job.

Bonnette's mother, who appears as speaker D in Texts 15b and 15c, apparently did not have any formal education as a child, and Bonnette believes
that not knowing how to read or write had limited her mother's ability to
"face the world." By that she means, in part, her ability to go beyond the

network of familiar friends and relatives in Cane Walk, and her ability to make a good impression on unfamiliar, often higher-status and highly judgmental people in Georgetown and elsewhere. For Bonnette, being educated enables you to "know how to really go around."

One potential effect of education—if a person remains in the system long enough—is that he or she may develop competence in varieties closer to SE, both directly by correction and instruction and indirectly by contact with more standard-like speakers. This competence may become, in turn, a wedge to help open traditionally closed doors as one "faces the world." Most estate-class members do not buy the door-opening part of this argument (not surprisingly, given the limited avenues for upward mobility available to them), but non-estate members do. Bonnette expressed the opinion, for instance, that how you talk *is* important—that while speaking "good English" would not necessarily help you to get a better job, it would help you to make a better impression, especially with strangers. She cited an interesting parallel in support of this: "You ever find, when you go somewhere, with strange people, the way you dress or the way you look—[on the basis of that] people assess how to treat you?"

Whether or not increased use of SE-like speech in everyday interactions is primarily cause (as non-estate-class members argue) or effect (as estate-class members argue), it is clear from local sociolinguistic research that it correlates with upward and outward mobility—from backdam to village front, from country to town, from illiteracy to education, and from low-status to high-status jobs and networks. Bonnette is a good example of this relationship.

Bonnette's recorded language use is decidedly acrolectal. In the nine singular pronoun subcategories that we have been using as a touchstone for individual comparisons in these introductions, Bonnette failed to use the appropriate acrolectal morphological forms in only two subcategories (first-person singular subject and possessive)—and then only less than 2 percent of the time in those subcategories. And in the English-to-Creole Correction test, she gave no evidence of knowing the correct basilectal form in five of the nine subcategories. In both respects—her natural performance and her tested competence—she is most similar in the Cane Walk sample to Katherine. Like Katherine, Bonnette has more friendship networks and daily contacts outside of Cane Walk (particularly in Georgetown) than within it.

The resemblance between Katherine and Bonnette is also obvious in Bonnette's texts, especially Text 15a, which deals with an academic topic and is taken from the first few minutes of the interview, when the participants were still speaking quite formally. Note the English plurals (*paasiz* 'passes' 780, *peerens* 'parents' 788), the modal perfectives (*shud ov left* 787), the non-contracted negative (*shud nOt hav ritn it* 786), and the *bii* passive (*ai wuz kep bak dheer* 783). There is a good deal of consonant-cluster simplification in this text and elsewhere: as Katherine also shows, nonstandard phonological elements persist into the upper-mesolect and acrolect, and are especially frequent in rapid, excited speech (as in Texts 15b and 15c).

The morphological marking of possession is a good gauge of a person's linguistic level within the continuum because it is one of the last features to be acquired in decreolization and one of the least frequent in informal speech. Bonnette does have some marked noun possessives (for instance, *chaps vOis* 815–16), but also some unmarked cases (*man vOis* 818). This is also true of her pronominal possessives. Alongside inflected *iz* and *mai* (803), the acrolectal singular-pronoun forms that we encounter least frequently in everyday speech, Bonnette uses noninflected *yu* (788) and *mo* (855).[41]

Bonnette's use of the English copula is characteristic of upper-mesolectal speakers. The copula occurs often, appropriately inflected for person, number, and tense, in Bonnette's texts: *aim* 'I am' 792, *dis iz* 'this is' 790, *yuur* 'you are' 794, *ai wuz* 'I was' 783, *yuu wor* 'you were' 787. The instances of zero copula in her texts are typically nonpast rather than past, and are particularly common before continuative verb + "-ing" (e.g. *di Ø jringkin* 831–32). This accords with previous findings that past forms of the SE copula typically come in first in decreolization (Bickerton 1973b), and that verb + "-ing" favors copula absence in nonstandard English dialects more than any other following environment except "gon(na)," a diachronically reduced form of "going to" (Labov 1969; Baugh 1983: 100–102; Holm 1984). It should also be noted that even though Bonnette clefts with *iz* and *wuz* instead of basilectal *a*, she often omits the dummy *it* or *ii* subject, just as basilectal speakers do: compare her *iz huu* (845) with Irene's *a wa* (391) and *a somting* (389). That the form *iz* in line 845 is a reduction of *it iz* (see Allsopp 1958a: 88; Labov 1969; Rickford 1979: 316ff) is unlikely because the final sibilant here is voiced rather than voiceless (see also Bickerton 1975: 3) and also because we have a clear example of a *wuz* cleft in line 805 without a dummy subject. Note, however, that one occurrence of dummy *it* does occur with *iz* in the more complex question construction in line 812.

Before we leave the copula, note that Bonnette's sentence *ai sii dee lifin dis chap* (846–48) provides a good example of the embedding of one sentence in another without the subject-raising process that, in SE, would have made the subject noun phrase of the embedded sentence (*dee*) the object of the matrix sentence (*dem*: "I saw them lifting this chap"). In this case it is the distinction in the mesolect between *dee* as third-person plural subject and *dem* as third-person plural object that allows us to recognize the absence of subject-raising, whereas in basilectal speech, this is signaled by the distinction between *ii* and *am* as third-person singular subject (e.g. *mii sii ii a lif dis chap*).

The final grammatical feature in Bonnette's texts to be discussed—and we will cover it in some detail—is past-tense marking. Past-marking is most pronounced in Text 15a, drawn from the formal opening section of the interview, and least obvious in Text 15c, drawn from a more spontaneous section of the interview nearly three hours later. In Text 15c, less than a third of Bonnette's semantically past verbs are marked (12/43),[42] and there are other indications that her speech has shifted away from the acrolect, such as her use of Creole lexical items like *wohn taim* ('once' 829), *skrambl* ('grab hurriedly,' 'roughly,' 863), and *siiz up* ('become constricted' 855).

A close analysis of past-marking in Text 15c is at first disappointing, for it defies most of the constraints on mesolectal past-marking that have been proposed to date. For instance, Bickerton (1975: 105) identifies past participles and weak syllabic verb-stems (those that end in *t* or *d* and mark past tense with syllabic -*id*) as two of the most favorable environments for past-marking in the mesolect. The two past participles in Text 15c are both marked (*skeerd* 829, *setld* 865), but the four weak syllabic verbs are all unmarked (*shout* 850, *somosohlt* 860, *staart* 868, and *nOt* 871). Bickerton (1975: 143ff) also identifies strong verbs as less favorable to past-marking than weak syllabics, but more favorable than weak nonsyllabics. The first half of this claim is patently untrue of the data in Bonnette's text, given the absence of any marked syllabics. The second is certainly true, on the face of it, since none of the weak nonsyllabics (apart from the past participles) are marked, whereas we find four strong verbs that are: *had* 830, *keem* 834, and *went* (twice) 837. But there are also 15 unmarked strong verbs (e.g. *see* 834, *kiip* 836, *kom* 844), leaving us with only 22 percent (4/18) of all the strong verbs marked.

Bickerton also finds (1975: 151) that phonological factors are of some importance with weak nonsyllabic past forms: that, as Labov et al. (1968), Wolfram (1969), and Fasold (1972) have found to be true of VBE, a following vowel favors the insertion of "-ed" more than a following consonant does. However, this is not the case in Bonnette's narrative: of the eight unmarked weak pasts, seven come before a vowel (e.g. *jomp ohn* 835). Finally, let us consider the constraint that Bickerton (1975: 149–51, 163) regards as the most significant one in the Guyanese mesolect and as one that might be used to reexamine the VBE data: the use of ∅ and "-ed" to mark nonpunctual and punctual, respectively.[43] That this is irrelevant in the case of Bonnette's text is clear from the fact that all of her unmarked pasts (beginning with *jrOp*) occur from line 834 onward, that is, from the point at which we start getting punctual predicates, telling us what specific actions took place on the day of the accident. Overall only one of Bonnette's 27 past punctuals in Text 15c is past-marked, compared with 11 of her 16 past non-punctuals.[44] This is the exact opposite of what Bickerton's analysis would lead us to predict.

The one factor that does appear significant is something Bickerton (1975) does not mention: the possibility that the unmarked cases might represent instances of the historical present. Let me preface this discussion by pointing out the tendency in the field of creole studies to resist analyses that minimize the difference between the creole and the lexically related standard language, whether this involves the postulation of similar underlying phonological forms or the operation of comparable semantic/syntactic constraints. This tendency is understandable as a reaction against the older tendency to regard *everything* in creole systems as standard-derived; but to adhere to it even where the facts dictate otherwise, and even where we are dealing with mesolectal varieties, is misguided. The suggestion that Bonnette is using a historical-present system similar to that used by speakers of American English may immediately raise the hackles of some creolists, but I hope they will be broad-minded enough to follow the argument through to its conclusion. I hope to show that the historical-present interpretation works better than the customary proposals, but I will also indicate where I still have reservations.

To appreciate the relevance of a historical-present interpretation, we need first of all to distinguish between narrative clauses and nonnarrative clauses, following the analytical framework introduced by Labov and Waletzky (1967) and Labov (1972b), and adopted by Schiffrin (1981) for the analysis of the historical present. *Narrative clauses*, those that contain the complicating actions and carry the narrative forward, are marked by a relation of temporal juncture: "a change in their order will result in a change in the temporal sequence of the original semantic interpretation" (Labov 1972b: 360). *Nonnarrative clauses* may include an *abstract* at the beginning of the narrative summarizing the story, *orientation clauses*, which set the scene and tell you where the various characters were and what they were doing at various points, as background information for the main narrative, *evaluation clauses*, in which the narrator explains the point of the story, and a *coda*, signaling that the story is finished, and returning the listener to the real world and the present (Labov 1972b: 363–70). The significance of the narrative/nonnarrative distinction is that the historical present is rarely found in nonnarrative clauses, where one tends to find instead either marked pasts or nonhistorical present forms; for example, "He *is* still there, up to this day." In the American English narratives of personal experience examined by Schiffrin (1981: 51), the historical present was used about 30 percent of the time in narrative clauses, compared with only 3 percent for nonnarrative clauses.

Interestingly enough, it is precisely in the nonnarrative clauses of Bonnette's Text 15c—where she digresses from the main action to say where she was or what she was doing at the time, or how she felt—that the past is usually marked. Note, for instance, the marked pasts in the embedded orientation clauses: *ai wuz in di baat* (839) and *ai went in do baat* (837).[45] Past-marking in orientation and other nonnarrative clauses like these is 56 percent (9/16), but only 9 percent (2/22) in the narrative clauses, where, with the exception of *keem* at the beginning of the action sequence (834) and *wudn staart* (836), all of the verbs are unmarked (*jrOp* 834, *hosl* 844, etc.).[46]

Another factor that supports the analysis of the unmarked forms in Text 15c as instances of the historical present is the fact that this narrative is replete with direct quotes ("*momii iz huu?*," "*momii iz huu?*," "*iz o maan, an di maan ded!*," 838–40). As Schiffrin (1981: 58–59) shows, direct quotes work together with the historical present as an "internal evaluation device," allowing the narrator "to present events as if they were occurring at that moment, so that the audience can hear for itself what happened, and can interpret for itself the significance of those events for the experience."[47]

One difficulty with adopting a historical-present analysis for this text is the fact that none of the historical-present forms with third-person singular subjects—nine of them in Text 15c—have the unambiguous "-s" suffix of SE. But Bonnette's marking of third-person present "-s" is very infrequent even in other clear cases (note the free variation in lines 794–98 and 816–18 of Text 15b), and we know from studies of VBE (such as Labov et al. 1968) that third-person present "-s" can remain infrequent and irregular in dialects even closer to SE. The majority of the unmarked pasts in Text 15c involve non-third-person subjects, which of course would not take a third-person-present suffix in SE either.

Finally, a word about the application of a historical-present analysis to variation in creole-speaking communities more generally, and about the relation of such an analysis to unmarked verb forms in creole languages. Unmarked verb forms in French-based Seychelles Creole have been described in terms of the historical present by Corne (1977: 102), who notes that "after an initial use (or uses) of *ti*, much of the remainder of the story may be told with verb forms unmarked for Past (i.e., a sort of 'historical present')." A similar description of Seychelles Creole is provided by Bollée (1977: 55), but Bickerton (1981: 83–84), examining variation between marked and unmarked past forms in a short extract from one of Bollée's texts, notes that the unmarked forms therein are nonstatives, and the forms marked with *ti* (the equivalent of *bin* in the English creoles) are all statives.

In short, the Seychelles Creole verb forms appear to follow the same rules of anterior marking as stative and nonstative predicates do in GC and other creoles (Bickerton 1975: 46–47).[48]

In the case of Bonnette's Text 15c, most of the unmarked predicates are nonstative, and most of the marked predicates are stative. But it is difficult to argue that Bonnette is following the Creole anterior system when her speech is, overall, so close to SE. Indeed, according to Bickerton (1975: 101, 1981: 85), the loss of the stative/nonstative distinction and the transition from anterior to past-marking is one of the *earliest* steps in the decreolization process. Bonnette certainly does not use the basilectal anterior marker *bin*, and even though Bickerton (1975: 109) finds one instance of mesolectal "-ed" that appears to be anterior rather than simply past, this is an exception for the speaker who uses it, and the speaker himself is regarded as exceptional.

But there is another reason why we would not want to discard a historical-present analysis of Bonnette's text in favor of an anterior analysis: the dimensions on which these alternatives depend are in fact strikingly similar, making us wonder whether they are not in fact different formal realizations of a common underlying system. To see this, recall the observation of Corne and Bollée that narratives often begin with marked past forms, then shift to unmarked "historical presents." Bickerton's (1981: 84) retort to this is that "folktales almost invariably begin with one or several of these [statives]: 'Once upon a time there *was* a girl...she *was called* such and such...she *had* two sisters....' It is this simple coincidence that has given rise to the hard-dying creole myth about 'narrative tenses' and 'historical presents.'"

But in the light of Labov's (1972c: 354–96) analysis of narrative and Schiffrin's (1981) analysis of how the historical present functions in narrative, it is clear that what Bickerton is describing here as a coincidental occurrence at the beginning of narratives could be described as—is in fact equivalent to a statement in terms of—the use of orientation and other non-narrative clauses at the beginning of narratives, before the introduction of the complicating actions. The temporally ordered narrative or action clauses typically employ nonstative or action verbs, and it is these in which the English historical present typically occurs. As Schiffrin (1981: 51) notes: "The almost total restriction of the HP [historical present] to complicating action clauses is not surprising. It is only here that tense is freed from its main job of providing a reference time: events can be understood as having occurred prior to the moment of speaking, with or without the past form." However, the temporally unordered orientation and other nonnarrative clauses typically contain a higher proportion of stative verbs (including modals and passives), and it is here that the historical present typically does *not* occur. It is therefore not a "coincidence" that stative verbs come at the beginning of narratives, and that they are usually marked. And far from ruling out a historical-present analysis, Bickerton's observation about where stative verbs occur in narratives only makes a historical-present analysis more persuasive.[49]

Givón (1982) argues that Bickerton's description of the functions of Ø and *bin* in creoles should be restated in discourse/pragmatic terms—terms that are similar to those of Labov (1972c) and Schiffrin (1981) even though Givón makes no reference to either, and developed his analysis quite independently. Furthermore, he draws a parallel between the use of creole Ø and *bin* and the SE historical present and perfect that is similar to the parallel noted above. The relatedness is clear from Givón's description of Ø (based on Hawaiian Creole data): "The Ø form is used to mark the verbs in clauses which carry the *backbone* of the action narrative (as against lacunae, side trips, background information, stable states, etc.)."

Although Givón's analysis is also similar to the one proposed above in comparing the creole Ø verb-stem to the SE historical present, and contrasting Ø with *bin* within the creole system, it differs in contrasting the historical present with "anterior" perfect forms ("has verb + en" and "had verb + en") alone. What I am suggesting instead is that the historical present, marked by either "verb + Ø" or "verb + s," stands in discourse/pragmatic contrast with "verb + ed" and *any other marked past* (regardless of whether it is "anterior" or not, and thus of whether it requires "had" or "had verb + en" or not), along the lines originally suggested by Schiffrin.

Clearly, more work remains to be done in this area. The exact nature of the formal oppositions within both the SE and the creole systems needs further clarification, with a careful attempt to mesh the discourse/pragmatic dimensions of Schiffrin (1981) with those of Givón (1982) and Wolfson (1982). Until then, we need to be cautious in the extent to which we would want to say that Bonnette is using the historical present as SE speakers do, especially in view of her limited third-person present "-s." And even though basilectal speakers do mark non-anterior with the stem form, it is inappropriate to describe them as using the historical present when they have no explicit "present" marking. A further argument against reinterpreting the basilectal anterior/non-anterior distinction as a use of the historical present is the fact that the former applies across all kinds of discourse whereas the latter is primarily restricted to narrative (Bickerton and Traugott, personal communications).

What seems clear is that, in narrative at least, basilectal and upper-mesolectal speakers mark and unmark their predicates in pragmatically similar if formally different ways. This awareness by itself reduces the tremendous conceptual gulf that Bickerton (1975: 194) sees between the poles of the Guyanese Creole continuum ("sets of quite distinct rules," "distinct analyses of the underlying tense-aspect system") and edges us one step closer to an unraveling of one of the fundamental continuum paradoxes: how do speakers who control different ranges along the creole continuum continue to intercommunicate despite their surface differences?[50] We do not yet have a definitive or comprehensive answer, but our analysis of past-marking in Bonnette's text has hopefully drawn us closer to it.

Before we leave the analysis of Bonnette and the historical present, it remains to ask whether a historical-present analysis would work for some of the variation between marked and unmarked past forms in Katherine's Text 13a. The answer is yes, but less dramatically so than in the case of Bonnette's Text 15c. Omitting verbs followed by dentals and verbs in subordinate clauses for reasons given earlier, 40 percent of Katherine's verbs in complicating action or narrative clauses are unmarked (6/15)—a figure that compares favorably with Schiffrin's 30 percent figure in American English narratives. The figure is also, as we might expect, higher than for unmarked pasts in orientation and other nonnarrative clauses (27 percent or 3/11), but the difference is not statistically significant (chi square = .28, not significant at the .05 level). Essentially, Katherine may be thought of as not unmarking enough action-clause pasts to be like Bonnette, and not marking enough nonnarrative-clause pasts to be like Schiffrin's SE speakers. In either case a discourse/pragmatic analysis in terms of the historical present does not work as effectively for her text. However, it would be worthwhile to attempt the historical-present analysis with longer stretches of text, both for Katherine and for other speakers.

Turning now to the phonology of Bonnette's texts, we note that although her speech includes some of the nonstandard features of Guyanese speech, they are far less frequent than they are in the speech of estate-class people like Granny or Irene, and sometimes show the kinds of conditioning found in colloquial British or American speech. For instance, half (3/6) of her consonant clusters ending in t or d are simplified,[51] but this compares with virtually categorical simplification in similar environments for speakers like Irene (for whom the existence of the clusters in underlying structure is questionable), and the constraining effect of the following environment is even more regular than it is in the case of the urban North American speakers examined by Labov et al. (1968), Wolfram (1969), and Fasold (1972). The simplified cases all precede consonants (*kep mii* 779, *kep bak* 783, *jos heer* 837–38) and the nonsimplified cases all precede vowels (*weest ov* 778, *left im* 804, *impakt outsaid* 838). To take another example, one that is more peculiar to the Guyanese speech community, Bonnette shows evidence of vowel-laxing in open syllables, but generally not in words outside of the personal pronoun set (contrast her *goo* 825 with Reefer's *gu* 421 [Text 11a], her *see* 845 with her mother's *se* 849, her *biikoz* 783 with Granny's *bikaas* 492

[Text 12a]), and at a lower frequency than speakers like Irene or Granny (note the relatively high frequency of tense *d(h)ee* 'they' in the texts below). The following data on overall vowel-laxing in the speech of the Cane Walk members represented in this chapter (excerpted from Rickford 1979: 211–12 and drawing on many hours of tape-recorded speech) illustrate this last point, and show that differential frequencies of vowel-laxing distinguish estate- and non-estate-class speakers more generally.[52]

Estate class		Non-estate class	
Derek	72% (91/127)	Sheik	59% (74/125)
Irene	82 (84/102)	Katherine	39 (48/122)
Reefer	72 (73/102)	Bonnette	43 (54/125)
Granny	88 (76/86)	Ustad	35 (44/125)

Other examples of Bonnette's upper-mesolectal phonology include the preservation of postvocalic *t* (*dat* 795, *wOt* 832), the limited incidence of postvocalic *r*-lessness (restricted to unstressed syllables, and here only in about a third of all possible cases: contrast *wenevo* 794 with *ouwor* 802), and the consistent use of *O* and *oh* in words like 'until' (*Ontil* 850; cf. her mother's *antil* 849) and 'all' (*ohl* 833). Only in the closing lines of the narrative about her husband's car accident, where she becomes more involved and speaks more rapidly than anywhere else in her tape-recordings, does Bonnette show any movement toward Creole forms: note the emergence of isolated instances of *da* 'that' (864, but at best ambiguous as a case of deletion because before a following dental), *ad* 'hard' (869), and *aal* (869—although even here the vowel is not as low or as unrounded as Granny's *aal* 550).

At the same time it is clear that Bonnette is not giving an artificially English-like performance. (We will encounter speakers in Chapter Six who are much more prone to do so.) She uses an alveolar rather than a velar nasal in most of her present participial endings (16/22, or 73 percent of the cases, including *vizitin(g)* 832 and 833), and shares with speakers from every other level of the continuum the affrication of *t* and *d* before *r* (*chraiyin* 836, *jrongk* 834), the raised starting point for the diphthong in 'now' (*nou* 846, rather than the more typically British or North American *nau*), and the use of final *ong* rather than *oun/aun* in words like 'down' and 'around' (*dong* 826, *orong* 793). She also gives us, in the single pronunciation of 'up' as *Op* (871), one of the few clear examples in this volume of the use of *O* in SE *o* words. This feature is often cited as characteristic of Caribbean and West African English pidgins and creoles (Wells 1982, 3: 576, 582; Cassidy and Le Page 1980: lii; Todd 1982), but insofar as it involves the really rounded and backed articulation represented by *O*, I find it considerably rarer than might have been expected in Guyanese speech.[53]

Text 15a is from Tape SI78, tape counter nos. 089–095; 15b and 15c are from Tape SI79, nos. 076–090 and 377–401, respectively. In Texts 15b and 15c H. is Bonnette's husband, and D. is her mother. R. in Text 15b is a relative of Bonnette's. A. in Text 15c is Angela Rickford.

15a. The school-leaving exam she took in high school

B: an ai tingk is wuz n ohfl weest ov taim. an wai ai tingk dee	778
kep mii bak tu—am—rait it, iz biikoz ai felt di hedmaasto	779
wohntid tu hav oz moch passiz oz pOsibl ogeens iz neem.	780
yu noo wOt o miin?	781
J: aha.	782
B: biikoz ai wuz kep bak dheer—	783
J: yu din, yu din niid it? yu din, yu din tingk yu	784
niidid di skuul liivin, den?	785
B: noo. an ai felt dat ai—a didn—a shud nOt hav ritn it,	786
a shud ov left lohng biifoor. bot—yuu wor nOt ot o puzishon den	787
tu porsweed yu peerens, yu noo hou?	788
J: m-hm. m-hm.	789
B: wen dee diisaid wel, dis iz taim fu yuu tu goo, den yu gOtu	790
goo. yu noo hou?	791

Translation

And I think it was an awful waste of time. And why I think they kept me back to—am—write it, is because I felt the headmaster wanted to have as many passes as possible against his name. You know what I mean?	780T
Ah-hah.	
Because I was kept back there—	
You didn't, you didn't need it? You didn't, you didn't think you needed the school-leaving (exam), then?	785T
Nooo. And I felt that I—I didn't—I should *not* have written it, I should have left long before. But you were not in a position then to persuade your parents, you know how?	
Mm-hm. Mm-hm.	
When they decide well, this is time for you to go, then you have to go. You know how?	790T

15b. Spirits of the dead speaking through the living

B: wel lisn, aim telin yuu obou dis. diiz—aim—diiz piipl,	792
de—indyon piipl orong di plees, ool piipl, dee biliiv dhot if	793
—a—sombodii fu di famolii daiz, an wenevo yuur having o	794
rilijos fongkshon, dat spirit ov dat porsn ohlwiz kom bak	795
an vizit—	796

H: an beg somting.   797
B: an kom tu—if dee hav eniiting tu see, dee wud kom ohn tu   798
sombodii huu iz dheer in di fongkshon, som Odo kloos relotiv,   799
an see wOt dee hav tu see. . . . ai soh it twais! wit do famolii—   800
   R: wid—am—wi Z?   801
B: ye-e, de had—iz nOt reelii ouwor famlii, bot wii oon dem oz kloos   802
famlii, biikoz—wen mai fado wuz smohl ii—iz peerens daid an   803
left im, an diiz piipl r—broht im op. an dis ool leedii, hor   804
hozbond had daid, an, di had dis fongkshon, wuz sombodii geting   805
marid. an, yuuzhwulii wen di kuk ohl di fuud an soo, yu   806
hav tu teek out fors—fu do piipl huu or ded.   807
   H: ded.   808
B: an put it in o kohrno. an wails di wor duuwing dis litl serimonii,   809
bot teekin out n put it in o koh—putim in o korhno—   810
   H: kichin faal dong?   811
B: doz leedii stard sheekin az if shi gOt—wu iz it yuz hav wen   812
yu sheeyin, man?   813
   D: kool fiiva [laughs]. egyu. [Everybody present echoes "egyu."] 814
B: eegyuu. an den shi sit op, an shi staart tohkin in dis chaps   815
vOis—di vOis—an shi staart tohkin, wOt shi laik, wOt shi   816
dozn laik, wOt—wel—wel iz reelii do man, kOz iz di   817
man vOis yu heerin. wOt ii laiks, wOt ii doz—   818
   J: shi imiiteetn iz vOis on so?   819
B: ai doont noo, bot ai hord it, ai wuz deer an ai luk—   820
   J: bot o miin shi songin jos laik ii?   821
   D: ye-e, ha ha [nervous laughter].   822
B: ye-es, hiz vOis. wOt shi—wOt ii laik, wOt ii dozn laik,   823
wOt ii dozn laik huu iz duuwing, an soo an soo an soo! an den   824
wen ii finish, shi goo ohn ogeen. shi sheek an shi   825
fohl dong. an den wen shi fohl dong, yu—di fan or op   826
n soo, put laimokohl n so, an shi kach orself. an shi in   827
noo wohn ting dat went ohn.   828

Translation

Well listen, I'm telling you about this. These—I'm—these people,
the Indian people around the place, old people, they believe that if
—a—somebody in the family dies, whenever you are having a
religious function, the spirit of that person always comes back   795T
and visits—

And begs for something.

And comes to—if they have anything to say, they would enter
somebody who is there at the function, some other close relative,
and say what they have to say. . . . I saw it twice with the family.   800T
With—am—with Z.?

Yeah, they had—it's not really our family, but we regard them as close family,
because when my father was small he—his parents died and left him, and these

people brought him up. And this old lady, her husband had died, and, they had this
function, it was somebody getting   805T
married. And usually when they cook all the food and so, you have to take out first
for the people who are dead.
    Dead.
And put it in a corner. And while they were doing this little ceremony, about
taking out and putting it in a corn—putting (it) in a corner—   810T
    Kitchen fall down?
This lady started shaking as if she had—what do you have when you're shaking,
man? [what's the name of the illness?]
    Cold fever. Ague.
    Ague. And then she sits up, and she starts talking in this chap's   815T
voice—the voice—and she starts talking about what she likes, what she
doesn't like, what—well—well, it's really the man, cause it's the
man's voice you're hearing. What he likes, what he doesn't—
    She's imitating his voice and so on?
    I don't know, but I heard it, I was there and I looked—   820T
    But I mean she's sounding just like him?
    Yeah, ha-ha.
    Yes, his voice. What she—what he likes, what he doesn't like,
what he doesn't like who is doing, and so on and so on and so on. And then
when he's finished, she goes on again. She shakes and she   825T
falls down. And then when she falls down, you—they fan her up
and so on, put Limacol and so on, and she recovers herself. And she didn't
know one thing that went on.

15c. Her husband's car accident

    B: a noo wen—am—wohn taim o ku riimembo o wuz reelii skeerd. iz   829
o dee—am—B wuz jringking, ii had o mootosaikl den. an yuuzhwulii   830
ohn fraidi afnuunz wen di bOiz kom out from skuul an di   831
jringkin, deer from wohn plees to do Odo, yu noo, vizitin   832
ohl di shOps. an dis dee dhee wur viziting ohl oovo,   833
an hii keem in, jrongk, an ii jrOp iz bag an ii see ii iz goowin   834
out ogeen, an ii jomp ohn n do baisikl. an—am—do baisikl   835
wudn staart, yu noo, n ii kiip chraiyin n chraiyin n chraiyin.   836
wel dat taim ai went—bai dat taim ai went in do baat. and—ai jos   837
heer o big impakt outsaid deer, yu noo, an ai see, "momii iz   838
huu? momii iz huu?" ai wuz in di baat. shi see, "iz o maan, an   839
di maan ded!"   840
    A: oo mai gohd!   841
    D: wel, bai yu sii dii—di porsn hou ii lee dong on dii rood,   842
yu noo, ai kaan mek out iz hii, an wii—   843
    B: an ai stil—an ai—ai—ai—hosl an ai kom out—ai hosl an ai kom out   844
from di baat, yu noo, an ai see, "iz huu? iz huu? iz huu?"   845

an shii s—an wel wen ai ron deer nou an ai sii dee lifin   846
dis chap okroh—if yu sii piipl!—n ai sii dee lifin   847
dis chap okrohs di schriit, bot ai in noo iz huu!   848
    D: antil wen wii neebo oovo de se, "i—iz B!"   849
    B: Ontil wohn o di chaps shout an tel mii iz R!   850
    D: a—an den wii ron dong do step. e-he.   851
    J: . . . wuz hii in chruut?   852
    D: ye-es. rait in front o wii a di rood de.   853
    B: wel dat taim o kud riimembo—mo hool s—yee, it wuz him.   854
mo hool stomok siiz op. yu noo, o kudn—   855
    J: an yu modo don si ii ded?   856
    B: ye-e, shii tel mii, "iz o maan, iz o maan, an di maan ded," yu noo?   857
    D: wil—ye-es, aafto di maan lee dong so flat bai ii belii,   858
a di rood, kraas di rood, so wii kaan ge tu noo iz huu.   859
    B: wel mai hool stomok jus somosohlt rait owee, ai i—yu noo—   860
    J: m-hm.   861
    A: oo lohd!   862
    B: wel ai kudn duu eniiting bot rosh out, an wii skrambl him, kar   863
im tu di hOspitol, dis, dat, da, da, dat. an den wen ii   864
wuz kwait setld in di hOspitol an, an yu noo, an den ai   865
reelii kech maiself—   866
    J: iz yuu n hii nou!   867
    B: noo, wen ai reelii kech maiself, den ai reelii staart sObin hard,   868
ard, hard, ad, ard, bikoz aal di taim ai—yu noo, ai ku   869
reelii stan ting, bot dat taim o riimembo o wuz redii—   870
mo hool stomok jos siiz Op laik, jos nOt op.   871

Translation

I know when—am—I remember once I was really scared. It was
a day—am—B. was drinking, he had a motorcycle then. And usually   830T
on Friday afternoons when the boys come out from school and they're
drinking, they're from one place to the other, you know, visiting
all the shops. And this day they were visiting all over,
and he came in, drunk, and dropped his bag and said he was going
out again, and he jumped on the bicycle. And—am—the bicycle   835T
wouldn't start, you know, and he kept trying and trying and trying.
Well, that time I was—by that time I had gone into the bath. And—I just heard a
big impact outside there, you know, and I said, "Mummy, who is
it? Mummy, who is it?" I was in the bath. She said, "It's a man, and
the man is dead!"   840T
    Oh my God!
    Well, because, you see—from the way in which he lay down on the road,
you know, I couldn't make out it was him, and we—
    And I was still—and I—I—I—hurried and came out—I hurried out
of the bath, you know, and I said, "Who is it? Who is it? Who is it?"   845T

And she s—and well, when I ran there now, I saw them lifting
this chap across—if you see people!—I saw them lifting
this chap across the street, but I didn't know who it was!
  Until our neighbor over there said, "I—it's B.!"
  Until one of the chaps shouted and told me it was R.!   850T
  A—and then we ran down the step. Eh-heh.
  . . . Was it really him?
  Yes. Right in front of us [our house] on the road there.
  Well, I remember that at that time—my whole s—yes, it was him.
My whole stomach seized up [knotted up]. You know, I couldn't—   855T
  And your mother had already said that he was dead?
  Yes, she told me, "It's a man, it's a man, and the man is dead," you know?
  Well, yes, because the man was lying down so flat on his stomach
on the road, across the road, we couldn't get to know who it was.
  Well, my whole stomach just somersaulted right away, and I, you know—   860T
  Mm-hm.
  Oh Lord!
  Well, I couldn't do anything but rush out, and we grabbed him, carried
him to the hospital, did this, that, and the other. And then when he
was quite settled in the hospital, and, and you know, and then I   865T
really caught myself—
  It's you and him now! [You'll begin to quarrel with him now!]
  No, when I really caught myself, then I really started sobbing hard,
hard, hard, hard, hard, because all the time I—you know, I could
really stand anything, but at that time I remember I was ready—   870T
my whole stomach just seized up like, just knotted up.

16. Ustad (1974–1975)

Ustad, sixty-two years old when first interviewed in 1974, stands out in
the Cane Walk sample in several respects. For one thing, he was eventually
recorded more often and in more varied circumstances than any other person, for a total of nine hours. For another, he was one of the rare cases of an
estate-class worker who had ascended the sugar-estate job hierarchy, rising
from a boy-gang worker (see Text 16a) to field foreman. He had gone as far
as fifth standard in primary school, so he had not had much more formal
schooling than those whose careers began in the cane fields. But his father
had been a Hindu pandit, and he became a full-time pandit himself after he
retired from the field foreman position. Whether his religious connections
helped to propel his rise within the sugar-estate ranks is not certain, but it
helped to broaden the range of his social and linguistic contacts. Ustad frequently served as community leader and representative in contacts with important people from outside; but he was just as comfortable bicycling around

the village to help a shovel digger's family perform their "jhaandis" and other religious ceremonies. If, as DeCamp (1971a: 29) suggests, the breadth of an individual's linguistic span within the continuum depends on the breadth of his social activities, we would expect Ustad to have an exceptionally broad linguistic span. And he does.

Evidence for this comes first of all from his variation in the nine singular-pronoun subcategories we have discussed. In the total sample of 24 Cane Walkers, Ustad, Sheik, and Oxford were the only three who showed morphological variation in all nine subcategories, and Ustad was the only one who used *all* 21 variants in these subcategories.

Ustad's texts have a historical and cultural value in addition to their linguistic value, documenting the kinds of corporal punishment meted out by the old-time schoolmasters, and the way marriages were arranged among (Hindu) Indo-Guyanese. Neither of these institutions has disappeared from the Guyanese scene, but they have become less common and less compelling, especially near the urban centers. I can remember one teacher in my youth who made us place our palms face down on her desk and then rolled a baton over the knuckles on the back of our hands. Such "inducements to learning and discipline" are not offered with quite the same frequency or severity these days. Similarly, although many Hindu marriages are still arranged by parents and pandits, the old prohibitions against spouses-to-be associating with each other are less stringent, and they themselves have more choice in the matter.

In terms of morphosyntax Ustad's texts contain elements of the most acrolectal and the most basilectal levels. On the one hand, they include *d(h)eer iz* existentials (953, 954) and full "be" passives with their agent phrases (890, 914); on the other, highly marked basilectal elements like *awii/abii*, the first-person-plural pronoun (924), and *na/no*, the preverbal negator (913). In fact Bickerton's (1975: 187) observation about single-range speakers (who control contiguous lects and move fluidly between them) can also be made about Ustad: "For many such speakers, one gets the impression that conversation is an experimental art form, and that they take a positive delight in exploiting their wide linguistic resources to entertain and perhaps sometimes startle their listeners."

That Ustad's linguistic repertoire began, like Sheik's, with a basilectal base is clear from the fact that he does not just manipulate basilectal surface forms, but shows a knowledge of more subtle underlying basilectal rules. The bald *fren(d)* in lines 918 and 923, for instance, with no article or quantifier, and without plural-marking, represents the basilectal system for marking nonspecific noun phrases, in contrast to definite and indefinite ones (marked with *di* and *wan*, respectively; see Bickerton 1981: 23). Similarly, he uses *no biin noo* rather than *no noo* in line 913, where *biin* marks the fact that the lack of knowledge he and the young people of his day had had about "gyalfren an baifren" was anterior to the moment of speaking (see Bickerton 1975: 29ff). Note that even though Ustad uses a long, tense vowel in *biin*, this form functions here like the basilectal anterior form (usually *bin*, with a short, lax vowel) rather than like the upper-mesolectal past-participial form (see Bickerton 1975: 82–84). By contrast, although Ustad uses marked plurals and the other previously mentioned characteristics of acrolectal speech, there are signs of strain at this end of the continuum, in the form of hypercorrections like *menz* (879), *moo bigo* (925), and *deer nOt tu goo* (928).

In three subsystems—negatives, habitual markers, and passives—Ustad shows us almost the whole gamut of possibilities in the continuum. In addition to the basilectal negator *na/no*, Ustad uses the acrolectal post-auxiliary forms, including *kyaant* (926), *didn* (959), and *doont* (960). He marks habitual aspect in turn with mesolectal *doz* (904) and zero—more accurately, the SE present (*hool* 895). He alternates between the acrolectal "be" passives mentioned above, a somewhat more mesolectal *get* passive (956), and the basilectal system in which the appearance of a single noun phrase with a transitive verb is all there is to signal the fact that the surface subject or agent is really the underlying object or patient/recipient of the action (*dis fut kot* 950). This last system has been discussed by a number of scholars (DeCamp 1971b: 362–63; Alleyne 1980: 97–100; Allsopp 1983; Markey and Fodale 1983), but there are intercreole differences and no single agreed-on analysis. In GC the passive interpretation of noun phrase–verb structures is strongest when the noun phrase is nonhuman and the verb requires a human subject; human underlying objects are usually passivized with *get*, even in the basilect (e.g. *di man ge(t) nak dong*).

Finally, the interpretation of unmarked verbs becomes particularly problematic when we are dealing with a speaker whose range is as broad as Ustad's. In some cases (e.g. *giv* 875), there is little question of a historical-present interpretation, but in others (e.g. *kom* 918) it is the most likely interpretation. The latter case occurs in Text 16c, in which the orientation clauses (913–14) most frequently have marked pasts and the narrative clauses, which carry the complicating action (916–28), most frequently have unmarked verbs. The argument for a historical-present interpretation of Text 16c is further strengthened by the occurrence of marked present forms: *ogriiz* (918), *kyaant* (926), and *iz* (928).

Ustad's phonology, like his morphosyntax, contains both acrolectal and basilectal elements. His use of voiceless interdental fricatives where required in SE words (*footh* 877, *thingz* 912, *nothing* 952) is almost flawless; only in one case (*tingking* 954) does he substitute the creole stop. The voiced interdental fricatives are proportionally less frequent—particularly in the

common definite article, which occurs most of the time as *di;* but in Text
16a, taken from the first minutes of my first taped interview with Ustad, and
representing some of the most careful speech I recorded from him, *dh*'s occur quite frequently (*dhat* 872, *fadho* 873, *dhen* 877, *dheer* 878), more so than
in any other text of comparable length in this chapter. At the same time,
Ustad exemplifies several typical GC pronunciations, including *maninjo*
('manager' 884), *aaks* ('ask' 917, but cf. *ask* 928), *labii* (919, <*le(t) awii*), and
marid ('marry' 907). This last example should really come under morphosyntax, of course, since it is an instance of a creole infinitival stem form
modeled on an SE past; compare *lef* 'leave' and *brok* 'break.' The form
schrenknos (880) is perhaps idiosyncratic, but it is an interesting folk etymology for 'strenuous,' involving analogical extension (*schrengk* + adjectival
nos) from 'strength.'

No single area of Ustad's phonology better exemplifies his oscillation between basilectal and acrolectal norms than his use (and avoidance) of basilectal "broad-mouth" pronunciations involving *a(a).* He uses the basilectal
Creole variants in many instances (*kaal* 894, *waan* 923, *flag* 900, *nak* 920,
baiz 918), but the acrolectal English variants almost as often, including different occurrences of the same word (*kohl* 939, *dOk* 885, *bOiz* 894). In some
instances (such as the words transcribed as *ohf* in line 896 and *otohl* in line
909), the actual pronunciation is intermediate between the two, just as we
found to be the case with Sheik. Unlike Sheik's texts, however, Ustad's include some examples of hypercorrection, cases in which he uses *O* or *oh*
where *a* or *aa* is normal in acrolectal or standard Guyanese English: *hohf*
'half' (904), *Obsent* 'absent' (899), and *Ofto* 'after' (878). Like *menz* and the
other instances of morphosyntactic hypercorrection cited above, these betray some degree of insecurity or uncertainty about the applicability of acrolectal norms.

Texts 16a, 16b, and 16c are from Tape SI18, tape counter nos. 028–044,
080–090, and 278–301, respectively; 16d is from Tape SI19, nos. 315–44.

16a. The different kinds of jobs he has held

U: ai lef skuul at—am—sik standard. wol yu noo, juurin dhat	872
taim mai fadho daid, soo ai tuk oovo di priishud in charj o	873
XXX hinduu chorch. . . . an wen den orong twentii-wohn,	874
wel, ai giv op di—am—chorch work, an went in di fiil.	875
wel ai staartid tu work in di fiil az—am—bai gang, kliinin	876
konohlz, wiiding daamz, chrenchiz, an soo footh. dhen from dheer nou,	877
a went intu dhi wiidin gang, tu—wi dhi fiimil gang. Ofto dheer,	878
iz wuz nOt suutid tu mii, ai went in di shOvl gang, weer pyoo menz	879
work, big men, moor schrengknos work, wid fohk an shovl. and—am—	880
J: m hm. wOt yu ohl ad tu duu—am—kliin out—jreenz an so?	881

U: wel, yu fohk an mool keen. yu plant keen, yu pripeer   882
siid bedz, yu plant keenz. from dheer nou, ai wuz—e—promootid   883
tu—am—Ondo di maninjo, misto F, az a—wot wi kohl—aam—cheking   884
ponts in di dOk. . . . and—am—afto deer, o yeer afto, ai wuz   885
promootid osistont jraivo, Ondo—dhi hed jraivo, wich wuz di   886
kohl fu di gang, woz G.   887
    J: m hm. wuz di jraivoz jOb? wodii—wudii haz tu duu?   888
    U: wel, suupovaiz work in di fiil. sii det sortn standord o   889
work iz biin don bai di—bai di workoz.   890

Translation

I left school in—am—sixth standard. Well, you know, during that
time my father died, so I took over the priesthood in charge of
X.X.X. Hindu church. . . . And when then around twenty-one,
well, I gave up the—am—church work, and went into the fields.   875T
Well, I started to work in the fields in the—am—boy gang, cleaning
canals, weeding dams, trenches, and so forth. Then from there now
I went into the weeding gang, to—with the female gang. After that,
it was not suited to me, I went into the shovel gang, where only men
work—big men, more strenuous work, with fork and shovel. And—am—   880T
    Mm-hm. What did you guys have to do—am—clean out drains and so on?
    Well, you fork and mould [sugar] cane.* You plant cane, you prepare
seed beds, you plant canes. From there now, I was—ah—promoted
to—am—under the manager, Mr. F., as a—what we call—am—checking
punts in the dock. . . . And—am—after that, a year after, I was   885T
promoted to assistant driver, under—the head driver, which was the
name for [the supervisor of] the gang, was G.
    Mm-hm. What's the driver's job? What he—what does he have to do?
    Well, supervise work in the field. See that a certain standard of
work is being done by the—by the workers.   890T

16b. Corporal punishment in school

U: JGG wuz o veri schrik man. wich—aam—marning ii put On di   891
blak suut, wel wi noo liks laik piiz in di klaas, from hari   892
raim tu harii rait. . . . wi get—wii kyar tambrin wip. den   893
leetor ohn wii get wail keen. wol di kaal it benchin. tuu bOiz   894
hool yu tu f—fiit an schrech yu okrohs o teebl, an tuu Odho baiz   895
hool yu tuu han. an from yu butok rait ohf di lash on yu.   896
    J: m hm. m hm. m. wo ii—wo ii yuustu biit yu fu? laik—fu laik wo?   897
    U: wel, if yu—am—kOgin from sombOdii els sleet, and yur nOt   898
peeying otenshon tu yu work, ohr, yu Obsent from skuul. di hav   899

---

*See the entry in Cassidy and LePage (1980: 306) for *mould (up)*: "cf. OED *v.*[1] 2.→1837. To
heap mould or earth around the roots of a plant."

tu ron yu dong in dooz deez an kach yuu. soor—soo di flag yu.   900
   J: huu yuustu ron yu dong? dee had—am—?   901
   U: wel di Odho bigo bOiz in—in di klaas. soo di skuulmasto   902
sen yu wel, "goo an sarch fu soo an soo, an bring him."   903
somtaim yu doz spen til hohf dee. sontain yu doz—di na   904
kach yu fu di dee. di neks dee dee goo bak ogen. wen   905
di bring yu, wel, liks laik piiz on yu.   906

Translation

   J.G.G. was a very strict man. Any morning he put on the
black suit, we knew (to expect) licks like peas in the class. From Harry
Rine to Harry Right. . . . We had—we had a tamarind whip. Then
later on we had a wild cane. Well, they call it "benching." Two boys
hold your two feet and stretch you across a table, and two other boys   895T
hold your two hands. And from your buttocks right off they lash you.
   What he—what did he use to beat you for? Like—like for what?
   Well, if you were—am—cogging [cribbing] from somebody else's slate and not
paying attention to your work, or were absent from school. They had
to run you down in those days and catch you. So—so they flogged you.   900T
   Who used to run you down? They had—am—?
   Well, the other, bigger boys in—in the class. So the schoolmaster would
send you, saying well, "Go and search for so and so and bring him."
Sometime you would spend half a day. Sometimes you would—they wouldn't
catch you all day. The next day they'd go back again. When   905T
they brought you back, well, [it would be] licks like peas on you.

16c. Arranged marriages in the old days

   U: an dipenz—if dii modho n fadh see, "yu gOtu marid dis   907
gyorl," yu gOtu marid it. an if di tel di gyorl, "yu gOtu   908
marid dis bOi," yu gOtu marid it. noo ton bak otohl. . . .   909
   J: . . . biifoor yu kom tu d—cheej wee di telin yu tu—huu   910
tu marii n su—yu on hav noo bOifrenz or gyorlfrenz or so? noo—   911
   U: wel wii hardlii heer dooz thingz. wii hardli heer bout gyalfren an   912
baifren. yu no biin noo wo di kaal soo. . . . mai porsonol   913
marij wuz reenj bai—bai mai fadho. an—am—ot dat taim, wii wor   914
living at XXX, an dhi gyorl aim goowin tu   915
marid at L. an jos di gyorl fadho kom hoom,   916
an aaks mai fadho fu mii in marij. mai fadho see, "ookee." hii   917
ogriiz. frend kom n tel mi se, "maan, luk maan"—bigo baiz   918
moo dhan mii—see, "maan, luk maan, labii gu sii yu gyaal." mii se,   919
"bai, mi dadii goo nak mii!" "noo," i se, "maan, go an tel yu   920
dadii." an ai goo an tel mi dadi. mii se, "dadii, o wohn tu goo sii   921
di gyaal." waan baks! rait ohf di reel, bifoo di w—laas word kom   922
out! waan baks a mii f—fees hee! wol, o staatid tu krai. fren   923

se, "aarait, maan, doon worii wi da, maan, labii gu L."   924
wel, yu noo, ai wor—dee woz moo bigo chap, an dee inkorij   925
mii tu goo tu sii di gyaal. an wi went tu L. wel, wii kyaant   926
goo in di ous. wii stanop a daam, wii sii plentii gyorl, bo wii   927
no noo wich wohn iz huu. wii deer nOt tu goo n ask."   928

Translation

And it depends—if the mother and father say, "You've got to marry this
girl," you've got to marry her. And if they tell the girl, "You've got
to marry this boy," you've got to marry him. No turn back at all. . . .
. . . Before you come to the stage where they are telling you to—who   910T
to marry and so on—you don't have boyfriends or girlfriends or so? No—
Well, we hardly hear those things. We hardly hear about girlfriend and
boyfriend. You didn't know what those things were. . . . My personal
marriage was arranged by—by my father. And—am—at that time we were
living at X.X.X., and the girl I'm going to   915T
marry at L. And it's just that the girl's father comes home,
and asks my father for me in marriage. My father says, "Okay." He
agrees. Friends come and tell me, "Man, look, man"—bigger boys
than me—they say, "Man, look, man, let us go and see your girl." I say,
"Boy, my daddy will knock me!" "No," they say, "Man, go and tell your   920T
daddy." And I go and tell my daddy. I say, "Daddy, I want to go and see
the girl." One box! Right off the rail, before the last word comes
out! One box across my face here! Well, I started to cry. My friends
say, "All right, man. Don't worry with that, man. Let us go [to] L."
Well, you know, I was—they were bigger chaps, and they encouraged   925T
me to go and see the girl. And we went to L. Well, we can't
go in the house. We stand up on the dam, we see plenty girls, but we
don't know which one is who. We did not dare go and ask.

16d. How a woman possessed by a jumbie diagnosed his illness

U: ai wuz neer dis wumon, nOt noowin dhat dis wumon nou, shiiz   929
goowin tu plee jombii tuu. bot dis wumon luus hor heer, yu noo,   930
oopm out hor heer an soo ohn, teek aaf or korchif. ai si dong   931
neer dis wumon. an sins zis wumon smel dat lohoban, dis   932
wuman mek—shii sprang op wid wohn kaino bloowin. se, "e?"   933
wol, ai get o bit fraikn, yu noo, bikohz On—Onekspektid dis ting   934
hapm. wel, dis iz di wee dee goo ohl—di—o man kom n ii tel   935
hor, "shantii! shantii! shantii!" wich miinz, "kwaiyet! kwaiyet!   936
kwaiyet!" wol, di kohl mii in. mi sisto n loh—tel di man de   937
wohn tu sii wo hapm tu mii an soo On. di man kohl mii in ogen.   938
wen dis man kohl mii in, ii see, wel, mai taim iz shohrt, dot dis   939
man—do—iiz o schrohng oobyo man, an ii haz sen dis oobya tu kil   940
mii, an hii kanot manij dis otohl, dot—am—aim goowin tu   941

dai. dis ting wil kom tu blod paizn, and—am—an soo On. wel,   942
dis wumon wu stil sid—sidn dong outsai sheeking hor hed. wol,   943
woz shii torn nou tu goo On dii ohlto tu plee dis jombii. an   944
suun az shii goo tu di ohlto, wit or lohng heer, shi staatu   945
tuu an froo, yu noo, sheeking hor hed an soo ohn, an shi meek   946
o big lohf. shi twist—iis, wes, naart, sout, iis—shov op   947
hor badii an ohl kaino thing. and—am—wel de staatu ask hor,   948
dot—am—ai am sik fu soo lohng yeer—aa—month. soo menii taim   949
dis fut kot, di waan fu noo, wel, wO reeli hapm tu   950
mii. wol dis wumon nou . . . dis wumon nou see, "yes." dis   951
wumon meek o laf, ii se, "luk, nothing rohng wit yuu. an   952
deer iz noo wohn kan duu yu somthing. and yu hav—yu wen tu menii   953
pleesiz, tingking dat sombOdi oobyo yuu. bot dheer iz nothing   954
laik di kaind. and wOt ai am teling yuu nou iz tu—" dis taim shi   955
pleeying, yu noo. ii see, "yu fut haz tu get kot—twais moor.   956
tuu taim moor di fut haz tu ge kot, den yu fut goowin tu get—   957
am—beto. an di fut na kot a di rait spOt." dis woz   958
di egzak word from dis wumon. . . . ai didn tel dis wumon nat   959
o word. ai did nat tel dis wumon nat o word. ai doont noo hor.   960

Translation

I was near this woman, not knowing that this woman, now, she is
going to play jumbie too. But this woman let out her hair, you know,   930T
opened out her hair and so on, took off her kerchief. I sat down
near this woman. And since this woman smelled that lohban,* this
woman made—she sprang up with a kind of blowing. I said, "Eh?"
Well, I got a bit frightened, you know, because unexpectedly this thing
happened. Well, this is the way they went on. The—a man came, and he told   935T
her, "Shanti! Shanti! Shanti!," which means "Quiet! Quiet!
Quiet!" Well, they called me in. My sister-in-law told the man they
wanted to see what had happened to me and so on. The man called me in again.
When this man called me in, he said, well, my time is short, that this
man—he is a strong obeah man, and he has sent this obeah to kill   940T
me. And he cannot manage this at all, that—am—I'm going to
die. This thing will come to blood poisoning and—am—so on. Well,
this woman was still sit—sitting down outside shaking her head. Well,
it was her turn now to go on the altar to play this jumbie. And
as soon as she went to the altar, with her long hair, she started to,   945T
to and fro, you know, shaking her head and so on. And she gave
a big laugh. She twisted east, west, north, south, east—shoved up
her body and all kinds of things. And—am—well, they started to ask
her, that—am—I am sick for so many years—ah—months. So many times

---

*"Lohban" is an aromatic substance (cf. Hindi *lohban* or *loban*), which Chaturvedi and
Tiwari 1975: 683 gloss as "(gum) benzoin, oil creosote." "Shanti," four lines below, is also from
Hindi: *sha:nti* 'peace, calmness, quiet' (ibid., p. 739).

this foot has been cut, they want to know, well, what really happened to   950T
me. Well, this woman now—ah—so this woman now said, "Yes." This
woman gave a laugh and said, "Look, nothing is wrong with you. And
there is no one can do anything to you. And you have—you went to many
places, thinking that somebody put obeah on you. But there is nothing
of the kind. And what I am telling you now is to—" Meanwhile she's   955T
playing, you know. She says, "Your foot has to get cut twice more.
Twice more the foot has to get cut, then your foot is going to get—
am—better. And the foot was not cut at the right spot." These were
the exact words of this woman. . . . I didn't tell this woman
a word. I did not tell this woman a word. I don't know her.   960T

5

Recordings of Natural Speech: Other Areas

In the last chapter all the speakers came from one small face-to-face com-munity and from a single ethnic group. The texts in this chapter have been specifically chosen to represent different regions and to represent the Afro-Guyanese as well as the Indo-Guyanese sectors of the Guyanese speech community.[1] Several of the selections are from recording of speakers from Georgetown, the capital city. Others come from various regions that are interesting or significant for one reason or another. For instance, Lohtan is from Port Mourant, Corentyne, a region popularly associated with dis-tinctively basilectal speech. Dhanish is from Bush Lot, a primarily Indo-Guyanese village in the West Coast Berbice region where Arnold Persaud did extensive fieldwork for his (1970) B.A. thesis, and to which his the-sis supervisor, Derek Bickerton (a visiting professor at the University of Guyana at the time), returned to do reinterviews of his own. The Bush Lot data collected by Persaud and Bickerton figured prominently in Bickerton's subsequent analyses of the Guyanese Creole continuum (1971, 1973, 1975), and Dhanish is in fact one of the speakers from the original sample, located with Persaud's kind cooperation. Anna is from Buxton, a primarily Afro-Guyanese village on the East Coast, Demerara, famous for its history of self-determination and for its strong African cultural survivals, like the queh-queh and ring-play traditions (W. Edwards 1982), which are exemplified in part in the folksongs of Chapter 6. Buxton is only a few miles from Cane Walk, and provides a good basis for comparison in terms of ethnicity. Finally, Basil is our lone representative of the Essequibo region, now famous as the site of "Skepi Dutch" (Robertson and Jaganauth 1976). Together with Anna, he also represents the most basilectal Afro-Guyanese speech in the spoken texts in this volume, allowing us to assess the claims and counterclaims of other researchers concerning the relationship between ethnicity and lan-guage use (Bickerton 1973; Devonish 1978; W. Edwards 1983).

The bulk of these speakers can be classified as working class, the most limited of Guyana's three classes (Raymond Smith 1962: 114–17; Robinson 1970: 58–59) in terms of income, education, occupational prestige, and institutional power. In these respects, they are equivalent to the Cane Walk estate-class field laborers.[2] Two—a small businessman and the wife of a skilled tradesman—might be classified as lower middle class, equivalent to the Cane Walk non-estate class. There are no representatives of the Guyanese upper middle class (professionals and administrators) in this chapter, but Chapter 6 does include some representatives of this highest socioeconomic stratum (the lawyers, for instance), and their speech is recognizably closer to the acrolect. As indicated in Table 5.1, the sexes are evenly represented in this chapter, but only two of the three age groups delimited in Chapter 4 are included; none of the speakers is from the under-eighteen group.

Since these speakers come from quite different areas and backgrounds, should they be considered part of a single Guyanese speech community, along with Cane Walkers? The answer is yes—at least on Hymes's (1972: 54–55) definition of a speech community as one "sharing rules for the conduct and interpretation of speech, and rules for the interpretation of at least one variety." For Guyanese from almost every region appear to share a common understanding of the local variety of SE and common norms for the social evaluation of English and Creole varieties. They also share rules for such Guyanese speech events as *rowing* and *tan'lize*.[3] Yet there are internal differences within this speech community, and some of these will be noted as they come up in the following texts.

TABLE 5.1
Speakers in This Chapter by Area, Ethnicity, Social Class, Age, and Sex

Text set number and name	Area	Ethnicity	Social class	Age	Sex
17. Ali	Georgetown, Demerara	Indo-Guyanese	LMC	37	M
18. Ayisha	Georgetown	Indo-Guyanese	WC	39	F
19. Lohtan	Port Mourant, Berbice	Indo-Guyanese	WC	49	M
20. Dhanish	Bush Lot, Berbice	Indo-Guyanese	WC	70	F
21. Anna	Buxton, Demerara	Afro-Guyanese	WC	36	F
22. Basil	Wakenaam, Essequibo	Afro-Guyanese	WC	70	M
23. Damon	Cumberland, Berbice	Afro-Guyanese	WC	78	M
24. Mother	Georgetown	Afro-Guyanese	LMC	80	F

NOTE: LMC is lower middle class; WC is working class.

17. Ali (1975)

Ali is unusual in combining many of the demographic categories that typically distinguish different sectors of the Guyanese population. Although he was born in a rural area (on the Corentyne), his family moved to the capital city of Georgetown when he was two, and he lived there until he was sixteen. Since the period from age four to age thirteen is usually considered critical in the formation of a person's vernacular (Labov 1972b: 138), we have to classify him as a Georgetown speaker, but his residence in Plaisance and Cane Walk from his late teens into his early twenties, and his frequent trips into other rural areas on business in later years, give him a closer acquaintance with rural life and language than the average urban resident enjoys. Growing up in predominantly Afro-Guyanese communities (Albouystown, Georgetown, then Plaisance, East Coast Demerara) he has also had closer associations and interaction with Afro-Guyanese than many Indo-Guyanese (although this pattern is not all that unusual). The whole point of Text 17a is that although he was Indo-Guyanese, his close contacts within the Afro-Guyanese community prevented him from being beaten up during the racial/political disturbances at the beginning of the 1960's, just as Afro-Guyanese with good Indo-Guyanese contacts were protected in areas where Indo-Guyanese were the instigators.

Ali also mediates socioeconomic classes. Although he grew up in an economically depressed, tough working-class area and did not have the opportunity to go higher than fourth standard in primary school, he now runs a flourishing small garment factory and has contacts with the higher-class businessmen in whose stores his products are sold. When he says, in line 963, "I live very nice with people," he is referring to his ability to get along successfully ("maneuver" 986) with people from a variety of ethnic, socioeconomic, and geographical backgrounds. This ability is positively valued in the society at large, but it is especially important for businessmen. Significantly, the other person who makes a similar claim in this volume ("I live good with everybody, right?," Text 14b, 727) is Sheik, another businessman.

Ali's speech is characteristically mid-mesolectal. His personal pronouns, for instance, contain enough occurrences of the SE variants (*ai, de(e)/di* as subject pronouns) to establish that he is comfortable at this end of the continuum. However, at particularly expressive or emphatic parts of his narrative (e.g. *mii iz o maan, mii na groo op* 963–94) he occasionally switches to basilectal forms. This is particularly the case with pronominal possessives (*mi brodo* 972, *di wee* 981), basilectal forms of which typically lie within the competence of mesolectal speakers. Sharply marked basilectal pronoun features, like the use of *ii* for masculine, feminine, and neuter gender or sex reference, do not occur in his recorded speech.

Similar examples are evident in other subsystems. Although we see a few examples of *bin* in Ali's texts, they are before locative prepositional phrases (973, 1001), instances of the main verb use of *bin* that continues fairly high into the mesolect. Note that in preverbal position Ali uses *wuz* and *di(d)* instead of *bin* (987, 1007), just as he uses *gun* instead of *gu* as his future auxiliary (970). Similarly, although he uses *dem* as a plural demonstrative adjective, the noun it modifies appears at least once with plural *-z* (*dem baiz* 971). And although Ali gives us a perfect example of creole topicalization via sentence-clefting (*iz oonii wohn hous di gOt* 995–96, as against untopicalized *di gOt oonii wohn hous*), it is mesolectal *iz* rather than basilectal *a* that serves as the topicalizing, sentence-initial morpheme.[4] However, there are clear uses of the creole passive without *bii* or a participial suffix (*wohn hOspitolaiz* 1001) and of preverbal completive or perfect *don* (983, one of the rare examples not in a *wen* clause). Note, too, that apart from auxiliary forms like *wuz* and *di(d)n* and main verbs *(h)ad* and *bin*, none of which occur in narrative or complicating action clauses (see the discussion of Bonnette's texts in Chapter 4), past-reference verbs are unmarked. The only exceptions are the syllabic forms *staartid* and *admitid* (974, 1003), which lend support to Bickerton's (1975: 102ff) hypothesis that this is where English past-marking of weak verbs is strongest in mesolectal grammars.

There are a few syntactic/pragmatic features of interest in Ali's texts. One is the counterfactual conditional in line 1007 (*if hii di goowin faas, hid bi don tu*), which employs *di* to mark the anterior condition in the antecedent clause or protasis, and *(wu)d bi don* to mark the hypothetical result in the consequence clause or apodosis.[5] Counterfactuals, which allow the speaker to speculate about what might have been the consequence if something other than what actually happened had happened, seem to serve as a common coda or closing line for narratives: compare the poignant counterfactual with which Ayisha closes her narrative (Text 18, line 1057).

Note also that the "if" clause in line 979 is used as a dramatic discourse device, equivalent to SE "You should have heard the commotion out there!" In both cases a conditional is used, and the construction is restricted to sense or perception verbs ("see," "hear," "smell," and so on). The Guyanese construction always employs the "if" clause or protasis without an accompanying "then" clause or apodosis, however. An analysis of what the unstated apodosis might be and how the conditional construction achieves its dramatic effect in narrative is presented in connection with another example in Mother's Text 24d (lines 1331–32).

Ali's texts also include a number of interesting GC lexical items and discourse features. Lexical items of interest include the use of *sodn so* (978) as a connective, equivalent to 'as soon as,' the use of *stoorii* in the sense of 'commotion, bedlam,' and *konsorn sombadii* in the sense of 'belonging to some-body other than the person spoken to, and therefore not to be touched, harmed, or otherwise tampered with.' Two of Ali's favorite expressions are the discourse markers *maan*, used as an empathetic means of relating or ap-pealing to an addressee (970, 973, 975),* and *rait*, which occurs postsenten-tially (962, 963, 971, 976), with rising intonation. This latter form helps the speaker to check that the meaning or significance of the proposition in the preceding sentence has been grasped by the addressee. It also provides the speaker/narrator with additional composition time between sentences. It is most commonly used in the texts in this volume by mesolectal speakers (cf. Sheik, Katherine). Basilectal speakers like Reefer use *yu noo* more fre-quently, although neither expression is restricted to one or the other end of the continuum.

Note also the use of the evidential construction in lines 970–71, *aal wii stan op n sii: dem baiz paas*, and compare it with Reefer's equivalent in Text 11c, line 482: *mi sidong de an mi witnis da*. In both cases the "evidential" consists of a description of the speaker standing or sitting at a vantage point from which the events can be witnessed firsthand, and occurs at a point in the narrative in which out-of-the ordinary, almost unbelievable events (in these two cases unjust and violent events) are being reported. Another com-mon evidential expression is *mi sii da wid mii oon tuu ai!* 'I saw that with my own two eyes!' Like the other examples, it represents a dramatizing stylistic option and is not required by the grammar, unlike Hopi and other languages in which evidential distinctions are morphologically marked in the verb, along with tense-aspect distinctions.

Ali's texts exhibit many previously discussed phonological features of GC. The only features worth noting again are the affrication of alveolar stops before *r*, as in *jringk* ('drink' 983) and *chreen* ('train' 997), and the extreme morphophonemic condensation evident in *aat* ('all right' 971) and *hOstil* ('hospital' 1004). Despite the order of presentation, Text 17a was recorded later in the interview than Text 17b, and it consistently contains the creole "broad mouth" *a(a)* pronunciations (*bikaaz* 966, *bai* 970, *shap* 976), in con-trast to some earlier uses of the corresponding SE *O* and *oh* pronunciations (*gOt* 996, *mohrnin* 989). This, like other phonological and morphosyntactic features, reflects the fact that the speaker became more involved and spoke more informally as the recording session went on.

Text 17a is from Tape SI33, tape counter nos. 565–91; 17b is from the same tape, nos. 252–67.

---

*Like *bai*, it is often used regardless of the sex of the addressee, but *gyorl* is sometimes substituted for female addressees, especially when the speaker is also female.

17a. Experiences in the 1962–64 disturbances

J: am—di distorbons n soo—it din of—efek yu tu moch?   961
A: wel ai yuustu liv in plezaans, rait? wel o ad som verii   962
gu—wel ai liv verii nais wi piipl, rait? mii iz o maan, mii na   963
groo op wi dis rees toorii an—gat tingz in maind, yu noo. op   964
tu nou, if ai gad o fren, iz o fren, huusuevo ii bii. ai in   965
gat yu, yu noo, wel se wel, bikaaz yur o niigroo chap, yu noo,   966
a gun liv bikaaz yu kin gi mi somting, or ai kin giv yu   967
somting. wen di ha di distorbons, wii liv in plezaans, neer   968
tu i seem leedii, di ool aig leedii? wii liv de.   969
dem bai se, "maan, wee yu gun muuv n gu?" aal wii stan op n   970
sii: dem baiz paas, rait, biitin piipl n ting. di se, "aat,   971
iz wi bai livin de, maan." mi brodo n mii, rait?   972
wii liv verii nais wi piipl, maan. an di paas, rait? o nait, wii   973
bin in di sinimo won dis ting staartid, in plezaans. . . . wii kom   974
out. dem baiz tel wi, dem bai se, "maan, heer. aalyu gu lang hoom   975
orlii, rait? kom ou di plees orlii." an wii ad o shap jos in   976
plezaans de. wii goo in di shap di nait, an wii si dong. oopn   977
o tin o kaan biif, n biskit, n wii iit. an sodn so, yu sii   978
sim oovo, w—if yu heer d—stoorii ou dee! wen dem bai   979
don, di kom n di tek tuu pak o bri—bristol. an di   980
gyaaf wid wii lil, an di gaan di wee. bot som tong baiz   981
kom op, an de brok di shap, di tek ot o baril o wain, an di   982
jringk n ting. wel dem bai don tel dem, yu noo, dat   983
dis shap konsorn sombadii dot, yu noo. wii din ad noo aard taim.   984
sins ai groowin op, o nevo ad o aard taim, maan. ai liv in   985
albaistong tortiin yeez, n doz o haad plees tu monuuvo.   986

Translation

Am—the disturbances and so on—they didn't affect you too much?
Well, I used to live in Plaisance, right? Well, I had some very
good—well, I lived very nicely with people, right? I'm a guy, I didn't
grow up with this race story, with animosity in my mind, you know. Up
to now, if I have a friend, he's a friend, whoever he may be. I don't   965T
have you typed as, you know, well, because you're a Negro, you know,
I'll live good just because you can give me something or I can give you
something. During the disturbances, we were living in Plaisance, near
the same lady [mentioned before], the Ole Higue lady. We lived there.
The guys said, "Man, where will you move and go to?" We stood up and   970T
saw: the guys passed, right, beating people and so on. They said, "All
right, the chap living there is our friend." My brother and I, right?
We live nicely with people, man. And they passed, right? A night, we
were in the cinema when this thing started, in Plaisance. . . . We came
out. The guys told us—they said, "Man, hear. You guys go home   975T

early, right? Come out of the place early." And we had a shop right in
Plaisance there. We went in the shop that night and sat down. Opened
a tin of corned beef and biscuits and ate. And suddenly, as soon as the
cinema was over, if you heard the bedlam out there! When they were
done, the guys came and took two packs of Bristol [cigarettes]. And they   980T
conversed a little and went on their way. But some [George-]town guys
came up and broke into the shop and took out a barrel of wine, and they
drank it and so on. Well, the guys had already told them, you know, that
this shop was special, you know. We didn't have a hard time. Ever
since I was growing up I've never had a hard time, man. I lived in   985T
Albouystown for thirteen years, and that's a hard place to maneuver.

17b. His stepbrother's car accident

A: mi stepbrodo bou tuu wiiks—bot—bot chrii wiiks bak, ii wuz	987
gun op borbiis. wel ii ad o red maazdo. . . . bai jril torn do,	988
yu noo, maikoonii, jril torn? ii se do mohrnin, it wuz, obout—jos	989
kwohrDo tu siks taim nou, goowin op. ii sii o jiip komin rong di	990
torn in waan spiid. ii se di neks ting hii noo, di jiip smash	991
op dis kyaar! . . . di ad tu—di tek haaf n ou fu get ii ou	992
di kyaar.	993
J: wo!	994
A: bika yu noo, do—jril torn dem—iz oonii wohn hous di	995
gOt a di esteet. alang de nou, iz di schreet rood afto	996
yu jomp di chreen lain. dem piipl on livn de. an til bak	997
nou, bai di haaf-wee kOnvoseeshon chrii—do di chrii—do big	998
chrii, dee yu gon fain piipl livin de, orong de. wel di	999
chrai—di wachmaan chrai n ting, in, bika aal chrii o dem	1000
wo bin in di kyaar, wohn hOspitolaiz and o neks bai—am—	1001
J: bo wo—huu bin in—yu bodii kyaar?	1002
A: ye-e. ye. an faiv porson from di jiip admitid at—am—	1003
gu at—am—maikoonii hOstil de. wel hii ge o stich in ii	1004
hed, ohl hee blak n bluu—	1005
J: hii di jraivin?	1006
A: o-he. . . . ii si if hii di goowin faas, hid bi don tu!	1007

Translation

My stepbrother, about two weeks—about—about three weeks ago, he was
going up to Berbice. Well, he had a red Mazda. . . . By Drill Turn there,
you know, in Mahaicony, Drill Turn? He said that morning, it was, just
about quarter to six now, going up. He saw a jeep coming around the   990T
turn at great speed. He said the next thing he knew, the jeep smashed
into this car! . . . They had to—they took half an hour to get him out
of the car.
    What!

Because, you know, that—Drill Turn there. There's only one house   995T
on the estate. Along there now it's just one straight road after
you cross the train line. People don't live there. And way back
now, by the halfway Conversation Tree—that big tree—that big
tree, there you'll find people living, around there. Well, they
tried—the watchman tried and so on—because the three   1000T
that were in the car, one was hospitalized, and another boy—am—
    But what—the one who was in your buddy's car?
    Yeah, yeah. And five persons from the jeep were admitted to—am—
went to—am—Mahaicony Hospital there. Well, he got a stitch
in his head. All here was black and blue.   1005T
    He was driving?
    Eh-heh. . . . He said if he was going fast, he'd have been done for too!

18. Ayisha (1974)

I have never met anyone who suffered as much, forgave as much, and survived as many trials as well as Ayisha did. (Like the other names in this volume, Ayisha is a pseudonym.) She was the first person I tape-recorded when
I returned to Guyana in 1974 to take up a university appointment and do
fieldwork for my dissertation, and she served to remind me that outside of
the comfortable university environment in which I had done my graduate
work, gathering facts and experimenting with ideas, there was a different
world, where people hurt and hungered and tried simply to survive and remain sane. As I went beyond Ayisha and interviewed other Guyanese, I encountered other examples of great pain (like Lohtan's narrative on the death
of his daughter, which follows Ayisha's text), and of course other examples of
great joy (like the childhood games and pleasures that Mother recounts at
the end of this chapter). But no single person moved or affected me as
deeply as Ayisha, and I share her story in this volume with great feeling.
    The racial/political disturbances of 1962–64 constitute something of a
watershed in Guyanese history—not because, as some might say, they contributed to a change of government in 1964 and the achievement of independence in 1966, but because they represented, for many of us, our first
significant loss of innocence. People who had never done like things before
looted, burned, murdered, harmed, and hated. Others became the victims
of this vindictiveness or transfixed witnesses. There are several descriptions
of these euphemistically named "disturbances" (see Reno 1964; Daly 1966;
Despres 1967; Glasgow 1970; Manley 1979). What still remains to be catalogued are the personal experiences of the thousands of Guyanese who
served as agent, victim, or witness during those terrible times. Some of
these experiences have surfaced more or less fortuitously while linguists

were tape-recording interviewees (A. Persaud 1970; Bickerton 1975). The eyewitness accounts of Ali and Ayisha add to our knowledge of this period; other such accounts will hopefully be gathered in a more systematic way in the future.

Like Ali, Ayisha is an Indo-Guyanese who grew up in Georgetown. She married early, at age fifteen, and moved with her husband to the largely Afro-Guyanese mining town of Mackenzie (later renamed Linden). It was her misfortune to still be there in 1964, when Afro-Guyanese attacked Indo-Guyanese in the area in reprisal for the killing of an Afro-Guyanese couple on the East Coast, Demerara. (See lines 1009–13 below.) Which race actually threw the first stone is virtually impossible to trace in the swirl of events that occurred in this period, and is in any event irrelevant. For Ayisha, who did not have Ali's contacts or his luck, the aftermath was the loss of a husband and two daughters; others had similar personal losses (*dee gat onado leedi laas tuu* 'there's another lady who lost two' 1027). Note how she at first avoids the details (*wel aafto do stoorii don* 'well, after that was finished' 1020), and then decides to backtrack and tell all (*o gun te* 'I will tell' 1028). And note the details about the precise day of the week it was when she got the fateful news that the doctor had given up hope for her daughters and wanted her consent to, euphemistically, 'take them,' and the perhaps unintentional but grim irony of her description of him as a *nais felo* (1043). The closing lines of the text document her struggle afterward to recover from the experience, and the painful memories and flights of imagination that came back to haunt her from time to time.

What the text does not document is the fact that Ayisha continues to undergo other daily sufferings. She is a huckster, like her mother and father before her, who were both from India. She walks the streets daily selling huge laundry baskets, which she buys in Essequibo and transports to Georgetown by boat, taxi, and foot. She makes only a small profit in the process, but every now and again she is the victim of muggers who beat her up and take all her money. Ali and Ayisha may have started life in the same boat, but unlike him, she continues in the working-class status in which she was born, with all its tribulations, and she was in no position to escape the wrath of the mob in the disturbances. In terms of socioeconomic status and family life, he has succeeded, but—to use a Guyanese metaphor—she continues to "suck salt."

Ayisha's text would be worth including in this volume on the basis of its content alone, but it also illustrates some significant features of Guyanese speech. Beginning with lexicon and morphology, we may note that by *miit bak* (1021) she means 'recover,' by *beer cheef* (1038) she means 'endure difficulties' or 'suffering,' by *gaan* (1052) she means 'gone off' ("lose control"), and by *gud saiz gyorl* (1056) she means 'full-grown' (teenagers, like hers).

The use of nominal *laif* as a verb in line 1044 is an example of the multi-functionality for which pidgins and creoles are well known. The form *aaz* in line 1050 is a connective meaning 'as soon as' and in fact represents a reduction of this longer phrase (cf. *asunaz* in line 578 of Granny's Text 12c). The form *mosii* ('must be' 1036) is the usual GC equivalent of the SE modal perfective "must have."

The phrase *goo ohndo Oporeeshon* (1032–33) reveals that "undergo" is perceived not as a unit, as it usually is (synchronically, at least) for SE speakers, but as a combination of free forms that can be permuted. We are reminded by this example of the creole penchant for morphological atomization reflected in such terms as *wantaim*, *wa mek*, and *wisaid* (see the introductions to the texts of Derek, Irene, and Bonnette in Chapter 4), and of the factorization principle that is commonly associated with pidgins but is represented also in creoles: "Express each invariant, separately intuited element of meaning by at least one phonologically separate, invariant stress-bearing form" (Naro 1978: 340).

Note also the use of *se* in line 1045 as a connective roughly equivalent to 'as if' or 'in the sense that,' serving to maintain the euphemism involved in the doctor's use of *teek dem*. By 'taking them' he does not mean savagely slaughtering or killing them; it is medication that will—mercifully, he argues—'take' the suffering children. Related, but commonly used to mock rather than placate, is the use of *se(e)* in expressions like *ii ronin op an dong di rood, se ii eksosaizin* 'He is running up and down the road as if he's exercising.' Here *se* does not necessarily introduce what the person said he was doing (although it might mean this), but can refer instead to what his activity, described in the preceding clause, seems to be "saying." There is a strong element of skepticism in this *se* construction, expressing the speaker's belief that the person under discussion is trying to project a certain image to the world, but is not really committed to or knowledgeable about what he claims to be doing. *Se* facilitates folk-philosophizing about the gap between people's external appearances and their true character.

The preceding uses of *se(e)* should be compared with its use as a sentence complementizer or serial verb, as in Derek's Text 14a, line 687 (see Alleyne 1980: 169–70 and Cassidy and Le Page 1980: 396 for possible West African sources; Bickerton 1981: 105ff for a discussion of its syntactic status). Compare also its use as a hypothetical or conditional marker, as in Text 27b, line 1434 (Chapter 6).[6] Alleyne (1980: 116–19) has demonstrated that the exploration of creole lexical fields can be revealing; the semantic field of *se(e)* seems very rich and should repay further exploration.

A few syntactic features are worth noting. The constructions *di had* (1008) and *dee gat* (1027) are both existentials, following the creole pattern noted earlier of an impersonal subject followed by a verb of possession. The sentence *dee gat onado leedi laas tuu* (1027) contains a relative clause without a subject relative pronoun (see pp. 150 and 176, above for further discussion). The mesolectal construction for pronominal absolutes—pronoun + *oon*—is exemplified by *mii oon* in line 1057; compare basilectal *mii waan* and acrolectal or SE "mine." As noted in the introduction to Granny above, prepositions are frequently absent in locative and temporal expressions where they would be expected in SE (*op Ø bukston* 1009, *Ø di satodee* 1014).

The long complex sentence beginning at line 1038 has embedded complements that begin with *mos* instead of *tu*, recalling a similar example in Derek's Text 9c, line 282: *shi in waan yu mos stodii*. The Derek line was introduced to exemplify the absence of nonfinites in creoles to which Bickerton (1980) first drew our attention. If we accept a similar analysis in this case, we have to provide for the deletion of the subject of the embedded sentences under identity with the objects of their matrix sentences (*nors* 1039; *peerons* 1040 and 1041). But the rule of Equi-Noun Phrase Deletion that provides for this in analyses of SE normally applies only to infinitival complements, which have no auxiliary (Culicover 1976: 217). The fact that Ayisha's embedded complements have auxiliary *mos* like their basilectal equivalents, but no overt subjects like their acrolectal infinitival equivalents, is perhaps representative of their status as a halfway mesolectal point on the road to acquisition of true nonfinites.[7]

Interesting also is the absence of the definite article with *dOkto/dakto* in lines 1030, 1033, and 1037, contrasted with its use elsewhere (e.g. 1028, 1038). This articleless use of the occupational category in indirect reference might represent nothing more than an extension of its similar use in direct address ("Doctor, . . ."). But the phenomenon occurs also in Lohtan's Text 19, below, where the definite article or demonstrative—otherwise used in conjunction with *piknii* (1061, 1105)—is omitted in two climactic pieces of dialogue (1095, 1098). Bearing in mind that zero usually represents non-specifics in the creole article system (Bickerton 1981: 56), the occasional use of articleless nominals by Ayisha and Lohtan might represent a conceptual distancing from the characters in their tragic narratives, a means of deliberately blurring their outlines, so as to somehow make the remembering or the recounting more bearable.

Ayisha appears to be typical of the mesolectal stage described by Bickerton (1975: 104) in which *had* and *wuz/woz* are the only affirmative past forms to have been acquired, apart from *staartid* (p. 108). These are the only forms consistently past-marked in Ayisha's text (*staartid* in three of four occurrences). The other past forms are main verb *bin* (1055) and preverbal *did* (1009), which is an anterior equivalent of basilectal preverbal *bin*. Note also the combination of a past and an irrealis/future form—*wuz in* (< *gun*)—in the apodosis or consequence clause of the counterfactual conditional in line

1057. Basilectal GC uses a similar device—anterior *bin* plus irrealis *gu* or *sa* (see McTurk Text 5b, line 150, in Chapter 3)—whereas SE uses a past form of the future or irrealis form plus the present perfect: "would have." The complexity and impact of this counterfactual conditional (which leaves Ayisha's audience silent for a while) is increased by the fact that adverbial *jos so* is fronted and topicalized with *iz*.

As before, we will restrict our phonological comments to features that are exemplified in particularly clear or interesting ways in this text, or that have been only touched on up to now. Several features of this type are illustrated only once in Ayisha's text, including *h* insertion in initial prevocalic position (*heebl* 1019), which—in this instance as in the earlier *hool aig* examples (349, 498)—seems to represent copying or transfer from an adjacent word beginning with *h*. Other one-time uses are the affrication of word final *z* in *wuj* (1048); the raising of the vowel in *kyer* (1029) from *a* to *e*, which must be ordered after velar palatalization to produce this result; and the reduced vowel of the negative particle in *no, maan* (1037), which is more frequent in phrases like this than when it occurs in isolation (see p. 151, above).

Ayisha alternates between *aa/a* (*aal, badii* 1030) and *oh/O* (*johrjtong* 1014, *Oporeeshon* 1033); but the former are generally not as low or unrounded as they are in truly basilectal speech (cf. Dhanish below) and the latter not as raised and rounded as they are in upper-mesolectal speakers (cf. the radio announcer in Chapter 6), and their classification as one or the other was sometimes not very clear-cut. The pan-creole rule involving the loss of initial voiced stops in tense-aspect markers (Rickford 1980a) is illustrated in *mosØii* (< *mos bii* 1036), *Øin* (< *gon* 1057), and *Øoz* (< *doz* 1021). The last example is interesting, because it sounds almost like a reduced form of "usually," which is quite possible by GC condensation or reduction rules. The form *oz* could also be a reduction of *yuuz tu*, and in this set of possibilities, we see yet another example of how phonological processes contribute to ambiguities about and shifting between the levels of the creole continuum.[8] Both "there" and "here" are frequently realized without final *r*, but the fact that the syllable-final vowel of the former is sometimes lax, whereas the final vowel of the latter is always tense, is a consequence of the relative strength and deletability of the preceding consonant. This point was discussed in some detail in the introduction to Derek's texts in Chapter 4, but it is nicely illustrated in the contrast between almost adjacent *hee* and *de* in line 1049.

One final phonological feature of interest that is not indicated in the transcript (as in most transcription systems) is the dramatic variation in voice quality, tempo, and volume throughout this narrative. For instance, at both points where Ayisha recalls giving her consent to the 'taking' of her daughters—lines 1031 and 1046—she speaks more slowly and softly, with a creaky voice, as if the memory itself were aging and tiring. It is features like this,

springing naturally from personal experience rather than artistically contrived, that allow the listener to share the impact of that experience.

Text 18 is from Tape OA1, tape counter nos. 068–078, 093–115, and
432–45.

18. Her family's death in the 1962–64 disturbances

A: wel it staart—noo, o-hou dis stoorii okor: riimembo di had o—am—	1008
som ool leedii an som ool maan op bokston—aam—did workin	1009
di faarm wen di se indyonz goo n kil dem insai di faarm?	1010
J: oo-oo yes, yes, yes, ye. di ad tuu blak piipl di livin op	1011
dee, no, n di—som chiron de, no?	1012
A: m-hm. an di se tuu indyonz goo op deer an kil dem.	1013
soo dat wuz di torzdi. an di satodee di bOiz dem from johrjtong	1014
gu op wi di b—lanch.	1015
J: di went op tur—am—mokenzii? e-he.	1016
A: mokenzii. an di satodee, orong haaf paas foor di mii deer.	1017
an faiv o klak di staartid—hool dee s—hool nait sa—sadee	1018
nait an sondi. an den di pleen goo n pik op huu heebl. . . .	1019
wel aafto do stoorii don, ai kom owee dis said an ai beg orong n	1020
ting n get o lil help, an o staartid tu work n miit bak. a oz	1021
bai dis baskit an sel. nou yu si o de wi dis baskit work nou.	1022
J: m-hm. bo yu hozbon din get kil, an yu ho—yu tuu	1023
dohtoz di ge kil den, no?	1024
A: noo, mi hozbon tuu. . . .	1025
J: su yuu laas aal chrii wohn dee?	1026
A: ohl chrii wohn dee. dee gat onado leedi laas tu. . . .	1027
di dOkto—aam—o gun te—B si ii wuz tu chra—ii gun	1028
chrai o lat wit dem. ii kyer den—O—di goo chruu tuu Oporeeshon.	1029
bot, dOkto se aal di gots, aal di paart ov di badii damij. . . .	1030
soo di dakto se ii gun tek dem. an ai grii. . . . ai kyaant	1031
waach dem otaal. kaaz dii maarnin, di torzdii maarnin di goo	1032
ohndo Oporeeshon. dOkto—torzii? yes, di torzdii. wel di	1033
fraidii, a din ge tu goo di torzdii—di fraidii maarnin o liiv	1034
orlii n o goo. wen o gu, o si dem. an di staartid tu krai.	1035
wel di nors mosii tel dem.	1036
bot ai tel dem, "no, maan. dakto in gun du yu do." o se,	1037
"ayu gun beer cheef, an ayu gun fiil gud." bot wen di dOkto	1038
tel di nors mos tel di modo or huu evo di p—di oo—di kloosis	1039
peerons o di children mos weet fu wohn o klak vizit,	1040
mos kom n miit im in di aafis, wel aafto n—di nors	1041
tel mi so, a see, "aarit, o gon gu n weet." wel o goo an	1042
weet. wel iiz o v—nais felo. ii kaal mi n ii shoo mi	1043
out n ting. ii se, "noo sens diiz chilren laif. a wudn	1044
teek dem, se, a wud kil dem. a wud giv dem somting tu teek dem,	1045

kaaz diz noo yuus living." an o—a gi ii di konsent. . . .   1046
yu noo, laik o get i shak, an afto o ge dis shak o get   1047
nohrmol bak. o wuj norvii fu kopl wiiks wel. if o wohk from   1048
de tu di kar—from hee tu de, el o gatu, iz laik a sidong   1049
an goowin so—sheekii. aaz o mek so an o luk—luk rong   1050
n ting, aiz riimembo diiz tuu gyorlz in din. laik o imajin dem in   1051
front o mii, an o gaan. . . . luk, dong so gat o chrii, yu noo   1052
wen yu goyin schreet hee to di—wen yu—   1053
    S: kOnvoseeshon chrii.   1054
    A: aiz go de an sidong. op tu jos nou o bin de kraiyin.   1055
laik is—a sii tuu gud saiz gyorl kaalin fu dee mamii. a se,   1056
"ou, if mii oon di livin, iz jos so di wuz in kaal!"   1057

Translation

Well, it started—no, how this story occurred: remember there was a—am—
an old lady and an old man up at Buxton—am—who'd been working on
their farm, and people said that Indians went in and killed them?   1010T
    Oh yes, yes, yes, yeah. There were two black people living up
there, right, and they—some children were there, right?
    Mm-hm. And people said that two Indians went up there and killed them.
So that was the Thursday. And on the Saturday the boys from Georgetown
went up with the b—launch.   1015T
    They went up to—am—McKenzie? Right.
McKenzie. And on the Saturday, around half past four they met there.
And at five o'clock they started—whole day S—whole night Sa—Saturday
night and Sunday. And then the plane went to pick up whoever was able
[to escape]. . . . Well, after that was finished, I came here and begged and 1020T
so on and got a little help, and I started to work and recovered. I
buy and sell these baskets. Now, as you see, I'm with this basket work.
    Mm-hm. But your husband didn't get killed, and your hu—your two
daughters got killed then, right?
    No, my husband too. . . .   1025T
    So you lost all three in one day?
    All three in one day. There's another lady who lost two. . . .
The doctor—am—I will te[ll]—B. [doctor's name] said he was to try—he'd
try a lot with them. He carried them—they went through two operations.
But the doctor said all their guts, every part of their bodies was damaged. . . . 1030T
So the doctor said he would take them. And I agreed. . . . I couldn't
watch them at all. Because the morning, the Thursday morning they under-
went the operation. The doctor—Thursday? Yes, the Thursday. Well, the
Friday, I didn't get to go the Thursday—the Friday morning I left
early and went. When I got there, I saw them. And they started to cry.   1035T
Well, the nurse must have told them [i.e. about the doctor's plans].
But I told them, "No, man. The doctor wouldn't do that to you." I said,
"You'll bear your chafe [pain], and you'll feel better." But when the doctor

told the nurse to tell the mother or whoever is the p—the—the closest
relative of the children that they must wait for a one o'clock visit,   1040T
that they must come and meet him in his office, well after n—the nurse
told me so, I said, "All right, I'll go and wait." Well, I went and
waited. Well he's a v[ery]—nice fellow. He called me in and showed me
out and so on. He said, "It's no sense these children live. I wouldn't
take them by killing them. I'd give them something to take them,   1045T
because it's no use their living." And I—I gave him the consent. . . .
You know, like I got the shock, and after I got this shock I became
normal again. I was nervy for several weeks. If I walked from
there to the car—from here to there—well, I'd have to, like, sit down,
and I'd be going so—shaky. As soon as I make so and look—look around   1050T
and so, I remember these two girls. It's as if I imagine them in
front of me, and I go off. . . . Look, there's a tree down so, you know,
when you're going straight here to the—when you—
    Conversation Tree.
    I usually go there and sit down. Up to just now I was there crying.   1055T
It's as if—I saw two biggish girls calling for their mother. I said,
"Ow, if mine were living, that's just how they would have called!"

19. Lohtan (1975)

A forty-nine-year-old Indo-Guyanese farmer and cattleman from Port
Mourant, Corentyne, when I interviewed him in 1975, Lohtan had had the
opportunity to go no higher than second standard in primary school. He is a
markedly basilectal speaker, as indicated by his use of genderless pronominal
ii and *am* (in reference to his daughter in lines 1061 and 1101) and first-
person plural *awii* (1081); his use of clause-final *don* (1082) and several
varieties of serial-verb construction (directional in line 1100, purposive in
line 1105); his use of continuative *a* (1061) and demonstrative/definite article *(?)a* (<*da* 1059, 1065); and his use of *na/no* as a preverbal-negative
(1087) and emphatic-positive (1099) marker. Some of these features vary
with their mesolectal equivalents (for instance, *komin* instead of *a kom* in line
1080), but this does not detract from our clear impression that we are in the
presence of someone who is competent at the basilectal end of the continuum, someone who, in the words of J. J. Thomas (1869: 105, quoted in
Todd 1974: 88), "is master of, and understands how to manage" the resources of a creole language.

Even more significantly, Lohtan impresses us not only as a competent
basilectal speaker, but as a competent narrator. Against those who suggest
that "linguists do not have the evidence to assert with confidence that speakers of creole languages are not handicapped by their language" (Whinnom

1971: 110), Lohtan establishes his credentials as a thinking, feeling, poetic human being who can exploit the resources of his language to the highest degree in the expression and communication of his experiences and reflections. In order to convey this, I will concentrate in this introduction on the analysis of his text as a narrative.

First, a word about the setting. Lohtan and his wife are sitting on their upstairs veranda, taking turns telling me and two of my University of Guyana students (both of whom grew up in the Port Mourant area and were acquainted with Lohtan) this narrative (and others). Their children are inside the house, working, playing, and talking. In the middle of this narrative (at the ellipses in line 1072), an old woman enters the yard and begins a noisy tirade, claiming that the Lohtans' goat had strayed into her garden and eaten up her green vegetables. Lohtan's wife excuses herself and goes downstairs for a heated, high-pitched argument about whether it was her goat or someone else's that had done the damage. The house itself is virtually emptied as the children stand around downstairs and on the steps as witnesses and contributors to the argument. Lohtan himself remains upstairs with us, listening, occasionally making comments on the incident (including a reminder to one of the students that the old lady is the student's aunt), and resuming his story once the old lady had stormed out of the yard. A little later his breathless wife returns upstairs, and after a few explanatory remarks about the goat incident, continues interweaving her contributions to the story of their daughter's death. (Since she covered a lot of the same ground, except for a few details, like the daughter's request for some of her favorite foods before going to the hospital—a harbinger, in retrospect, that her death was near, only Lohtan's portion of this long narrative is presented here.)

Hymes (1982) has pointed to the significance of three in the structure of Chinook narratives (in the American Northwest). In Lohtan's case two is the significant structural number. There are two main scenes: the hospital, at night, and Lohtan's home, early the next morning. There are two primary characters in each scene: the watchman and Baka in the first, Lohtan's wife and his neighbors (as an undifferentiated group) in the second. Baka also figures in the other scene, but he serves primarily as a pivotal connection between the two episodes, providing the complication that allows the second scene to unfold. Two households are juxtaposed in this narrative, each with activities that keep them busy at a time when most people are sleeping, but of a very different sort: against the unfolding of the death news in Lohtan's home, the hysterical reaction of his wife and their hasty preparations for burial, are juxtaposed the wedding eve festivities in the neighbor's home, which rocks with loud music and merriment.

Even more pervasive is the repetition of propositions in pairs throughout the narrative.[9] Sometimes this involves a slightly different rephrasing: *mi hool ii yam, mi fiil o ii aan stee* (1062) and *mi de de til nain a klak a nait. . . . til nain a klak a nait mi de de* (1067–68). In other cases the exact wording is repeated: *gaan bak kwik* (1087, 1088). The overall effect is to slow down the pace of the narrative, to let the individual events sink into consciousness slowly and in elaborate detail, as they have a way of doing when tragedy is unfolding.[10] At some critical points—like the moment just before Lohtan gets the news from Baka and the moment when his wife reacts—the repetition is in threes (the mouth-washing in lines 1079–82, the wife's shouting, and the references to *piknii ded* in 1092–98), slowing us down even more. (Recall how Ayisha fusses about the details of whether it was Thursday or Friday morning that she got her fateful news, in lines 1032–34, above.) All of this is in contrast to lines 1100–1102, where the repetition is arrested, and contrary devices—like the piling up of predicates in the serial-verb construction and the omission of subject pronouns—are used to convey the speed with which arrangements for the burial were made and executed.

Lohtan is a consummate verbal craftsman, selecting just the right points of detail for elaboration. For instance, in lines 1062–65 the details about *shub*ing his hand underneath the child's *batii* and feeling *ʔa pii hat laka faiya* highlight his relationship to the subject of his narrative as parent to child, privileged and unhesitant to interact with her in this intimate, private way. The heat of the pee is both physical (the result of her raging fever) and metaphorical (symbol of her life, her last struggle, in Dylan Thomas's words, to "not go gentle into that still night/Rage, rage against the dying of the light"). By contrast, details are omitted, just as effectively, in line 1098, where the neighbors are told simply, *piknii ded*, and their reaction is conveyed, not in long expressions of sympathy, but in the bald statement, *wel di myuuzik stap*.

This is, in fact, the theme of the story: cooperation and mutual consideration among neighbors and human beings. Despite the argument that Lohtan and his wife have with their neighbor about straying goats (inserted as a counterpoint in the middle of this story by some sort of divine ordination), the fundamental principle illustrated in this narrative is the importance of interpersonal cooperation and consideration: the watchman allows Lohtan to go in, although it is apparently after visiting hours; Baka agrees to come and tell Lohtan about his daughter if and when anything further develops; the neighbors halt their music as soon as they get the news of the girl's death (note how the cessation of the music is emphasized in line 1106 by fronting and topicalizating *noo myuuzik*); and Lohtan, in return, hurries to bury his daughter and not 'humbug the wedding' next door.

The proliferation of *yu noos* and *yu onstan*s in the last seven lines of the narrative represent direct, insistent appeals to the listeners to understand why the narrator acted as he did in real life (burying the child within seven hours of receiving the news of her death) and to grasp the larger thematic significance of the narrative. He succeeds in this attempt, I think, just as he succeeds in conveying the texture and feel of the very personal experience that he underwent. Contrary to what Whinnom fears, this ordinary farmer and cattle-breeder, far from evidencing any intellectual handicap from his language, shows a clear capacity to harness it for effective rhetoric and poetics.

Finally, a few phonological notes. Lohtan's text exemplifies the markedly basilectal use of (ʔ)a as a definite article or demonstrative adjective. According to Hancock (n.d.a), this is a feature of "archaic Guyanese," found also in the anglophone Creoles of Suriname. In this volume it occurs otherwise only in the texts of Derek (9b, line 264) and Dhanish (20, line 1144). In every case it occurs with secondary or primary stress, unlike the deletion of initial voiced stops in tense-aspect auxiliaries, which is more frequent in unstressed syllables. The occurrence of one instance of *do* (1083) and several of *ʔa* (1059) suggests that this form derives from *da(t)* 'that,' synchronically if not diachronically. Note one occurrence of *is* (1067) for the corresponding proximal demonstrative, 'this.' These examples show the need for an adequate understanding of the phonetics and phonology of Guyanese speech for syntactic and semantic analysis, a point reinforced by the occasional operation, in Lohtan's speech, of a rule palatalizing voiceless alveolar sibilants. The evidence of *shi* for 'see' in line 1061 leads us to consider the form *sho* in line 1071 a possible instance of the rare basilectal irrealis marker *sa*, although its interpretation as a reduction of *shud* 'should' is also possible.

Forms like *o* (< *hou* 1062) and *bo* (< *bout* 1072) reveal that condensation of dipthongal *ou* usually involves loss of the second or unstressed segment, whereas forms like *aarit* (< *aarait* 1070) reveal that in the case of *ai* it is the first, stressed segment that is lost. There are a few instances of the voicing of intervocalic voiceless stops, as in *gid op* (1078) and *bigaa* (1087), and of the realization of *w* as *b* (*abi* 1073) or Ø (*el* 1068). Vowels are often elided in the course of morphophonemic condensation, as in *ma* (< *mii a* 1070) and *lagoo* (< *le(t) awii goo* 1090). In this category we might include the variation between *a* and *aa*, evidenced by *pas* vs. *paas* (1058, 1072), *baka* vs. *baaka* (1069, 1077), and *an* vs. *aan* (1063, 1062). One relatively rare feature that is largely restricted to basilectal speech (unlike vowel-laxing) is vowel-tensing, as in *iif* ('if' 1070).

Text 19 is from Tape PM4, tape counter nos. 351–64 and 428–65.

19. The death of his daughter

L: mi goo bot—aa pas eet. yu noo, mi wachman am	1058
aspital. wel mi aaks o—ʔaʔ—ʔaʔ—ʔa geetmaan, se,	1059
"le mi goo in lil bit, no maan?" wel ii lou mi fu goo	1060

in. wel wen mi gu mi shi di—di piknii a sliip, ii shot   1061
ii ai. wel mi hool ii yam, mi fiil o ii aan stee,   1062
yu noo—if ii a biit. . . . seem taim mi o—mi o sh—mi o shub mi an   1063
andaniit dii batii, yu noo? wel shi pii seem taim.
ʔa pii hat laka faiya, maan. a yuurin hat laka faiya. mi   1064
sta—mi ge—mi a taak in mi hoon main see,   1065
"is piknii gu ded." mi de de til nain a klak a nait. . . .   1066
til nain a klak a nait mi de de. el, notn na   1067
rang. el, wan chap neem baka, wel hii granpiknii bin aspital   1068
tu. su mi tel ii se, "aarit, ma gu oom. an, iif yu   1069
de li bit moo leet an if eniting rang yu sho kom tel   1070
mi." yu noo? wel mii mos lef bo aaf paas nain an ting. . . .   1071
el abii neebo marid di nait. yu no onstan,   1072
di bin marid di—am—di in pleeyin myuuzik a di nait.   1073
    J: di seem nait do di chail ded?   1074
    L: ye-e. di seem nait chail ded. wel, mi tel di—am—mi   1075
fren baakaa, see, wen ii kom maanin taim, if eniiting otaal   1076
ii mos ron kom tel mii. wel mii gid op bout—   1077
tuu o klak a maanin. mi wash mi mout an ting . . . an mi—de   1078
pon wash mi mout. wel mi sii wan lait komin bai—   1079
bai awii schriit. wen di lait komin nou, mi wash mi   1080
mout don. wel a chap kom. . . . mi se, "ʔa piknii ded." chap   1081
kom, ii tel mi se—am—"do piknii ded, bai. ton, mi   1082
si di piknii ded." wel, mii na taak notn. di mischris   1083
a kuk a kichin. dem a kuk.   1084
    J: ii na heer yet?   1085
    L: no, ii no hee, bigaa gu—gaan bak kwik. mi   1086
no mek ii sii yam. ii . . . gaan bak kwik. wel mi   1087
wash mi mout an ting kli—don. el mi kom iizii,   1088
mi tel am se, "yu noo apm? lagoo sii a piknii. . . .   1089
oniihou mi biliiv si di piknii ded." yu eer? . . . ʔel—ʔe—ʔel—   1090
ʔel—ʔel, shii tel mii see ii sii wan lait kom. sii won lait   1091
kom antil wen ii ton bak. ii se ii sii dii   1092
lait. se, "piknii ded fi chruu." ii jom rait   1093
owee, e, "piknii ded fi chruu!" wel ii staatu halo—   1094
shout n ting. el ii staatu shout, an wel—aal di pii—   1095
wel di myuuzik stap rait owee. dem se, "wo hapm?"   1096
el—aal—mi tel am se, "piknii ded." wel di myuuzik   1097
stap. wel di bai no ga fi marid maaning taim?   1098
goo an ori bring di piknii kom. aada kaafn n   1099
ting, faas, yu noo, n wii berin am jes nain o klak,   1100
bikaz di piipl ge weding, yu onstan? yu noo, az di   1101
piknii ded, wi kyaan ombog di wedin, yu   1102
onstan? an aal abi liv neebo, yu onstan? su—   1103
mi see, "di piknii ded aredii. le wi kyar bering   1104
am." bo di piipl dem—noo myuuzik dee na plee no moo. dem   1105
stap, yu noo?   1106
                                                                          1107

Translation

I went at about half past eight. You know, I was watching over her at
the hospital. Well, I asked that—that—that—that gateman, I said,
"Let me go in for a little while, please." Well, he allowed me to go   1060T
in. Well, when I went I saw that the—the child was sleeping, she'd shut
her eyes. Well, I held her arm, I held her hand to see how it felt,
you know—if it was beating. . . . At the same time I—I—I shoved my hand
underneath her behind, you know? Well, she peed at that very moment.
That pee was hot like fire, man. That urine was hot like fire. I   1065T
sta—I got—I kept thinking to myself [talking in my own mind],
"This child will die." I stayed there until nine o'clock at night. . . .
Until nine o'clock at night I stayed there. Well, nothing went
wrong. Well, a chap named Baka, well, his granddaughter was in hospital
too. So I told him, "All right, I'm going home. And if you're   1070T
here a little longer and anything goes wrong, you must come and tell
me." You know? Well, I must have left about half past nine or so. . . .
Well, our neighbor got married the [same] night. You understand,
they were married the—am—they were playing music that night.
      The same night that the child died?   1075T
      Yeah. The same night that the child died. Well, I'd told the—am—my
friend Baka that when morning came, if anything at all [was wrong],
he must come and tell me. Well, I got up at about—
two o'clock in the morning. I rinsed my mouth and so on . . . and I—was
in the process of rinsing my mouth. Well, I saw a light coming up—   1080T
up our street. As the light was coming now, I finished washing my
mouth. Well, the guy came. . . . I said, "The child is dead." The guy
came and told me—am—"The child is dead, boy. [When I] turned, I
saw the child was dead." Well, I didn't say anything. The wife
was cooking in the kitchen. They were cooking.   1085T
      She hadn't heard yet?
      No, she hadn't heard, because—go—he'd gone back quickly. I
didn't make her see him. He . . . went back quickly. Well, I
finished washing out my mouth and so on, clean. Well, I came in quietly,
I said to her, "You know what? Let's go and see that child. . . .   1090T
Anyhow, I believe the child is dead." You hear? . . . Well—wel—wel—
well—well, she told me that she'd seen a light coming. Seen the light
come and seen it turn back. She said that she'd seen the
light. She said, "The child is dead—for real!" She took off right
away, shouting, "The child is dead—for real!" Well, she started to holler—   1095T
shout and carry on. Well, she started to shout, and well—all the pe[ople]—
well, the music stopped right away. They said, "What happened?"
Well—all—I told them, "The child is dead." Well, the music
stopped. Well, the boy still had to get married in the morning.
We hurried and brought the child home. Ordered a coffin and   1100T
so on fast, you know. And we buried her at nine o'clock,

because the people had a wedding, you understand? You know, as the
child was [already] dead, we shouldn't humbug [spoil] the wedding, you
understand? I mean, we all lived as neighbors, you understand? So—
I said, "The child is dead already. Let's carry her and bury
her." But the people—no music did they play anymore. They
stopped, you know?

1105T

20. Dhanish (1976)

Seventy years old when I interviewed her, Dhanish is a retired cane-cutter.
Her mother had also been employed as a laborer in the cane fields, and her
father, who came from India, was probably a sugar-estate laborer too. Born
at No. 16 Village, just a few miles away from Bush Lot, Dhanish had lived in
Bush Lot since the early 1940's. She was one of the members of Arnold Persaud's (1970) Bush Lot sample, and it was through his courtesy that both
Bickerton and I were able to reinterview her subsequently (Bickerton in
1970 or thereabouts).

Dhanish is perhaps the most distinctly basilectal speaker in this volume.
Not only does she regularly employ the four tense-aspect markers (*don, bina,
bin*, and *a*) that Bickerton (1975: 27) treats as the criteria for identifying
basilectal, or most markedly creole, speakers, but she also consistently employs the basilectal variants in other grammatical subsystems. For instance,
her personal pronouns correspond to the classic basilectal system: *mi(i)* as
first-person-singular subject and possessive (1108–9); *ii* and *am* as genderless third-person nonobject and object forms, respectively (1109, 1119,
1153); undifferentiated *awii* as first-person plural (1142), *ayu* as second-
person plural (1135), and *dem* as third-person plural (1122). It should be
noted that the occasional occurrences of third-person plural *de(e)* (as in
1149) all occur before *na*, and in fact represent part of a more general
basilectal rule in which the final *m* of *dem* is assimilated and lost before a
following *n*.[11] This in turn is part of an even more general rule in which final
nasals are subject to assimilation to the place of articulation of the following
consonant, and subsequent loss by simplification of geminates (Rickford
1980a). Where the pronominal vowel is *ee* (as in *dee* 1144), this probably represents the subsequent application of a tensing/raising rule that produces (in
this case but not always) a form closer to the acrolect.

What is refreshing about Dhanish's text is that it exemplifies several
basilectal features that we have not yet discussed. For example, this text provides evidence that numeric plurals can take the form pronoun + numeral in
GC (*awii trii* 1146) and are in this respect more versatile than SE, which
normally employs the form numeral + "of" + pronoun, as in "(the) three of

us." Dhanish also uses *eniiting* in line 1117, where we would expect "something" in SE, the form of the quantifier when it is not in the scope of a negative (e.g. "She bought something" vs. "She didn't buy anything"). The explanation for this usage may have to do with the fact that creole negative-concord rules yield *notn* ('nothing') as the form of the quantifier in the scope of a negative, instead of *eniiting* ('anything'). As a result, the latter form is deprived of its SE function and becomes eligible for positive uses, as in line 1117. Irene's *yu na noo eniibadii kyan kom kom nak yu dong de* (Text 10d, 386) is similar.[12] While we are on the subject of negatives, note that Dhanish's use of *noo* for the isolated negative particle uttered in response to a question (1134), but *na/no* for preverbal negation (1134, 1149), reinforces the observations that were made in the introduction to Reefer's texts about the present-day functional distribution of these two forms.

Note also the impersonal construction involving *don* in line 1114: *ii don bot wan mont an ting*. This may be derived from *wan mont an ting don* by a rule of subject-to-object-raising similar to the insertion of the impersonal "there" in SE. The latter rule derives "There arose a storm" from "A storm arose" (Culicover 1976: 224–25). Since *ii* is a common creole equivalent of SE impersonal "there," it is relatively easy to analyze the creole transformation as similar, with the appropriate lexical substitution:

$$X \quad \text{noun phrase} \quad \text{verb} \quad Y \quad \Rightarrow$$
$$X \quad ii \quad \text{verb} \quad \text{noun phrase} \quad Y.$$

However, more work remains to be done on the class of verbs that can undergo subject-to-object-raising of this type in GC, and the exact nature of the structural change. For one thing, sentences with nondefinite noun phrase subjects followed by *be* commonly undergo "there"- insertion in English: "Water is on the ground" ⇒ "There is water on the ground." But in the equivalent GC structures the locative copula *de* is replaced by *gat* in the course of raising: *waata de pon di grong* ⇒ *ii gat waata pon di grong*. Another consideration is that GC sentences with impersonal *ii gat*, *dee gat*, or *di had* often seem to involve the grafting of the impersonal construction onto the front of another sentence with neither movement nor replacement of the sentence's main verb, as in Ayisha's *dee gat onado leedi laas tuu* (Text 18, 1027) and Sheik's *di had bogii yustu teek piipl dong ongtong* (Text 14a, 725–26, Chapter 4). In all of these cases the impersonal construction serves to focus the underlying subject of the embedded sentence (*onado leedi*, *bogii*), and in this respect it is similar to clefting and topicalization with *a* or *iz*.[13]

As noted in the introduction to Derek's texts, Dhanish's text contains two apparent exceptions to Bickerton's (1975: 30–33) claim that nonpunctual aspect markers do not occur in temporal clauses, for the two *wen* clauses in lines 1127 and 1152 both contain continuative *a*. But two qualifying remarks need to be made about these apparent exceptions. One is that they are continuative and not habitual aspect markers, providing little support for Walter Edwards's (1983) claim that habitual-aspect markers—in particular, *doz*—can occur in temporal clauses. Second, these *wen* clauses do not have the sense of "whenever," "on any occasion on which," that Bickerton specifies as necessary for the deletion or nongeneration of the aspect marker; instead, they are equivalent to "while," describing processes in progress when the event in the main clause takes place. In this sense they are like the *wail* clause in line 1117 (which also contains *a*) and unsatisfactory as counterexamples to Bickerton's claim. However, the passive in the sentence *mi heer wan big naiz a mek* (1123) is a clear counterexample to Bickerton's claim that nonpunctual aspect markers like *a* and *doz* are deleted in creole passives, and on the basis of this and other examples like it, Bickerton has agreed in a personal communication that his claim on this point was overstated.

Dhanish's text also includes an example of locative *dee* + continuative *a* in the sentence *dem stil dee a daab* (1122), which is comparable to Lohtan's *mi—de pon wash mi mout* (1079–80). In both cases, whether *de(e)* is combined with prepositional *pon* or continuative *a*, the effect is to add duration to the continuative or progressive action referred to in the main verb, to represent it as ongoing over an extended period of time. Both examples testify to the close relationship between locatives and progressives (a point raised in the introduction to Sheik's texts, Text set 14, Chapter 4).

Lohtan's example, in fact, recalls the Middle English progressive construction with "on" + verb "-ing": "King Henrie the eight with all his Lordes *on hunting* in his forrest at Windsore" (Nashe 1958, 2: 258, l. 23). Traugott (1972: 143), from whose work the Nashe quotation is taken, has followed Jespersen (1933: 53) in suggesting that the reduction of prepositional "on" to schwa gave rise to *a*-prefixed gerundials ("A-hunting we will go") in the history of English, and may have contributed to the more general development of English progressive "-ing." The phenomenon of *a*-prefixing in Appalachian English and other English dialects, as in "he come a-runnin' out there," is usually seen as a development from earlier "on" + verb "-ing" too (Jespersen ibid.; Krapp 1925: 268; Wolfram and Christian 1975: 99, from whom the preceding example is taken). Note that in pointing to these examples in other dialects, I am merely emphasizing the relationship between locatives and continuatives that is independently exemplified in Lohtan's and Dhanish's texts. *A*-prefixing of the type just discussed does not occur in GC, even though one might expect it as a possible intermediate stage in the transition from basilectal *a* verb (*bil a ron*) to mesolectal verb + *in* (*bil ronin*). Mufwene (1982) has suggested, however, that New World slaves might have been exposed to, and learned, the English *a*-prefixing construction; he also argues that the prepositional and verbal uses of *a* are identical in GC and JC, representing one "spatio-temporal" morpheme.

One final point about preverbal *a* in Dhanish's text. In at least one occurrence (1155) it has a more plausible punctual than nonpunctual interpretation. It is true that the laughter referred to in line 1155 might have been continuous, but the starting itself could only have been punctual, suggesting that *a* sometimes functions as a simple past-marker. Careful scrutiny of other examples should help to shed further light on this issue, and reveal the relation of this use of *a* to its more conventional nonpunctual aspectual function.

There are many other points of interest in Dhanish's text, but for the sake of brevity I will restrict myself to some lexical and phonological observations. The reduplication of *fos* in line 1142 and *bihin* in line 1143 serves the function not only of indicating the order in which Dhanish and her daughters mounted the stairs, but of simulating the sound of their alternate footsteps. In another section of her recorded interview, Dhanish was equally creative in her use of reduplication, saying *mii duu kain kain wok* to suggest that she did all kinds of work (= 'work of this kind, that kind, the other kind'). The expressions *a tap* and *a batam* (1123, 1124) are classic creole prepositional phrases for 'above' (or "upstairs" in this case) and 'below' (or "downstairs"). The form *duu* in line 1110 is an emphatic discourse marker, which I translate as "please." The form *le(t)* in the same line functions as a conjunction/complementizer, parallel to the form *mek* discussed earlier (p. 158); and *an ting* (1109) may be regarded as a postverbal equivalent of the postnominal comitative or associative pluralizer *(an) dem* (as in *jaan dem*). The *noun phrase (an) dem* construction signifies "the specific entity (usually a person) referred to in association with unspecified others" (Rickford 1985b: 46), whereas the *verb phrase an ting* construction signifies a specific action or process together with unspecified others. The form *betii* (1155) is a Bhojpuri/Hindi kinship term, generalized in Guyana to refer to all female relatives of a younger generation than one's own, including daughters, nieces, granddaughters, and daughters-in-law (Rampaul 1978: 144–45). Possibly also of Indic origin are *baab* (1134) and *khaj* (1153).

Phonologically, Dhanish's text is valuable for its evidence of the assimilation and deletion of initial *d* in the demonstratives *da* and *dis*. Full forms of these occur in lines 1150 and 1151, an example of *da* with the *d* assimilated to a preceding nasal (*na*) occurs in line 1108, and examples of *dis* with the *d* completely deleted (*is*) occur in line 1144 and elsewhere. Line 1140 indicates that the deletion can also extend—in Dhanish's speech at least—to the comparative conjunction *dan*. The raising of *e* to *i* is exemplified in several words, including *til* (1128) and *yit* (1122), and we need to recall the creole rules for the reduction of dipthongs (discussed in the introduction to Ayisha's text, 18) to interpret *ot* as 'out' (1152) and *deetim* as 'daytime' (1130). The realization of underlying *v* as *b*—attested in Irene's texts and in some of the eighteenth- and nineteenth-century texts—is attested below in *kubr/koba* ('cover' 1119). One respect in which Dhanish differs from other GC speakers in this volume, however, is in her tendency to produce *tr* sequences without affrication (*chr* is the more common GC pronunciation). The *r* in this and other postconsonantal occurrences is sometimes trilled; this is sometimes the case with older Indian speakers and, like the non-affrication of *tr* sequences, may represent Bhojpuri influence.

Text 20 is from Tape BL2, tape counter nos. 006–038.

20. A hassar jumbie story

D: wel, wen dis ool maan, mi ool maan ded—wel wen na ool maan	1108
deed an ii a gu fi beriyin an ting, mii taak se, "ool maan,	1109
duu, yu mosn kom fraikin awii, le awii sii yuu. wen awii	1110
gu sii yu, awii gu fraikin. yu ken kom, bikaaz dis a yu hous,	1111
bot awi mosn si yu." wel, so, a trii dee wuk	1112
don, ten dee wok don, totiin dee wok don.	1113
wel, ii don bot wan mont an ting. wel, waan dee, mii tuu	1114
gyal dem a daab batm hous.	1115
an mii goo a shap. mi se mi a gu gu—bai lil bit	1116
eniiting a shap. bot wail mi a gu, mii sii wan leedi a	1117
sel hasa, an mi bai dis hasa, an, mi put am	1118
pon wan bukit. an mi tek wan beesn an mi kubr am, mi koba—a	1119
hasa. an mi gu wee a shap. wel mi bai	1120
an ting an kom, soo kwik, dem piknii na	1121
don daab yit. dem stil dee a daab. soo dem see—em—	1122
mii—mii kom a tap. mi heer wan big naiz a mek. dem tuu gyal	1123
a daab batam ous a batam. an mii heer won	1124
big naiz mek. mi taak, "ʔeʔ—eʔ—eʔ!" mi gu, mi put	1125
mi paasl. mi taak—mi na taak notn. mi put mi paasl	1126
wo mii gu bai. wen mi a kom bak a kichin,	1127
dis naiz meek ageen. mi se, "au, ool maan, mii na bina til yu,	1128
see yu mosn kom, see—em—awii gu fraikin, an	1129
luk hou hai hi deetim yu a fraikin mi. da	1130
na rait, yu no." an mi kom dong a batam.	1131
su den gyal a taak se, "maa, yu goo a tap, yu iit brekfos?"	1132
se, "yu kyaan iit brekfos su kwik yit!"	1133
mi se, "noo, baab. mi no iit brekfus." se, "mii kom se,	1134
'le mii help ayu—daab!'" bot dis taim mi fraikin. mii taak se	1135
"le mii help ayu daab, den aal awii gu goo	1136
wan taim." su mi help dem daab an ting, an aal—aal	1137
awii wash awii han an fut an ting an awii goo op a tap. bo	1138
mii na tel dem, bikaaz dem gu fraikin	1139
moo an mii!	1140
J: moo dan yuu, m-hm.	1141

D: wel awii goo a tap. ho—ou! dem piknii dee fos fos, mii   1142
de bihin bihin. bot dee na noo wo hapn. wel, dem tuu,   1143
dem heer is naiz. a hasa a jom pon a bokit! dee   1144
na taak notn. bot mi a taak pon mi main. mi si no—se,   1145
"ou ool maan, aal awii trii kom op a tap an if yu gu   1146
duu da, dem piknii gu fraikin, den   1147
trobl pan mii. bika aal gu faal pon mii! de na gu—   1148
den gu fraikin, de na gu waan duu dis wuk, de na gu   1149
waan duu da wuk, an awii na ge noobadii fi duu   1150
wok." dis bai bina lil.   1151
wel, wen dem a tek ot brekfos, agin dis naiz mek.   1152
bo mii na taak. den ii se, "maa"—see—"khaj"—   1153
see—em—"di hasa dis a jom pon a bukit!"   1154
an mii a staat laaf. mi se, "truu, betii! oo mi   1155
gaad, a hasa a jom!" bot mii na taak   1156
wa hapn.   1157

Translation

Well, when this old man, my old man died—well, when that old man
died and he was going to be buried and so on, I said, "Old man,
please, you mustn't come and frighten us, or let us see you. When we   1110T
see you, we'll be frightened. You can come, because this is your house,
but we mustn't see you." Well, the three-day post-burial formalities
were completed, the ten-day formalities, the thirteen-day formalities.
Well, about a month had gone by. Well, one day, my two
daughters were daubing [with mud and cow dung] the yard under the house. 1115T
And I went to the shop. I said I was going to—buy a little
something from the shop. But while I was going, I saw a lady
selling hassar [fish], and I bought this hassar, and I put it
in a bucket. And I took a basin and covered it, I covered—that
hassar. And I went away to the shop. Well, I bought [the things]   1120T
and so on and came back so quickly that the children hadn't
finished daubing yet. They were still daubing. So they said—em—
I—I came upstairs. [Laughs.] I heard a big noise! Those two girls
were downstairs daubing the yard under the house. And I heard a
big noise! I said to myself, "Eh—eh—eh!" I went and put down   1125T
my parcel. I said—I didn't say anything. I put down the parcel
that I'd gone to buy. As I was coming back into the kitchen,
I heard this noise again. I said, "Ow, old man, didn't I tell you
that you mustn't come, that—am—we would be frightened, and [yet]
look how in the broad daylight you're here scaring me! That   1130T
isn't right, you know." And I came downstairs.
So the girls said, "Ma, you went upstairs, did you eat breakfast?"
They said, "You couldn't have eaten breakfast so quickly!"

I said, "No, dears. I haven't eaten breakfast." I said, "I came to
say, 'Let me help you—daub!'" But actually I was afraid. I said,   1135T
"Let me help you daub, then all of us will go [to eat breakfast]
at the same time." So I helped them daub and so on, and all—all
of us washed our hands and feet and so on, and we went upstairs. But
I didn't tell them [what had happened] because they would be more frightened
than me!
    More than you, mm-hm.   1140T
    Well, we went upstairs. Ow! The children went in front, I
went behind. But they didn't know what had happened. Well, they
heard this noise too. That hassar was jumping in the bucket! They
didn't say anything. But I was thinking to myself. I said no—said,
"Ow, old man, all three of us have come upstairs and if you're going   1145T
to do that, the children will be scared, and then I'll really be in
trouble. Because everything will fall on me! They won't—
they'll be scared, they won't want to do this chore, they won't
want to do that chore, and we don't have anybody else to do
the work." This boy was small.   1150T
Well, while they were putting out breakfast, we heard this noise again.
But I didn't say anything. Then she said, "Ma"—she said—"Ah"—she
said—am—"The hassar is jumping in that bucket!"
And I started to laugh. I said, "That's true, my daughter. Oh my   1155T
God, that hassar is really jumping!" But I didn't say
what had happened.

21. Anna (1974)

As the first spoken texts from an Afro-Guyanese speaker in this volume,
Anna's two selections allow us to begin considering the issue of ethnic differences within the Guyanese Creole continuum. Thirty-six years old when
this recording was made, Anna was born and raised in historic Buxton village, East Coast, Demerara, about ten miles outside the capital city of
Georgetown. Buxton, originally a cotton plantation named Orange Nassau,
was one of the first plantations to be bought by former slaves after emancipation, being purchased just two years later, in 1840, for the sum of 11,000
pounds sterling by a group of 128 of them. Ever since, the village has been
associated with fearless political activism, including a nineteenth-century
incident in which Buxtonians stopped the governor's train to protest property taxes (Abrams 1970: 120). The village has also been associated with the
maintenance of distinctive Afro-Guyanese cultural traditions, and has produced generations of schoolteachers, orators, politicians, and others who
have distinguished themselves in their respective fields.[14] When Anna says

in lines 1163–64, *mii kom out from boksn, rait? mii a taak di chruut*, it is the integrity and reputation of her native village that she is appealing to as authority for her claims.

Anna is a popular huckster of fruits and vegetables in one of the open-air markets in Georgetown, and the recording from which these extracts were taken was part of a series of interviews I did with various hucksters for a newspaper feature story on market conditions. These interviews were done in front of the hucksters' stands, usually with a small crowd of other hucksters, customers, and passersby looking on, interjecting their own comments, laughing and providing appropriate audience reaction throughout. It was a perfect setting for public oratory and dramatic performance, and Anna's performance was among the best. One would need a videotape to appreciate the full range of the skills that Anna displayed on this occasion, but her texts will have to suffice. Among her dramatizing strategies, note the effective repetition of short sentences that state and restate the bald truth (*ting baad, notn na a sel*), the use of juncture and stress to emphasize particular words (*luk, yuu doon aaks mii notn!*), and the constant use of the discourse marker *rait?* to maintain contact with the assembled crowd of listeners and onlookers. The microphone she was wearing did not inhibit or impede her at all. She gestured and moved about vigorously in the stall that constituted her stage, even lying down on the counter at one point and closing her eyes to demonstrate how the hucksters sometimes slept in their stalls overnight to prevent their produce from being stolen.

Linguistically, one is perhaps struck first of all by the presence in Anna's texts of such basilectal creole features as negative *na* (1179), continuative *a* (1163), pronominal *mi(i)* as first-person subject and possessive (1164, 1189), unmarked noun plurals (1191), and zero copulas (1158). We have of course encountered such features repeatedly in the spoken texts above, but Bickerton's (1973a) discussion of the relationship between ethnicity and language use in Guyana would not have led us to expect such basilectal features from a modern-day Afro-Guyanese.[15] It is true that Anna spends her days among Indo-Guyanese hucksters, many of whom are basilectal speakers. But her home and her network of family and friends are in Afro-Guyanese Buxton, and it is not necessary to appeal to Indo-Guyanese contacts to account for basilectal features in her speech, as the evidence of Devonish (1978) and W. Edwards (1983) from other nearby Afro-Guyanese villages has shown.[16]

Although it is clear that Anna is capable of dropping below the mesolectal floor that Bickerton (1973a: 656–67) establishes as a baseline for Afro-Guyanese speakers, what she displays in these extracts is not pure basilect, but variation between basilectal and nonbasilectal forms, the proportions varying from one feature to the next, as the following data show:

Plural suffix (n = 23)		Negators (n = 15)		1st-person subject pronoun (n = 16)	
∅	-s	na	in/en	mi(i)	ai
91%	09%	33%	67%	38%	62%

In the case of the plural suffix, Anna is almost categorically basilectal, avoiding the SE suffix in all but two cases.[17] In the case of the negators, mesolectal *in/en* seems to be her primary form, but the five cases in which she uses basilectal *na* are interesting: all but one of them precede the basilectal continuative marker *a*, representing extremely close covariation if not co-occurrence (Labov 1971a: 462). Note, incidentally, that *a* is not automatically assimilated to the final vowel of *na* as Bickerton (1975: 29) predicts; such assimilation or coalescence does occur sometimes with other speakers, but it is not obligatory. (Compare Cooper 1980: 46.)

In the case of the first-person subject pronoun, pooling statistics across the two texts is quite misleading, because *mi(i)* is used categorically in the first text (five occurrences of *mi(i)*, none of *ai*), but only once in 11 occurrences in the second. No environmental or stylistic constraints on this variation are immediately obvious. Anna appears to be as involved and excited in Text 21a as she is in 21b, and since the second text is farther into the interview we might have expected it to have more informal speech and a higher incidence of Creole variants. It may be, of course, that Anna used a higher incidence of basilectal forms right at the beginning of her interview because she was trying to validate her status as one of the hucksters and an appropriate spokeswoman of their cause, and this became less necessary as the interview wore on. A detailed analysis of the entire interview might shed further light on this issue. Other mesolectal features in Text 21b are the use of *(h)ii* instead of basilectal *am* for the two occurrences of the third-person-masculine object pronoun (1199, 1200), and the use of *yuu oon* rather than basilectal *yuu waan* for the absolute pronoun in line 1203.

Anna's variation in the choice of copula forms is equally interesting, but it is important to keep the different following environments separate, and we will also ignore the negative cases, which would force us to reconsider *in/en* and *na*. Following locatives are generally marked with the basilectal creole form *de(e)* (1184, 1190), although there is none in the complex sentence in 1167–68. The 11 cases before an adjective all have basilectal zero (1158 and elsewhere). The five cases before verb + "-ing" (1165) are also instances of zero copula or auxiliary, but zero in this case is the mesolectal variant, the basilectal equivalent being *a* + verb (Bickerton 1973a), as used in line 1163. Finally, of the six cases before a noun phrase, one has zero (1202), but the other five all contain either *iz* or *wuz* (three cases in 1189, one each in 1190 and 1203). These are the only cases of the acrolectal or SE copula in the text, and significantly enough, they occur in the very position—before noun phrases—where inflected "be" is retained most often in VBE, JC, and Gullah (Labov 1969: 735–36; Stewart 1969: 243–44; Bickerton 1971: 491; Holm 1984: 291–92). Note that I have counted as cases of prenominal *iz* the topicalizing instances of this form in lines 1190 and 1203. Not included in the count, but worthy of separate mention, is the absence of the "be" copula in clause-final or exposed position in line 1194, after *aal di puliis seyin*. This is one of the cases where SE cannot contract "is," and where, following Labov (1969), we would not expect VBE or other nonstandard English dialects to be able to delete either. If VBE indeed has a creole history, as seems likely (Stewart 1968; Dillard 1972; Rickford 1977a; Baugh 1983; Holm 1984), it might have passed through a stage in which zero copulas as radical as this one were permitted.

Two tense-aspect markers are absent from Anna's texts where they would normally be expected. The absence of habitual *a* or *doz* before *gu* in the *wen* clause in line 1194 supports the part of Bickerton's (1975) Main Stative Rule that excludes nonpunctuals from temporal clauses.[18] An irrealis marker (*gu*, *wil*, or *wud*) is also absent where it would be expected in the consequence clause of the conditional sentence in lines 1187–88. This may be the result of phonological (rapid speech) elision, but it is not predictable from any currently existing grammatical description of GC or other creoles.

The final morphosyntactic feature to which I wish to draw attention is the occurrence of the sentence-final adjectival construction in lines 1167–68: *de na waan notn a maakit gud*. Conventional word-order rules might have led us to expect instead *de na waan notn gud a maakit*, with the adjective preceding rather than following the prepositional phrase. The marked word order Anna employs here is, however, similar to an example in Reefer's Text 11c: *waan maan a tek out waan o ii kozn from di rom shap swiit* (457–58). In both cases delaying the adjective until the very last constituent slot in the sentence serves as an emphatic or focusing device, but it does so by making the focused-on element the comment, and everything preceding it in the sentence the topic.[19] This construction has not been discussed before in the literature on creole languages, and we would do well to keep our eyes and ears open for other occurrences. It clearly needs to be considered together with the other focusing devices that we have come across in these texts—fronting, clefting, and the use of impersonal or existential expressions.

The clearest phonological equivalent of the basilectal morphosyntactic features in Anna's speech is the categorical use of *a(a)* where mesolectal speakers more typically have *O* and *oh*: *baks* (1190), *gaad* (1179), and so on. Her speech also includes the other phonological features used by the basilectal Indo-Guyanese speakers in this volume, except that she does not delete *d* on demonstrative *da* and *dis* as Derek, Lohtan, and Dhanish do. The very

noticeable absence of *h* on the proper name in line 1198 (*aak* 'Hack') is stereotypically associated with Afro-Guyanese speech from certain rural areas,
but Derek, Granny, Reefer, and even Katherine—all Indo-Guyanese—
show us many examples of *h*-deletion, in a wide range of word classes, so the
validity of the stereotype is open to question.

Text 21a is from Tape OA5, side B, tape counter nos. 145–46; 21b is from
this same tape and side, nos. 205–34.

21a. Complaints about business being bad in the market

A: ting baad! notn en selin at dis maakit! evrii maanin	1158
yu gafu week op chrii o klak—langtaim, ting yuuztu sel.	1159
nou, it w—wos. piipl in waan bai notn. aaz	1160
yu tel dem ou di prais goowin, de se, "ting deer.	1161
ii deer. shap ting deer. maakit ting deer.	1162
aal ting deer." notn na a sel. rait? mii kom out from	1163
boksn, rait? mii a taak di chruut. notn na a sel. rait?	1164
evriibadii kraiyin se ting baad. an govoment se,	1165
"fiid yuself, klooz yuself," an dem a plaant, an wo evo	1166
den get, dem a sel, an de na waan notn	1167
a maakit gud. . . . noting en selin fu chuut! nou, yu	1168
on noo mont en, yu on	1169
noo wiik a deez, yu on noo nootaim, bikaa di ting	1170
baad! yu on noo satodee, sundi, mondi, chuuzdi or notn—	1171
ting baad! ting baad! aal di—luk. [She points to	1172
unsold produce at her market stall.] luk.	1173
J: o—yes.	1174
A: waach. aal dem lood dong de. luk dong de, aal dem	1175
lood dong de mii bai, an aal mi a chro we! luk—aal.	1176
wach dong de—aal dem kyukyombo mi a chro wee! aal!	1177
ting na a sel!	1178

Translation

Things are bad! Nothing is selling at this market! Every morning
you have to wake up at three o'clock. Long ago, things used to sell.
Now, it's w—worse. People don't want to buy anything. As soon as   1160T
you tell them what the price is, they say, "Things are dear.
It is dear. Things are dear in the shop. In the market.
Everything is dear." Nothing is selling. Right? I come from
Buxton, right? I'm talking the truth. Nothing is selling. Right?
Everybody is crying out that things are bad. And the government says,   1165T
"Feed yourself, clothe yourself," and they are planting, and whatever
they reap, they are selling, and they don't want anything good
to be at the market. . . . Really, nothing is selling! Now, you

don't know month-end [when things are normally better], you don't
know weekdays, you don't know any [special] time because things are   1170T
bad! You don't know Saturday, Sunday, Monday, Tuesday, or nothing.
Things are bad! Things are bad! All the—look. [She points to
unsold produce at her market stall.] Look.
    Yes.
    Look at all those loads down there. Look down there, all those   1175T
loads down there I bought, and all I am throwing away! Look—all.
Watch down there—all those cucumbers I'm throwing away. All!
Things aren't selling!

21b. Stealing in the market

    A: tiif? oo gaad! na taak bou tiif! ho ha! shh! hool op!   1179
yu on taak bot tiif hee? yu waan fu taak?   1180
wen yu don, put om pon shii.   1181
wen yu don, pi—put it pon shii. tiif?   1182
    J: wai—di tiif from shii di ada dee?   1183
    A: wen yu lok—tiif! rait hee a di maakit wii de rait hee an   1184
sii piipl snachin out piipl baangl, out o dem aan, an yu   1185
kyaan taak! bika aaz yu taak, dem gu kil yu! . . .   1186
if wii wo de ee sii, wii kyaan se notn, ka dem   1187
kil yu! . . . luk, a gon tel yu dis nou. laas yeer   1188
wuz sevntichrii? dis iz mii staan. oovo de iz mii staan.   1189
yu sii we da baks de? fu laas yeer, iz   1190
chrii saikl ai laas rait in bitwiin deer.   1191
    J: rait in front yu ai?   1192
    A: rait in front mi aiz, an aal chrii gaan a fraidi maarnin.   1193
an wen yu gu a dii steeshon, aal di puliis seyin, "bring   1194
di riisiit." an wen yu kyaar di riisiit, yu on eerin—   1195
dem en komin bak an tel yu se de fain dii baisikl.   1196
dii laas baisikl ai laas de, a tek it out   1197
bot chrii mont, an a di oo aak—sevnti   1198
siks daalo. an wen a gu an tel ii, ii see   1199
ii en biznis, a ad tu pee ii sevnti siks daalo! . . .   1200
an di laas taim a kii—o laas di baisikl de, an di maan   1201
kom an aks mi, "we yu risit?" a se, "luk, yuu doon   1202
aaks mii notn! iz mii baisikl, na yuu oon! bika wen mi—kyaari   1203
di risiit ayu na a duu notn." an mii finish at dat!   1204

Translation

    Thieves? Oh God! Don't talk about thieves! [Laughs.] Shh! hold up!
You'll talk about thieves here? You want to talk [about them]?   118
When you are finished [with me], put it [the microphone] on her [another
vendor]. When you're finished, put it—put it on her. Thieves?

Why—they stole from her recently?

When you look—thieves! Right here at the market we are, and
we see people snatching people's bangles off their hands, and you
can't talk! Because if you talk, they [the thieves] will kill you! . . .   1185T
If those of us who are here see, we can't say anything, because they
would kill you! . . . Look, I'm going to tell you this now. Last year
was 1973? This is my stall. Over there is my stall.

You see where that box is? During last year it's   1190T
three bicycles I lost right in between there.

Right in front your eyes?

Right in front my eyes, and all three went on a Friday morning.
And when you go to the police station, all the police say is, "Bring
the receipt." And when you carry the receipt, you don't hear—   1195T
they don't come back to tell you that they've found the bicycle.
The last bicycle I lost there, I'd bought it
about three months before, and I owed Hack [Hack's cycle store] seventy-
six dollars. And when I went and told him [what had happened], he said
he wasn't interested, I [still] had to pay him seventy-six dollars! . . .   1200T
And the last time I ca—I lost the bicycle there and the (police)man
came and asked me, "Where is your receipt?," I said, "Look, you don't
ask me anything! It's my bicycle, not yours! Because when I—carry
the receipt, you guys don't do anything." And I left it at that!

22. Basil (1963)

Basil's jumbie ("ghost") story is taken from a recording made by Wordsworth McAndrew in 1963, one of several he made over a period of two and a
half days with the person pseudonymously referred to as Basil. His subject,
an Afro-Guyanese who was seventy years old at the time, had been born and
raised in Wakenaam, Essequibo, and in earlier days had been, among other
things, a "pork-knocker" (a prospector for gold and/or diamonds), a "timber-
man" (woodcutter), a "Kali Mai" man (a practitioner or officiating person in
the Madrasi Indian Kali Mai religious tradition), and a village cricketer. Two
other people were present during the interview from which this jumbie story
is taken: a farmer who was a "guitar man" and folksong leader and a young
male teacher. According to McAndrew, both sometimes influenced the interview, the farmer by challenging Basil's authority on particular issues and
the teacher by failing to shift into a deeper or more basilectal Creole. One
effect was to cause Basil to shift from time to time into a more mesolectal
variety of Creole and give respectful responses ("Evidently," "Thank you,
sir!") to their questions and comments. Their influence is particularly
marked in the passage following the narrative, where they challenge his definition of *jombii*; it is not very pronounced in the narrative itself.

The phonemic transcript below represents a conversion from McAndrew's transcript, made in a nonphonemic dialect-spelling system. Although it cannot, therefore, be as true to the fluctuations of actual speech as a transcript made directly from the tape-recording, it can be considered a reasonably accurate approximation to the real-life speech event, since McAndrew used numerous devices to represent the pronunciation and explained these in detail.[20] Where his transcript provided no specific guidance—as, for instance, with respect to the relative length or tenseness of the vowel in *awii*—I tended to use the basilectal full form or spellings that were conventional in other studies rather than artificially introducing variation for its own sake. As is true of dialect-spelling systems in general, the original transcript contained more devices for indicating consonant quality than vowel quality, and the text below should therefore be considered more authoritative with respect to the former than the latter.

Basil's jumbie story is representative of a larger genre of narratives about supernatural beings and events, particularly about local folk spirits such as the jumbie and the Old Higue.[21] Like many such stories, it is set on a moonlit night, and the human figure who encounters the "spirit" is someone who likes to "walk late," someone whose breaking of conventional morals or norms sets him or her up for a hair-raising, almost punitive encounter. In this case, however, the "spirit" the man encounters is not a genuine supernatural being, but a group of unspecified people who appear to be over-concerned about his habit of walking late. Note that this habit is not presented in a negative light. Rather, Basil gives it a potentially positive interpretation: maybe the man simply used to go and visit his sweetheart. The narrator's attitude, in fact, is that he does not know what the protagonist used to do, and does not care, and that the group of nosey people who try to "perform as jumbie" should not care either. In the end it is they who run away in terror, as the protagonist, pushed into a corner, retaliates by "firing a wild lash" with his stick. The moral of *this* jumbie story is not that one should not walk late, but that one should mind one's own business and leave supernatural judgment and punishment to supernatural beings.

Naana, a word that recurs in the refrain (*tunait awii gu berin awii naana*), is a Hindi term for the maternal grandfather (cf. *na:na:*; Chaturvedi and Tiwari 1975: 360). It is one of the many Hindi kinship terms that have survived among Indo-Guyanese (see Rampaul 1978: 143). Its use here suggests that the narrative might have been transmitted to Basil in this form from an Indo-Guyanese, or that he himself had extensive contacts with Indo-Guyanese. The latter seems likely since, as noted above, Basil had been a Kali Mai man in earlier times. Elsewhere in his interview, he also describes himself as performing other activities more typical of the Indo-Guyanese than the Afro-Guyanese tradition, such as the invoking of spirits to increase one's chances of winning a cricket match. He also uses other Hindi or Bhojpuri words in the interview, for example, *bal* 'strength, power' (Chatur-vedi and Tiwari 1975: 503). One consequence of Basil's apparently intimate contacts with Indo-Guyanese is that the basilectal elements in his speech cannot be taken as clear evidence on the question of whether the Creole of Afro-Guyanese is as basilectal as that of Indo-Guyanese. There is, of course, an irony in this point, if the Indo-Guyanese essentially picked up their Creole from the Afro-Guyanese as the two groups worked together on nineteenth-century sugar plantations, as noted in Chapter 2 above.

Basil uses a more basilectal variety of GC than Anna. This can be seen by comparing their use of some of the features we considered in her introduction. Preverbal *na* constitutes only a third of Anna's negators, for instance, but Basil uses it categorically, as he does also the subject pronoun *mi(i)* and the prenominal copula *a*.[22] Preverbal continuative *a* is more frequent in Basil's text than in Anna's, especially when compared with its mesolectal equivalent, "∅ verb + *in*" (*a waak* vs. *waakin*); the frequency of the *a* form is 62 percent (8/13) in his case, 38 percent (3/8) in hers. Finally, he uses *awi(i)* categorically as his first-person-plural pronoun, whereas she just as cate-gorically uses *wi(i)*.[23]

At the same time Basil's speech also contains nonbasilectal elements. Al-though his narrative contains examples of the basilectal use of *wan* as indefi-nite article (*wan maan* 1207, *wan gruup* 1218), these two occurrences are matched by two occurrences of mesolectal *o* (1209, 1222). Similarly, basilectal *dem piipl dis*, with the proximal indicator following the noun phrase (1229), is matched in line 1226 by mesolectal *diiz piipl dem*, with the proximal indicator preceding the noun phrase and the pluralizer following.

With respect to Bickerton's Main Stative Rule, Basil's text includes both supporting examples and counterexamples. For instance, the *wen* clause in line 1209 includes no habitual *a*, as Bickerton's rule would predict, but the *wen* clause in 1216—where *wen* means "while"—does contain continuative *a*, providing the same kind of weak counterexample as Dhanish's text did.[24] Basil also has one example of continuative *a* preceding the locative copula *de* (1242), which, as noted in the discussion of a similar example in Irene's Text 10b (338), is treated by Bickerton as an unusual exception to his Main Stative Rule.

On the question of the existence of nonfinite clauses in GC and other creoles, the sentence *awii gu stap YU FROM WAAK LEET* (1211–12) is par-ticularly interesting. The capitalized portion at first seems like yet another example of the finiteness of GC verb complements, since the subject pro-noun is not raised into object position of the matrix sentence. This is not obvious from a pronoun like *yu*, which is never case-marked in the basilect, but if the subject of the embedded complement were a third-person-singular pronoun, it would have to be *ii* (subject) rather than *am* (object) in a comparable position (*awii gu stap II FROM WAAK LEET*). However, in other respects the complement behaves like a true nonfinite clause. It does not permit tense- or modality-marking (**awii gu stap YU FROM GU WAAK LEET*), and unlike the *mek* complements discussed in Bickerton (1981: 103ff), it is not governed by Chomsky's (1977) Propositional Island Constraint against moving constituents outside of a finite clause. For instance, it is possible to move the subject of the embedded clause in line 1211 to the front of the sentence for topicalization (*a yuu awii gu stap FROM WAAK LEET*) and to WH-question it (*a huu awii gu stap FROM WAAK LEET?*). The interaction of phonological with syntactic constraints in constructions of this type also needs to be considered. For instance, with a third-person pronoun only the full form—*hii*—would be acceptable in the primary stress slot that topicalization or clefting creates (*a hii awii gu stap FROM WAAK LEET*); the *h*-less *ii* form, as in Bickerton's (1981: 104) Example 160 (**a i mi mek ha wok*), would be unacceptable. As suggested by our recurring references to it, the whole subject of sentential embedding and complementation in GC and other creoles is a fascinating topic. Bickerton deserves credit for having raised some of the initial questions about this area so pointedly, but the answers are not yet all in.

One other area that seems to require further research is the details of GC topicalization, in particular, the question of what kinds of elements are eligible for sentence fronting and topicalization with and without *a* or *iz*. In Basil's text we see two rarely topicalized elements: adverbial *ya* in line 1247 and modal *kyaan* in line 1250. The modal example is the rarer of the two—and the more unusual, since it seems to involve the copying of the modal rather than mere fronting, but without the initial *a* or *iz* that usually accompanies such copying.

Finally, note Basil's extensive use of *wel* as a discourse device (1207, 1210, 1224, 1225, etc.), reminiscent of Lohtan's frequent use of the same connective in his narrative.

Text 22 is from a tape-recording made by Wordsworth McAndrew in 1963.

22. The jumbie story "Tonight We Will Bury Our Nana"

W: yu noo enii ado jombii stoorii? tel wii di won bout "tunait	1205
awii gu berii awii naana." . . .	1206
B: wel, aa. wan maan yuuztu waak leet at nait, evri nait a ii	1207
kostom—waak leet. mi na noo if ii doz gu a ii swiitaart	1208

ar wo, bot ii o maan a waak out leet wen di nait kom.   1209
wel it opeer laika dem waan shoo dis maan sortn—aa—tookin,   1210
se yu mosn waak su leet, an awii gu stap yu from   1211
waak leet a nait. . . . dat abii gu profaarm az jombii.   1212
abii jombii gu stap yu. . . .   1213
bina muunlait nait, jentlmen. dis maan gaan. an   1214
wen ii lef ii . . . di plees we ii kom fram, ii a kom   1215
hoom. wen ii a kom hoom, e—e? wails waakin,   1216
waakin, waakin, wen ii luk—tuwadz we ii a gu   1217
hoom, yu noo, ii sii wan gruup o piipl a kom. . . .   1218
"tunait awii gu berin awii naana. tunait awii   1219
gu berin awii naana. tunait awii gu berin awii naana." . . .   1220
ii se, "wel, livin piipl kyaan de a dam fu gu kyai kaafn   1221
a berin grong dis taim a nait. dis . . . mos bii o jombii,   1222
ar goos." "tunait awii gu berin awii naana. tunait awii gu—"   1223
wel hii goowin tuwordz dem, dem komin tuwordz hii.   1224
wel biifoor di miit ii, deer wuz o brij. wel ii se,   1225
"fu seev miself from diiz piipl dem—diiz piipl—dis a spirit,"   1226
ii gu aaniit di brij an haid de. ii se, "wel dem   1227
gu paas an dem no gu sii mii." . . .   1228
dem piipl dis nou, jombii a piipl a sii,   1229
yu noo? wen, wen—di noo wo a hapn. wel dem kom   1230
an dem res dem kaafn pan di brij. wen dem res dem   1231
kaafn pan di brij: "oo, ii de a batam de? oo, ii de a batam   1232
de?" [Mumbled jumbie conversation:] . . . "tunait awii gu   1233
berin awii naana. tunait awii gu berin awii naana. tunait—." wel   1234
wen dem don dem pik op di kaafn nou. wel . . .   1235
di maan se ii fiil dat diiz piipl dem gu paas am. [Jumbies   1236
speak among themselves:] "rait andaniit dis brij hee tunait.   1237
rait andaniit dis brij hee tunait. rait andaniit dis   1238
brij hee tunait," noowin dis maan de de a haid   1239
fram dem. "rait andaniit dis brij hee tunait."   1240
wel wen di maan sii diiz piipl dem kontinyu fu kom   1241
we ii a de, ii pik—yu noo, ii a waak wid ii   1242
stik fu daag. ii gat ii stik—ii se, "wel le mi   1243
tel alyu somting: nat wan dam ting laika da na gu hapm ya!   1244
tunait? gaadamit!" ii rosh pan dem. wen ii rosh pan dem—   1245
ai! dee start fu ron! ii se, "luku, ayu   1246
jombii! yu tingk mi fraikin ayu? tunait? ya yu gu   1247
bring na(na)—?" ii se, "kom le abii gu!" ii faiya, ii a faiya   1248
wail lash! luku jombii dong—ii de biyain   1249
dem! "tunait dis naana gun berin berin de? kyaan   1250
naana, kyaan berin de tunait!—naana kyaan berin,   1251
nat yet." ii ron dem tu el! . . . finish de, bodii.   1252

Translation

    Do you know any other jumbie [ghost] stories? Tell us the one about "Tonight   1205T
We Will Bury Our Nana [maternal grandfather]."
    Well, ahh. A man used to walk late at night. Every night it was his
custom—to walk late. I don't know if he would go to his sweetheart
or what, but he was a man who would walk late when the night came.
Well, it appears as if they wanted to teach this man a lesson, to tell   1210T
him that you mustn't walk so late, and we are going to stop you from
walking late at night. . . . that we are going to perform as jumbies.
Our jumbies will stop you. . . .
    It was a moonlight night, gentlemen. This man had gone out. And
after leaving his . . . the place he had come from, he was coming   1215T
home. While he was coming home, eh-eh [surprise]! While walking,
walking, walking, as he looked—toward the place where he was going,
toward home, you know, he saw a group of people coming. . . .
"Tonight we will bury our nana. Tonight we
will bury our nana. Tonight we will bury our nana." . . .   1220T
    He said, "Well, living people couldn't be on the dam carrying a coffin
to the cemetery at this time of night. This . . . must be a jumbie,
or ghost." "Tonight we will bury our nana. Tonight we will—"
Well, he was going toward them, and they were coming toward him.
Well, before they reached him, there was a bridge. Well, he said,   1225T
"To save myself from these people—these people—these are spirits,"
he went underneath the bridge and hid there. He said, "Well, they
will pass by and they won't see me." . . .
    These people now, jumbies are people who can see [through anything],
you know? When, when—they knew what was going on. Well, they came   1230T
and they rested their coffin on the bridge. After resting their
coffin on the bridge: "Oh, he's underneath there? Oh, he's underneath
there?" [Mumbled jumbie conversation:] . . . "Tonight we will
bury our nana. Tonight we will bury our nana. Tonight—." Well,
when they were finished, they picked up the coffin now. Well . . .   1235T
the man felt that these people would pass him by. [But then he
hears them continue:] "Right underneath this bridge here tonight.
Right underneath this bridge here tonight. Right underneath this
bridge here tonight," knowing that this man was there hiding
from them. "Right underneath this bridge here tonight."   1240T
Well, when the man saw these people continuing to come toward
where he was, he picked—you know, he used to walk with his
stick to fend off dogs. He has a stick—He said, "Well, let me
tell you something: nothing of the sort is going to happen here!
Tonight? Goddamit!" He rushed in on them. When he rushed them—   1245T
Aie! They started to run! He said, "Look, you
jumbies! You think I'm scared of you? Tonight? Here you'll
bring nana?" He said, "Come, let's go!" He fired, he was lashing

out wildly! If you see how the jumbies went down—he was right behind
them! "Tonight this nana will be buried there? No way can   1250T
Nana be, he can't be buried there tonight!—Nana can't be buried,
not yet!" He ran them to hell! [The story is] finished there, buddy.

23. Damon (1977)

Damon, seventy-eight years when interviewed in 1977, fits the stereotype
of the upper-mesolectal speaker better than any of the Afro-Guyanese in
this chapter. He was born and raised in the village of Cumberland, on the
northern bank of the Canje River, just across from the city of New Amsterdam, East Coast Berbice. One of the reasons his speech is as close to SE as it
is is undoubtedly the network of people with whom he has worked all his life.
His earliest job, at the age of fourteen, was as a live-in houseboy or assistant
butler to a wealthy dentist in the town of New Amsterdam. His duties included showing patients into the surgery and reminding them "to be careful
not to put they feet on the chair." In using these very words, probably much
as they were used in explaining his duties to him, Damon reflects the pre-
tentiousness and snobbishness of the upper-middle-class family for whom
he worked. For a while he was even referred to by his employer's surname, a
practice that was common in slavery days, but one that Damon mentioned
with little apparent resentment.

At the time he was interviewed Damon was serving as caretaker for the
playhouse of an amateur drama group in which English and American expatriates and members of the Georgetown middle class figured prominently.
He had been thoroughly exposed to their speech patterns and had obviously
assimilated a good deal of them. In this respect his experience was similar to
that of an old Indo-Guyanese Cane Walker who had been a house servant
and chauffeur for English sugar-plantation managers, and who said, in one
of his interviews with me: "I used to, you know, associate with pure white
people—the English people and Scots people and so—and through that, I
pick up they ways, you know, in living. . . . So, ah haven't got so much o'
education, but I take up the language from them" (Rickford 1979: 126).

We will take a closer look at Damon's language in a moment, but first we
should examine his text for its value as a contribution to Guyanese history
and folklore. From these perspectives, two points stand out. First, incredibly
enough, in 1977 this seventy-eight-year-old man was able to pinpoint the
area and the tribe in Africa from which his great-grandfather is believed to
have come (recalling Alex Haley's *Roots*). And second, the fantastic story he
tells about slaves flying back to Africa cries out for further interpretation.
I will discuss each of these points in turn.

Working backwards from Damon's birth date in 1899, and allowing for about 30 years a generation, Damon's great-grandfather must have been born around 1809. He may, of course, have been born earlier, perhaps in the last decade of the eighteenth century, and in this case may indeed have come to Guyana before the British slave trade was abolished in 1807. Alternatively, he may have come to Guyana with the wave of African indentured workers who immigrated in the 1840's, but this is contrary to Damon's claim that he was a slave, and would also make him older than many of the indentured Africans who arrived during this period.

It was Damon's great-aunt, who raised him from birth, who told Damon about his great-grandfather, and the information he shares with us is a testimony to the value of oral history. Besides the story of his great-grandfather's Middle Passage recounted here, Damon's great-aunt told him that this ancestor from the Popo tribe had been the son of a king or prince and had been enticed to join a slaving ship along with other friends while he was sitting near the shore with some books. Damon recalls that his great-uncle, son of this legendary great-grandfather ("Roger Stewart from Guinea"), used to speak their ancestral African language. But all that he remembers of it is the phrase with which his great-uncle used to greet him: *pitii pitii bOi, tambong* 'Pitty, pitty boy, tambung!' Damon suggests that *pitii* meant "small," like French *petit*, and that *tambong* meant something like "Good morning" or "Good afternoon," but in seeking a possible etymology and interpretation, we will obviously need to consult West African languages.

Which "Guinea" Damon's great-grandfather came from is difficult to determine, since the term is used in many place-names in West Africa. It may refer to the Republic of Guinea or to Equatorial Guinea, countries separated by several thousand miles of coastline, or to the Gulf of Guinea, stretching from Cape Palmas to Cape Lopez, or to the Guinea Coast, including everything from the Republic of Guinea to Equatorial Guinea. The most likely candidate is the Gulf of Guinea, and within this the country of Benin, formerly known as Dahomey. Popo was an important settlement on the Slave Coast; shown on modern maps as Grand Popo, it is just west of Ouidah, both in Benin.

According to Le Page (1960: 36–41), the term Popo is also used to refer to people from this region: "It is the central and Eastern Ewe, especially those near the coast, who are called *Popo* by the Yoruba, but the name was applied by the Europeans to any slave coming from the Slave Coast west of the Yoruba country, the region in which the Ewe languages and their related dialects are spoken." [25] Bryan Edwards (1793) is quoted by Le Page (p. 79) as saying that the Papaws, or people of Ouidah, "are unquestionably the most docile and best-disposed Slaves that are imported from any part of Africa. Without the fierce and savage manners of the Koromantyn Negroes, they are also happily exempt from the timid and desponding temper of the Eboes. . . . That punishment which excites the Koromantyn to rebel, and drives the Ebo Negro to suicide, is received by the Papaws as the chastisement of legal authority, to which it is their duty to submit patiently."

Be this as it may—the Popos in Damon's narrative certainly do not seem as docile as Edwards suggests—it appears that, in the case of both Jamaica and Guyana, most slaves from Popo, Ouidah, and elsewhere on the Slave Coast were imported in the early part of the eighteenth century (Le Page 1960: 75; Postma 1970: 220; Devonish 1978: 11). If Damon's great-grandfather arrived in Guiana at the beginning of the nineteenth century, the Slave Coast contingent in which he would have been included would have been relatively small, compared with the larger contingents being imported from the Windward and Gold coasts at the time.

The motif of slaves flying back to Africa recurs in narratives, myths, and anecdotes among black populations in the New World, but has attracted little scholarly attention to date. I first encountered it on one of the South Carolina Sea Islands in 1970, from a middle-aged schoolteacher who told me that her great-grandparents had flown back to Africa after receiving a whipping on the Sea Island cotton plantation where they were working. She told me this, not as a folktale or legend, but as a statement of historical fact. As she passed on this bit of ancestral lore, she squinted at me closely to be certain that I was taking it seriously and deserved to be taken into her confidence.

Subsequently, I came across other references to this motif—in the book of Suriname legends by Breinburg (1971), to which St. Claire Drake drew my attention, and in *Drums and Shadows* (1940), a book based on interviews with South Carolinian and Georgian slaves conducted in the 1930's as part of the Writers' Program, Georgia. John Szwed, who drew my attention to this book, also pointed out that the motif was present in the autobiography of the Cuban runaway slave Esteban Montejo (1973: 43), who told his interviewer, Miguel Barnet, that unlike the Indians, who committed suicide to avoid being Christianized by the Spanish colonizers, "the Negroes . . . escaped by flying. They flew through the sky and returned to their own lands."

Wordsworth McAndrew (personal communication) has pointed out that the concept of human flight is paralleled in the blood-sucking folk spirits Ole Higue and Fire-Ass (or Fire-Rass), who fly through the air in search of victims. The same connection was suggested by Damon, who said that he did not doubt the story about his great-grandfather flying back to Africa because he himself had seen a Fire-Ass in the 1950's—a male figure, flying through the air, with a blue flame coming out of his mouth. Esteban Montejo (1973: 43–44) also related the ability to fly to witchcraft and magic, for the preceding quote continues:

The Musundi Congolese were the ones who flew the most; they disappeared by means of witchcraft. They did the same as the Canary Island witches, but without making a sound. There are those who say that the Negroes threw themselves into rivers. This is untrue. The truth is they fastened a chain to their wrists which was full of magic. That was where their power came from. I know all this intimately, and it is true without a doubt.

Warner-Lewis (1982: 78), discussing the flying-back-to-Africa motif as well as the commonly reported belief that "slaves who were being beaten could have their hurt telepathically transferred to the slave master's wife," notes that these magical occurrences were induced by incantations of African languages and served as tools of rebellion against slavery. Both of these points receive support from Damon's text. The motif may also symbolize the fervent desire of the Africans to return home (Schuler 1980: 19; Warner-Lewis 1982: 76) or their belief in the transmigration of the soul to Africa after death (Van Berkel 1695). In any case Damon's narrative should not be mistaken for a fond bit of family folklore. It has rich connections with similar narratives and other aspects of African-derived folk culture in the New World.

In comparison with its intriguing details for the historian, anthropologist, or folklorist, the linguistic characteristics of this text are relatively unremarkable. Although Damon and I lived across the street from each other and had met, talked, exchanged garden produce, and otherwise maintained good neighborly relations for almost three years prior to the interview, he continued to monitor his output in this interview to display the careful, upper-mesolectal speech that his occupational networks over the years had taught him. This is evidenced in the occasional repetitions that do not seem to be there for dramatic or rhetorical effect, as they are in Lohtan's text, but seem intended to convey greater precision for its own sake (*in di nait, juurin di nait* 1267–68). Another evidence of this concern is Damon's occasional hesitation on, and replacement of, what he perceives as stigmatized Creole expressions, as in line 1262, where the words that are interrupted and replaced by *set o piipl* are *rees* 'race' and *neeshn* 'nation.'[26] Still another is his qualification and explanation of individual words, as in line 1267 (*wen o se yat, o boot, seelin boot*).

The speaker's enterprise, in terms of grammatical characteristics at least, is successful, with SE plural and possessive noun inflections (*deez* 1265, *tiichoz rezident* 1254), English copulas and auxiliaries (including passive auxiliaries, as in lines 1254 and 1265), and past-marking all in force. Past-marking is clearest with syllabic and strong verbs, like *staartid* (1290), *boht* (1256), and *keem* (1265). Weak verbs like *taar* and *riich* in lines 1293 and 1295 appear to lack the past-tense suffix but cannot be counted as such because they are followed by alveolar *d*, an environment in which it would be difficult to hear whether the verbs in question really had a final alveolar stop.

These uninflected weak verbs also occur in the section of the narrative in which Damon is most involved, however. From around line 1269 onward, Damon reduces his own audio-monitoring and puts down my interruptions instead of tolerating or encouraging them: *noh, ai doon noo dat* (1275), *wit, weet. yu gun heer* (1281). It is in this section that a few, more non-standard features emerge. The four instances of zero "be" copula (1269, 1287, 1291, 1292) all occur in this section (note that three of the four are before "verb + *in*," one of the most favorable zero-copula environments), tense-marking becomes more nonstandard (*din yuuztu* 1292–93, *wudo biin* 1295), the historical present is deployed for past habituals (*komz* 1284), and stem forms like *taar* (1293) and *disopeer* (1287) emerge.[27]

It would be interesting to follow this speaker's production in other portions of the recording in which his careful monitoring is reduced, or in which he quotes other speakers, to gauge the limits of his competence. I think that it stretches farther into the lower-mesolect than the text below suggests. For instance, in another section of the recording, Damon talks about his father (whom he rarely saw) striding down the street in a long coat and top hat on the way to his second marriage. As Damon quotes the teasing he received from his friends on this occasion, his language veers sharply toward the basilect: "*bai, luk yu dadii—yu na gu tel ii houdii?*" ("Boy, look at your daddy—aren't you going to tell him 'howdy'?"). This is only one of several examples of the dangers of making generalizations about the linguistic competence of individuals—or the groups they represent—without reference to a variety of samples, preferably recorded in many different contexts and supplemented by open elicitation.[28]

Although Damon's speech in this narrative includes many morphosyntactic features typical of the upper-mesolectal or SE end of the continuum, his speech includes phonological features that identify him clearly as a Guyanese, and a participant in the Guyanese Creole continuum. The *O* and *oh* pronunciations he uses in line 1262 and elsewhere are not basilectal, as we have noted several times before, but only once do we encounter English *dh* rather than Creole *d* (*dhem* in line 1267, compared with *dem* in line 1292 and *em* in line 1262). Similarly, the presence of final postvocalic *r* in *deer* (1273) and *heer* (1295) is not basilectal, but the monopthongal vowel and velar nasal in *dong* (1269) and *orong* (1272) reveal Damon's adherence to Guyanese norms rather than those of the English and North American expatriates with whom he has worked. As noted in the introduction to Bonnette's texts (Text set 15), the final *ong* pronunciation is characteristic of all levels in the Guyanese continuum, and provides yet another indication that social stratification and differentiation are weaker with respect to phonology than morphosyntax in creole continuum communities (cf. Traugott 1981; Escure 1981).

Text 23 is from Tape C1, tape counter nos. 129–39 and 265–94.

23. Stories passed down about his great-grandfather, a slave from Guinea

D: an—aa—pliiz tu tel yu dat chorch an skuul an	1253
tiichoz rezident wuz bilt bai mai greet granfaado, a sleev.	1254
J: oo, o-ho?	1255
D: yes. hii boht dat bildin from di esteet bai di neem o	1256
smitsn, an bilt dat chorch.	1257
J: wo wuz hiz neem?	1258
D: rohjo schoort. . . . rohjo schoort, from ginii. hi woz from di	1259
papeeyon chraib, sii? . . . pepeeyon. di se—	1260
di se poopoo. bot ii reel neem iz popeeyon. sii? reel neem fu di	1261
chr— . . . and—em—onOdo ree—nee—set o piipl de kohl em ookuu,	1262
steeshii. yu noo, evri chraib had di oon neem, wel hii wuz from	1263
di popeeyon chraib. . . . di kom from ginii, man. . . . sleevrii	1264
deez. a kyan tel yu o litl hou di keem heer. hii wuz—broht	1265
dong bai—a dunoo if iz poochogiiz ar som piipl, in o yach.	1266
wen o se yat, o boot, seelin boot. menii ov dhem, in di nait,	1267
juurin di nait, di wur put On di dek. bot, juurin di dee, de	1268
wor dong in di hach. wen di nait iz kuul an dee On di	1269
dek, di yuuztu hav o pastaim.	1270
J: e he? wo di iz pastaim? wo di yuuztu du?	1271
D: sit orong in o ring. laik wo wii se, ring plee. sii? ring plee.	1272
den de—staartu sing, yu noo? sing in deer konchrii wee.	1273
J: yu nevo rimembo enii o dem sangz?	1274
D: noh, ai doon noo dat. dis iz wOt o hord. naido a doon noo	1275
moch ov—a doonoo eniiting ov im.	1276
J: bot o miin dis—wen di o—de an dis dek an su, di yuuz	1277
tu bii stil cheen an so, ar di jos yuuztu—?	1278
D: noh, o biliiv—noh, di doon—wozn cheen.	1279
J: bika di kyaan—	1280
D: wit, weet. yu gun heer. soo, wen de staartu sing, az yul	1281
—wud staart a ring plee, wen di sing for o taim, waan outdo di	1282
sorkl gun goo n sit in di midl o di ring. den di tempoo	1283
komz greeto an greeto an greeto an greeto, an hii jos	1284
disopeer! mek o noot o dat!	1285
J: ii wo?	1286
D: ii jos disopeer. nOt kidin yu. ii jos disopeer.	1287
J: o heer somtin laik dis biifoor.	1288
D: hi jos disopeer. it woz goowin ohn soo, for o litl wail.	1289
it wuz—goowin ohn for o litl wail. soo wen de staartid tu nootis	1290
dis ting—di s—sleev oonorz, ar di piipl baarginin piipl—di	1291

bringin dem tu sel. soo wen de nootis dis ting, de din   1292
yuuz tu put dem—de taar di boot. de taar di boot, an   1293
kep dem deer ohl di taim from den ohn. biikohz bifoor di   1294
riich dong heer, di wudo biin—em—akchulii—   1295
    J: yu miin dee in komin bak?   1296
    D: noh, di gohn bak. di gohn bak, maan. . . . yes, gohn bak tu afriko.   1297

Translation

And—am—I'm pleased to tell you that that church and school and
teacher's residence was built by my great-grandfather, a slave.
    Oh, uh-huh?
    Yes. He bought that building from the estate owned by someone named   1255T
Smithson, and built that church.
    What was his name?
    Roger Stewart. . . . Roger Stewart, from Guinea. He was from the
Papayan tribe, see? . . . Papayan. They say—   1260T
They say Popo. But it's real name is Papayan. See? The real name of the
tribe. . . . And—em—another ra—na—set of people were called Oku,
Stayshee. You know, every tribe had its own name. Well, he was from
the Papayan tribe. . . . They came from Guinea, man. . . . In slavery
days. I can tell you a little about how they came here. He was brought   1265T
down by—I don't know if they were Portuguese or what, in a yacht.
When I say a yacht, a boat, sailing boat. Many of them, in the night,
during the night, they were put on the deck. But during the day, they
were down in the hatch. When the night was cool and they were on the
deck, they used to have a pastime.   1270T
    Eh-heh? What was their pastime? What did they do?
    Sit around in a ring. Like what we call a ring-play. See? Ring-play.
Then they would start to sing, you know? In their native way.
    You don't remember any of those songs?
    No, I don't know them. This is just what I heard. Nor do I know   1275T
much about—I don't know anything about him.
    But I mean—this—when they were on—they were on deck and so on, they used
to be still chained and so on, or they just used to—?
    No, I believe—no, they don't—weren't chained.
    Because they couldn't—   1280T
    Wait, wait. You'll hear. So, when they started to sing, as you would—
would start a ring-play, after they'd sung for a time, one person in the
circle would go and sit in the middle of the ring. Then the tempo
would become faster and faster and faster and faster, and he'd just
disappear! Make a note of that!   1285T
    He what?
    He would just disappear. I'm not kidding you. He'd just disappear.
    I've heard something like this before.
    He'd just disappear. It was going on like this for a little while.

This was going on for a little while. So when they started to notice   1290T
this thing—the s—slaveowners, or the people trading in people—they
were bringing them to sell. So when they noticed this, they didn't
continue putting them—they tarred the boat. They tarred the boat, and
kept them [down] there all the time from then on. Because before they
reached down here, they would have—em—actually—   1295T
    You mean they [the slaves] weren't coming back?
    Naw, they went back. They went back, man. . . . Yes, went back to Africa.

24. Mother (1982)

Eighty years old when she was interviewed, Mother comes from strong
working-class roots. Her father, who immigrated to Guyana from Barbados
as a young man with his father, was a market vendor. Her mother was a
Georgetown housewife, and she herself grew up in the same working-class
sections of the city and its environs—Albouystown, La Penitence—in which
Ali (Text set 17) was raised several decades later. Like many working-class
youngsters of the time, she was taken out of school at a relatively young age
to help around the home, at approximately the third-grade level. Her classification as a member of the lower middle class rests largely on the fact that
her husband was a skilled tradesman—a mechanic/engineer—and on the
fact that she has been upwardly mobile, in terms of place of residence and
other status characteristics, since her early twenties (again like Ali). For the
last several years she has been living with one of her children in the United
States.

I ended up selecting four brief texts from Mother's interview rather than
one long one because each of the topics we covered seemed valuable in one
way or another. The first text, for instance, is both a sentimental evocation of
pleasurable school-day experiences and a snapshot, as it were, of the colonial experience: children of the sun dressed in white dresses and blue serge
pants marching in procession, singing paeans of praise to distant kings and
queens. It is a testimony to the strength of the colonial preparation for such
occasions that Mother's only *oh* tokens occur in this text (*kohz, johj* 1307,
gohd 1309), where she is giving us a sample of the coronation songs she
sang seven decades earlier. The acrolectal target is not always reached—
basilectal *aa* intrudes in *maarnin* (1305) and *naat* (1306)—and there is at
least one instance of hypercorrection (*lohnz* 1306), but since Mother uses
a(a) categorically elsewhere, the shift to English norms in this one section is
noteworthy.

Text 24b provides a rare glimpse of distinctive Portuguese speech patterns in Guyana. As represented by Mother, the patterns include the ab-

sence of affrication on initial *ch* (*shaild* 1318) and the absence of the initial glide in 'with' (*id* 1319). The latter feature is attested in the speech of several Indo-Guyanese in this volume (Reefer, Granny, Katherine), and Mother may be simply giving us a stereotypical nonstandard pronunciation to symbolize the nonnative English of the Portuguese woman from Lisbon. But it is important to note that Mother lived with this woman for several years, and the stereotype she draws—if such it is—is well tempered with direct experience. In any case the linguistic and cultural assimilation of the Portuguese and other "minority" ethnic groups in creole communities is a topic deserving of further investigation. It is one that is likely to contribute much to our larger understanding of linguistic diffusion across ethnic boundaries (see Labov 1984; Rickford 1985a).

Text 24c is valuable for its representation of the widespread folk belief that Ole Higues hide their skins in mortars before taking off on their blood-sucking missions, and are often sabotaged by people who put salt and pepper in the skins to torment them when they return to assume their normal form. Nichols (1982) reports an almost identical story from South Carolina, and cites references to stories with similar content and a similar refrain from North Carolina and the Bahamas, Mississippi/Michigan, and among the Vai in Liberia, West Africa (Parsons 1917; Dorson 1956; Ellis 1914). In the case of Mother's text the formulaic character of the Ole Higue's complaint (*skin, da mii!!*)—handed down almost exactly in this fashion from earlier generations—has preserved one occurrence of the otherwise obsolete *da* form of the copula. In Rickford (1974) I suggested that the *a* form of the present-day preverbal-aspect marker in GC might have been a relatively recent innovation, replacing an earlier *da* form of the type still found in Gullah. Mother's text agrees with the evidence of McTurk (1881; see Text 5a) in confirming the hypothesis, but extends it to include the creole copula as well.

Text 24d is a fine example of Mother's skill as a narrator, demonstrating her ability to make past events come alive, complete with visual and sound effects. It also includes an example of *tu* ('to' 1331) as a locational rather than a directional preposition, equivalent to English "at." This feature is more conventionally associated with Gullah or Sea Island Creole (Nichols 1982) than with GC, where it is more common to find *a* (perhaps derived in part from "at") used for both functions.

The most important feature of this last text—from the viewpoint of the linguist, at least—is the protasis-only conditional in lines 1333–34: *if yu sii di faiyo goowin in n komin out*. Two previous examples have occurred in this volume: Bonnette's *if yu sii piipl!* (847) and Ali's *if yu heer stoorii ou dee!* (979, false starts excluded). As noted in the discussion of the Ali example, this distinctive GC construction, in which the protasis is used without any apodosis or consequence clause, is limited to verbs denoting the five primary senses. (It is in fact more common with *sii* and *heer* than any others.) To this observation we can add the following:

1. At the simplest level these constructions serve as intensives, as a way of saying "The fire was intense!" or "There was a *lot* of people!" or "The commotion outside was terrifying, deafening!" In this respect, as noted before, they are roughly equivalent to SE constructions with modal "should": "You should have seen the fire!" and so on.

2. Unlike the SE modality expressions, the GC construction can only have "you" as its subject. "He should have seen the fire!" may be grammatical in SE, but *if hii sii faiyo*! is not grammatical in GC.

3. In its restriction to subject "you," the GC construction is also different from the protasis-only regret conditional that is possible in SE: "If only I hadn't given her the car keys" (Akatsuka 1983). A related point is that although this SE type can occur in soliloquy, the GC type cannot; an addressee or hearer must always be present.

4. The GC construction is limited to narratives of past events personally experienced by the narrator. Although the verb is always unmarked—*sii*, *heer*, and so on—its past reference follows from conventional rules for the interpretation of creole nonstative stem forms (Bickerton 1975: 28). Use in philosophizing or argument, as in *if yu sii mi paint*! ('If you could only see my point!'), is impossible, but the construction may be used in nonpersonal narrative (for example, traditional folktales) if presented as though the narrator were actually there. Sometimes the prefatory phrase *mi heer* or *a heer* ('I hear') is used when reporting events at which the narrator was not present in person, the warrant for the use of the construction lying, then, in the first-person experience of another: *a heer if yu sii piipl*.

Putting these observations together, we might say that the function of this construction is not simply to denote intensives of various kinds, but to make the events under description more vivid and immediate for the hearer. In this sense, the construction is an evaluative device (Labov 1972b: 366; Schiffrin 1981: 58–59) of the type that narratives of personal experience often contain to indicate they are worth the telling. This last point is in fact crucial for explaining how the intensive function comes to be conveyed by this partial conditional. The unstated apodosis is roughly equivalent to "You would have been surprised!" Or, in even more detail, "You would have been surprised, and you would have found it as worthy of reporting in a narrative as I do now." The narrower intensive function, in short, derives from the larger obligation that narratives be worth telling, by this approximate chain of logic: "If you had seen the fire going in and out, you'd have been amazed, and you would have found it as worthy of reporting in a narrative as I do now. Since I mention this fire going in and out in a narrative, a genre reserved for reportable events, be assured that it was burning in a remarkable (reportable) way." No speaker would say this much explicitly, of course, but it is part of the unstated meaning of the "simple" protasis-only conditional that Mother uses in lines 1333–34.

Turning from this intriguing conditional construction to the analytic conventions of the preceding introductions, we find that, overall, Mother's speech in these texts is representative of the mid-mesolect. SE plural-marking is extensive (about 75 percent) but use of the SE copula is lower (about 50 percent), and SE past-marking is virtually nonexistent, limited to *wuz* and *had*. The classical mesolectal preverbal forms—habitual *doz*, anterior *di(d)*, negative *din* and *in/en*—are used frequently, and Mother shows us an instance of *kud* used for nonpast rather than past-marking (1303), recalling similar examples from Trinidadian Creole English discussed in Solomon (1972). Mother's texts contain several examples of subject-pronoun deletion that are not of the usual second-person type (no *ai* before *hoop* in line 1318, no *wii* before *maach* in 1301, no *shi* before *kudn* in 1319).

There are several distinctive GC lexical items in Mother's texts, including *out* ('put out' 1335), *weeri* ('to be satisfied, satiated' 1314), and *priven* ('stop' 1330). But Mother's most distinctive creole trait is her use of *a(a)* rather than *oh* in such words as *kaarneeshon* (1298) and *taak* (1319); as noted above the songs contain exceptions. This is the feature most stereotypically associated with creole phonology (see p. 152 and elsewhere in this volume), and it is largely responsible for the overall auditory impression of "creole" speech that one picks up strongly from Mother but less so from Bonnette or Katherine. Like most mesolectal Guyanese speakers, Mother shows the deletion of unstressed syllables in words like *kaarneeshon* and the simplification of final *ld* and *nd* consonant clusters (*ool* 1321, *stan* 1300—but not in *and* 1298 or *chaild* 1328, both of these exceptions occurring before a pause). Her variation on these features should remind us, however, that the neatly invariant texts of creole speech we often encounter in publications—modern ones as well as those from earlier periods—may sometimes represent idealizations rather than reality.

Texts 24a and 24b are from Tape OA16, tape counter nos. 717–63 and 908–14, respectively. Texts 24c and 24d are from Tape OA17, nos. 688–92 and 509–51, respectively.

24a. The coronation of King Edward: children's parade

M: wii had kaarneeshon: di gyorlz in wait dresiz and—yu lil medol,   1298
an di baiz in wait short wid—aam—sorj paants, an wi—wii had   1299
a—kyarol ii did neem, di banmasto, misto kyarol stan op hai pon do   1300
ting di dee wen wii goo. maach til from sharpol   1301

skuul aal dii wee dong tuu hai striit, an kom in tu di—di—di laa   1302
koots. ye-es! an wii sing, ai kud riimembo dii fors sing—saang   1303
wii sing wuz, "let cheerz ring faar n waid." [Singing:] "let   1304
cheerz ring fa-ar an waid/en jai an brait dis haapii maarnin. . . .   1305
sing from di naat tuu di sout pool/sing ov di lohnz biitwiin/   1306
kohz ov johj an meerii/heel tuwo king an kwiin!" da iz di   1307
fors won. den wii had, "among our eenshent mongtinz/an from ouwo   1308
lovlii hilz/oo let di preerii ekoo/gohd bles di prins ov weelz!" . . .   1309
bot eniihou, o no wo—do kaarneeshon dee, maan, su moch o bonz!   1310
do taim laik di din gat iiriiyeetid jringk su moch lek nou!   1311
di gi wii waan baril o shigo waato an laim. di gi wii gud fu di   1312
wedo a di taim, ka di son wuz hat. wii jringk til wii   1313
weeri, an som bonz, maan! som big bonz wid shigo on tap. . . .   1314
dem baiz seyin, "ai in get! ai din get non!" hii lai!   1315
de get, oredi. an di—oovo an oovo yu kin tekin yu bonz, maan!   1316

Translation

We celebrated Coronation: the girls in white dresses and—little medals,
and the boys in white shirts with—am—serge pants, and we—we had
a—Carol was his name, the bandmaster, Mr. Carol stood up high on that   1300T
thing on the day that we went. We marched all the way from Sharples'
school down to High Street, until we came into the—the—the Law
Courts. Yes. And we sang, I can remember the first sing—song
we sang was, "Let Cheers Ring Far and Wide." [Singing:] "Let
cheers ring far and wide/And joy and bright this happy morning. . . .   1305T
Sing from the North to the South Pole/Sing of the lands between/
Cause of George and Mary/Hail to our King and Queen!" That is the
first one. Then we had, "Among our ancient mountains/And from our
lovely hills/Oh let the prairie echo/God bless the Prince of Wales!" . . .
But anyhow, I know that Coronation Day, man, there were so many buns!   1310T
At that time aerated [carbonated] drinks weren't as plentiful as they are now.
They gave us a barrel of lemonade. That was good for the
weather at the time, because the sun was hot. We drank until we were
weary, and there were buns, man. Some big buns with sugar on top. . . .
The boys kept saying, "I didn't get any! I didn't get any!" Lies!   1315T
They'd gotten some already. And—over and over you could take buns, man.

24b. The speech of a Madeira Portuguese woman at Bartica

M: and a gu nou tu baartiiko tu dis leedii. and o miit—di leedii soo   1317
laik mi! shi se, "a, foriino, dii shaild nais. hoop yu stan gud   1318
id mii, shail." kudn taak ingglish pleen, yu noo.   1319
ye-es. . . . shii iz lizbon pootugiiz, yu noo.   1320

Translation

And I went now to Bartica to this lady. And I met—the lady liked me so! She said, "Ah, Farina, the child is nice. Hope you get on well with me, child." She couldn't speak English clearly, you know. Yes. . . . She's a Lisbon Portuguese, you know.   1320T

24c. Chant of the Ole Higue

M: boʔ wii yuuztu plee ool haig. . . . di se di ool haig doz tek aaf ii   1321
skin an les it, an huu kin kech it tek it an put it—   1322
J: put saalt.   1323
M: put an kovo it aando maato n aal. ai in noo if piipl   1324
kyan—en—an di doz tek salt n pepo n put it,   1325
su wen di ool haig gu, ii doz se, "skin, da mii!!   1326
yu no noo mii? skin, skin, yu noo noo mii?" [Laughs.]   1327

Translation

But we used to play Ole Higue . . . they say the Ole Higue takes off her skin and leaves it, and whoever catches it would take it and put it—
Put salt.
Put it in a mortar and cover it up and all. I don't know if people can—and—and they take salt and pepper and put it [on the skin]   1325T
so that when the Ole Higue returns, she would say "Skin, it's me! Don't you know me? Skin, skin, don't you know me?" [Laughs.]

24d. A fire in Leopold Street

M: a riimembo wen o woz o chaild, a krismostaim, di fos faiyo ai sii   1328
in gayana. ai in noo wo yeer wuz do. a heer waan skwib,   1329
an from do di priven skwib from komin in di   1330
konchrii. waan skwib—di chainii di duuwin skwib tu—tu   1331
leopool sriit kaarno an lambord schriit, an di hool plees bloo op!   1332
an ii bon out di hool o lambord schriit. heer, do dee, if yu   1333
sii di faiyo goowin in n komin out, so: "pshh!"—laik sombadi   1334
senin it. an notn kun out it. iz a danamait di—di—di   1335
piipl from di baksait had to drap o banam—m—o donomait—   1336
an lik op eviiting bifoor di get tu out dii faiya.   1337
ka dii faiyo swiipin from waan plees tu di neks.   1338

Translation

I remember one Christmas when I was a child, the first fire I saw in Guyana. I don't know what year that was. I heard a firecracker,

and that led them to ban firecrackers from being imported into the   1330T
country. One firecracker! Some Chinese were exploding firecrackers at
the corner of Leopold and Lombard streets, and the whole place blew up!
And it burned down the whole of Lombard Street. Hear, that day, if you
saw the fire going in and coming out, so: "Pshh!"—as if somebody were
sending it. And nothing could put it out. It was dynamite the—the—the   1335T
people from the bauxite company had to drop a—bomb—a stick of dynamite
and demolish everything before they were able to put the fire out.
Because the fire was sweeping from one place to the next.

6

Modern Texts
from Diverse Domains

In this final chapter I have selected a sample of modern texts (dating from the 1930's to the 1970's) representing the broader use of Guyanese varieties of English—in newspapers and the radio, in folksongs and literature, in the classroom and the law courts.[1] Such texts, drawn from both oral and written channels, make an interesting counterpoint to the tape-recorded extracts in Chapters 4 and 5, since they were produced not in response to any query or stimulus from the investigator, but in the spontaneous fulfillment of the language users' own communicative or expressive needs. To be sure, the speech used in, say, the lawyers' summations (Text set 31) may not be "natural" in the sense that it is language adopted for a formal occasion, but even texts like these are useful as snapshots of naturally ongoing activities rather than dramatic reenactments for the researcher's benefit. Valuable as tape-recordings of oral conversation are, we need to draw on other sources to round out our understanding of a speech community's code matrix and verbal repertoire (Gumperz 1964). This seems to me to be a major need of modern sociolinguistics.

The texts in this chapter differ from the texts in Chapter 3 in another important respect. Apart from the obvious difference that those texts were all written and drawn from earlier periods, most of them were penned by outsiders to the Guyanese speech community, expatriates reporting to their countrymen in Europe what the "natives" in this part of the world were doing or saying. The pervasive we/they spirit of the early texts ("we" the European writers, "they" the local African and Indian populace) is captured in Kirke's observation (Text 4a, line 88): "Their speeches are as wonderful as their letters." This distanced stance is absent from the texts in this chapter, which feature the subjects of the earlier travelogs in the role of the authors, creators, and language users themselves.

25. Evelyn Moe Newspaper Column (1930–1940)

Evelyn Moe's newspaper column, "Uncle Stapie pon de People," appeared regularly in Georgetown's *Sunday Argosy* in the 1930's and 1940's and was reportedly very popular. As the nineteenth-century *Argosy* cartoons in Chapter 3 demonstrate, there has always been a place in the mass media for creole. "The Sam Chase Show," broadcast over Radio Demerara in the 1950's and 1960's (see Rickford, ed., 1978: 232–36 for excerpts), the Seymour comic strips published in newspapers and as separate books in the 1960's and 1970's, and the column "Laugh with Lucius and Then Think," which appears currently in the Georgetown *Sunday Chronicle*, are more recent examples.

Unfortunately, the thrust of all such works is a stereotypical association of creole with humor and gossip—as if this were all that nonstandard varieties were good for. The phenomenon is not unique to Guyana, of course; it is virtually universal.[2] In Guyana, as in many other pidgin-creole areas, news reports and serious editorializing have always been done in the standard language. Signs of potential change are evident, however, in the work of Guyanese artists and writers. The production "Tragic Frontiers in the Caribbean," staged in Georgetown a few years ago, and featuring Johnny Agard, Ken Corsbie, Marc Matthews, and Henry Mootoo, is only one of several recent demonstrations that creole can be successfully used for serious and philosophical themes.[3] Elsewhere in the Caribbean poets and oral performers like Louise Bennett, Edward Braithwaite, Paul Keens-Douglas, and Michael Smith (see Braithwaite 1984) have been making—and exemplifying—the same point. Of course the texts of many of the speakers featured in the preceding chapters also demonstrate this (see Lohtan's Text 16 and its introduction), as do the verbalized reflections and philosophies of thousands of creole speakers worldwide. But the everyday poetry and rhetoric of folk like these usually go unnoticed and unappreciated by the literary/academic establishment.

One of the difficulties of using creole in the newspapers or literature is how to represent it in writing. Moe chooses to represent many of the standard creole features: the realization of English "th" as *t* or *d* ("dis" 1339, "tink" 1362), progressive participial "-ng" as *n'* ("starvin'" 1341), consonant-cluster simplification ("almos'" 1342), vowel-opening or -lowering ("lang" 1339), vowel-shortening or -laxing ("tek" 1349), and metathesis ("aks" 1355). However, perhaps for the sake of maintaining readability, other potential creole features are not represented. For instance, the *l* in "already" (1342) is retained although it would be absent in all but the most acrolectal Guyanese speech, and "letter" (1343) would almost certainly not show retroflexion or *r*- constriction. Another example is the absence of final *t* in demonstrative and interrogative pronouns like "what" and "that." But what makes this case interesting is that the final consonant is retained only in the narrative section in lines 1339–49 ("dat," "what" 1340). It is carefully deleted in the dialogue between the two Indo-Guyanese boys from line 1351 onward ("wha'" 1354, "dah" 1358).

This is not the only evidence of a shift toward basilectal creole norms in the boys' dialogue. The English copula is present in the narrative section ("is" 1347, "was" 1348) but is absent in the dialogue before adjectives, and replaced by "ah" before noun phrases (1357) and in continuative/progressive constructions (1353). Pronominal "ah" (1343) is replaced by "me" (1352); the English plural suffix is dropped (contrast "times" 1345 with "lick" 1359); negative "ent" (1345) gives way to "no" (1351); and perfect "has" (1346) is replaced by "done" (1362). In the dialogue, creole idioms ("kill am wid lick" 1359) and transformations (such as topicalization with "ah" in 1351) begin to appear for the first time.

It should be noted that the language of newspaper writing is rarely this basilectal, as a glance at any of the other columns or comic strips referred to above will attest. This may be partly because the writers themselves are typically from middle-class backgrounds and may not control this level of the continuum, or because they see their primary (or most important) audience as middle-class readers who might find basilectal creole objectionable or hard to follow, especially in print. In any case is it purely coincidental that Moe uses his most basilectal creole for the dialogue of Indo-Guyanese, or is he suggesting that the basilect is most characteristic of this ethnic group? As noted earlier, this is a popular stereotype, but it is challenged by new data on Afro-Guyanese speech, including the texts of Anna and Basil, and the folksongs in this volume.

Apart from the boys' dialogue, there are only one or two distinctly creole features in these texts. In Text 25a there is a single occurrence of the emphatic pronominal "we dis," a basilectal feature more frequently realized as "a-we dis." Copula absence, a characteristically mesolectal creole feature (Bickerton 1973a), is also widespread in this text, a form of "be" occurring only once ("is" 1340) in a total of seven possible environments. In the narrative portion of the second text, the English copula is present in all three potential environments, and negative "ent" (1345) is the only grammatical feature with creole roots. There are two examples of nonstandard verb agreement—"gets" (1343) and "is" (1347)—but the latter is not very frequent in speech, and the former does not seem well motivated. It may be that "gets" is intended as a historical present, but it does not occur in a complicating narrative clause, where the historical present would be most likely to occur.[4] It is also unlikely as an instance of overgeneralization of the (nonhistorical) present-tense suffix, since the reference here is clearly past rather

than present, and punctual rather than habitual or generic.⁵ Its main function seems to be to contribute "nonstandard" coloring. Other features that
seem out of place are "hasn" and "here it is again" (1346–47), which are
pitched too high, in terms of continuum level, for the surrounding text. Examples like these remind us how difficult it is for writers trained and accustomed to writing in SE to write in creole. Moe's touch is masterly in some
sections—particularly in the Boodoo Ram/Sanchar dialogue—but goes
awry in others.

25a. From the Sunday Argosy, Feb. 2, 1930

Well, well, dis a funny place. But how we gettin' lang in	1339
truth? . . . Dat part is alright but Uncle Stapie what bout poor we dis?	1340
While de grass growin' de horse starvin'. It starvin' so	1341
bad already dat it almos' pon dyin'.	1342

25b. "The Ten Commandments," from the Sunday Argosy, May 5, 1940

Ah gets a letter from Canada las' week from a lady askin' me to	1343
write dat joke bout "de Ten Commandments."	1344
Well if ah ent write it already bout ten times in de las' ten 'ears,	1345
ah hasn' write it once.	1346
Anyhow, ah is always ready to oblige a lady. So here it is again.	1347
Somewhere up Eas' Coas' ah little Eas' Indian boy named Boodoo Ram was	1348
hurrin from school an' de followin' conversation tek place between	1349
them!	1350
Boodoo Ram: "Hi, Sanchar, Ah wheh you ah go? You no ah go school?"	1351
Sanchar: "Boy, me getaway, Me ah go 'skult.'	1352
Teacher bad like a sword today. He ah tear lick."	1353
Boodoo Ram: "Boy, ah wha matter wid am?"	1354
Sanchar: "Boy, he ah aks how much Commandment dem got, an' dem	1355
boy no know."	1356
Boodoo Ram: "Dem no know ah ten?"	1357
Sanchar: "Ten? You know dah boy Mungul? Mungul tell am twenty.	1358
He wan' kill am wid lick. Dah boy Bissoon tell am	1359
thirty. Me Gawd! Me no know how Bissoon go able si'down.	1360
You know dah boy Harilall? Harilall tell am hundred.	1361
Boy, me no tink he done lick Harilall yet. Ten?	1362
You tell am ten, leh he bus' you ----."	1363

Translation

I got a letter from Canada last week from a lady asking me to
write that joke about "the Ten Commandments."

Well if I haven't written it already about ten times in the last ten
years, I haven't written it once.

Anyhow, I am always ready to oblige a lady. So here it is again.
Somewhere up the East Coast a little East Indian boy named Boodoo Ram was
hurrying from school and the following conversation took place between
them!

"Hi, Sanchar, where are you going? Aren't you going to school?"

"Boy, I got away, I am going to play truant.
The teacher is as bad as a sword today. He is flogging a lot."

"Boy, what is the matter with him?"

"Boy, he was asking how many Commandments there were, and those
boys didn't know."

"They didn't know it was ten?"

"Ten? Do you know that boy named Mungul? Mungul told him twenty.
He wanted to kill him with licks. That boy Bissoon told him
thirty. My God! I don't know how Bissoon will be able to sit down.
Do you know that boy Harilall? Harilall told him a hundred.
Boy, I don't think he's finished flogging Harilall yet. Ten?
You tell him ten, let him burst your ----."

26. Guyanese Folksongs (1950's – 1970's)

The Guyanese folksongs in this volume, like the Uncle Stapie newspaper
extracts, are part of a larger selection printed in Rickford (1978), but without the detailed commentary provided here. This particular text set is one of
three in this volume that we owe to Wordsworth McAndrew (the others are
Basil's texts in Chapter 5 and the birthday requests below). McAndrew is
deservedly regarded as the expert on Guyanese folklore: the richness of his
collected materials, the length of his experience, and the depth of his exper-
tise on diverse aspects of Guyanese folklore and culture are virtually un-
matched. The folksongs presented below are from a collection he recorded
in Guyana between the 1950's and the 1970's, and aired on "What Else?"
and other popular radio programs. He frequently refers to the full set of
Guyanese folksongs as a "book," and to its subgenres as "chapters," a practice I follow here.

Folk material is of particular potential value to the linguist—I say "potential" because it is so infrequently exploited—because it often preserves the
patterns of earlier times. For instance, Speirs' (1902) collection of Guyanese
proverbs contains several features rarely attested in modern GC, such as
nonpunctual/copulative *da*, prepositional *na*, and the realization of intervocalic *v* as *d*, as in "cassada." [6]

Of the three folksongs printed here, Text 26a from the "Queh-Queh" chapter is probably the oldest, containing lexical items like "moushay" and "cammalamma" that are rare today.* Its basilectal grammatical features, however, including demonstrative "dem" and continuative "ah," are very common, as their recurrence in the spoken texts in this volume attests. Text 26c is from what McAndrew frequently describes as the newest and most active chapter of the Guyana folksong book—the "Rhyming Songs" and "Blend Tunes" that mix musical and verbal elements from the Indian and Afro-Creole traditions. Its basilectal creole features include negative "na," indefinite "wan," and lexical "mumma."[7] Note that Text 26a (like Text 26b) comes out of the Afro-Guyanese tradition, while Text 26c is Indo-Guyanese—demonstrating once again that the basilect is used by both groups.

One feature of Text 26c worth noting is the upward style-shift in the last line: the double connective "until when" is nonstandard, but pronominal "I" and modal/future "will" are acrolectal. One likely explanation is that the entire last verse, beginning with "Fish in da water," is a formulaic love verse of the kind exchanged among schoolmates and included in love letters. These love verses often have SE morphology and syntax ("Roses are red/violets are blue/sugar is sweet/and so are you"), preserving the form in which they were originally introduced to the community, via greeting cards and other written sources.

Text 26b represents a mesolectal level of the continuum, evident in the fact that it uses subject pronoun "ah" (a monophthongal reduction of "I") where Text 26c typically uses "me," and demonstrative "dese" where Text 26a uses "dem." Note, however, that it shares with Text 26c the absence of the English copula (1372, 1388), the use of possessive *me*, and the use of the nonstative verb-stem without "has" or "have" ("come" 1370, "tu'n" 1386) to signal perfect aspect—past with present relevance (see Comrie 1976: 52).

Finally, a word or two on the phonological features represented in McAndrew's orthography. In addition to nonstandard consonantal features such as consonant-cluster simplification and *th*-stopping, the orthography represents the lowering of SE *O* and *o* to *a*, as in "baderation" ('botheration' 1372) and "da" (1388), the absence of postvocalic retroflexion in unstressed syllables ("tomorra" 1379; but cf. "dollar" 1377), and the laxing of the high front vowel in "marrid."[8] As we found to be true of the "Uncle Stapie" texts above, not every potential feature of creole phonology is represented ("when" in line 1373, for instance, might have been represented as "wen"), but the orthographic conventions are easy for the reader already literate in English

---

*"Moushay" is French creole for *monsieur* (see Faine 1937: 269). "Cammalamma" is defined by McAndrew (1978: 240) as "To 'wind up' or gyrate oneself, as in dancing." This may be related to French Creole *calimangnole* and *calinda*, both of which refer to popular forms of dancing in Haiti (Faine 1937: 219). Compare also JC *calembe*, which like *calinda* refers to a "dance of African origin" (Cassidy and Le Page 1980: 89).

to follow, and—for Guyanese and Caribbean audiences at least—they provide a good guide to the appropriate creole pronunciation.

All the folksong texts are from Wordsworth McAndrew's collection, as indicated in the introduction to this text set.

26a. From the "Queh-Queh" chapter

Moushay moushay	1364
Moushay moushay	1365
See dem gal ah cammalamma an ah laugh	1366
Moushay	1367
Moushay (repeat)	1368

26b. From the "Ring-Play" chapter

Good morning Mistress Crosby	1369
Ah come to make a statement	1370
Bout dese two little chilrun	1371
Because dey baderation	1372
Ah when ah put on me lang coat	1373
Dey call me Mistress Ramgoat	1374
An when ah put on me lang boots	1375
Dey call me Mistress Pussy-in-de-Boots	1376
Ah gwine to pay a dollar	1377
To put dem in de station	1378
An when ah come home tomorra	1379
Ah comin home to see dem.	1380

26c. From the "Rhyming-Song" chapter (sung by Shani Sahadeo)

Nineteen sixty-two, the early part of June	1381
Me mumma binna tell me na marrid so soon.	1382
Nineteen sixty-two, the early part of June	1383
Me mumma binna tell me na marrid so soon.	1384
When me binna lil gal, me mumma gie me dhal an rice	1385
Now me tu'n wan big gal, me marrid legalize.	1386
Nineteen sixty-two, etc. (repeat here and after next verse)	1387
Fish in da water, an' bird in da sky	1388
I will love you until when I die.	1389

27. Jan Carew Novel, 'Black Midas' (1958)

The two extracts from Jan Carew's *Black Midas* given here are representative of the use of Creole in Guyanese literature. Some younger writers—poets and dramatists especially—have been writing more extensively in creole in recent years, but in fiction the use of creole is usually confined to the dialogue, the narrative remaining in SE as it does below. Guyana's best-known writers—novelists such as Wilson Harris, Edgar Mittleholtzer, and Jan Carew, and poets such as A. J. Seymour and Martin Carter—have generally published in SE. This is true of other Caribbean and British Commonwealth territories as well, reflecting in part the effects of the British-derived educational and sociocultural systems in these territories and the fact that many of the writers come from middle-class, nonbasilectal backgrounds, and in part the constraints of publishing in Europe and North America and trying to reach a larger English readership.

Braithwaite (1984: 45 – 46) notes that for recent "sound poets" like Michael Smith, Paul Keens-Douglas, Linton Kwesi Johnson, and Oku Onuora, "nation language is no longer anything to argue about or experiment with; it is their classical norm, and comes out of the same experience as the music of contemporary popular song." In Caribbean drama, too, the use of creole is traditionally strong, but in fiction it is restricted, as noted above, primarily to dialogue. Samuel Selvon's novels and short story collections, such as *The Lonely Londoners* (1956), *Ways of Sunlight* (1957), and *Moses Ascending* (1975), represent a rare attempt to incorporate the syntax and lexicon of creole speech—in his case mesolectal Trinidadian varieties—in fictional prose (see Rohlehr 1978; Bernhardt 1983).[9]

The limited use of creole in Caribbean literature is illustrated also in the orthographies adopted to represent it. In these extracts from *Black Midas*, we find very few of the orthographic conventions exploited by Moe, McAndrew, and others in the mass media. The ubiquitous realization of SE interdental fricatives as stops in GC is not represented ("the" 1392), nor is the absence of retroflexion in "Doctor" (1394), nor the low, unrounded, "broad mouth" realization of the vowels in this word and elsewhere ("got" 1398). The only phonological feature represented, curiously enough, is the loss of unstressed initial syllables, as in "'bout" (1396) and "'way" (1404). From examples like "chile" (1397) and "lef'" (1404), it at first appears as if consonant-cluster simplification is being represented. But we encounter many cases in which the final, postconsonantal *t* or *d* is intact ("rest" 1397, "second" 1401), and the marking of this feature appears to be lexically rather than phonologically conditioned; the word "lef'," for instance, occurs invariably in Text 27b without final *t*. Apart from these cases, the only lexical items given non-English spellings are those that have non-English roots, like "pick'ny" (1400;

a reduction from "pickaninny"), or that are used in non-English ways, like the preverbal negator "nah" (1429).

One of the reasons for the limited tinkering with conventional English orthography found in Caribbean literature is that extensive modification may make the text difficult for an English-literate audience to read, even if that audience includes creole speakers.[10] However, several Caribbean writers have shown that, even without dialect spelling, it is possible to convey the rhythm and feel of creole speech effectively through the use of creole lexicon and syntax. The extracts from Carew's *Black Midas* are a case in point.

Text 27a provides a fictional (but certainly true to life) representation of doctor talk, rounding out the picture of professional language use in Guyana that we get from the texts of the teacher and the barristers below. The discourse in this extract shows some evidence of the kind of asymmetrical power relationships that others have found in interactions between men and women, parents and children, and doctors and patients in the United States (see Zimmerman and West 1975; West and Zimmerman 1983). Carew's fictional doctor interrupts ("The doctor cut her short" 1396), expresses impatience with his questioner's attempt at elaboration ("Yes, yes" 1398), and gives orders (1417–18). It could be argued that these features reflect the urgency of the communicative situation, but the fact that they show up in more leisurely doctor-patient interaction, and in similar dyads, points to a deeper set of conventions.

At the same time a measure of mutual respect is expressed by the forms of address that the principals use toward each other. The old woman addresses the doctor by his professional title, "Doctor," and he addresses her as "My" (cf. Hindi *ma:i:* 'mother; an old woman'; Chaturvedi and Tiwari 1975: 588), paying homage both to her age and to her status as the female head of the household.[11] In calling her My, he is also, in effect, addressing her as if she were his mother, which is compatible with his being, like her, Indo-Guyanese.

There is abundant evidence in Text 27a that the doctor is accustomed to and comfortable with the mores of rural populations, and is attempting to relate to My in accord with those mores. Note that he suggests payment in kind rather than cash for his services ("Bring chicken and egg to me house" 1430) and is familiar with local folk remedies such as rubbing cow dung on a sick child (1419). His use of Creole is explicitly commented on by the author/narrator: "The doctor spoke in dialect and his voice took on the sing-song lilt of an Indian villager" (1392–93). His "taking on" this sing-song lilt (as Daizal Samad has noted in a personal communication) suggests an act that is effortless and unconscious rather than contrived. This is also suggested by the doctor's use of "me" (1408) as a subject pronoun where the average urban speaker would have mesolectal "I" or "Ah," and by his use of Creole idioms like "How much year she got?" (1398) to inquire about the daughter's age.

The old woman, like the doctor, uses subject pronoun "me" (1422); her perfectives, like his, do not require auxiliary "has" or "have" (1405, 1406), and her speech includes an example of the absence of an article with a noun phrase whose reference is nonspecific ("other doctor" 1402). The congruence between her dialect and his (when speaking to her) reinforces the general impression that his use of Creole is nonartificial and noncondescending, and is intended simply to help her understand better, feel more comfortable, and provide more information. Had the doctor addressed the old woman as he addressed the nurse (in SE, and with professional terminology, 1414–15), communication between them might have been less effective. This pattern of linguistic down-shifting for basilectal and lower-mesolectal Creole speakers is common among Guyanese doctors, although it tends to vary depending on their individual backgrounds, personalities, and linguistic competence.

Text 27b is included partly because it shows the speech of an Afro-Guyanese, Bullah. Like the Indo-Guyanese characters in Text 27a, Bullah uses many morphosyntactic creole features, including "say" as a conditional marker (1434); unmarked past participials ("plan" 1433) and passives ("call" 1437); deictic/plural "them" (1435); existential "it got" (1439); and habitual "does" (1440). One minor difference between him and the old woman in Text 27a is that he uses mesolectal "en't" as negator while she uses basilectal "nah."

Text 27a is from Carew (1958), pp. 50–53; 27b is from the same edition, pp. 152–53.

27a. A doctor's conversation with an old woman whose daughter is in labor (Mocha, East Bank Demerara)

An old Indian woman stood in the doorway blinking at the torchlight.	1390
"Me glad you come, Doctor," she said, shading her eyes.	1391
"You is the girl mama?" The doctor spoke in dialect and his voice	1392
took on the sing-song lilt of an Indian villager.	1393
"Yes, Doctor. You is a good man; you lef' you house	1394
this time . . ."	1395
"Tell me 'bout the girl." The doctor cut her short.	1396
"She is me one-chile, Doctor; all the rest dead . . ."	1397
"Yes, yes. How much year she got?"	1398
"She got fifteen year, Doctor."	1399
"This is the first pick'ny?"	1400

"Second time she having pick'ny, Doctor; first one dead in   1401
she belly. Other doctor tell she 'No more pick'ny, Teena,' but she   1402
husband is a no-good man, get drunk, beat she, now he go   1403
'way lef' she."   1404
   "How long the girl got pain?"   1405
   "Two day, Doctor; pick'ny should come July month; now   1406
September." . . . The doctor felt for her pulse and turned round.   1407
   "Me want plenty water, My, plenty boiling water," he said, and the old   1408
woman's bare feet slapped the mud floor as she ran out with an iron pot   1409
in each hand. The nurse stuck a thermometer into the girl's mouth.   1410
   "Don't bite it," she said close to her ear.   1411
   "What's her temperature?" the doctor asked when she held the 1412
thermometer up to the light. . . .   1413
   "I'm going to puncture the outer membrane, and if that doesn't   1414
work, we'll have to use an anaesthetic and forceps. Aron!" . . .   1415
   "The nurse going to visit the girl and the pick'ny every day," the   1416
doctor said, and he handed her a bottle of liver extract. "Give the girl   1417
this three times a day and keep the pick'ny clean.   1418
If you rub cow-dung on the pick'ny it will die, you hearing me?"   1419
   "Yes, doctor."   1420
   "You got milk, My?"   1421
   "Yes, doctor, me got two cow."   1422
   "You must boil the milk before you give it to the pick'ny. . . .   1423
You understand?"   1424
   "Yes, Doctor." . . .   1425
   "You got money, My?"   1426
   "How much, Doctor?"   1427
   "Five dollar."   1428
   "Ow, me God! Me nah got five dollar, Doctor."   1429
   "All right. Bring chicken and egg to me house;   1430
me got to live too, you know."   1431
   "Yes, Doctor."   1432

27b. A shopkeeper at Perenong Creek in the diamond-prospecting interior

   "Me got it all plan," Bullah said, shading his eyes and looking through   1433
the window at the sun. "About ten mile from here is the hills. Say they   1434
lef' here at three o'clock, then they should reach them hill   1435
by afternoon. Them two goin' try get over them hill   1436
fast, and b'time they cross that last hill call 'Ham Nah   1437
Jai,' en't going to be much breath lef' in them, and even   1438
if they got any lef' then it got some bad anaconda snake;   1439
you can smell them far off if the wind up, and you does   1440
hear them snoring like man."   1441

28. Birthday Requests from Radio Listeners (1970's)

The five texts below are extracts of letters from Guyanese who wrote to Wordsworth McAndrew in the 1970's with requests for musical selections on his "What Else?" and "East Meets West" radio programs. Although I have labeled these "birthday requests," listeners in fact asked to have a certain record played for a particular person or group of people on all sorts of occasions and even just in friendship. The five extracts below are drawn from a large collection that McAndrew kindly made available for analysis of the extent to which, and the ways in which, patterns of speech are carried over into writing.

Given the pattern of Haiti and other diglossic speech communities (Ferguson 1959), we might expect that the standard or "high" variety would be used for virtually all kinds of writing, from newspaper editorials to personal letters. But in these examples, though the writers basically follow the conventions of SE, we find some interesting intrusions from the Creole vernacular.

One could of course look for creole transfer or "interference" (Weinreich 1953: 1) in the written work of schoolchildren, as Craig (1969), Cave (1971), Tyndall (1974), Haynes (1978), and Rickford and Greaves (1978) have done. In school the pressure to use SE in written work is greater, but it is precisely the relative absence of external pressure that makes these letters interesting. They are written not as a classroom assignment, but as a spontaneous act. In this sense the function of the material is closer to that of ordinary speech than school compositions typically are, and the letters also share more of the textual quality of the spoken language.

The comparison of written and spoken, planned and unplanned, integrated and involved discourse has become a major enterprise of linguists in recent years (Ochs 1979; Chafe 1981; Tannen 1982), and the analysis of these birthday requests can simultaneously benefit from and contribute to this research. The letter in Text 28a, for instance, is characterized by the kind of involvement associated with oral conversation, including a direct appeal to share the writer's indignation: "Well, I must say . . ." Though written, it lacks the integration that usually accompanies writing; note the deictic, context-bound reference to "that boy" (1444). This involvement and lack of integration may be characteristic of informal personal letters, but it is not what we would expect of a written request to the program director of a radio station.

Part of the reason that we find these textual qualities and the presence of some Creole features in these letters is that the radio personality in this case (McAndrew) encouraged in his programs a preference for the informal over the formal and the spontaneous over the pretentious. For instance, he would usually read the letters "live" on the air, and the letters themselves were often written in a register suited to this purpose ("Greetings goes her way" 1460). In addition, he was well known for his use of Creole on the air—a mesolectal or "Georgetown" variety, as he would say. As we shall see in Text 29a, other radio talk-show hosts in Guyana follow SE more closely.

Yet when we look more closely at the language of these letters, we discover that they contain very few basilectal features, a point noted by Rickford and Greaves (1978) in regard to school compositions. The writers are clearly trying to adhere to the convention that SE should be used in writing. Note in this connection that there are no instances of first-person subject "me" or third-person object "am." There are instances of possessive "you" (1443) and "they" (1450), but as we have seen, unmarked possessives persist further into the mesolect than other pronominal forms, and their nonstandard character may often pass unrecognized due to the application of *r*-deletion or other phonological processes. The copula is present in two of these letters where it would be required in SE, in both past and present forms, and with appropriate person-number agreement ("am" 1443, "is" 1444, "was" 1446, "are" 1449). But two writers do not use SE present forms of "have" (1452) and "go" (1460); even some university students have difficulty with the suppletive forms of these verbs, and with the use of English third-person "-s" more generally.

Two nonstandard features show up in Texts 28b–28d: the use of the verb-stem instead of an inflected past participle in post-auxiliary and other positions ("marry" 1450, "know" 1451, "stick" 1453), and the absence of past conditionals in conditional expressions ("will" instead of "would" 1454, "can" instead of "could" 1455). Particularly interesting in Text 28d is the subordinate clause in the second sentence, with a pronominal subject and a finite verb, and without the insertion of "it" at the boundary between the main and subordinate clauses: "I will like ∅ *if you can put over this birthday request*" (1455; see also 1459–60). The fact that this finite phrasing occurs and its nonfinite equivalent does not ("I would like you *to put over this birthday request*") might be taken as evidence of the relative rarity of nonfinite clauses in Guyanese speech. For further discussion on this point see the introduction to Sheik's texts (Text set 14, Chapter 4).

Two other nonstandard features each occur only once: the use of prepositional "at" instead of "to" in line 1454,[12] and the clefting/topicalization in lines 1445–46: "Is every Wednesday you hear some sort of request for him." Such a marked Creole feature does not normally occur in written compositions, and its presence here conveys once again the flavor of spoken usage.

Despite the overlapping of spoken and written conventions in these texts, many of the letters in McAndrew's collection contain conventions unique to the epistolary genre, such as the salutation in Text 28e: "I hope my lines will

not fail in finding you O.K." Another letter begins similarly: "I do hope that
the arrival of my few lines will reach you under the best of luck and pros-
perity as it leaves me enjoying your wonderful programme."* The incidence
of this kind of ornateness in Guyanese letters, especially those written by
younger people, is probably lower than it was a few decades ago, reflecting
both changes in the conventions handed down in the schools and changes in
the oral conventions in the society at large. Such flowery salutations are the
written equivalent of the grandiloquent speech-making and "fancy talk" traditional at weddings and other formal events discussed in the introduction
to Kirke (Text set 4, Chapter 3).

All the extracts happen to be from Indo-Guyanese listeners.

28a. From a listener in Johanna Cecilia, Essequibo

Hello, Mac,	1442
I am a regular listener to you fantastic programme "What Else." Well,	1443
I must say that, that boy G. of B. Street, Reliance is trying to be a	1444
well-known person on your programme. Is every Wednesday you hear some	1445
sort of request for him. And I sent a lot of requests and was never	1446
successful. . . .	1447
Your regular listener	1448

28b. From a listener in Vreed-en-Hoop, West Coast Demerara

We are two sisters and four brother and my sisters are getting	1449
marry . . . and we are kindly asking to request they wedding greeting.	1450

28c. From a listener in Black Bush, Corentyne, Berbice

Also a very special greeting from her boy-friend B know as D.	1451
Hoping she have a happy get together on that special occasion of her	1452
birthday on the 6th October. The cake will be stick at 12 o'clock.	1453

28d. From a listener in Albion Estate, Corentyne, Berbice

I am a regular lissenor at your programme (East Meat West) I will like	1454
if you can put over this birthday request for me on the 19th October	1455

*Even more elaborate salutations ("I hope that the arrival of this letter finds you under the
golden boughs of love and happiness") are possible. These ornate salutations have parallels
elsewhere, as in this opening from a letter written by a nineteenth-century Irish immigrant to
America: "Dear Father and Mother, I take this favorable opportunity to write these lines
hoping the arrival of this letter finds you in good health as it leaves me at present, thanks be to
God for his kind mercies to us all" (quoted in Wakin 1976: 19).

1977. Happy birthday greeting go out to S. of Albion . . . Wishing you   1456
lots of love and manny more birthday in the future.   1457

28e. From a listener in Soesdyke, East Bank Demerara

Hi! You Mac.,
    I hope my lines will not fail in finding you O.K. Sir I wish if   1458
you can please publish my sister R. 13th Birthday. . . . Greetings goes   1459
her way from her three loving Brothers.   1460
                                                                                 1461

29. Radio Announcer (1975)

    This text provides a good example of the relatively standard varieties of English that are characteristic of radio broadcasts. The announcer, B., is an ethnically mixed ("mulatto") middle-class woman with long experience in radio broadcasting, and her interviewees are a number of Afro-Guyanese calypso singers who were competing in the 1975 Mashramani celebrations to be held in Georgetown. Mashramani is the local version of the Mardi Gras or Carnival celebrations held in New Orleans and many other parts of the world. It includes colorful street parades and pageants as well as steel-band and calypso competitions.

    The full-time occupations of these particular calypsonians are not known, but traditionally, most have come from the working and lower-middle classes and from the Afro-Guyanese community.[13] They tend to compose their own songs and to exploit the resources of mesolectal Creole in their compositions, certainly more so than local pop singers, who depend more heavily on imported (American, British, Caribbean) material. By contrast, the average radio announcer is expected to avoid nonstandard varieties of English, especially in syntax. Occasionally, commercials, dramatic productions, and comedy shows aired on the radio are couched in mesolectal Creole rather than SE, but this is the exception rather than the rule.

    We have in this interview, then, interaction between participants whose typical public registers lie in different areas of the continuum, and it is interesting to observe the extent and nature of their mutual adjustment. We have only a few lines from the calypsonians in this sample, but the acrolectal nature of S.'s grammar in lines 1471–72 is very different from the mesolectal grammar he uses in the calypso that he sings moments later. X.'s repetition of the announcer's past participle (*invohlvd*, complete with *oh* and the final consonant cluster) and his series of "yesses" in line 1481 likewise attest to his accommodation to the relatively standard speech of the interviewer and the formal conventions of a radio interview. At the same time the announcer adjusts her speech in the direction of her interviewees' mesolectal Creole dialogue. Grammatically, this is most marked in lines 1473–75, where she is joking and where her remarks are addressed specifically to her guests rather than to her radio audience.[14] It is in lines 1473 and 1474 that the present-perfect "have" auxiliary, which occurs elsewhere (1463, 1467, 1468, 1484), disappears before *gOt*. It is also here (in line 1475) that one of her two examples of zero copula (*ai ∅ spOilin*)[15] and her only two cases (of ten) of omitting the complementizer "that" occur. It is in this line, too, that she wavers between the conventions of direct and reported speech: the use of *doon sing* rather than nonfinite *nOt tu sing* is appropriate for direct rather than indirect speech, but the use of first-person *ai* rather than *yuu* immediately after is not. Her avoidance of the nonfinite form may relate to the general rarity of nonfinite subordinate clauses in GC.

Phonologically, B.'s nonstandard features include eight (of 43) uses of an alveolar stop instead of an interdental fricative (e.g. *dat* 1462, *diiz* 1473, *dee* and *deer* 1474), two (of 8) uses of alveolar *n* (instead of velar *ng* in the participial ending (e.g. *telin* 1475), and three (of 14) uses of word-final consonant-cluster simplification (e.g. *doon* 1464). These are strikingly low frequencies (19–25 percent). Recall the much higher incidence of these and other nonstandard phonological features in the conversational speech of Katherine and Bonnette, who have comparable socioeconomic status but were recorded in a less formal context.

Note further that *orongd* (1466), involving a monopthongal rather than a dipthongal medial vowel, and a velar rather than alveolar stem-final nasal, is nonstandard in British and American speech but is characteristic of standard speech at the very highest levels of the Guyanese continuum. It is common to find affricate (*chr*) pronunciations of SE *tr* sequences across the continuum too, however, and the fact that B. uses *thr* and *tr* pronunciations instead (1467, 1477) is a measure of her approximation to SE norms in her broadcasting register. She is also very consistent in her use of SE *oh*, *O*, and *Oi*, rather than *aa* or *a* and *ai* in words like *wohn*, *klOk*, and *enjOi* (1463, 1466, 1462). The use of reduced schwa instead of *O* in *biikoz* (1474) is more common in middle-class than working-class speech and in the mesolect than the basilect; we will see some more examples of this purportedly "elegant schwa" replacing other full forms below.

B.'s lexicon includes items like *infekshos* (1476), *yuu jentlmen* (1483), and the indefinite pronoun *wohn* (1477). Like her use of standard phonetic variants, these remind us that despite her apparent camaraderie, she is an educated speaker performing in a formal context.

One final note. Lakoff (1973), Conklin (1978), and others claim that hyperbolic adjectives like "wonderful" and "lovely," and the frequent use of sentence qualifiers or hedges like "I think" and "I feel," are characteristic of women's speech, and that these features both contribute to and reflect women's relative powerlessness and nonassertiveness. Both features are characteristic of B.'s speech; there are seven instances of sentence qualifiers like "think," "feel," and "I'm afraid that" in this short extract. But the independent variables go beyond gender. Contrast the relatively powerful and self-assured language of the schoolteacher addressing her pupils in the next extract, and compare the conventionalized humility and powerlessness of the lawyers in the extract after that, who use "sir" and "your honor" to the judge, and frequently preface their statements with qualifiers like "think" and "respectfully submit." B.'s use of "I think" and "I feel" may, like her use of "you gentlemen," be part of a more general convention of deferring to the guest in a public interview, especially when the person knows more than the interviewer about the topic under discussion. The study of gender-related and discourse-governed variation of this type in Caribbean and other pidgin/creole speech communities has scarcely begun.

Text 29 is from Tape CAS2, side B, tape counter nos. 101–6, 139–47, 179–85.

29. From an interview with local calypsonians

B: oooo, verii verii gud. aa yes, ai enjOi dat. . . . dhi wondoful thing	1462
obout booth ov dhooz dhat aiv hord iz dhat wohn wohnts tu heer moor.	1463
yu doon wohnt it to en. dhis iz—dhis iz lovlii. ai thingk dhat wii	1464
reelii geting dhii spirit ov dhi rood maarch nou. rait. tuu minits	1465
tuu ilevn oo klOk. and—am—wir geting muuvd orongd nou so dhat. . . .	1466
oo yes, verii nais. soo nou, wiiv hord thrii ov dhii rood	1467
maarchiz—aa—vaiying fOr dhi rood maarch taitl, and nou wi hav gOt	1468
widh os dhii—Onorobl S. . . . yes and—om—wol, tel mii obout yoor	1469
rood maarch, S.	1470
S: e-e—mai rood maarch iz—am—am invaitin mai waif out tu jOin di	1471
band in—plee mash olong in sevnti-faiv.	1472
B: o-ha. and, yuu thingk dhat yuu gOt it tuu. diiz jentlmen fiil	1473
dee gOt it, yu noo. ai wun laik tu bii o joj, biikoz deer	1474
ohl gud. . . . wel, P wuz telin mii doon sing, ai spOilin	1475
di hool stoorii. bot am ofreed dhat ohl di chuunz ar soo infekshos	1476
dhat—aa—wohn fiilz dhat wohn most meek o litl kOntribuushon.	1477
an ai thingk dhot dhis iz dhi hool pOint ov o rood maarch	1478
kOmpitishon. yuu wohn tu get evriibOdii—dhi hool poblik, dhi	1479
hool neshon invohlvd, and—	1480
X: invohlvd. yes, yes. yes, B.	1481
B: —an singing an biiting tu dhi—yu noo—tu di chuunz az dhee goo.	1482
wel, ai wud laik tu thangk yuu jentlmen verii—verii verii moch	1483
indiid. am—ai thingk dhat aiv had o verii hapii mohrning. ai jos	1484
wohn tu heer moor. dis iz dhi thing.	1485

Translation

Ooh, very very good. Ah yes, I enjoyed that. . . . The wonderful thing
about both of those that I've heard is that one wants to hear more.
You don't want it to end. This is—this is lovely. I think we're
really getting the spirit of the road march now. Right. Two minutes   1465T
to eleven o'clock. And we're getting moved around now so that. . . .
Oh yes, very nice. So now, we've heard three road
marches—ah—vying for the road march title, and now we have
with us the—Honorable S. . . . Yes and—um—well, tell me about your
road march, S.   1470T
    Eh—my road march is—I'm, I'm inviting my wife out to join the
band and play Mash along in [nineteen] seventy-five.
    Oh-ho! And you think that you've got it too. These gentlemen feel
they've got it, you know. I won't like to be a judge, because they're
all good. . . . Well, P. was telling me not to sing, that I was spoiling   1475T
the whole story. But I'm afraid that all the tunes are so infectious
that one feels that one must make a little contribution.
And I think that this is the whole point of a road march
competition. You want to get everybody—the whole public, the
whole nation involved, and—   1480T
    Involved, Yes, yes. Yes, B.
    —and singing and beating to the—you know—to the tunes as they go.
Well, I would like to thank you gentlemen very—very very much
indeed. I think that I've had a very happy morning. I just
want to hear more. This is the thing.   1485T

30. Schoolteacher (1977)

Although the problem of teaching English to Caribbean creole speakers
has been much discussed,[16] very little work has been devoted to the teacher's
language use and the structure of verbal interaction in the classroom. This
brief extract from the classroom session of a schoolteacher in the village of
Golden Grove should therefore provide some useful insights.

The teacher is a thirty-year-old Afro-Guyanese woman, possibly from
Victoria village, given her positive references to it at several points. Victoria
and Golden Grove, both largely Afro-Guyanese villages, are about 18 miles
out of Georgetown on the East Coast, Demerara. The teacher was a teacher-
trainee at the time, and Fitzroy Lewis, a University of Guyana student, vis-
ited the classroom to observe and tape-record the lesson. The teacher would
therefore have been attempting to perform as well as possible for the occasion, presumably trying to use "good English" and to demonstrate that she
could control and stimulate her class effectively. After the class, Lewis dis-

cussed the lesson and other aspects of education in the area with her, in the presence of the school's headmaster.

Although the session was held in the secondary school in Golden Grove, the class being observed was form 1, and the 42 pupils in the class were only between ten and twelve years old. This accounts for some of the teacher's seemingly patronizing remarks, such as the reference in lines 1488–89 to culture as a "big word" that needs to be broken into "nice little tiny bits." The class has just returned from a field trip to Victoria and is discussing some of its highlights. Note the fairly typical characteristics of formal class-room discourse: numerous long questions from the teacher followed by short responses from the students. The students take turns at the teacher's choice; even when she issues an apparently open invitation to respond, she quickly follows up on this by calling on a particular student (as in lines 1499–1500). She refers to students by their first names or by familiar references to where they come from (*O, viktooryo gyorl* 1486, *F, linden* 1512), whereas they refer to her respectfully as *mis* (1487)—a good example of the nonreciprocal address pattern characteristic of asymmetrical power situations (see Brown and Ford 1961).

In addition to requests for information, the teacher's speech acts include commands and rebukes (1507–8), repetitions of pupil's answers as a signal of approval and an invitation to continue (1490), and commendation (1498). Discourse analysis of this type might have useful implications for teacher training, demonstrating, for instance, the need for the teacher to encourage longer and more diverse student participation, and to seek to minimize the position-oriented or authority-centered character of classroom discourse (see Bernstein 1972). It might also be useful in sociolinguistics and the analysis of linguistic variation. Some of the most venerable Guyanese teach-ers, like the late C. A. Yansen, author of *Random Remarks on Creolese* (1975), used to conduct the serious, instructional part of their lessons in SE, but would make a dramatic switch into GC for jokes, rebukes, and classroom management. There is an element of this in Text 30, too. Note the more standard phonology and more complex syntax where the teacher is making a pedagogical point to the class as a whole (e.g. the final-consonant clusters and passives in lines 1488 and 1502), and the less-standard phonology and syntax where she is rebuking a specific student (e.g. the zero copula in line 1495).

Despite the teacher's attempt to maintain "good English," her speech contains several nonstandard or Creole features. Her passives, noun plurals, and third-person "-s" marking are all in accord with the rules of SE; two of her five yes-no questions (1499, 1512) show no subject-auxiliary inversion, although the second of these need not involve inversion in SE either. SE features of her phonology include the nonpalatalization of the velar in *kan*

(1504; cf. *gyorl* in line 1486) and the use of low-mid *O* and *oh* (*wOt, tohk* 1486, 1495). But her nonstandard phonological features are even more evident. They include a high frequency of *d* and *t* stops for the SE interdental fricatives *dh* and *th*, respectively (only two of the 12 cases in this extract are fricatives), the absence of final *t* in *da* and *wo* (1507, 1503), nonretroflexion in *sento* and *kolcho* (1486, 1488), and the realization of *tr* as *chr*, as in *chrip* (1512). These provide some support for Le Page's (1968) claim that teachers themselves are sometimes unsure of correct usage. However, since some of these features, such as the last three, are characteristic of all but the most formal and "correct" local usage, their classification as "nonstandard" in the Guyanese context is open to question. In her basic use of SE syntax and avoidance of the most distinctly Creole phonological features, the schoolteacher in this extract is probably characteristic of many others of her geographical and educational background. To make valid generalizations about the nature and level of teachers' classroom language use in Guyana as a whole, however, we need to draw on other samples, controlling for possible differences between urban and rural schools, and between primary and secondary levels.

Text 30 is from Tape CAS1, side A, tape counter nos. 086–114. T. is the teacher.

30. A classroom discussion, Golden Grove, East Coast Demerara

T: O, viktooryo gyorl. wOt gooz ohn in—di kolchorol sento?	1486
O: mis, kolcho.	1487
T: kolcho. kolcho. doz o big word, soo wii wohnt it brookn dong into	1488
nais litl tainii bits. bai kolcho wii miin— [rising intonation]	1489
O: daansin.	1490
T: daansing.	1491
O: paartiiz.	1492
T: paartiiz. verii gud. yes, izo paartii o paart ov yoor kolcho, G?	1493
G: ye, mis.	1494
T: oo. wai yu laafin at O? giv or o chaans tu tohk.	1495
[To O:] ye-es [continue].	1496
O: spoorts.	1497
T: spoorts. verii gud. verii gud. doz viktooryo gyorl. shii nooz	1498
wOt gooz ohn in or vilij. verii gud. eniibOdii els wud wohn tu	1499
ad somting tu O wOt gooz ohn in di kolchorol sento? M?	1500
M: mis—aam—spoorts.	1501
T: spoorts. hiiz o viktooryo bOi. ii didn wohn tu bii left out. hii	1502
wohnts tu tel yuu dhat. A, duu yuu ohndostan wo gooz ohn in di	1503
kolchorol sento? kan yuu riimemo wot O sed, wOt gooz ohn	1504
at di kolchorol sento?	1505

A: mis, daansiz.   1506
    T: daansiz an paartiiz. yes, doon plee wi da pensil. yu wur   1507
peeying otenshon. lets liiv di kolchorol sento, and, tohk o   1508
litl obout di kindogaardn skuul. nou, huu wohnts tu see   1509
somthing obout di kindogaartn skuul?   1510
    M: mis, mii!   1511
    T: noo, M. [Sighs:] F, linden. yu went On di chrip, rait?   1512

Translation

O., Victoria girl. What goes on in the Cultural Center?
Miss, culture.
Culture. Culture. That's a big word, so we want it broken down into
nice little tiny bits. By culture we mean?
Dancing.   1490T
Dancing.
Parties.
Parties. Very good. Yes, aren't parties a part of your culture, G.?
Yeah, miss.
Oh. [Then] why are you laughing at O.? Give her a chance to talk.   1495T
[To O.:] Yes [continue].
Sports.
Sports. Very good. Very good. That's a Victoria girl. She knows
what goes on on her village. Very good. Would anybody else want to
add something to O. about what goes on in the Cultural Center? M.?   1500T
Miss—am—sports.
Sports. He's a Victoria boy. He didn't want to be left out. He
wants to tell you that. A., do you understand what goes on in the
Cultural Center? Can you remember what O. said, about what goes on
at the Cultural Center?   1505T
Miss, dances.
Dances and parties. Yes, don't play with that pencil. You were
paying attention. Let's leave the Cultural Center and talk a
little about the kindergarten school. Now, who wants to say
something about the kindergarten school?   1510T
Miss, me!
No, M. F., from Linden. You went on the trip, right?

31. Barristers (1977)

Texts 31a and 31b, from a court hearing, illustrate some of the characteristics of professional language use in the Guyanese Creole continuum. The
recording from which they are taken was made in Justice Aubrey Bishop's
court in Georgetown in 1977 by Lennox Foster and Francis Callender, two

University of Guyana students. Unfortunately, background information about the two barristers is unavailable.

As in the British legal system, to which Guyana adheres, the barrister is the person who represents clients in court, as against the solicitor, who draws up wills and performs other out-of-court duties. Medicine and law have traditionally been two of the primary avenues of upward mobility for the locally born in Guyanese society; until independence in 1966 the highest positions in government and commerce were largely monopolized by expatriates, with the result that many of the brightest students, given the opportunity to go abroad for higher education, chose to specialize in medicine and law. High school graduates today tend to choose higher education and careers in a wider variety of areas, but lawyers and doctors still command good salaries and high prestige. And although members of the Georgetown elite occasionally joke about people in prominent positions who lack social and linguistic "polish," we would expect the language of the average lawyer or doctor, especially as used in formal settings, to be representative of the acrolectal pole of the continuum.[17]

This expectation is basically borne out in these two extracts, especially in the syntax and lexicon. The barrister for the plaintiff (Text 31a) has only one obvious nonstandard grammatical feature—the absence of the past suffix on participial *damij* (1517)—and it appears to be phonologically motivated, the result of *t/d* deletion after an affricate and before another consonant. The barrister for the defendant is more nonstandard generally, but his delivery is also more animated. At the level of syntax, his speech contains only three nonstandard features: the absence of possessive case-marking in the first-person pronoun (*mi* 1528), the absence of the third-person-present suffix (*see* 1529), and the absence of the copula (*yu nOt bong* 1529–30). Each of these occurs only once in the extract, and each is matched by at least one occurrence of the expected acrolectal form or feature: possessive *iz* (1528), *yoor* (1531), and *its* (1533); the intact third-person-present suffix in *bohrooz* (1532), and the occurrence of the copula in both present and past forms (*ar*, *iz*, *wuz* 1536).

Furthermore, both speakers not only adhere to SE syntax in other grammatical subsystems, but also employ features associated with more elaborate and formal discourse (see Bernstein 1966, 1972). These features include a predominance of passive over active forms (*wuz sed, ar fongd* 1523, *ar don*, *wuz yuuzd* 1536), a relatively high frequency of conditionals and hypotheticals (1523, 1533), a penchant for abstract nominalizations rather than active verbs (*dhi thingking* 1521, *dhi ripleesment* 1525, *som oreenjment* 1530), and complex sentences with multiple complements and conjunctions (like the long sentence beginning in line 1521). The choice of lexical elements like *rendo* rather than "make" (1520) and *volishn* rather than "choice" (1533) is also in keeping with the education of the speakers and the formality of the setting, just as the forms of address and the terminology indicate that we are dealing with the register of the legal profession: *yoor Ono* (1531); *mi lornid fren* and *steetment ov kleem* (1528); *jojment* (1537).

Nonstandard phonological features, however, are more common, as we found to be true also of the speech of the radio announcer and the school-teacher in this chapter, of Mother and Damon in Chapter 5, and of Bonnette and Katherine in Chapter 4. This is in keeping with the general fact that social stratification is sharp with respect to syntactic features in the Guyanese Creole continuum, but gradient with respect to phonological ones (Rickford 1981; but cf. Fasold 1970). In the samples below both barristers occasionally realize English interdental fricatives as stops, although this happens more frequently with the definite article (*di* 1524) than with complementizers or demonstratives (*dhat, dhiiz* 1525), and more frequently in the speech of the defendant's barrister than in the speech of the plaintiff's. Both also use a monopthongal vowel and velar nasal in words like "found" and "bound" (*fongd* 1523, *bong* 1530), lending support to our earlier suggestion that this feature spans the entire continuum.

But there are also quantitative—sometimes qualitative—phonological differences between these two lawyers. The barrister for the plaintiff almost never simplifies his syllable-final consonant clusters (*damij* 1518 is a rare exception), whereas the barrister for the defendant does so quite frequently, particularly with *st* clusters; the occurrence of plural *kOsiz* in 1529 is the result of applying plural-formation rules to a stem ending in a sibilant instead of a stop, and is similar to examples like "wasses" and "desses" (plurals for "wasp" and "desk," respectively) in VBE (Labov 1967). Interestingly enough, the two environments in which the barrister for the defendant does not simplify his clusters are where the members of the cluster differ in voicing (as in *steetment* 1528) and where the second member of the cluster is the past-tense morpheme (*yuuzd* 1536). Mixed-voice and past-tense clusters have been found to act as disfavoring environments for consonant-cluster simplification in many earlier studies (see Fasold 1972). The barrister for the defendant also shows a high frequency of nonretroflexion after vowels—"sir," for instance, is almost invariably *so*, with a mid-central nonretroflex vowel—whereas his adversary shows nonretroflexion only occasionally, as in *rendo* (1520). Finally, the barrister for the plaintiff, in his pronunciation of "accident" as *aksodint* (1521), uses the "elegant schwa" that was mentioned in the introduction to the radio announcer's Text 29; compare its use in the upper-middle-class expression of indignation: *nOnsons* (not *nOnsens* 'nonsense!'). Note that in Atlantic creole varieties of English more generally, central or reduced vowels are not very frequent, certainly less so than in standard varieties of English in the Caribbean, Britain, and North America

(Wells 1982, 3: 570). This may be one of the striking exceptions to the general truth that phonological reduction is characteristic of informal or vernacular speech.

Text 31a is from Tape CAS4, side A, tape counter nos. 201–21; 31b is from the same tape and side, nos. 239–50.

31a. From the summation of the barrister for the plaintiff

ai—ai riispekfulii sobmit, sor, dhat di—di—di paarts riipleest wur	1513
riizonebl, and ail sait o kees, sor, wich—diilz wid dhis sOrt ov	1514
riipeerz ishuu—B vorsos R, naintiin sevnti wohn, eetiin, west	1515
indyon riipoorts, peej nainti-siks. . . . dhis wuz o kees weer o lOrii wuz	1516
damij, sor. it wuz held—di kOst ov di riipeerz wuz—wuz hai. an	1517
it wuz held in dhat kees dhat di kOst ov kompliit riipeer—ohl damij	1518
wuz riikovorebl. nOtwitstanding dhat di riizolt ov di kompliit riipeer	1519
mee bii tu rendo di vihiikl moor valyuuebl dan it woz biifoor dii	1520
aksodint. a tingk—at wohn steej, sor, . . . it wuz dhi thingking ov dhi	1521
baar, sor, dhat yuu wud bii put bak tu di ekstent ov yoor akchul lohs,	1522
bot, in dhis kees it wuz sed dhat—if sortn riipeerz ar fongd	1523
nesoserii, . . . iivn dhoo di valyuu ov di viihiikl mait bii enhanst	1524
bai dhi ripleesment ov dhiiz paarts, sor, dheer seeying dhat dhats o	1525
riizonebl—dhats riizonebl.	1526

Translation

I respectfully submit, sir, that the parts replaced were	
reasonable, and I'll cite a case, sir, which deals with this sort of	
repairs issue: B. versus R., 1971, Eighteen, West	1515T
Indian Reports, page 96. . . . This was a case where a lorry was	
damaged, sir. It was held—the cost of the repairs was—was high. And	
it was held in that case that the cost of complete repair—all damage	
was recoverable. Notwithstanding that the result of the complete repair	
may be to render the vehicle more valuable than it was before the	1520T
accident. I think, at one stage, sir, . . . it was the thinking of the	
bar, sir, that you must be put back to the extent of your actual loss,	
but, in this case it was said that—if certain repairs are found	
necessary, . . . even though the value of the vehicle might be enhanced	
by the replacement of these parts, sir, they're saying that that's	1525T
a reasonable—that's reasonable.	

31b. From the summation of the barrister for the defendant

On di inchres, so, ai wud se di kyaan bii oloud nou, so,	1527
onles mi lornid fren iz gun tu omend iz steetment ov kleem. di	1528
buk see kwait pleenli, so, iivn kOst—if yu doon ask fo kOsiz, yu	1529

nOt bong tu get dem. so, yu mait have som oreenjment   1530
wid di Odo said. . . . yu sii, yoor Ono, dis iz nOt o—o det, in   1531
di sens dhat a man bohrooz monii from yuu an ii dozn giv yuu bak,   1532
an di koort ov its oon volishn ken see wel, if—di pleentif had iz   1533
monii in di bangk, iid ov at liist gOt siks posent ohr wOtevo   1534
di inchre—di koort oloud. dis iz n aksident wich wuz—di   1535
ripeerz ar don, di kar wuz yuuzd. wOt iz—wOt iz di inchres fohr?   1536
jos tu bild op di jojment? dat iz nOt di eem ov inchrest, so.   1537

Translation

   On the interest, sir, I would say they can't be allowed now, sir,
unless my learned friend is going to amend his statement of claim. The
book says quite plainly, sir, even costs—if you don't ask for costs,
you're not bound to get them. Sir, you might have some arrangement   1530T
with the other side. . . . You see, your Honor, this is not a debt, in
the sense that a man borrows money from you and doesn't give it back,
and the court of its own volition can say, well, if the plaintiff had his
money in the bank, he'd have earned at least six percent or whatever
the interest—the court allowed. This is an accident which was—the   1535T
repairs are done, the car was used. What is—what is the interest for?
Just to build up the judgment? That is not the aim of interest, sir.

32. Christmas Greetings from Guyanese in England (1976)

   The practice of recording Christmas greetings from Guyanese living
overseas and airing them on local radio stations during the Christmas season is an old one. For the overseas Guyanese who send these greetings, it is
far more than an opportunity to say "Merry Christmas!," since they could
do this as well by letter or phone. It is also an opportunity to number themselves among the few who are working or studying "abroad"—in the metropolitan societies that, in the eyes of a developing and ex-colonial community,
are the source of so many of the "good things" of life: power, privilege, position, higher education, material goods, films, records, the latest fashions,
and so on. Note, in this connection, that the second speaker whose greetings
are excerpted below introduces herself as "from London" rather than from
No. 7 Village, the place where she was apparently born and raised.
   Most interesting from our point of view, this is an opportunity for the
overseas Guyanese to show how contact with the metropolis has "improved"
them, and since the form of one's speech is the primary medium for doing
this in a radio broadcast, there is a tendency to use SE syntax as far as possible, and even to display traces of a British or North American accent. For
those back home these broadcasts provide an opportunity to hear their ab-

sent relatives and friends in person, to hear their own names on the radio, and to inform or remind others in the local community that one of their own is "abroad," claiming in the process the small increase in status that this may entail.

The greetings themselves, which are usually read from a prepared script, have a fairly consistent structure. One by one the speakers introduce themselves by name and go on to list the intended recipients of their greetings, usually including a self-protective clause like "other relatives and friends" (1539–40) or "friends and relatives whose names time does not permit me to mention" (1561). In the heart of the greeting, the hope is expressed that the folks back home will remain in good health, have a good time, and remember the speaker, who is frequently pictured as at a disadvantage compared with those at home. To a certain extent this last sentiment is real, because Christmas is *the* festive season in the Guyanese calendar, celebrated much more assiduously than is usually the custom in England and North America, but it sometimes sounds contrived. Some speakers, like the first one below, take the opportunity to deliver didactic or philosophical remarks on the meaning of Christmas. It is customary for all speakers to include some reference to meeting again in the future and to conclude the greeting by "performing" the wish (a subset of Austin's 1962: 159 "behabitives") for the last time.

The three excerpted Christmas greetings below exemplify this general structure well, and also illustrate the tendency to maintain SE syntax. The speaker in Text 32a displays the verbosity and use of big words often associated with educated speech (see Labov 1970), and also draws heavily on the "be"-passive and the very formal use of participial "in being so" for anaphoric sentential subordination (1541). One possible trace of his Creole background is the absence of a plural suffix on *frend* (1540), but this is within the realm of colloquial SE, since the suffix here would have constituted the final member of a triple-consonant cluster itself followed by a consonant. The other speakers use less pretentious syntax and lexicon, but also follow SE morphosyntax throughout, except for the deployment of a present perfect in line 1558 instead of a simple preterit.

Phonologically, these excerpts show us many of the nonstandard features we have found in other samples of acrolectal and upper-mesolectal Guyanese speech in this volume: the nonretroflexion of the central reduced vowel (represented here as *o*) in *kapcho* (1544) and *bacholoz* (1555); the frequent realization of interdental fricatives as stops, particularly voiced *dh* (realized as a fricative only five of 22 times in these extracts, compared with four of five for voiceless *th*); the simplification of syllable-final homophonous voice clusters (more frequent with *nd* than with *st*). The speaker in Text 32c "enunciates" well throughout, but the absence of initial *h* on *oom* (1560) reveals that she is from an area in which *h*-dropping is common. The dropping of word-initial *h* is common on pronominal, auxiliary, and other unstressed forms in general Guyanese speech, but *h*-dropping on full nouns and open-class items is more geographically restricted, reportedly most common in East Coast Demerara villages like Victoria and Bachelor's Adventure, although I know of no systematic data-based analysis of its distribution.

Most interesting, and representative perhaps of British dialect patterns, is the tendency to use a monopthongal unreduced *a* instead of *ai* in *ma* ('my' 1544), *al* ('I'll' 1554), and *am* ('I'm' 1559) and to reduce other unstressed vowels to schwa (*konOt* 1553, *dimoraro* 1556). Particularly marked in this regard, but suggestive of an American accent rather than a British one, is the occasional use by the speaker in Text 32a of a voiced flap instead of a voiceless alveolar stop (represented by *D*, as in *eksaiDing* 1545). With pronunciations like these, one announces that one has not simply reached the farthest pole of the Guyanese continuum, but has even gone beyond it. However, as noted in Chapter 1, post-independence nationalism has brought an increasing tendency to mock such "imported" accents. Nowadays, many Guyanese who return home intending to stay make some effort to get rid of an acquired foreign accent.

Text 32a is from Tape CA3, side B, tape counter nos. 510–38; 32b and 32c are from the same tape and side, nos. 431–36 and 487–508, respectively.

32a. Male Afro-Guyanese, Seafield, West Coast Berbice

aa—dis iz W.O. ov—aa—siifiil, wes koos bobiis spiiking. mai deer mum,	1538
dad, V, R, an C, n famolii, . . . an tu ohl mai Odo relotivz n	1539
frend bak hoom. . . . krismos iz riigaardid bai menii az n okeezhn ov	1540
greet jOi n hapiinis, an in biiying soo, wii mos nOt olou di rilijos	1541
signifikons tu bii lOst. ai hoop dat yuu wil ohl hav o wondofol	1542
taim, az wii wil bii duuwing our oon thing heer, chraiying veri moch tu	1543
kapcho di reel spirit ov gayoniiz krismos. ma memoriiz ar stil	1544
fresh . . . tu i verii eksaiDing mooments wii had wail dheer. boDai kon	1545
oshoor yuu dhat ai wil ohlwiz kiip dooz memoriiz olaiv. ai mos vencho	1546
tu ad dat wi di dohning ov yet onOdo nyuu yeer, a wud laik tu	1547
wish yuu ohl di veri best in yoor endevoz, wODevo dee mee bii. ai	1548
shal rimembo yuu ohl, an luk fOword tu di dee, wen wii shal miit	1549
ogeen. mee gohd bles yuu ohl. thengk yu.	1550

Translation

This is W. O. of Seafield, West Coast Berbice speaking. My dear mum, dad, V., R., and C., and family, . . . and to all my other relatives and friends back home. . . . Christmas is regarded by many as an occasion of   1540T

great joy and happiness, and in being so, we must not allow the religious
significance to be lost. I hope that you will all have a wonderful
time, as we will be doing our own thing here, trying very much to
capture the real spirit of Guyanese Christmas. My memories are still
fresh . . . of the very exciting moments we had while there. But I can   1545T
assure you that I will always keep those memories alive. I must venture
to add that with the dawning of yet another new year, I would like to
wish you all the very best in your endeavors, whatever they may be. I
shall remember you all, and look forward to the day, when we shall meet
again. May God bless you all. Thank you.   1550T

32b. Female Indo-Guyanese, No. 7 Village, East Coast Berbice

dis iz C M from lOndon kohling misto n misiz M ov nombo sevn vilij,   1551
iis borbiis. hai mom, dad an J, hoop yuur wel an having o nais   1552
krismos at hoom. sorii wii konOt bi dheer, bot teek thingz iizii, an   1553
doont worii tuu moch. if evriting gooz wel, al bii hoom neks yeer.   1554

Translation

This is C. M. from London calling Mr. and Mrs. M. of No. 7 Village,
East Berbice. Hi, mom, dad, and J.; hope you're well and having a nice
Christmas at home. Sorry we cannot be there, but take things easy, and
don't worry too much. If everything goes well, I'll be home next year.

32c. Female Afro-Guyanese, Bachelor's Adventure, East Coast Demerara

diz iz V K sending krismos griitingz tu di Nz ov bacholoz   1555
odvencho, iis koos dimoraaro. heloo mom, dad, L, . . . ohldhoo wii ar   1556
having o wait krismos oovo heer, wiir chraiying tu meek di best ov   1557
it. ai most see at dis mooment ai av enjOid ma laas krismos with   1558
yuu, and am sohrii am nOt spending dis wohn with yuu. an a soo—ohlsoo   1559
see—dhat av mist evriiwohn at oom. . . . an fainolii, tu ohl mai   1560
frenz an relotivz huuz neemz taim doz nOt pormit mii tu menshon,   1561
al wish yu ohl o merii krismos an prOspros nyuu yeer.   1562

Translation

This is V. K. sending Christmas greetings to the N.s of Bachelor's   1555T
Adventure, East Coast Demerara. Hello Mom, Dad, L. . . . Although we are
having a white Christmas over here, we are trying to make the best of
it. I must say at this moment I have enjoyed my last Christmas with
you, and am sorry I'm not spending this one with you. And I should—also
say—that I miss everyone at home. . . . And finally, to all my   1560T
friends and relatives whose names time does not permit me to mention,
I'll wish you all a Merry Christmas and prosperous New Year.

Notes

Notes

Introduction

1. In 1901 an educator in Sierra Leone referred to the local Creole as "largely defective and sadly wanting in many of the essentials and details that make up and dignify a language." As recently as 1981, a government minister referred to GC as a "vulgar, rough and ready mode of description." For a review of these and other attitudes toward pidgins and creoles, see Rickford and Traugott (1985).

2. Although Hymes's definitions have been accepted as a working base within pidgin-creole studies for the past decade and a half, and resemble the definitions of both predecessors (Hall 1966) and successors (Mühlhäusler 1980) in several respects, definitional and theoretical questions continue to provoke considerable discussion and controversy within the field. The controversies include whether and how pidgins and creoles might be distinguished from other varieties that exhibit part but not all of their component processes (convergence or mixture, for instance, but not reduction); whether the putative instances of "simplification" associated with pidginization should be described as such; how much of a role language transfer or mixing plays in the pidginization process; whether the grammatical expansion associated with creolization may come about through extension in functional role by adults without nativization; and whether creolization reflects the influence of an innate bioprogram. Hymes (1971a) discusses some of these questions himself, in the course of introducing papers by Whinnom, Samarin, Ferguson, and others in Hymes (1971b). Subsequent discussions of these themes include Todd (1975); Bickerton (1977a, 1984); DeCamp (1977); Rickford (1977b); Alleyne (1980: 120–35); Mühlhäusler (1980); Corder (1981); Andersen (1983: 1–56); Christie (1983); Versteegh (1984: 35–58); and Muysken and Smith (1986).

3. Andersen's (1983) integrative introduction is particularly valuable in this respect.

4. As Ian Hancock has noted (personal communication), Haitian, Papiamentu, and Tok Pisin are ahead of GC in terms of the amount of published material. This is certainly true; the Reinecke, Tsuzaki, et al. (1975) bibliography of pidgins and creoles lists 1,213 publications for Papiamentu, 428 for Haitian, 253 for Hawaiian, and only 84 for GC. But not only are many of the works listed written *in* the pidgin or creole rather than *on* it; these numbers do not reveal how centrally GC data have figured in demonstrating the importance of pidgin/creole data for sociolinguistics and variation theory—and for language acquisition and evolution as well—in the 1970's and 1980's. Bickerton's (1975) *Dynamics* deals specifically with GC, and his (1981) *Roots* draws primarily on GC and Hawaiian data. Note, however, that Jamaican, Hawaiian,

Belizean, Trinidadian, St. Lucian, and San Andres data have also come to the focus of pioneering quantitative, implicational, or sociopsychological studies.

5. The speakers in Chap. 4 are all Indo-Guyanese, since Cane Walk is an overwhelmingly Indo-Guyanese community.

Chapter 1

1. The concept of a "language mastery continuum" was introduced by Reinecke and Tokimasa (1934) in reference to Hawaii; Schuchardt had apparently articulated a similar concept as early as 1914, but without using the term (see Schuchardt 1979: 130). Works in the 1960's and early 1970's that endorsed the characterization of English-speaking Caribbean communities in terms of a continuum include DeCamp (1960: 135, 1971), Le Page (1960: 116), Cassidy (1960: 2), Alleyne (1963: 25), Craig (1963, 1971), B. Bailey (1964: 105), and Bickerton (1971, 1973a,b). Of these, DeCamp (1971) and Bickerton (1973a) were the primary developers of the continuum model, linking it to synchronic methods of analysis (implicational scaling) and interpreting it in diachronic terms. Subsequent critiques of the continuum model include Haynes (1973, 1979), Washabaugh (1977), Devonish (1978), Le Page (1978, 1980a, 1984), Gibson (1982), W. Edwards (1984a,b), and Escure (1981, 1984a,b).

2. Compare Quirk (1965) and Sag (1973) with respect to other grammatical categories.

3. Building on Stewart (1965), Bickerton (1975: 24) provided the following definitions, which have become fairly standard in the field: "*basilect* will be used to refer to that variety of Guyanese Creole most distinct from English, *acrolect* to refer to educated Guyanese English (a variety which differs from other standard varieties of the language only in a few phonological details and a handful of lexical items), and *mesolect* to refer to all intermediate varieties."

4. For instance, Text 14c (Sheik's) would fall between 21b and 15c. Including the frequencies with which each feature were used would show the transitions between outputs in even finer detail, and of course frequencies themselves (without an implicational array) could be used to illustrate continuous transition between standard and creole.

5. Despite this criticism, B. Bailey's suggestion that we assign different weights to lexical, phonetic, morphophonemic, and syntactic variables for the purpose of placing samples on the continuum is a good one and deserves further investigation. What it amounts to is a claim that some creole/standard differences make more of a difference than others, and this is precisely what the ordering of linguistic variables in an implicational scale indicates: although the use of a stop consonant in "the" and the use of preverbal *no ben* are both "creole" features, the latter is more distinctively creole than the former, and can be used to predict the occurrence of the former (but not vice versa). Bailey's suggestion includes the interesting additional prediction that morphosyntactic variables always make more of a difference than phonological ones. This receives some support from the fact that phonological variables tend to occur in the leftmost or less markedly basilectal columns in implicational scales like those in Tables 1.1 and 1.2, and from the fact that phonological creole variants tend to be used by speakers across the continuum, in contrast with morphosyntactic ones. However, highly marked phonological variables like *aa* show that the situation is more complex.

6. DeCamp presents the data of Table 1.4 as an unordered set of outputs and variables and describes how to scale it, but does not give us the finished scale. Table 1.3 is arranged as an implicational scale too: a basilectal index alone implies basilectal

indexes to the left, but a nonbasilectal index, alone or otherwise, implies nonbasilectal indexes, alone or otherwise, to the right (see Bickerton 1973a: 646).

7. Bickerton (1971, 1973a), Day (1973), Washabaugh (1977), Rickford (1979), Akers (1981), Escure (1982), and Nichols (1983) are examples of implicational studies of continua that extended DeCamp's original model in several ways: by allowing (1) for more variants per variable, (2) for split cells (as in Table 1.1 above), (3) for attention to quantitative differences, and (4) for interpretation of synchronic patterns in terms of C.-J. Bailey's (1973) dynamic or wave model. Pavone (1980) has shown, however, that some of the scales in the Bickerton and Day studies do not satisfy statistical criteria for scalability, and that other scales in the continuum literature need to be reexamined against these criteria (which are more stringent than the ones linguists typically employ).

8. Of course, implicational scaling, a favorite technique of continuum advocates, depends on co-occurrences of features too (DeCamp 1971: 356). But while advocates of discrete co-system analyses envisage very strict co-occurrence restrictions, such that many or all variable features must simultaneously shift from "+" to "−" values, allowing only two varieties, continuum advocates assume that co-occurrence restrictions can shift one at a time in sequence across the entire property-item space, permitting a continuous spectrum of minimally different varieties, as in Figs. 1.2 and 1.4.

9. One could argue, to be sure, that basilectal *am* realizes the same three gender categories as mesolectal *ii/shii/it*, but since there is no formal basis for this division in the basilect itself, the argument is no more convincing that if we distinguished masculine and feminine "they" in English by comparison with *ils* and *elles* in French.

10. Valdman (1971: 61) and Alleyne (1980: 187) both indicate that the Haitian situation is more variable than is usually assumed. Lefebvre (1974) provides similar evidence for Martinique, but there are obvious differences between Martinique and Guyana: *none* of Lefebvre's Martinique subjects possessed only the intermediate varieties or mesolects (pp. 57, 74), and *all* were competent in the Creole basilect (p. 61). Contrast, on these points, Bickerton (1973a: 664) and Rickford (1979: 481–500).

11. In the light of variation in the literature, the terminology used in addressing this issue requires clarification. Terms like "unidirectional" or "bidirectional"—open to diachronic interpretation—are sometimes used in the literature, but are avoided here. "Linear" is sometimes used instead of "unidimensional" (for instance, DeCamp 1971b: 353–54). Sometimes "bidimensional" or "two-dimensional" is used where bipolar variation along a single dimension is clearly intended (e.g. Bickerton 1973b: 20, Le Page 1980a: 127). Bidimensional scaling—involving four poles, as in Figs. 1.1 and 1.2 above—is a subset of multidimensional scaling, one of the commonest types in the social sciences literature.

12. Contingent changes are contrasted with constrained rule changes, in which "adoption of a rule Rj is impossible before a rule Ri has been adopted, or conversely, the adoption of Ri automatically and necessarily enforces the adoption of Rj."

13. Washabaugh (1977) further suggested that the grammatical variation between *fi* and *∅* on Providence Island, not apparently attributable to Stampean natural processes, was also "horizontal," but Bickerton (1977b: 355) reanalyzed his data and suggested that *∅* might be better considered an intermediate phase in the development of the linear continuum, between basilectal *fi* and intermediate *tu*.

14. The English/book learning dimension is not explicitly represented in Fig. 1.3. This is to some extent because of the difficulty of representing four dimensions si-

multaneously, but also because it seems likely that Creole and SE can be treated essentially as poles of one dimension, so that [−Creole] is more or less equivalent to [+English]. In the quantitative Belizean data in Le Page (1984: 7), high values on nasalization, the Creole variable (speaker SM, 53%; speaker SH, 67%), are matched by low values on r-coloration, the English/book-learning variable (speaker SM, 21%; speaker SH, 30%), and low values on nasalization (speaker FN, 2%; speaker DG, 2%) are matched by high values on r-coloration (speaker FN, 67%, speaker DG, 75%). In analyzing the St. Lucian data on 100 informants, Le Page (1980) tabulates corresponding Creole and SE features separately, but it is clear from the frequencies that they are the plus and minus values of a common variable. For instance, cluster A2 uses feature SE2 (correct use of plural inflection on nouns) 94.4% of the time, and feature C3P2 (invariability of count nouns as to number) 5.6% of the time, and Le Page (p. 136) explicitly describes Creole feature C4P3 as the reciprocal of its English equivalent SE3. In this respect, his analysis is like Washabaugh's: the attempt to represent Creole and English as two separate dimensions rather than poles of a single dimension is not persuasive.

15. Le Page's (1984: 15) conclusion that "almost any kind of mixing can take place" suggests that the entire three-dimensional solid is populated, but it also hints at a disquieting degree of random variability from a descriptive and explanatory point of view.

16. This assumption was also explicit in Bickerton's work on the Guyanese continuum. For instance, his (1971) paper on complementizer variation contains a hypothetical model in which the *fu* forms are invariant in all environments in the middle of the 19th century. Admittedly the model is simplified and the dates approximate, but if the evidence of Text 1b in Chap. 3, below, is reliable, *tu* was a part of slave speech at least half a century earlier. The *tu* form attested there (line 91) is even more problematic for the model because it occurs in a purposive clause, where it would be expected to come in latest.

17. Because of the historical centrality of Emancipation in Caribbean communities, it is usually interpreted as a major trigger of decreolization. But preceding and successive events may have been equally important, or even more important, and W. Edwards (1975: 285) has made the intriguing suggestion that the physical separation of blacks from plantations following Emancipation "removed the master-slave relationship and this removed much of the pressure for linguistic acculturation." The issue deserves rethinking and research.

18. Hancock (1969) had suggested earlier that creole speakers always had a metropolitanized version of their language for use with Europeans.

19. But Bickerton's new position—made clearer in a later paper (1984b)—differs from Alleyne's, for he assumes that mesolectal varieties came in first and basilectal ones later, given low proportions of blacks to whites and good access to English norms by slaves in the formative years. Alleyne's more complex characterization of the early situation (i.e. virtually all lects present from early on) still strikes me as sociolinguistically plausible and in accord with available evidence.

20. Even under the most ideal conditions, second-language acquisition is not instantaneous, and Cruickshank (1916: 14–16) includes two reports from indentured 19th-century African immigrants to Demerara that reveal the gradualness (although not the structural course) of their acquisition of English. One of the reports— reprinted in part in Chap. 2 below—is from an African who came to Guyana as an adult and learned his English from a fellow slave. The other—closer to the ideal house-slave situation hypothesized for earlier periods—is from a young Ondo woman who was "taken as a house girl by a family in New Amsterdam."

21. W. Edwards (1984a: 88), drawing on Alleyne (1980: 190), observes that "linguistic acculturation does not entail 'decreolization.'" One can agree, but still inquire about the extent to which, and the ways in which, the processes are similar. The answers bear on the question he asks (ibid.) about whether mesolectal continuum varieties represent evolutions from earlier basilectal stages.

22. Of course, even where intermediate models were already available, their acquisition would involve a process of creative internalization. But the creative element would be stronger and the similarities in the resulting output more remarkable if speakers followed independent but similar routes in going from basilect to acrolect, without already available intermediate models.

23. See Eersel (1971: 320), and the discussion of Christmas messages from overseas Guyanese in Chap. 6, below. Allsopp's (1958a) *ai tOuld him*, with a received pronunciation (RP) diphthong in 'told' (Wells 1982, 2: xix), no longer constitutes the Guyanese acrolect. Appropriate educated or acrolectal usage is now his no. 2: *ai toold him*. Older Guyanese professionals who were educated abroad years ago and still have British accents often seem anachronistic by the new standards.

24. Winford (1985b) makes an interesting argument, however, that Haitian-type creole situations and Jamaican-type creole continua both satisfy and challenge the classic and conventional criteria for diglossia.

Chapter 2

1. Locally born Portuguese are not regarded as European, perhaps because their 19th-century forebears came to Guyana as indentured workers rather than colonizers (R. Smith 1962: 102). According to Bronkhurst (1883), the Madeira Portuguese immigrants used to be "taunted with the appellation '*white nigger*' by the Negro population of the colony."

2. The list included Elmina, the principal Portuguese stronghold on the Gold Coast, in existence since 1486.

3. And, to a lesser extent, St. Eustatius: see Le Page (1960), Hancock (1980), and Williams (1983).

4. The practice of picking up slaves at other ports, however, was more characteristic of Dutch free traders operating on the Windward Coast than of WIC ships being supplied from lodges on the Slave and Gold coasts (Postma 1970: 189–90).

5. However, Ian Hancock (personal communication) suggests that there was more Dutch activity in the Senegambia than normally acknowledged; the issue will be discussed in a book he is currently preparing on the origin and spread of the Atlantic anglophone creoles.

6. Devonish (1978: 11–14) gives the total as 15, apparently overlooking one shipment.

7. As Hancock (1986: 88) notes, "The Dutch did not, apparently, establish households with the Africans in the same way as did the British, Portuguese, and French, and there is no clear evidence of a Dutch-derived domestic creole having developed on the coast, although a Dutch pidgin may have been used at some time in Calabar."

8. Ian Robertson has recently done work in the Netherlands along these lines that should contribute much to our knowledge of this early period.

9. Compare Baudet (1981: 106): "Historical documentation does not exclude the possibility that some slaves could have learned a Portuguese pidgin, yet we have no actual reports of such a pidgin being spoken by slaves going to the New World."

10. The older (Bloomfieldian) polygenetic hypothesis does not seem likely to me: that New World pidgins and creoles arose from the masters' deliberate attempts to

simplify their usage, perhaps combined with imitations of their slaves' own imperfect attempts. See Taylor (1961), DeCamp (1971a), Todd (1974: 30–31), and Bickerton (1976) for persuasive rebuttals.

11. References to "English" colonists and planters in historical accounts of Guyana mask the fact that many of the settlers were Scottish. The frequency and salience with which the Scottish figure in local folklife and folklore (Brackette Williams, personal communication) suggest that they may have had a bigger impact on Afro-Guyanese culture than is normally recognized.

12. Netscher (1888: 64) reports that only four WIC cargoes came into Essequibo and Demerara between 1749 and 1765.

13. Hancock himself has observed (1980: 32, n. 15) that "only a tiny minority of slaves would have come into prolonged contact with GCCE in Africa." He sees them as having had a greater linguistic impact in the New World than their numbers might suggest "because they were African and they knew some form of the language of the European" and therefore served as "models for the others." As noted above, this is an issue that merits further research.

14. Slaves who had merely been transshipped from Africa via Barbados or those who had been there for a short while would, once again, probably have spoken little or no English. According to Niles (1980: 156), "New Africans generally did not speak English, but were in a position to learn Barbadian English in a few years." (This claim is supported by newspaper references in her Appendix A, pp. 177–78.)

15. Compare Alleyne's (1971, 1980) suggestion—discussed in Chap. 1, above—that considerable variation must have been present from early on.

16. On this point, compare the present-day sentiments of Reefer, a cane-cutter, quoted in the introduction to Text set 11 in Chap. 4.

17. For details on slave resistance in general, see Price (1973) and Craton (1982).

18. Hancock (n.d.*a*) has suggested that 19th-century African indentured immigrants to Trinidad might have been one source of the basilectal features attested in an 1845 sample of Trinidadian Creole. This is plausible if the immigrants arrived speaking a variety of GCCE linguistically similar to that of the sample, but is less so if they arrived with little or no Creole English and learned it in the colony, as Cruickshank's old African did.

19. If Sister Mary Noel Menezes of the History Department of the University of Guyana is able to pursue her interest in researching the history of the Portuguese of Guyana, we may be able to flesh out our very limited information about the linguistic competence of 19th-century Portuguese immigrants.

20. W. Rodney (1981: 184) refers to the refusal of Indians to live next to Africans on the plantation Huis t'Dieren in 1881, and Bickerton (1970: 8) argues that the migration of Indians into separate rice villages isolated them from the rest of Creole society even more decidedly than estate residence had done.

21. Before that, however, thousands of French Creole speakers from St. Lucia came to the colony in the late 19th and early 20th centuries to work in the interior or on sugar estates. According to Ian Robertson (personal communication), many of them have remained; some have not returned to St. Lucia for 50 years. A description of their speech, by Robertson and University of Guyana students, is available from him c/o the School of Education, University of the West Indies, St. Augustine, Trinidad.

22. As a practical matter, though, true independence has been limited to some extent by Guyana's reliance on external loans; and the direction of migration has been reversed to some extent by emigration to North America, Europe, and the Caribbean.

23. Devonish (1978: 127–35) argues that widespread endorsement by the intellectual and ruling classes of the use of Standard English rather than Creole as the official language of the country is based on unconvincing rationales reflecting support for the existing economic, social, and political order. For more general statements about the reluctance of the Caribbean middle classes to introduce reforms that threaten their own privileges and positions, see Bell (1980) and Lewis (1983).

24. As independently suggested in Devonish (1978: 105) and Rickford (1983b); see the latter for a stage-by-stage quantitative model of the process.

25. Nath (1970: 247–48) shows that in 1931 only 25.06% of the Indian population was literate in English, compared with 80.8% of the "Negro" population; by 1946 these figures had increased to 55.98% and 97.3%, respectively.

26. In Rickford (1986b) I relate the class structure of Cane Walk to the sociological categories of Marx, Dahrendorf, and Weber.

27. See the introductory remarks on Katherine and Bonnette (Text sets 13 and 15) in Chap. 4.

28. On this point, I agree wholeheartedly with Hancock's observation that "creole language maintenance has always been more vigorous than is usually acknowledged; . . . pressures to retain the creole, for some people, should be seen as being equally important as pressures to metropolitanize are for others" (n.d.*a*: 3).

29. Although Mandle (1973: 98) shows that the proportion of urban Indians remained around 5.8% between 1911 and 1946, the tabulation on p. 76, above, shows that the urban proportion more than doubled in the next 14 years.

Chapter 3

1. Cox (1938) is a good but not exhaustive bibliographical source on New World travelers' accounts.

2. Stewart (1970: 367, fn. 26) reminds us, however, that such prejudice did not necessarily impugn the accuracy of the linguistic record.

3. Citing the example of a magistrate who misinterpreted "haag" as 'hawk' instead of 'hog,' Bronkhurst (1883: 221) notes: "Sometimes the Creole *patois*, as spoken by the people, can scarcely be understood by strangers, and by even those who have been long residents in the colony."

4. I have just discovered (in Bronkhurst, 1883: 83) another possible source of information on this period—a manuscript by Stephen Grellet (a Quaker missionary from England who was in the Guiana colonies around 1794), which I have not yet seen.

5. Biographical details from Lee (1896: 310).

6. In the second edition of Pinckard's *Notes* (London, 1816; 2: 167–68), as in the (1942) Guiana edition based on it, "for" occurs in both pre-infinitival slots in line 12, along with other minor editorial changes in the text.

7. Ian Hancock (personal communication) has raised the question of whether this ubiquitous word ("backra") could have been independently introduced into each of these different creoles by Igbos and Efiks. It seems more likely that it was diffused along slave-trade routes and in slave-based communities of the Old World and the New, but "white man" would have been a fairly salient concept at the time, and the diffusion of this single item does not necessarily establish the diffusion of a West African pidgin as a whole. Why an Ibo/Efik source? This may have something to do with the fact that the proportion of slaves from Ibo- and Efik-speaking areas brought into the Caribbean via the British slave trade had increased sharply in the second quarter of the 18th century (Le Page 1960: 74–75), since this is precisely the period

in which the first attestations of the word in Antigua and Jamaica occur (Cassidy 1971: 155). But one could just as well have expected a source in one of the Senegambian, Windward Coast, or Gold Coast languages, given the fact that slaves from these areas had arrived in significant numbers earlier.

8. "Nyam" is a clear pan-Africanism, with similar or identical forms in Wolof, Fula, Hausa, Efik, Twi, Tshiluba, Umbundu, Mandingo, Zulu, and Twi (see Turner 1949: 199; Cassidy and Le Page 1980: 325). Hancock (1969: 38–39) lists occurrences in Krio, Sranan, Saramaccan, Jamaican, and Gullah in addition to Guyana. In DeCamp's (1971b: 355) implicational scale (see Table 1.4), "nyam" is the most distinctive basilectal variant, its use implying the use of basilectal variants for each of the other variables.

9. And, in fact, Pinckard is alone among the early-19th-century observers to include "'em" as a feature of contemporary black speech (7 of 8 cases, overall). However, Pinckard generally represents nonstandard phonological features (the realization of SE *th* as *t* or *d*, the realization of SE *v* as *b*) more consistently than either Bolingbroke or St. Clair; and some features that must have been characteristic of contemporary Creole pronunciation, such as final-consonant-cluster reduction (the realization of "fast" as "fas'"), are not represented by any of the three observers.

10. If early-19th-century GC were like modern GC, *bin* would be optional (but not obligatory) before "tell" (31) because it is anterior to the other predicates in the sentence, but not out of sequence. See Bickerton (1975: 35) and the detailed discussion preceding Irene's texts (10a–d) in Chap. 4.

11. These and other possibilities are explored in detail in a paper entitled "19th Century Guyanese Creole: Three Views" that I presented at the Creole Workshop at the 1986 Linguistic Institute, held at the City University of New York.

12. See Traugott and Romaine (1985) for the challenges of conducting sociohistorical linguistic research on earlier periods.

13. Biographical details from Stephan (1896).

14. A less persuasive possibility is that "handsome" is a nominal form, equivalent to "handsomeness." Craig (1980) reports copula-less predicate nominals in JC: *ai waan nors*, 'I want (to be) a nurse.'

15. The source is Portuguese *sabé* or *sabeir* (see Hancock 1969: 69, fn. 77) or Spanish *sabe* (Webster's Third: 2020).

16. See also Hancock's (n.d.*a*: 17) observation that Jamaica "has had considerable later [post-17th century] influence throughout the Caribbean, probably because of the size and mobility of its population."

17. See Cassidy and Le Page (1980: 422) for JC entries, and Holm and Shilling (1982: 193) for Bahamian. Compare also the account in Allen et al. (1867: xxvii), cited in Stewart (1968), of the Gullah schoolchildren who did not respond to a question about the color of the sky until it was rephrased by one of their parents as, "How sky *stan*'?"

18. For other examples of wedding toasts and fancy talk, see Allsopp (1980: 104; Tobago), Abrams (1970: 123–24; Guyana), and Lynch (1964; Barbados).

19. There are other examples in Kirke's (1898) book, including the following one, attributed to a "respectable black gentleman" (p. 267): "massa, me make you know that *for me* wife confine Tuesday gone."

20. See Traugott (1976) on the prevalence of parataxis in pidgins.

21. The news media of the 19th century played an important role in bringing "dialect" material before the public.

22. Although these forms are described in terms of the processes required to produce them from standard forms, this is not to say that the processes could only

have originated with the local Creole-speaking populations. As Hancock (personal communication) points out, *gie* may have been present in metropolitan (southwestern) varieties of English to begin with. Regardless of where or when they originated, the forms yielded by these processes were characteristic of contemporary black speech in the Guiana colonies.

23. The example in line 137 is actually a topicalizing/clefting copula (also *a* in modern basilectal GC) rather than a nonpunctual aspect marker, showing that the alternation extended to this form/function too.

24. Note that the sample of *Suriname* (Negro-English appearing as an appendix in Bolingbroke (1807: 400) includes one example of "de" as a continuative/habitual marker ("den de mekie too mooso bawli bawli" = 'they make too much noise') and three examples of "da" as a copula (including "da mie" 'It's me').

25. Contrary to the claim in Bickerton (1975: 41) that "done" is not found in Quow's book.

26. As noted in Chap. 2, however, his further conclusion that "the massive influx of Indian indentured labourers into 19th-century Guyana did not bring about any significant repidginization or recreolization of pre-1837 Creole" is more controversial. See also the introduction to Cruickshank's Text 8 for further discussion.

27. For permitting and assisting me to consult the collection of over a thousand "Argus" cartoons in the National Archives, Georgetown, thanks are due to Jean Craigwell and Tommy Payne. I am also grateful to Joel Benjamin of the University of Guyana library, who first made copies of some of these cartoons available to me, and to Lennox Foster, who photographed the two reprinted here.

28. On the last two points, contrast the lax short *i* in English "miss"; GC often has tense vowels in closed syllables and lax vowels in open syllables where SE has the opposite. And see p. 101, above, on "sheketary" and "shail."

29. Compare the modern Guyanese equivalent: *Ah fire de wuk.*

30. Compare the use of "hot" as both adjective and verb in GC, and see Mühlhäusler (1975) for Tok Pisin examples.

31. Compare *manz* as the plural of *man* in Gullah, reported in Turner (1974: 307).

32. See Rickford (1985b) for evidence from Gullah or Sea Island Creole.

33. Compare "unu-all" in Providence Island Creole, discussed in J. Edwards (1974).

34. In any case, it is worth noting that the purposive environment in which "for to" came in earliest and remained longest in English is also the environment in which *fu* is the most tenacious (or the last in which it is replaced by *tu*) in GC and other Caribbean creoles. See Bickerton (1971) and Washabaugh (1974, 1977).

35. In other books—*Among the Common People of British Guiana* (Georgetown, 1897) and *Scenes and Sketches of Demerara Life* (Demerara, 1899), neither of which I have been able to consult—Van Sertima apparently uses more basilectal Creole. See the assessment in Reinecke et al. (1975: 424).

36. For a different view, however, see W. Edwards (1983).

37. Selections from this correspondence—the originals of which are available in the Tsuzaki/Reinecke Collection at the University of Hawaii's Hamilton Library—appear in Gilbert (1983).

38. Compare Rickford and Rickford (1976) on this point.

39. Two examples do occur, however, in a Barbadian song in Marryat (1834: 220–22), cited in Morrow (1984: 12): "Nebba see *um* night/Dat Rodney cannot fight/Nebba see de day boy/Pompey lick*um* de Caesar." And there is an additional VBE example in Dillard (1972: 98) as well: "He full *um* fote [fort] wid cotton bale." Given these examples, we might ask whether the form might not have been more

widely distributed among New World Africans, borrowed from them by indentured Indians arriving in the Caribbean from the 1830's onward, and preserved by the Indians after the Africans had stopped using it. But before accepting this possibility, we need more detailed documentation and analysis of 19th-century-African use; "see," for instance, does not occur in our list of Indo-Guyanese verbs that take object agreement *um*, and the first and third examples of *um* given in this note could conceivably have been instances of the unstressed indefinite article "one."

40. Jenkins (1871: 103–4), cited in Adamson (1972: 117); Collens (1888: 48), cited in Warner-Lewis (1982: 64); Argus (1891); Kirke (1898: 249) and a modern Indo-Guyanese rhyming song, both cited in Devonish (1978: 40–41).

41. However, Bresnan and Mchombo (1985: 1) suggest that while there is "substantial synchronic evidence of the close relation between grammatical and anaphoric agreement, . . . it is possible to predict clear syntactic differences between a grammatical agreement marker and a morphologically incorporated anaphoric pronoun."

42. The parentheses around (*ke*) signify that it is optional in the sentence. However, "when marked by an object marker *ke*, a human object noun carries some emphasis" (Shukla 1981: 98).

Chapter 4

1. All of the speakers represented in this chapter were tape-recorded by me in Guyana between 1974 and 1976.

2. See Macaulay (1981), Wolfson (1982), and Romaine (1984) for further discussion.

3. For a discussion of the classes in this community from a conflict perspective, see Rickford (1986b; n.d.).

4. However, several of the Cane Walk children listening to Derek's tale volunteered the right explanation when I asked what *naso* meant, suggesting that it was quite familiar to them.

5. The noninterrogative equivalents occur also: *disaid, dasaid, da mek*.

6. See Bickerton (1971: 479–80) and Gibson (1982: 189–99) for further discussion of *gat/get*.

7. I except my own use of *don* in a conversation with Bonntte, line 856.

8. Both of the examples given here occurred in the spontaneous speech of a mesolectal Guyanese speaker.

9. See, however, G. Sankoff and Laberge (1974) and Rickford (1980b).

10. See Washabaugh's (1974: 156) discussion of *mi* and the popularity of the spelling "yuh"—suggesting invariant laxness—in cartoons and other printed material. Compare *mii* 229; and see Rickford (1979: chaps. 6 and 7) for a detailed discussion.

11. See Rickford (1981: 205–7) for more discussion, including reference to parallel examples in Canadian French discussed by G. Sankoff (1974: 32), which point to the cross-language validity of this analysis.

12. See Sebba (1983) for recent detailed analysis.

13. Compare Gibson (1982: 148–49).

14. This is a violation of the Main Stative Rule discussed in the introduction to Derek's texts, and one that is not as exceptional as Bickerton (1975: 34–35) suggests.

15. See Allsopp (1976: 13–15), Alleyne (1980: 103–4), Bickerton (1981: 52), Huttar (1981), and Gibson (1982: 137–39) for further discussion. See also the entry "Topicalization" in the Line Index for additional examples.

16. I wish to thank Derek Bickerton, Dwight Bolinger, Bernard Comrie, Chris Corne, Talmy Givón, Deborah Schiffrin, and Elizabeth Closs Traugott for helpful

comments on an earlier draft of this "anterior" discussion and the discussion of the historical present in Bonnette's Text 15c. They should of course not be held responsible for the formulations presented in either discussion.

17. Compare Bickerton's (1975: 41) discussion of the Guyanese native-speaker's intuitions concerning *bin* vs. *don*.

18. Just as it can be with "used to" in English. As Comrie (1976: 29) notes, "One can quite reasonably say, without self-contradiction, in answering a question whether or not Bill used to be a member of a subversive organisation: *Yes, he used to be a member of a subversive organisation, and he still is.*"

19. If Irene had said *mi granfaada ga plees a filisti bilid*, we would have to assume that he still did.

20. Irene's sentence in line 354 more so than Bickerton's sentence, perhaps because the anteriority of the former is more solidly supported by the discourse context, in particular, the opening line 352.

21. Bickerton (personal communication) argues that the issue of appropriate narrative sequence "applies only to point actions; if a prolonged action was in progress prior to a series of point actions, then it will get *bina* marking no matter where it comes." This argument is not convincing, however, because both *bina lai dong* and *a lai dong* seem acceptable in lines 365–66, and Bickerton himself concedes (1975: 37) that he would not risk ruling out *a* instead of *bina* in a similar GC sentence: "(2.58) *wan nait awi* bina *kom fram raisfiil, when awi miit goolingroov ton, soja blak awi wi dem taachlait* 'One night we were coming from the ricefield, when we reached Goldengrove intersection, soldiers with electric torches stopped us there.'"

22. Here as elsewhere, events referred to in quoted, direct speech have to be considered in relation to other events referred to in direct speech in preceding or following clauses, and not to the descriptive events in the narrative, since their reference points are different.

23. Bickerton (personal communication) suggests that if the speaker had said *wan man heng iself*, this leaves open the possibility that he might still be alive. On the contrary, I think there would be no question of his being dead in either case.

24. Gibson (1984: 125) claims that it is possible to say *di buk faal dong an mi* bin *pik it op*, but I do not share her intuitions about this sentence if the picking up is non-anterior, and would be more convinced by attestations recorded in real life. Overall, I think it is useful to make restrictive predictions about *bin* marking and modify them only in the face of incontrovertible evidence, and then only to the minimum necessary. The traditional claim that *bin* and *∅* are freely interchangeable everywhere is obviously incorrect, and we need to avoid regressing too easily to a similar conclusion.

25. Note that the requirement that *bin* be marked would be upheld even where connectives provide the correct ordering, as in *biifo ii gu tu di spat, ii bin plant di siid* 'Before he went to the spot, he planted the seed.'

26. See Rickford (1974, 1980b) for discussions of this point.

27. Hancock (personal communication) notes: "Palatalization of velar stops preceding *a* isn't a creole feature especially; it was common in the English of the period (and so was the lowering of *o* to *a* in words like 'form' = "farm"); Africans repeated what they heard. English speakers up until 1725 would have pronounced "court" as *kart* but "cart" as *kyart* too. This is still true in some areas of Britain, e.g. in Ulster."

28. See Rickford (1983b) for more discussion.

29. See Rickford and Greaves (1978) for further discussion of this feature and its effects on children's written English.

30. The parallels to this in English child-language seem to me worth exploring;

but that is *not* to say that I subscribe to a baby-talk theory of pidgin or creole formation.

31. The variation between *wee*, *we*, and *wi* as realizations of 'way' is paralleled in the variation between *dee*, *de*, and *di* as realizations of pronominal 'they.' Examples like *sim* and *intaitl* in lines 406 and 441 indicate that variation between *ee* or *e* and *i* occurs in closed syllables too.

32. When the *h* does show up, it's on 'old' rather than 'Higue': *hool aig*, lines 498, 516, just as in line 349 above.

33. Why neighboring Trinidad is non-rhotic and why Krio is non-rhotic while Sranan is rhotic are questions worth investigation (Hancock, personal communication).

34. Shields (1984: 5) notes that Jamaican speakers sometimes produce forms like *sailonto* 'silent' and *lasto* 'last,' with an enclitic schwa, when attempting to retain their final clusters by "emphatic aspiration."

35. Her use of *imself* for 'herself' in line 656 is nonstandard, but it appears to be a true performance error, with no local Creole model that might lead us to consider it an instance of interference instead. Basilectal GC personal pronouns do not distinguish between masculine and feminine third-person singular pronouns; the form for both is *ii* (subject and possessive) or *am* (object). Lower-mesolectal GC uses *(h)ii* for masculine referents (all cases). Upper-mesolectal GC introduces *(h)im*, but only for object case marking. Unlike JC, GC never uses *(h)im* for nonobjects (subjects, possessives, or reflexives).

36. See Labov (1969) for discussion; and see Granny, Text 12c, line 583—after *fens*—for another example.

37. It should be noted that the rule for past marking of strong verbs in Bickerton (1975: 151) incorrectly lists "+temporal" as a variable constraint instead of "−temporal." (Cf. pp. 149–50 and rule 14 on p. 163 of the same work.)

38. See line 708; and also Reisman (1970) for a similar play on "nansi" and "nonsense" in Antigua.

39. This may result from a conflation of *you might find, you see . . .* or from the phonological raising of the vowel in *see*—compare *si* (691).

40. Compare the old transformational rule of "Equi-NP Deletion," by which the underlying noun phrase subject of the infinitival complement of verbs like "try" is deleted under identity with the main verb subject ("John tried John leave = John tried to leave").

41. The last two forms could, however, represent phonological reduction from inflected *yoor* and *mai*, since Bonnette's competence clearly includes the inflected forms. In the case of a speaker like Granny, who never uses the inflected forms, this possibility would be ruled out, at least from a synchronic point of view.

42. In addition to semantically nonpast verbs like *noo* (829) and *kom out* (831), and verbs that occurred in the speech of the other speakers, some verbs in Text 15c were excluded from the count because they were indeterminate with respect to past marking. Excluded cases include *in noo* (848), and instances of modal *ku(dn)* (nonpast in 829, past in 869).

43. More precisely, what Bickerton hypothesizes is that "-ed" will be most common with predicates that are not in a *wen* clause (i.e. that are "+punctual," "−temporal"). Note in this connection "+temporal" in his (1975: 151) variable rule should really be "−temporal," as suggested by the preceding discussion and by his rule 14 on p. 163.

44. The nonpunctuals include the stative modals and copulas, which like other statives are regarded as nonpunctual (cf. Bickerton 1975: 46). Contrary to Bickerton's hypothesis in the preceding note, the single punctual in a *wen* clause—*kech* in 868—is unmarked.

45. Here, *went* is static, not dynamic, equivalent to *wuz in di baat*.

46. Note that, following the usual convention (Labov 1972c: 362), the subordinate clauses beginning with *iz* in lines 834, 848, and 850, and with *wen* in lines 864 and 868 have been excluded from the count because they do not advance the action of the narrative.

47. Alternatively, Wolfson (1979, 1982) has suggested that speakers switch between past and historical present to mark off important events within the narrative. This hypothesis works for Text 15c to the extent that the narrative clauses containing the unmarked verbs are clustered together in the middle of the story (lines 834–63). But it is less persuasive than Schiffrin's analysis because only one narrative clause is marked with the past form.

48. Corne (personal communication) notes that Isle de France Creole (covering the Creole of Mauritius, the Seychelles, and Rodrigues) generally conforms to the classic creole system: *ti* marks the verbal as anterior—past for statives and past-before-past for nonstatives, while the unmarked verbal is non-anterior—present for statives and past for nonstatives. However, the completive marker *fin* has modified the system along the lines sketched by Bickerton (1981: 88–97) and Corne (1983), and the presence of unmarked past statives argues in favor of a historical present. As Corne puts it (personal communication): "It seems to me largely irrelevant whether one refers to unmarked past nonstates as being in the historical present or as being an archaic story-telling convention, but the presence of unmarked past *states* seems to me to argue in favor of the former. Otherwise they would remain unaccounted for. But nor do I see any real conflict here. If unmarked past nonstates derive from the bioprogram, then one would expect them to occur in the process of creolization in Mauritius, and since the major input language (the original 'target') uses the historical present, particularly but not exclusively in narratives, the bioprogram would be (a) reinforced in the case of past states, and (b) modified in the case of unmarked past states. *And* the whole works is further under pressure from the inclusion of *FIN* in Aux."

49. Schiffrin (personal communication) writes that a preliminary reexamination of her data suggests that discourse function (the fact of being in an orientation or complicating action clause) seems to have more to do with tense marking than stativity per se. None of the past-reference active verbs in her orientation clauses were in the present. There were not many past-reference stative verbs in her complicating action clauses, but her guess is that "they would be likely environments for historical present—not only because they're in the complicating action clause, but because they're some kind of high point in the story, and likely to be evaluated." The unmarked past statives reported for Isle de France Creole narratives by Corne (see preceding note) may provide some support for this possibility.

50. As noted in Chap. 1, Gibson (1982) proposes that basilectal and mesolectal GC systems share underlying semantic and syntactic structures. Such sharing, where established, might help to explain the fruitful intercommunication across levels.

51. Mixed-voice cases like *nt* and *lt* were not considered, nor were cases like *jomp* (line 835), which may represent the historical present.

52. The fact that Sheik's relative frequency is 16%–24% higher than that of the other non-estate-class speakers but still 13%–29% lower than that of the estate-class speakers is yet another indication of his checkered background and ambiguous sociolinguistic allegiance.

53. Note that even in the same line (871), Bonnette uses the more frequent *op* the second time.

Chapter 5

1. Except for Mother (Text set 24), whom I recorded in California in 1982, and Basil (Text set 22), who was recorded by Wordsworth McAndrew in Guyana in 1963, all the speakers in this chapter were tape-recorded by me in Guyana between 1974 and 1976.

2. See Rickford (1986b; n.d.) for the relationship of Cane Walk's classes to the stratification models of Marx, Dahrendorf, and Weber.

3. Further discussions of this issue, including Matched-Guise (Lambert 1967) evidence demonstrating the common evaluative norms referred to here, is provided in Rickford (1979: 167–83).

4. Note that the clefting or topicalizing morpheme is usually identical with the copula used before noun phrases, the entire sentence being treated as a noun phrase; in the basilect, the copula is invariant *a*, in the mesolect invariant *iz*.

5. This construction recalls VBE "be done verb + ed" constructions (see Baugh 1983: 77ff), although *don* functions in Ali's sentence as main verb rather than auxiliary.

6. See Traugott and Ferguson (1982) for parallels in Tok Pisin and other pidgins and creoles.

7. Recall, though, that, as I argued in the introduction to Sheik's texts in Chap. 4, basilectal and mesolectal speakers already do have at least one true nonfinite structure, in locative complements.

8. See the introduction to Derek's texts in Chap. 4 and Reisman (1970) for further discussion.

9. I am grateful to Elizabeth Closs Traugott for drawing my attention to this feature and leading me to reexamine the entire text for the significance of twos.

10. Those who have experienced the death of someone close might remember the sensation that everything is happening in slow motion as the news is taken in. Later, we can often recall the exact time, the beating of the heart, the smell of the bedsheets, the little bumps that we saw on the wall above our eyes.

11. See the discussion in the introduction to Irene's texts in Chap. 4.

12. Note that here the quantifier is not really within the scope of the preceding negative, for *yu na noo* is a separate prefatory clause, "You never know, it may be that . . ."

13. For relevant examples and discussion, consult the Indexes.

14. See the anecdotes about "Dem Bux'n Man" in Abrams (1970: 123).

15. That they were the norm among 18th- and 19th-century African and Afro-Guyanese speakers is clear from the written texts in Chap. 3.

16. Ian Robertson (personal communication) has suggested that basilectal varieties are alive and well in African villages like Sandvoort and Ithaca in Berbice.

17. Zero rather than postnominal *dem* is the appropriate basilectal pluralizer for the plural nouns in Anna's texts, since they are either indefinites or preceded by plural numerals or quantifiers.

18. See the introduction to Derek's texts in Chap. 4 for relevant discussion.

19. I am grateful to Heng-hsiung Jeng, who has worked extensively on the topic-comment construction; see Jeng (1982) for discussion on this point.

20. I am grateful to McAndrew for the time and effort he expended on the preparation of this transcript, and for making it available to me for use in this volume.

21. See S. Persaud (1978) for discussion. Other examples are Irene (Text 10c), Granny (12a), Ustad (16d), and Mother (24c).

22. His single instance of the English copula—the form *wuz* in line 1225—occurs in an existential construction, where the basilectal equivalent would be *bin gat* rather than *a*.

23. Interestingly, from the perspective of person-number reference, lines 1210–13 show some fluctuation—even confusion—in the choice of the pronoun forms.

24. Note that we still have no cases of habitual *a* in *wen* clauses.

25. Handler and Lange (1978: 27) observe that in historical sources "Whydah (or Ouidah) could refer to such people as the speakers of various Ewe languages (including Fon speakers, such as the Dahomeans, Gun, and Popo, and the Ewe proper), who were shipped from that major slaving port in Dahomey."

26. The word *neeshn* in creole has a wider range of referents than it does in SE, including animals of the same species, as well as people sharing a particular ethnic identity or phenotype.

27. The form *disopeer* might represent the absence of final -*d* or -*z*, or of a preceding modal auxiliary like *gun* or *wud*.

28. The issue is explored in greater detail in Rickford (1987).

Chapter 6

1. The speech samples in this chapter come from various sources. The radio announcer's speech (Text 29) and the overseas Christmas greetings (Text set 32) were recorded from radio broadcasts. The teacher's discussion (Text 30) was recorded by Fitzroy Lewis in 1977, and the lawyers in court (Text set 31) were recorded by Francis Callender and Lennox Foster in 1977. Wordsworth McAndrew recorded the Guyanese folksongs (Text set 26) and the birthday requests (Text set 28).

2. A headline in the *New York Times* of May 29, 1984, reads: "Pidgin Is the Language for Jokes in Cameroon." For additional examples of the stereotypical association of pidgin/creole varieties with the trivial and the humorous, see Rickford and Traugott (1985).

3. Excerpts from this and similar productions can be heard on Marc Matthews's record *Marc Up* (Tie Records, No. 001, 1978). It is available from Theatre Information Exchange, "The Playpen," Prospect, St. James, Barbados.

4. See the discussion in the introduction to Text set 15 (Bonnette), Chap. 4.

5. See Scott (1973), Roberts (1976), and Rickford (1980a) on the common habitual function of irregular -*s* in VBE.

6. For a discussion of the grammatical features of Jamaican proverbs, see Lawton (1984).

7. "Mammy" is also basilectal, but "mummy" and "mom" seem to be more typical of mesolectal speech.

8. The conventional English spelling "married" is presumably modified to "marrid" to indicate precisely this.

9. Interestingly enough, Haynes (1984) has independently identified Selvon as one of only two short-story writers in Andrew Salkey's anthology, *Island Voices* (1970), who "use Local and Mixed Speech for authorial comment, the others resorting mainly to Standard English in the narrative sections of their stories." The other writer she found to be outstanding in this respect (among the 17 represented in the collection) is R. O. Robinson—of Jamaica.

10. See D'Costa (1983)—herself a successful author—for a discussion of the orthographic and related challenges with which the Caribbean writer must grapple.

11. See Brown and Ford (1961) on the respect signaled in American English by the

use of professional title alone. I am grateful to Daizal Samad and Surendra Gambhir for information on the implications of the use of *mai*. Compare also standard Hindi *maiya:* 'mother' (Chaturvedi and Tiwari 1975: 620).

12. "At" is more common with verbs of motion, as in "He gone at the market"; its use here probably reflects an association with prepositional *a*, which is used for both stative and dynamic locatives in basilectal GC.

13. However, a number of East Indians have distinguished themselves as calypsonians over the years, in Trinidad as well as in Guyana.

14. Contrast lines 1465–66, where she uses the acrolect to give a time-check and to provide the radio audience with a visual description of what is happening in the studio.

15. Interestingly enough, the other example is also before a present progressive or continuative "-ing" participle (∅ *reelii geting* 1465). As noted several times above, the progressive is a favoring environment for auxiliary "be" or copula absence in VBE and other English dialects. The 11 cases of copula presence in this extract are before adjectives (5 cases), noun phrases (3), present progressives (2), and the infinitive (1).

16. See Le Page (1968), Cave (1971), Craig (1971, 1977, 1980), Carrington (1976), Carrington and Borely (1977), Rickford and Greaves (1978), and Roberts (1983), and the references therein.

17. It is noteworthy that Sir Lionel Luckhoo, one of the most vigorous spokesman for the anti-Creole and pro-SE position common among the middle class, is a member of the legal profession.

References

References

Abrahams, Roger D. 1970. "Traditions of Eloquence in the West Indies." *Journal of Inter-American Studies and World Affairs* 12: 502–27.
———. 1972. "The Training of the Man-of-Words in Talking Sweet." *Language in Society* 1: 15–29.
———. 1976. *Talking Black.* Rowley, Mass.: Newbury House.
———. 1983. *The Man-of-Words in the West Indies: Performance and the Emergence of Creole Culture.* Baltimore: Johns Hopkins University Press.
Abrahams, Roger D., and John F. Szwed. 1983. *After Africa. Extracts from British Travel Accounts and Journals of the Seventeenth, Eighteenth and Nineteenth Centuries concerning the Slaves, their Manners and Customs in the British West Indies.* New Haven, Conn.: Yale University Press.
Abrams, Ovid. 1970. *Guyana Metegee.* Buxton, Guyana: self-published.
Adamson, Alan H. 1972. *Sugar Without Slaves: The Political Economy of British Guiana, 1838–1904.* New Haven, Conn.: Yale University Press.
Akatsuka, Noriko. 1983. "Conditionals Are Context-Bound." Paper presented at the Symposium on Conditionals, Stanford, Calif.
Akers, Glenn. 1981. *Phonological Variation in the Jamaican Continuum.* Ann Arbor, Mich.: Karoma.
Allen, W. F., C. P. Ware, and Lucy McKim Garrison. 1867. *Slave Songs of the United States.* New York: A. Simpson and Co.
Alleyne, Mervyn C. 1971. "Acculturation and the Cultural Matrix of Creolization." In Hymes, ed., listed below, pp. 169–86.
———. 1980. *Comparative Afro-American.* Ann Arbor, Mich.: Karoma.
Allsopp, Richard. 1958a. "Pronominal Forms in the Dialect of English Used in Georgetown (British Guiana) and Its Environs by Persons Engaged in Non-Clerical Occupations." M.A. thesis, London University, Vol. 2.
———. 1958b. "The English Language in British Guiana." *English Language Teaching* 12 (2): 59–66.
———. 1962. "Expressions of State and Action in the Dialect of English Used in the Georgetown Area of British Guiana." Ph.D. thesis, London University.
———. 1972. "Some Suprasegmentals of Caribbean English." Paper presented at the Conference on Creole Languages and Educational Development, St. Augustine, Trinidad.

———. 1976. "The Case for Afro-Genesis." In Cave, comp., listed below.

———. 1978. "Washing Up Our Wares: Towards a Dictionary of Our Use of English." In Rickford, ed., listed below, pp. 173–94.

———. 1980. "How Creole Lexicons Expand." In Valdman and Highfield, eds., listed below, pp. 89–108.

———. 1983. "The Creole Treatment of Passivity." In Carrington, ed., listed below, pp. 142–54.

Andersen, Roger W., ed. 1981. *New Dimensions in Second Language Acquisition Research*. Rowley, Mass.: Newbury House.

———. 1983. *Pidginization and Creolization as Language Acquisition*. Rowley, Mass.: Newbury House.

Area Handbook for Guyana. 1969. Washington, D.C.: Johnson Research Associates.

Austin, J. L. 1962. *How to Do Things with Words*. New York: Oxford University Press.

Baber, Colin, and Henry B. Jeffrey. 1986. *Guyana: Politics, Economics and Society*. London: Frances Pinter.

Bailey, Beryl Loftman. 1965. "Toward a New Perspective in Negro English Dialectology." *American Speech* 40(3): 171–77.

———. 1966. *Jamaican Creole Syntax*. Cambridge: Cambridge University Press.

———. 1971. "Jamaican Creole: Can Dialect Boundaries Be Defined?" In Hymes, ed., listed below, pp. 341–48.

Bailey, Charles-James N. 1973. *Variation and Linguistic Theory*. Washington, D.C.: Center for Applied Linguistics.

Bailey, Charles-James N., and Roger W. Shuy, eds. 1973. *New Ways of Analyzing Variation in English*. Washington, D.C.: Georgetown University Press.

Barrett, W. G. 1969 (1848). Preface to Edwin Angel Wallbridge, *The Demerara Martyr. Memoirs of the Rev. John Smith, Missionary to Demerara*. New York: Negro Universities Press.

Baudet, Martha M. 1981. "Identifying the African Grammatical Base of the Caribbean Creoles: A Typological Approach." In Highfield and Valdman, eds., listed below, pp. 104–17.

Baugh, John. 1983. *Black Street Speech: Its History, Structure, and Survival*. Austin: University of Texas Press.

———. 1984. "Steady: Progressive Aspect in Black Vernacular English." *American Speech* 59(1): 3–12.

Beckwith, Martha W. 1929. *Black Roadways: A Study of Jamaican Folk Life*. Chapel Hill: University of North Carolina Press.

Bell, Wendell. 1980. "Equality and Social Justice: Foundations of Nationalism in the Caribbean." *Caribbean Studies* (University of Puerto Rico) 20(2): 3–36.

Bennett, Louise. 1966. "Candy Seller." In Louise Bennett, *Jamaica Labrish*. Jamaica: Sangster's Bookstores.

Bernhardt, Stephen. 1983. "Dialect and Style-Shifting in the Fiction of Samuel Selvon." In Carrington, ed., 1983 listed below, pp. 266–76.

Bernstein, Basil. 1966. "Elaborated and Restricted Codes, an Outline." In Stanley Lieberson, ed., *Explorations in Sociolinguistics*, pp. 254–61. *Sociological Inquiry* (special issue) 36(2).

———. 1972. "A Sociolinguistic Approach to Socialization, with Some Reference to Educability." In Gumperz and Hymes, eds., *Directions*, listed below, pp. 465–97.

Berry, Jack. 1976. "Tone and Intonation in Guyanese English." In A. Juilland, ed., *Linguistic Studies Offered to Joseph Greenberg*, 2: *Phonology*, pp. 263–70.

Bickerton, Derek. 1970. "Guyanese Speech." Unpublished Manuscript, main library, University of Guyana, Georgetown.

———. 1971. "Inherent Variability and Variable Rules." *Foundations of Language* 7: 457–92.

———. 1973a. "On the Nature of a Creole Continuum." *Language* 49: 640–69.

———. 1973b. "The Structure of Polylectal Grammars." In Roger W. Shuy, ed., *Proceedings of the Twenty-Third Annual Round Table Meeting on Language and Linguistics*, pp. 17–42. Monograph series 25. Washington, D.C.: Georgetown University Press.

———. 1975. *Dynamics of a Creole System.* Cambridge: Cambridge University Press.

———. 1976. "Pidgin and Creole Studies." *Annual Review of Anthropology* 5: 169–93.

———. 1977a. "Pidginization and Creolization: Language Acquisition and Language Universals." In Valdman, ed., listed below, pp. 49–69.

———. 1977b. "Putting Back the Clock in Variation Studies." *Language* 53(2): 353–60.

———. 1977c. *Change and Variation in Hawaiian English*, 2: *Creole Syntax.* Honolulu: Social Sciences and Linguistics Institute, University of Hawaii.

———. 1980. "Decreolisation and the Creole Continuum." In Valdman and Highfield, eds., listed below, pp. 109–28.

———. 1981. *Roots of Language.* Ann Arbor, Mich.: Karoma.

———. 1983a. "Creole Languages." *Scientific American* 249(1): 116–22.

———. 1983b. "Notice of P. Baker and C. Corne, *Isle de France Creole* (Karoma, 1982)." *The Carrier Pidgin* 11(4): 8–9.

———. 1984a. "The Language Bioprogram Hypothesis." *The Behavioral and Brain Sciences* 7(2): 173–88.

———. 1984b. "The Role of Demographics in the Formation of Creoles." Paper presented at the 13th Annual Colloquium on New Ways of Analyzing Variation, Philadelphia, Pennsylvania.

Birdwhistell, Roy L. 1970. *Kinesics and Context: Essays on Body Motion Communication.* Philadelphia: University of Pennsylvania Press.

Blom, Jan Petter, and John J. Gumperz. 1972. "Social Meaning in Linguistic Structures: Code-Switching in Norway." In Gumperz and Hymes, eds., *Directions*, listed below, pp. 407–34.

Bloomfield, Leonard. 1933. *Language.* New York: Henry Holt.

Bolingbroke, Henry. 1807. *A Voyage to the Demerary.* London: Richard Phillips.

Bollée, A. 1977. *Le Créole français des Seychelles.* Tübingen: Niemeyer Verlag.

Bosman, William. 1814 (1704). "A New and Accurate Description of the Coast of Guinea, divided into the Gold, the Slave and the Ivory Coasts." In John Pinkerton, ed., *Voyages and Travels in All Parts of the World*, 16: 337–547. London: Longman et al.

Braithwaite, Edward Kamau. 1984. *History of the Voice: The Development of Nation Language in Anglophone Caribbean Poetry.* London: New Beacon Books.

Brasch, Walter M. 1981. *Black English and the Mass Media.* Amherst: University of Massachusetts Press.

Breinburg, Petronella. 1971. *Legends of Suriname.* London: New Beacon Books.

Bresnan, Joan, and Sam A. Mchombo. 1985. "Topic, Pronoun, and Agreement in Mchombo." Unpublished manuscript, Department of Linguistics, Stanford University.

Bridenbaugh, Carl, and Roberta Bridenbaugh. 1972. *No Peace Beyond the Line—The English in the Caribbean, 1624–90.* New York: Oxford University Press.

References

308

Britton, Sanford. 1983. "An Example Using Several Scaling Techniques." In Peter Dunn-Rankin, *Scaling Methods*, pp. 409–17. Hillsdale, N.J.: Lawrence Erlbaum Associates.
Bronkurst, H. V. P. 1881. *The Origin of the Guyanian Indians Ascertained.* Georgetown, British Guiana: The Colonist Office.
———. 1883. *The Colony of British Guyana and Its Labouring Population.* London: T. Woolmer.
———. 1888. *Among the Hindus and Creoles of British Guiana.* London: Woolmer.
Brown, Roger, and Marguerite Ford. 1961. "Address in American English." *Journal of Abnormal and Social Psychology* 62: 375–85.
Byrne, Francis. 1984. "*Fi* and *Fu*: Origins and Functions in Some Caribbean English-Based Creoles." *Lingua* 62: 97–120.
Carew, Jan. 1958. *Black Midas.* London: Martin Secker and Warburg.
Carrington, Lawrence. 1976. "Determining Language Education Policy in Caribbean Sociolinguistic Complexes." *International Journal of the Sociology of Language* 8: 27–43.
———, ed. (in collaboration with Dennis Craig and Ramon Todd Dandaré). 1983. *Studies in Caribbean Language.* St. Augustine, Trinidad: Society for Caribbean Linguistics.
Carrington, Lawrence, and C. Borely. 1977. *The Language Arts Syllabus, 1975: Comment and Counter-Comment.* St. Augustine, Trinidad: School of Education, University of the West Indies.
Carter, Hazel. 1983. "How to Be a Tone Language." In Carrington, ed., listed above, pp. 90–111.
———. 1984. "Defining the Syllable in Jamaican Creole." Paper presented at the 5th Biennial Meeting of the Society for Caribbean Linguistics, Mona, Jamaica.
———. n.d. "Suprasegmentals in Jamaican and Guyanese: Some African Comparisons." In Gilbert, ed., listed below.
Cassidy, Frederic G. 1971 (1961). *Jamaica Talk: Three Hundred Years of the English Language in Jamaica.* 2d ed. London: Macmillan.
———. 1980. "The Place of Gullah." *American Speech* 55: 3–16.
Cassidy, Frederic G., and Robert B. Le Page. 1980. *Dictionary of Jamaican English.* 2d ed. Cambridge: Cambridge University Press.
Cave, George. 1971. *Primary School Language in Guyana.* Georgetown: Guyana Teachers' Association.
———, comp. 1976. *New Directions in Creole Studies.* Papers presented at the 1st Annual Conference of the Society for Caribbean Linguistics. Georgetown, Guyana.
Chafe, Wallace C. 1981. "Integration and Involvement in Speaking, Writing and Oral Literature." In Deborah Tannen, ed., *Spoken and Written Language: Exploring Orality and Literacy*, pp. 35–53. Norwood, N.J.: Ablex.
Chaturvedi, Mahendra, and B. N. Tiwari. 1975. *A Practical Hindi-English Dictionary.* 2d ed. Delhi: National Publishing House.
Chomsky, Noam. 1965. *Aspects of the Theory of Syntax.* Cambridge: Massachusetts Institute of Technology Press.
———. 1977. "On WH-Movement." In Peter W. Culicover, Thomas Wasaw, and Adrian Akmaijian, eds., *Formal Syntax*, pp. 71–132. New York: Academic Press.
Christie, Pauline. 1979. "Assertive 'no' in Jamaican Creole." *Occasional Paper* 10. St. Augustine, Trinidad: Society for Caribbean Linguistics.

————. 1983. "In Search of the Boundaries of Caribbean Creoles." In Carrington, ed., listed above, pp. 13–22.

Clark, Eve V. 1978. "Locationals: Existential, Locative and Possessive Constructions." In Joseph H. Greenberg, et al., eds., *Universals of Human Language*, pp. 85–126. Stanford, Calif.: Stanford University Press.

Clementi, Cecil. 1937. *A Constitutional History of British Guiana*. London: Macmillan.

Collens, J. H. 1888. *A Guide to Trinidad: A Handbook for the Use of Tourists and Visitors*. 2d ed. London: Elliot Stock.

Comrie, Bernard. 1976. *Aspect: An Introduction to the Study of Verbal Aspect and Related Problems*. Cambridge: Cambridge University Press.

Conklin, Nancy Faires. 1978. "The Language of the Majority: Women and American English." In Margaret A. Lourie and Nancy F. Conklin, eds., *A Pluralistic Nation*, pp. 222–37. Rowley, Mass.: Newbury House.

Cooper, Vincent O. 1980. "On the Notion of Decreolization and St. Kitts Personal Pronouns." In R. Day, ed., *Issues in English Creoles*. Heidelberg: Julius Groos.

Corder, S. P. 1981. "Formal Simplicity and Functional Simplification in Second Language Acquisition." In Andersen, ed., *New Dimensions*, listed above, pp. 146–52.

Corne, Chris. 1977. *Seychelles Creole Grammar*. Tübingen: Nan.

————. 1983. "Substratal Reflections: The Completive Aspect and the Distributive Numerals in Isle de France Creole." *Te Reo* (University of Auckland, N.Z.) 26: 65–80.

Cox, Edward Godfrey. 1938. *A Reference Guide to the Literature of Travel*, 2: *The New World*. Seattle: University of Washington Press.

Craig, Dennis. 1969. *An Experiment in Teaching English*. Kingston, Jamaica: Caribbean Universities Press.

————. 1971. "Education and Creole English in the West Indies: Some Sociolinguistic Factors." In Hymes, ed., listed below, pp. 371–92.

————. 1977. "Creole Languages and Primary Education." In Valdman, ed., listed below, pp. 313–32.

————. 1980. "Models for Educational Policy in Creole-Speaking Communities." In Valdman and Highfield, eds., listed below, pp. 245–66.

————. 1983. Review of David Sutcliffe, 'British Black English.' *Language in Society* 12(4): 542–48.

Craton, Michael. 1982. *Testing the Chains: Resistance to Slavery in the British West Indies*. Ithaca, N.Y.: Cornell University Press.

Cruickshank, J. Graham. 1905. *Negro Humor: Being Sketches in the Market on the Road, and at My Back Door*. Demerara, British Guiana: The Argosy Co.

————. 1916. *Black Talk, Being Notes on Negro Dialect in British Guiana with (Inevitably) a Chapter on Barbados*. Demerara, British Guiana: The Argosy Co.

————. 1930. "The Wreckage of an Industry." *The West India Committee Circular*, March 6, 1930, pp. 87–88.

Culicover, Peter W. 1976. *Syntax*. New York: Academic Press.

Curtin, Philip D. 1969. *The Atlantic Slave Trade: A Census*. Madison: University of Wisconsin Press.

Daly, Vere T. [1966]. *A Short History of the Guyana People*. Kitty, Guyana: self-published.

————. 1967. *The Making of Guyana. Independence Histories*, 1. Georgetown, Guyana: self-published.

Day, Richard R. 1973. "Patterns of Variation in Copula and Tense in the Hawaiian Post-Creole Continuum." *Working Papers in Linguistics* 5(2), Department of Linguistics, University of Hawaii.

D'Costa, Jean. 1983. "The West Indian Novelist and Language: A Search for a Literary Medium." In Carrington, ed., listed above, pp. 252–65.

DeCamp, David. 1971a. "Introduction: The Study of Pidgin and Creole Languages." In Hymes, ed., listed below, pp. 13–45.

——. 1971b. "Toward a Generative Analysis of a Part-Creole Continuum." In Hymes, ed., listed below, pp. 349–70.

——. 1977. "The Development of Pidgin and Creole Studies." In Valdman, ed., listed below, pp. 3–20.

DeCamp, David, and Ian F. Hancock, eds. 1974. *Pidgins and Creoles: Current Trends and Prospects*. Washington, D.C.: Georgetown University Press.

Despres, Leo A. 1967. *Cultural Pluralism and National Politics in British Guiana*. Chicago: Rand McNally.

Des Voeux, G. William. 1948 (1903). *Experiences of a Demerara Magistrate*. Georgetown, British Guiana: The Daily Chronicle, Ltd. [Part of a 2-vol. work originally published under the title *My Colonial Service*.]

Devonish, Hubert St. Laurent. 1978. "The Selection and Codification of a Widely Understood and Publicly Useable Language Variety in Guyana, to Be Used as a Vehicle of National Development." D. Phil. thesis, University of York.

——. 1983. "Towards the Establishment of an Institute for Creole Language Standardization and Development in the Caribbean." In Carrington, ed., listed above, pp. 300–316.

Dillard, J. L. 1971. "The Creolist and the Study of Negro Non-Standard Dialects in the Continental United States." In Hymes, ed., listed below, pp. 394–408.

——. 1972. *Black English: Its History and Usage in the United States*. New York: Random House.

Domingue, N. C. 1971. "Bhojpuri and Creole in Mauritius: A Study of Linguistic Interference and Its Consequences in Regard to Synchronic Variation and Language Change." Ph.D. dissertation, University of Texas.

Dorson, Richard M. 1956. *Negro Folktales in Michigan*. Cambridge, Mass.: Harvard University Press.

Dulay, Heidi, Marina Burt, and Stephen Krashen. 1982. *Language Two*. New York: Oxford University Press.

Dunn-Rankin, Peter. 1983. *Scaling Methods*. Hillsdale, N.J.: Lawrence Erlbaum Associates.

Edwards, Bryan. 1793. *The History, Civil and Commercial, of the British Colonies in the West Indies*, vol. 2. London: J. Stockdale.

Edwards, Jay D. 1970. "Social Linguistics on San Andrés and Providencia Islands, Colombia." Ph.D. dissertation, Tulane University.

——. 1974. "African Influences on the English of San Andrés Island, Colombia." In DeCamp and Hancock, eds., listed above, pp. 1–26.

Edwards, Vivian K. 1979. *The West Indian Language Issue in British Schools*. London: Routledge and Kegan Paul.

Edwards, Walter F. 1975. "Sociolinguistic Behaviour in Rural and Urban Circumstances in Guyana." D.Phil. dissertation, University of York.

——. 1977. *An Introduction to the Akawaio and Arekuna Peoples of Guyana*. Georgetown: Amerindian Languages Project, University of Guyana.

———. 1978. "Tantalisin' and Busin' in Guyana." *Anthropological Linguistics* 20(5): 194–213.

———. 1979. "The Sociolinguistic Significance of Some Guyanese Speech Acts." *International Journal of the Sociology of Language* 22: 79–101.

———. 1982. "A Description and Interpretation of the Kwe-Kwe Tradition in Guyana." *Folklore* 93(2): 181–92.

———. 1983. "Code Selection and Shifting in Guyana." *Language in Society* 12(3): 295–311.

———. 1984a. "A Community-Based Approach to the Provenance of Urban Guyanese Creole." In Sebba and Todd, eds., listed below, pp. 83–94.

———. 1984b. "Socializing the Continuum: Guyanese Sociolinguistic Culture as Social Networks." Paper presented at the 5th Biennial Meeting of the Society for Caribbean Linguistics, Mona, Jamaica.

Eersel, Christiann. 1971. "Varieties of Creole in Suriname: Prestige in Choice of Language and Linguistic Form." In Hymes, ed., listed below, pp. 317–22.

Ellis, George W. 1914. *Negro Culture in West Africa*. New York: Neale Publishing Co.

Escure, Geneviève. 1981. "Decreolization in a Creole Continuum: Belize." In Highfield and Valdman, eds., listed below, pp. 27–39.

———. 1982. "Contrastive Patterns of Intragroup and Intergroup Interaction in the Creole Continuum of Belize." *Language in Society* 11(2): 239–64.

———. 1984a. "The Acquisition of Creole by Urban and Rural Black Caribs in Belize." In Sebba and Todd, eds., listed below, pp. 95–106.

———. 1984b. "The Belizean Continuum in Apparent Time." Paper presented at the 5th Biennial Meeting of the Society for Caribbean Linguistics, Mona, Jamaica.

Faine, Jule. 1937. *Philologie créole*. Port-au-Prince, Haiti: Imprimerie de l'État.

Farley, Rawle E. G. 1954. "The Rise of the Peasantry in British Guiana." *Social and Economic Studies* 2(4): 87–103.

———. 1956. "Aspects of the Economic History of British Guiana: 1781–1852." Ph.D. thesis, University of London.

Fasold, Ralph W. 1970. "Two Models of Socially Significant Linguistic Variation." *Language* 46(3): 551–63.

———. 1972. *Tense-Marking in Black English*. Washington, D.C.: Center for Applied Linguistics.

———. 1973. "The Concept of 'Earlier-Later': More or Less Correct." In Bailey and Shuy, eds., listed above, pp. 27–58.

———. 1981. "The Relation Between Black and White Speech in the South." *American Speech* 56(3): 163–89.

Ferguson, Charles A. 1959. "Diglossia." *Word* 15: 325–40.

Fredericks, Esau. 1978. "Rice-Farming Terms in Guyana." In Rickford, ed., listed below, pp. 111–20.

Gambhir, Surendra Kumar. 1981. "The East Indian Speech Community in Guyana: A Sociolinguistic Study with Special Reference to Koine Formation." Ph.D. dissertation, University of Pennsylvania.

———. 1983. "Diglossia in Dying Languages: A Case Study of Guyanese Bhojpuri and Standard Hindi." *Anthropological Linguistics* 25(1): 28–38.

Gibson, Kean. 1982. "Tense and Aspect in Guyanese Creole: A Syntactic, Semantic and Pragmatic Analysis." D.Phil. thesis, University of York.

———. 1984. "Evidence Against an Anterior Tense System in Guyanese and Jamaican Creoles." In Sebba and Todd, eds., listed below, pp. 123–30.

Gilbert, Glenn. 1983. "Two Early Surveys of the World's Pidgins and Creoles: A Comparison of Schuchardt and Reinecke." Paper presented at the York Creole Conference.

———, ed. n.d. *Pidgin and Creole Studies: Essays in Memory of John E. Reinecke.* Honolulu: University of Hawaii Press. Forthcoming.

Givón, Talmy. 1975. "Focus and the Scope of Assertion: Some Bantu Evidence." *Studies in African Linguistics* 6(2): 185–205.

———. 1976. "Topic, Pronoun and Grammatical Agreement." In Charles Li, ed., *Subject and Topic,* pp. 151–88. New York: Academic Press.

———. 1982. "Tense-Aspect-Modality: The Creole Proto-Type and Beyond." In Paul J. Hopper, ed., *Tense Aspect: Between Semantics and Pragmatics,* pp. 115–63. Philadelphia: John Benjamins.

Glasgow, Roy A. 1970. *Guyana: Race and Politics Among Africans and East Indians.* The Hague: Martinus Nijhoff.

Goffman, Erving. 1972. *Relations in Public: Microstudies of the Public Order.* New York: Harper Colophon Books.

Goodman, Morris. n.d. "The Portuguese Element in the American Creoles." In Gilbert, ed., listed above.

Goslinga, Cornelis Ch. 1971. *The Dutch in the Caribbean and on the Wild Coast, 1580–1680.* Gainesville: University of Florida Press.

Graham, Sara, and David Beckles. 1968. "The Prestige Ranking of Occupations: Problems of Method and Interpretation Suggested by a Study in Guyana." *Social and Economic Studies* 17(4): 367–80.

Grice, H. P. 1975. "Logic and Conversation." In P. Cole and J. L. Morgan, eds., *Speech Acts,* pp. 41–58. *Syntax and Semantics* 3. New York: Academic Press.

Gumperz, John J. 1964. "Linguistic and Social Interaction in Two Communities." In Gumperz and Hymes, eds., *Ethnography,* listed below, pp. 137–53.

Gumperz, John J., and Robert Wilson. 1971. "Convergence and Creolization: A Case from the Indo/Aryan/Dravidian Border." In Hymes, ed., listed below, pp. 151–67.

Gumperz, John J., and Dell H. Hymes, eds. 1964. *The Ethnography of Communication.* Washington, D.C.: American Anthropological Association.

———. 1972. *Directions in Sociolinguistics.* New York: Holt, Rinehart.

Guttman, Louis. 1944. "A Basis for Scaling Qualitative Data." *American Sociological Review* 9: 139–50.

Guy, Gregory. 1980. "Variation in the Group and the Individual: The Case of Final Stop Deletion." In William Labov, ed., *Locating Language in Time and Space,* pp. 1–36. New York: Academic Press.

Haley, Alex. 1976. *Roots.* New York: Dell.

Hall, Robert A. Jr. 1966. *Pidgin and Creole Languages.* Ithaca, N.Y.: Cornell University Press.

Hancock, Ian F. 1969. "A Provisional Comparison of the English-Derived Atlantic Creoles." *African Language Review* 8: 7–72.

———. 1977. "Recovering Pidgin Genesis: Approaches and Problems." In Valdman, ed., listed below, pp. 277–94.

———. 1980. "Gullah and Barbadian: Origins and Relationships." *American Speech* 55(1): 17–35.

———. 1986. "The Domestic Hypothesis, Diffusion, and Componentiality: An Account of Atlantic Anglophone Creole Origins." In Pieter Muysken and Norval Smith, eds., *Substrata Versus Universals in Creole Genesis,* pp. 71–102. Amsterdam: John Benjamins.

————. n.d.*a*. "A Preliminary Classification of the Anglophone Atlantic Creoles." In Gilbert, ed., listed above.

————. n.d.*b*. *Littorally Speaking: Social and Linguistic Development on the Upper Guinea Coast.* Forthcoming.

Handler, Jerome S., and Frederick W. Lange. 1978. *Plantation Slavery in Barbados.* Cambridge, Mass.: Harvard University Press.

Harris, C. A., and J. A. J. de Villiers, eds. 1911. *Storm van's Gravesande: The Rise of British Guiana.* 2 vols. London: Hakluyt Society.

Haynes, Lilith M. 1973. "Language in Barbados and Guyana: Attitudes, Behaviors and Comparisons." Ph.D. dissertation, Stanford University.

————. 1978. "Words and Meaning in Guyanese Classrooms." Paper presented at the 2d Biennial Meeting of the Society for Caribbean Linguistics, Cave Hill, Barbados.

————. 1979. "A Note on Creolization and the Continuum." In Ian F. Hancock, ed., *Readings in Creole Studies*, pp. 335–38. Ghent: E. Story-Scientia.

————. 1984. "Language Variation in *Island Voices*." *English World-Wide* 5(1): 25–42.

Heine, B. 1970. *Status and Use of African Lingua Francas.* Munich: Weltforum Verlag.

Herskovits, Melville J. 1958. *The Myth of the Negro Past.* 2d ed. Boston: Beacon Press.

Herskovits, Melville J., and Frances S. Herskovits. 1934. *Rebel Destiny: Among the Bush Negroes of Dutch Guiana.* New York: McGraw Hill.

Highfield, Arnold, and Albert Valdman, eds. 1981. *Historicity and Variation in Creole Studies.* Ann Arbor, Mich.: Karoma.

Hintzen, Percy. 1983. "Social Stratification: The Caribbean Issue, the Guyanese Example." In Michael Parris and George Danns, eds., *A Sociology Text for the Caribbean.* Georgetown, Guyana: Institute of Development Studies.

Holder, Maurice A. 1972. "Word Accentual Patterns in Guyanese English (GE) Compared with British English (RP norm)." In *Proceedings of the 7th International Congress of Phonetic Sciences, Montreal, 1971*, pp. 897–99. The Hague: Mouton.

————. 1984. "The Compound Stress Rule in Guyanese English." Paper presented at the 5th Biennial Meeting of the Society for Caribbean Linguistics, Mona, Jamaica.

Holm, John (with Alison Watt Shilling). 1982. *Dictionary of Bahamian English.* Cold Spring, N.Y.: Lexik House.

————. 1984. "Variability of the Copula in Black English and Its Creole Kin." *American Speech* 59(4): 291–309.

————, ed. 1983. *Central American English. Varieties of English Around the World Text Series* T2, ed. Manfred Görlach. Heidelberg: Julius Groos Verlag.

Hooper, Joan Bybee. 1973. "Aspects of Natural Generative Phonology." Ph.D. Dissertation, University of California, Los Angeles.

Huttar, George. 1981. "Some Kwa-Like Features of Djuka Syntax." *Studies in African Linguistics* 2(3): 291–323.

Hymes, Dell H. 1964. "Introduction: Toward Ethnographies of Communication." In Gumperz and Hymes, eds., *Ethnography*, listed above, pp. 1–34.

————. 1968. "The Ethnography of Speaking." In J. A. Fishman, ed., *Readings in the Sociology of Language*, pp. 99–138. The Hague: Mouton.

————. 1971a. Introduction to Part 3: General Conceptions of Process. In Hymes, ed., listed below, pp. 65–90.

————. 1972. "Models of the Interaction of Language and Social Life." In Gumperz and Hymes, *Directions*, listed above, pp. 35–71.

——. 1982. "The Language of Myth." Presidential Address, 57th Meeting of the Linguistic Society of America, San Diego, Calif.

——, ed. 1971b. *Pidginization and Creolization of Languages*. Cambridge: Cambridge University Press.

Jayawardena, Chandra. 1963. *Conflict and Solidarity on a Guyanese Plantation*. London: Athlone.

Jeng, Heng-hsiung. 1982. "The Development of Topic and Subject in Chinese and English." In Linguistic Society of Korea, ed., *Linguistics in the Morning Calm*. Seoul: Hanshin Publishing Co.

Jenkins, Edward. 1871. *The Coolie: His Rights and Wrongs*. London: Strahan & Co.

Jeremiah, Milford Astor. 1977. "The Linguistic Relatedness of Black English and Antiguan Creole: Evidence from the Eighteenth and Nineteenth Centuries." Ph.D. dissertation, Brown University.

Jespersen, Otto. 1933. *Essentials of English Grammar*. University City: University of Alabama Press.

Kay, Paul, and Gillian Sankoff. 1974. "A Language Universals Approach to Pidgins and Creoles." In DeCamp and Hancock, eds., listed above, pp. 73–84.

Key, Mary Ritchie. 1975. *Paralanguage and Kinesics (Non-Verbal Communication)*. Metuchen, N.J.: Scarecrow Press.

Kirke, Henry. 1898. *Twenty-Five Years in British Guiana*. London: Sampson Low, Marston.

Krapp, George P. 1925. *The English Language in America*. New York: Frederick Ungar.

Labov, William. 1963. "The Social Motivation of a Sound Change." *Word* 19: 273–309.

——. 1966. *The Social Stratification of English in New York City*. Washington, D.C.: Center for Applied Linguistics.

——. 1967. "Some Sources of Reading Problems for Speakers of the Black English Vernacular." In A. Frazier, ed., *New Directions in Elementary English*, pp. 140–67. Champaign, Ill.: National Council of Teachers of English. [Reprinted in Labov 1972c: 3–35.]

——. 1969. "Contraction, Deletion, and Inherent Variability of the English Copula." *Language* 45(4): 715–62. [Reprinted in Labov 1972c: 65–129.]

——. 1970. *The Logic of Non-Standard English. Georgetown University Monographs in Languages and Linguistics* 22: 1–43. [Reprinted in Labov 1972c: 201–40.]

——. 1971a. "The Notion of System in Creole Studies." In Hymes, ed., listed above, pp. 447–72.

——. 1971b. "On the Adequacy of Natural Languages, I: The Development of Tense." Unpublished manuscript.

——. 1972a. "Some Principles of Linguistic Methodology." *Language in Society* 1: 97–120.

——. 1972b. *Sociolinguistic Patterns*. Philadelphia: University of Pennsylvania Press.

——. 1972c. *Language in the Inner City*. Philadelphia: University of Pennsylvania Press.

——. 1973. "The Boundaries of Words and Their Meanings." In Bailey and Shuy, eds., listed above, pp. 340–73.

——. 1980. "Is There a Creole Speech Community?" In Valdman and Highfield, listed below, pp. 369–88.

——. 1982. "Building on Empirical Foundations." In Winfred P. Lehmann and

Yakov Malkiel, eds., *Perspectives on Historical Linguistics*, pp. 17–92. *Current Issues in Linguistic Theory* 24. Philadelphia: John Benjamins.

———. 1984. "The Transmission of Linguistic Traits Across and Within Communities." Paper presented at the Symposium on Language Transmission and Change, Stanford, Calif.

Labov, William, and Joshua Waletzky. 1967. "Narrative Analysis: Oral Versions of Personal Experience." In June Helm, ed., *Essays on the Verbal and Visual Arts*, pp. 12–44. Seattle: University of Washington Press.

Labov, William, Paul Cohen, Clarence Robins, and John Lewis. 1968. *A Study of the Non-Standard English of Negro and Puerto Rican Speakers in New York City.* 2 vols. Philadelphia: U.S. Regional Survey.

Lakoff, Robin. 1973. "Language and Women's Place." *Language and Society* 2: 45–79.

Lalla, Barbara. 1979. "Sources for a History of Jamaican Creole." In Edward Baugh, ed., *Language and Literature in the Commonwealth Caribbean*, pp. 50–66. Kingston, Jamaica: West Indian Association for Commonwealth Literature and Language Studies.

Lalla, Barbara, and Jean D'Costa. 1984. "Voices in Exile: Jamaican Creole Songs, Stories and Sayings from the Eighteenth and Nineteenth Centuries." Unpublished manuscript, Department of English, Hamilton College.

Lambert, Wallace E. 1967. "A Social Psychology of Bilingualism." In John Macnamara, ed., *Problems of Bilingualism. Journal of Social Issues* (special issue) 23(2): 91–109.

Lawton, David. 1984. "Grammar of the English-Based Jamaican Proverb." *American Speech* 59(2): 123–30.

Lee, Sidney, ed. 1896. *Dictionary of National Biography*, vol. 45. New York: Macmillan.

Lefebvre, Claire. 1974. "Discreteness and the Linguistic Continuum in Martinique." *Anthropological Linguistics* 16(2): 47–78.

Le Page, Robert B. 1960. "An Historical Introduction to Jamaican Creole." In R. B. Le Page and David DeCamp, *Jamaican Creole*, pp. 1–124. *Creole Language Studies* 1. London: Macmillan.

———. 1968. "Problems to Be Faced in the Use of English as the Medium of Instruction in Four West Indian Territories." In Charles A. Ferguson, Joshua A. Fishman, and Jyotirindra Das Gupta, eds., *Language Problems of Developing Nations*, pp. 431–42. New York: Wiley and Sons.

———. 1978. *Projection, Focussing, Diffusion, or Steps Towards a Sociolinguistic Theory of Language. Occasional Paper* 9. St. Augustine, Trinidad: Society for Caribbean Linguistics.

———. 1980a. "Hugo Schuchardt's Creole Studies and the Problem of Linguistic Continua." In K. Lichem and H. J. Simon, eds., *Hugo Schuchardt. Schuchardt Symposium 1977 in Graz*, pp. 114–45.

———. 1980b. "Theoretical Aspects of Sociolinguistic Studies in Pidgin and Creole Languages." In Valdman and Highfield, eds., listed below, pp. 331–67. New York: Academic Press.

———. 1984. "The Need for a Multidimensional Model." Paper presented at the 5th Biennial Meeting of the Society for Caribbean Linguistics, Mona, Jamaica.

Le Page, Robert B., and Andrée Tabouret-Keller. 1985. *Acts of Identity*. Cambridge: Cambridge University Press.

Lewis, Gordon K. 1983. "Historical Conjuncture Between European and Slave Cultures: Manifestations for Viable Alternatives in the Caribbean." Paper presented at the Conference on Viable Economic and Social Alternatives in Central America and the Caribbean, Stanford, Calif.

Littlefield, Daniel C. 1981. *Rice and Slaves: Ethnicity and the Slave Trade in Colonial South Carolina.* Baton Rouge: Louisiana State University Press.

Lynch, Louis. 1964. *The Barbados Book.* London: Andre Deutsch Ltd.

McAndrew, Wordsworth. 1978. "Guyanese Folksongs." In Rickford, ed., listed below, pp. 237–40.

Macaulay, Ronald K. S. 1981. "The Rise and Fall of the Vernacular." Unpublished manuscript.

McTurk, Michael ["Quow"]. 1949 (1899). *Essays and Fables in the Vernacular.* Georgetown, British Guiana: The Daily Chronicle, Ltd. [Originally published in 1881; the 1899 edition is said to be identical with that edition.]

Mandle, Jay R. 1973. *The Plantation Economy: Population and Economic Change in Guyana, 1838–1960.* Philadelphia: Temple University Press.

Manley, Robert H. 1979. *Guyana Emergent: The Post-Independence Struggle for Non-Dependent Development.* Cambridge, Mass.: Schenkman.

Markey, Tom L., and Peter Fodale. 1983. "Lexical Diathesis, Focal Shift, and Passivization: The Creole Voice." *English World-Wide* 4: 69–84.

Marryat, Frederick. 1834. *Peter Simple.* Paris: Bandry's European Library. [Reprints N. Y. Franklin Library, 1835; E. P. Dutton, 1907.]

Mihalic, F. 1971. *The Jacaranda Dictionary and Grammar of Melanesian Pidgin.* Milton, Queensland: Jacaranda Press PTY Ltd.

Milroy, Lesley. 1980. *Language and Social Networks.* London: Basil Blackwell.

Mintz, Sidney, and Richard Price. 1976. *An Anthropological Approach to the Afro-American Past: A Caribbean Perspective.* ISHI Occasional Papers in Social Change 2. Philadelphia: Institute for the Study of Human Issues.

Mohan, P. R. 1978. "Trinidad Bhojpuri." Ph.D. dissertation, University of Michigan.

Montejo, Esteban. 1973 (1968). *The Autobiography of a Runaway Slave,* ed. Miguel Barnet, tr. Jocasta Innes. New York: Vintage.

Moreton, J. B. 1790. *Manners and Customs in the West India Islands.* London: Richardson, Gardner, and Walker.

Morrow, Todd E. 1984. "Bajan." B.A. (Hons.) thesis, Department of Linguistics, Stanford University.

Mufwene, Salikoko S. 1982. "Notes on Durative Constructions in Jamaican and Guyanese Creoles." Paper presented at the 4th Biennial Meeting of the Society for Caribbean Linguistics, Paramaribo, Suriname.

———. 1983. "Some Observations on the Verb in Black English Vernacular." *African and Afro-American Studies and Research Center Papers* 2 (5).

———. 1985. "Gullah and Jamaican: An Issue on Decreolization." Unpublished manuscript.

Mühlhäusler, Peter. 1975. "The Functional Possibilities of Lexical Bases in New Guinea Pidgin." Paper presented at the International Conference on Pidgins and Creoles, Honolulu, Hawaii.

———. 1980. "Structural Expansion and the Process of Creolization." In Valdman and Highfield, eds., listed below, pp. 19–55.

———. 1986. *Pidgin and Creole Linguistics.* Cambridge: Cambridge University Press.

Muysken, Pieter C., ed. 1981. *Generative Studies of Creole Languages.* Dordrecht: Foris Publications.

Muysken, Pieter C., and Norval Smith, eds. 1986. *Universals Versus Substrata in Creole Genesis.* Amsterdam: John Benjamins.

Naro, Anthony J. 1978. "A Study on the Origins of Pidginization." *Language* 54(2): 314–47.

Nashe, Thomas. 1958. *The Works of Thomas Nashe*, Vol. 2, ed. R. B. McKerrow. Oxford: Basil Blackwell.

Nath, Dwarka. 1970. *A History of Indians in Guyana*. 2d ed. London: self-published.

Neto, Serafim Da Silva. 1957. "Breves Notas para o Estudo da Expansão da língua Portuguêsa em África e Ásia." *Revista de Portugal* 22: 129–47.

Netscher, P. M. 1888. *Geschiedenis van de Koloniën Essequebo, Demerary, en Berbice*. 's Gravenhage, Netherlands: The Provincial Utrecht Society of Arts and Sciences.

Nichols, Patricia C. 1976. "Linguistic Change in Gullah: Sex, Age and Mobility." Ph.D. dissertation, Stanford University.

———. 1982. "Gullah and Caribbean Creole English." Paper presented at the meeting of the American Dialect Society/South Atlantic Modern Language Association, Atlanta.

———. 1983. "Black and White Speaking in the Rural South: Differences in the Pronominal System." *American Speech* 58(3): 201–15.

Niles, Norma A. 1980. "Provincial English Dialects and Barbadian English." Ph.D. dissertation, University of Michigan.

Ochs, Elinor. 1979. "Planned and Unplanned Discourse." In Talmy Givón, ed., *Discourse and Syntax*, pp. 51–80. New York: Academic Press.

Oppenheim, Samuel. 1907. "An Early Jewish Colony in Western Guiana, 1658–1666, and Its Relation to the Jews in Surinam, Cayenne and Tobago." *Publications of the American Jewish Historical Society* 16: 95–186.

Parsons, Elsie Clews. 1917. "Tales from Guilford County, North Carolina." *Journal of American Folklore* 30: 187–88.

———. 1918. *Folk-tales of Andros Island, Bahamas*. Memoirs of the American Folklore Society 13. New York: AFS.

Pavone, James. 1980. "Implicational Scales and English Dialectology." Ph.D. dissertation, Indiana University.

Perlmutter, David M., and Scott Soames. 1979. *Syntactic Argumentation and the Structure of English*. Berkeley: University of California Press.

Persaud, Arnold. 1970. *Some Salient Creole Features in Guyanese Speech*. B.A. thesis, University of Guyana.

Persaud, Satnarine. 1978. "Names of Folk-Spirits in Guyana." In Rickford, ed., listed below, pp. 63–74.

Pinckard, George. 1806. *Notes on the West Indies . . . Including Observations on the Island of Barbadoes, and the Settlements Captured by the British Troops upon the Coast of Guiana*. 3 vols. London: Longman, Hurst, Rees & Orme.

Pollard, Velma. 1983. "The Social History of Dread Talk." In Carrington, ed., listed above, pp. 46–62.

Postma, Johannes. 1970. "The Dutch Participation in the African Slave Trade: Slaving on the Guinea Coast, 1675–1795." Ph.D. dissertation, Michigan State University.

Price, Richard, ed. 1973. *Maroon Societies: Rebel Slave Communities in the Americas*. Garden City, N.Y.: Doubleday Anchor Press.

Quirk, Randolph. 1965. "Descriptive Statement and Serial Relationship." *Language* 41(2): 205–17.

Ramdat, Kuntie. 1978. "Indian Dishes and Cooking Terms in Guyana." In Rickford, ed., listed below, pp. 123–36.

Rampaul, Sayadam. 1978. "Hindi Kinship Terms in Guyana." In Rickford, ed., listed below, pp. 137–52.

Rauf, Mohammad A. 1974. *Indian Village in Guyana*. Leiden: E. J. Brill.

Reinecke, John E. 1937. "Marginal Languages: A Sociological Survey of the Creole Languages and Trade Jargons." Ph.D. dissertation, Yale University.

Reinecke, John E., and Aiko Tokimasa. 1934. "The English Dialect of Hawaii." *American Speech* 9: 48–58, 122–31.

Reinecke, John E., Stanley M. Tsuzaki, David DeCamp, Ian F. Hancock, and Richard E. Wood. 1975. *A Bibliography of Pidgin and Creole Languages. Oceanic Linguistics Special Publication* 14. Honolulu: University Press of Hawaii.

Reisman, Karl. 1970. "Cultural and Linguistic Ambiguity in a West Indian Village." In Norman F. Whitten, Jr., and John F. Szwed, eds., *Afro-American Anthropology*, pp. 129–44. New York: Free Press.

Reno, Philip. 1964. *The Ordeal of British Guiana*. New York: Monthly Review Press.

Rickford, John R. 1974. "The Insights of the Mesolect." In DeCamp and Hancock, eds., listed above, pp. 92–117.

———. 1976. "Communicating in a Creole Continuum." In Cave, comp., listed above.

———. 1977a. "The Question of Prior Creolization in Black English." In Valdman, ed., listed below, pp. 190–221.

———. 1977b. "The Field of Pidgin-Creole Studies. A Review Article on Loreto Todd's Pidgins in English." *World Literature Written in English* (MLA Division 33), 16(2): 477–513.

———. 1979. "Variation in a Creole Continuum: Quantitative and Implicational Approaches." Ph.D. dissertation, University of Pennsylvania.

———. 1980a. "How Does DOZ Disappear?" In Richard R. Day, ed., *Issues in English Creoles: Papers from the 1975 Hawaii Conference*, pp. 77–96. Heidelberg: Julius Groos Verlag.

———. 1980b. "Analyzing Variation in Creole Languages." In Valdman and Highfield, eds., listed below, pp. 165–84.

———. 1981. "A Variable Rule for a Creole Continuum." In David Sankoff and Henrietta Cedergren, eds., *Variation Omnibus*, pp. 201–8. Edmonton, Alberta: Linguistic Research, Inc.

———. 1983a. *Standard and Non-Standard Language Attitudes in a Creole Continuum. Occasional Paper* 16. St. Augustine, Trinidad: Society for Caribbean Linguistics.

———. 1983b. "What Happens in Decreolization." In Andersen, ed., *Pidginization*, listed above, pp. 298–319.

———. 1985a. "Ethnicity as a Sociolinguistic Boundary." *American Speech* 60(2): 99–125.

———. 1985b. "Some Principles for the Study of Black and White Speech in the South." In Michael Montgomery and Richard Bailey, eds., *Language Variety in the South: Perspectives in Black and White*, pp. 38–62. Tuscaloosa: University of Alabama Press.

———. 1986a. "Social Contact and Linguistic Diffusion: Hiberno English and New World Black English." *Language* 62(2): 245–89.

———. 1986b. "The Need for New Approaches to Social Class Analysis in Sociolinguistics." *Language and Communication* 6(3): 215–21.

———. 1987. "The Haves and Have Nots: Sociolinguistic Surveys and the Assessment of Speaker Competence." *Language in Society* 16(2): 149–77.

————. n.d. *Linguistic Variation and the Social Order*. New York: Academic Press. Forthcoming.

————, ed. 1978. *A Festival of Guyanese Words*, 2d ed. Georgetown: University of Guyana.

Rickford, John R., and Barbara Greaves. 1978. "Non-Standard Words and Expressions in the Writing of Guyanese School Children." In Rickford, ed., listed above, pp. 40–56.

Rickford, John R., and Angela E. Rickford. 1976. "Cut-Eye and Suck-Teeth: Masked Africanisms in New World Guise." *Journal of American Folklore* 89(353): 294–309.

Rickford, John R., and Elizabeth Closs Traugott. 1985. "Symbol of Powerlessness and Degeneracy, or Symbol of Solidarity and Truth? Paradoxical Attitudes Toward Pidgins and Creoles." In Sidney Greenbaum, ed., *The English Language Today*, pp. 252–61. Oxford: Pergamon Press.

Roberts, Peter A. 1976. "Hypercorrection as Systematic Variation." In Cave, comp., listed above.

————. 1980. "The Adequacy of Certain Theories in Accounting for Important Grammatical Relationships in a Creole Language." In Richard R. Day, ed., *Issues in English Creoles: Papers from the 1975 Hawaii Conference*, pp. 19–38. Heidelberg: Julius Groos Verlag.

————. 1983. "Linguistics and Language Teaching." In Carrington, ed., listed above, pp. 230–44.

Robertson, Ian E. 1974. "Dutch Creole in Guyana: Some Missing Links." *Occasional Paper* 2. Mona, Jamaica: Society for Caribbean Linguistics.

————. 1981. "Creole Dutch and the Guyana Venezuela Border Question." Unpublished manuscript.

————. 1982. "Redefining the Post-Creole Continuum." *Amsterdam Creole Studies* 4: 62–78.

————. n.d. *Berbice Dutch: A Description*. Forthcoming.

Robertson, Ian F., and Dhanishwari Jaganauth. 1976. "A Comparative Word List of Berbice and Skepi Dutch." Unpublished manuscript.

Robinson, Pat. 1970. "The Social Structure of Guyana." In Lloyd Searwar, ed., *Cooperative Republic: A Study of Aspects of Our Way of Life*, pp. 51–78. Georgetown: [Government of Guyana].

Rodney, Ruby V. 1981. "Analysis: Guyanese Creole and American Black English with Special Emphasis on Tense and Aspect." Ph.D. dissertation, Rutgers University.

Rodney, Walter. 1970. *A History of the Upper Guinea Coast, 1545 to 1800*. Oxford: Oxford University Press.

————. 1981. *A History of the Guyanese Working People, 1881–1905*. Baltimore: Johns Hopkins University Press.

Rodway, James. 1912. *Guiana: British, Dutch and French*. London: T. Fisher Unwin.

Rohlehr, Gordon. 1978. "Samuel Selvon and the Language of the People." In Edward Baugh, ed., *Critics on Caribbean Literature*. London: Allen and Unwin.

Romaine, Suzanne. 1982. *Socio-Historical Linguistics: Its Status and Methodology*. Cambridge: Cambridge University Press.

————. 1984. *The Language of Children and Adolescents: The Acquisition of Communicative Competence*. Oxford: Basil Blackwell.

Ross, John Robert. 1973. "A Fake NP Squish." In Bailey and Shuy, listed above, pp. 96–140.

Rouse, Irving. 1953. *Guianas: Indigenous Period*. Publication 55. Mexico City: Instituto Panamericano de Geografía e Historia.

Sag, Ivan A. 1973. "On the State of Progress on Progressives and Statives." In Bailey and Shuy, listed above, pp. 83–95.

St. Clair, Thomas Staunton. 1834. *A Soldier's Recollections of the West Indies and America*. 2 vols. London: Richard Bentley.

Salkey, Andrew, ed. 1970. *Island Voices: Stories from the West Indies*. New York: Liveright. [Originally published in 1965 as *Stories from the Caribbean*. London: Elek.]

Samarin, William. 1980. "Standardization and Instrumentalization of Creole Languages." In Valdman and Highfield, listed below, pp. 213–36.

Sankoff, David, and Henrietta Cedergren. 1976. "The Dimensionality of Grammatical Variation." *Language* 52(1): 163–78.

Sankoff, Gillian. 1974. "A Quantitative Paradigm for the Study of Communicative Competence." In Richard Bauman and Joel Sherzer, eds., *Explorations in the Ethnography of Speaking*, pp. 18–49. Cambridge: Cambridge University Press.

———. 1980. *The Social Life of Language*. Philadelphia: University of Pennsylvania Press.

Sankoff, Gillian, and Suzanne Laberge. 1974. "On the Acquisition of Native Speakers by a Language." In DeCamp and Hancock, eds., listed above, pp. 73–84.

Sankoff, Gillian, and William Labov. 1985. "Variation Theory." Paper presented at the 14th Annual Conference on New Ways of Analyzing Variation, Washington, D.C.

Schiffrin, Deborah. 1981. "Tense Variation in Narrative." *Language* 57(1): 45–62.

Schomburgk, Robert. 1922 (1847). *Travels in British Guiana, 1840–1844*, tr. and ed. Walter E. Roth. Georgetown, British Guiana: The Daily Chronicle Ltd.

Schuchardt, Hugo. 1914. *Die Sprache der Saramakkaneger in Surinam. Verhandelingen der Koninklijke Akademie van Wetenschappen te Amsterdam*, n.s. 14 (6). Amsterdam: Johannes Muller. [Preface translated in Schuchardt 1979: 73–108.]

———. 1979. *The Ethnography of Variation: Selected Writings on Pidgins and Creoles*, ed. and tr. T. L. Markey. Ann Arbor, Mich.: Karoma.

Schuler, Monica. 1980. *Alas, Alas, Kongo: A Social History of Industrial African Immigration into Jamaica, 1841–1865*. Baltimore: Johns Hopkins University Press.

Schumann, John H. 1978. *The Pidginization Process: A Model for Second Language Acquisition*. Rowley, Mass.: Newbury House.

Schumann, John H., and Ann-Marie Stauble. 1983. "A Discussion of Second Language Acquisition and Decreolization." In Andersen, ed., *Pidginization*, listed above, pp. 260–74.

Scott, Jerri C. 1973. "The Need for Semantic Considerations in Accounting for the Variable Usage of Verb Forms in Black Dialects of English." *University of Michigan Papers in Linguistics* 1(2): 140–46.

Sebba, Mark. 1983. "The Syntax of Serial Verbs: An Investigation into Serialisation in Sranan and Other Languages." D. Phil. thesis, University of York.

Sebba, Mark, and Loreto Todd, eds. 1984. *Papers from the York Creole Conference, Sep. 24–7, 1983. York Papers in Linguistics* 11. University of York.

Selinker, Larry. 1972. "Interlanguage." *International Review of Applied Linguistics* 10(3): 209–32.

Seymour, Arthur. 1978. "Opening Remarks." In Rickford, ed., listed above, pp. 16–18.

Shepard, Roger N., A. Kimball Romney, and Sara Beth Nerlove. 1972. *Multidimensional Scaling: Theory and Applications in the Behavioral Sciences*, 1: *Theory*. New York: Seminar Press.

Shields, Kathryn. 1984. "The Significance of Word-Final t/d Consonant Clusters in

Standard Jamaican English." Paper presented at the 5th Biennial Meeting of the Society for Caribbean Linguistics, Mona, Jamaica.

Shukla, Shaligram. 1981. *Bhojpuri Grammar.* Washington, D.C.: Georgetown University Press.

Simpson, Jane. 1983. "Warlpiri Syntax." Ph.D. dissertation, Massachusetts Institute of Technology.

Slobin, Dan Isaac. 1979. *Psycholinguistics.* 2d ed. Glenview, Ill.: Scott, Foresman.

Smith, M. G. 1965. *The Plural Society in the British West Indies.* Berkeley: University of California Press.

Smith, Norval, Ian Robertson, and Kay Williamson. n.d. "The Ijo Element in Berbice Dutch." *Language in Society.* Forthcoming.

Smith, Raymond T. 1962. *British Guiana.* London: Oxford University Press.

Smith, Reed. 1926. *Gullah.* Columbia: University of South Carolina Press.

Solomon, Dennis. 1972. "Form, Content, and the Post-Creole Continuum." Paper presented at the Conference on Creole Languages and Educational Development, St. Augustine, Trinidad.

Spears, Arthur A. 1982. "The Black English Semi-Auxiliary *come.*" *Language* 58(4): 850–72.

Speirs, James. 1902. *The Proverbs of British Guiana.* Demerara, British Guiana: The Argosy Co.

Stephen, Leslie, ed. 1896. *Dictionary of National Biography,* vol. 5. New York: Macmillan.

Stewart, William A. 1962. "Creole Languages in the Caribbean." In Frank A. Rice, ed., *Study of the Role of Second Languages in Asia, Africa and Latin America,* pp. 34–53. Washington, D.C.: Center for Applied Linguistics.

———. 1965. "Urban Negro Speech: Sociolinguistic Factors Affecting English Teaching." In Roger W. Shuy, ed., *Social Dialects and Language Learning,* pp. 10–18. Champaign, Ill.: National Council of Teachers of English.

———. 1970 (1967, 1968). "Toward a History of American Negro Dialect." In Frederick Williams, ed., *Language and Poverty,* pp. 351–79. Chicago: Markham.

———. 1974. "Acculturative Processes and the Language of the American Negro." In William W. Gage, ed., *Language in Its Social Setting,* pp. 1–46. Washington, D.C.: Anthropological Society of Washington.

Sutcliffe, David. 1982. *British Black English.* London: Basil Blackwell.

Tanna, Laura. 1984. *Jamaican Folk Tales and Oral Histories.* Kingston: Institute of Jamaica.

Tannen, Deborah. 1982. "Oral and Literate Strategies in Spoken and Written Narratives." *Language* 58(1): 1–21.

———, ed. 1981. *Coherence in Spoken and Written Discourse.* Norwood, N.J.: Ablex.

Taylor, Douglas. 1961. "New Languages for Old in the West Indies." *Comparative Studies in Society and History* 3: 277–88.

Thomas, J. J. 1969 (1869). *The Theory and Practice of Creole Grammar.* London: New Beacon Books.

Thompson, Claudith. 1980. "A Socio-historical Background to the Lexicon of Guyanese English." Paper presented at the 3d Biennial Meeting of the Society for Caribbean Linguistics, Aruba, Netherland Antilles.

Thompson, R. W. 1961. "A Note on Some Possible Affinities Between the Creole Dialects of the Old World and Those of the New. . . ." In Robert B. Le Page, ed., *Creole Language Studies* 2, pp. 107–13. London: Macmillan.

Tiwari, U. N. 1960. *The Origin and Development of Bhojpuri*. Calcutta: The Asiatic Society.

Todd, Loreto. 1974. *Pidgins and Creoles*. London: Routledge and Kegan Paul.

——. 1982. *Cameroon. Varieties of English Around the World* Text Series T1, ed. Manfred Gorlach. Heidelberg: Julius Groos.

Torgerson, Warren S. 1958. *Theory and Methods of Scaling*. New York: Wiley and Sons.

Traugott, Elizabeth Closs. 1972. *A History of English Syntax*. New York: Holt, Rinehart.

——. 1976. "Pidgins, Creoles and the Origin of Vernacular Black English." In Deborah Sears Harrison and Tom Trabasso, eds., *Black English: A Seminar*, pp. 57–93. Hillsdale, N.J.: Lawrence Erlbaum Associates.

——. 1977. "Pidginization, Creolization and Language Change." In Valdman, ed., listed below, pp. 70–98.

——. 1981. Introduction to Highfield and Valdman, eds., listed above, pp. 1–6.

Traugott, Elizabeth Closs, and Charles A. Ferguson. 1982. "Toward a Checklist for Conditionals." Unpublished manuscript.

Traugott, Elizabeth Closs, and Suzanne Romaine. 1985. "Some Questions for the Definition of 'Style' in Socio-Historical Linguistics." In *Folia Linguistica Historica* 6(1): 7–39.

Trotman, David V. 1976. "The Yoruba and Orisha Worship in Trinidad and British Guiana: 1838–1870." *African Studies Review* 19: 1–17.

Tsuzaki, Stanley M. 1971. "Coexistent Systems in Language Variation: The Case of Hawaiian English." In Hymes, ed., listed above, pp. 327–39.

Turner, Lorenzo Dow. 1974 (1949). *Africanisms in the Gullah Dialect*. Ann Arbor: University of Michigan. [Originally published by the University of Chicago.]

Tyndall, Belle. 1965. "Some Grammatical Aspects of the Written Work of Some Creolese-Speaking School Children in British Guiana." Thesis for the Diploma in the Teaching of English Overseas, Victoria University, Manchester.

——. 1974. *English Language Curriculum: BV and Lodge Experimental Projects*. Georgetown: Faculty of Education, University of Guyana.

Valdman, Albert. 1971. "The Language Situation in Haiti." In Hymes, ed., listed above, pp. 61–62.

——, ed. 1977. *Pidgin and Creole Linguistics*. Bloomington: Indiana University Press.

Valdman, Albert, and Arnold Highfield, eds. 1980. *Theoretical Orientations in Creole Studies*. New York: Academic Press.

Van Berkel, Adriann. 1941 (1695). *Travels in South America Between the Berbice and Essequibo Rivers and in Suriname, 1670–1689*, tr. Walter E. Roth. Georgetown, British Guiana: The Daily Chronicle, Ltd.

Van Sertima, J. 1897. *Among the Common People of British Guiana*. Georgetown, British Guiana: C. K. Jardine.

——. 1899. *Scenes and Sketches of Demerara Life*. Demerara: n.p.

——. 1905. *The Creole Tongue of British Guiana*. New Amsterdam, British Guiana: self-published.

Vaughn-Cooke, Anna Fay. 1980. "Lexical Diffusion: Evidence from De-Creolization." Paper presented at the 9th Annual Conference on New Ways of Analyzing Variation in English, University of Michigan.

Versteegh, Kees. 1984. *Pidginization and Creolization: The Case of Arabic. Amsterdam Studies in the Theory and History of Linguistic Science* 33. Philadelphia: John Benjamins.

References   323

Voorhoeve, Jan. 1957. "The Verbal System of Sranan." *Lingua* 6: 374–96.
Wakin, Edward. 1976. *Enter the Irish American.* New York: Thomas Y. Crowell.
Wallbridge, Edwin Angle. 1969 (1848). *The Demerara Martyr: Memoirs of the Rev. John Smith, Missionary to Demerara.* New York: Negro Universities Press.
Warner-Lewis, Maureen Patricia. 1982. "The Yoruba Language in Trinidad." Ph.D. dissertation, University of the West Indies.
Washabaugh, William. 1974. "Variability in Decreolization on Providence Island, Colombia." Ph.D. dissertation, Wayne State University.
———. 1977. "Constraining Variation in Decreolization." *Language* 53(2): 329–52.
Weber, Max. 1946. *From Max Weber: Essays in Sociology,* ed. H. H. Gerth and C. Wright Mills. New York: Oxford University Press.
Weinreich, Uriel. 1953. *Languages in Contact.* New York: Linguistic Circle of New York.
Weinreich, U., W. Labov, and M. Herzog. 1968. "Empirical Foundations for a Theory of Language Change." In W. P. Lehmann and Y. Malkiel, eds., *Directions for Historical Linguistics,* pp. 97–195. Austin: University of Texas Press.
Wells, J. C. 1982. *Accents of English,* 1: *An Introduction*; 3: *Beyond the British Isles.* Cambridge: Cambridge University Press.
West, Candace, and Don H. Zimmerman. 1983. "Small Insults: A Study of Interruptions in Cross-Sex Conversations Between Unacquainted Persons." In Barrie Thorne, Cheris Kramarae, and Nancy Henley, eds., *Language, Gender and Society,* pp. 103–17. Rowley, Mass.: Newbury House.
Whinnom, Keith. 1965. "The Origin of the English-Based Creoles and Pidgins." *Orbis* 14: 509–27.
———. 1971. "Linguistic Hybridization and the 'Special Case' of Pidgins and Creoles." In Hymes, ed., listed above, pp. 91–116.
Williams, Jeffrey F. 1983. "Dutch and English Creole on the Windward Netherlands Antilles: An Historical Perspective." *Amsterdam Creole Studies* 5: 93–111.
Winford, Donald. 1972. "A Sociolinguistic Description of Two Communities in Trinidad." D.Phil. thesis, University of York.
———. 1985a. "The Syntax of *fi* Complements in Caribbean English Creole." *Language* 61(3): 588–624.
———. 1985b. "The Concept of 'Diglossia' in Caribbean Creole Situations." *Language in Society* 14(3): 345–56.
Wolfram, Walt. 1969. *A Sociolinguistic Description of Detroit Negro Speech.* Washington, D.C.: Center for Applied Linguistics.
Wolfram, Walt, and Donna Christian. 1975. *Sociolinguistic Variables in Appalachian Dialects.* Arlington, Va.: Center for Applied Linguistics.
Wolfson, Nessa. 1976. "Speech Events and Natural Speech: Some Implications for Sociolinguistic Methodology." *Language in Society* 7: 215–37.
———. 1979. "The Conversational Historical Present Alternation." *Language* 55(1): 168–82.
———. 1982. *The Conversational Historical Present in American English Narrative.* Dordrecht: Foris Publications.
Writers' Program, Georgia. 1973 (1940). *Drums and Shadows: Survival Studies Among the Georgia Coastal Negroes.* Westport, Conn.: Greenwood Press. [Originally published by the University of Georgia Press.]
Wurm, Stephen A. 1971. *New Guiana Highlands Pidgin: Course Materials. Pacific Linguistics* D. 3. Canberra: The Australian National University.

————. 1980. "Standardization and Instrumentalization in Tok Pisin." In Valdman and Highfield, eds., listed above, pp. 237–44.

Yansen, C. A. 1975. *Random Remarks on Creolese*. Margate, Eng.: self-published.

Zenk, Henry. 1984. "Chinook Jargon and Native Persistence in the Grand Ronde Indian Community, 1856–1907: A Special Case of Creolization." Ph.D. dissertation, University of Pennsylvania.

Zimmerman, Don H., and Candace West. 1975. "Sex Roles, Interruptions and Silences in Conversation." In Barrie Thorne and Nancy M. Henley, eds., *Language and Sex: Difference and Dominance*, pp. 105–29. Rowley, Mass.: Newbury House.

Indexes

Line Index of
Selected Grammatical Features

For the benefit of the instructor who wishes examples of Creole forms for class use, or the researcher who wishes to verify or replicate an established analysis or to explore a new hypothesis, this index lists all the lines in which selected grammatical or morphosyntactic features are exemplified in the texts. (The separate general index lists the page numbers on which these and other features are discussed.) Two classes of variables have been selected for indexing: those that have already attracted attention in the literature (like the tense-aspect markers or the infinitival complementizers), and those that can be expected to interest researchers in the future because of their centrality or uniqueness in the Creole semantic system (like relative clauses or the simultaneous verb phrase construction).

Features are listed in this index first in terms of general subcategory or variable (in small capital letters, e.g. COMPLEMENTIZERS, INFINITIVAL), and then in terms of specific subtypes or variants thereof. Citation forms are given both in the phonemic orthography used for the spoken texts (italic) and in the English or dialect spellings used for the written texts and folksongs (in single quotation marks). Brief definitions or descriptions are included in parentheses where they seem necessary. Occurrences of the features in the narrative or introductory lines of the written texts are not included unless these are written in Creole rather than Standard English. In general, occurrences of the features in my contributions to the dialogue in the spoken texts are not included either, except in some subcategories where the sample is limited or could otherwise benefit from their inclusion; in such cases examples from me are included in parentheses, with the notation J. Only one line number is given in the few instances where a feature occurs more than once in a line. Note, finally, that a semicolon rather than a comma marks the boundaries between lines from different chapters. For convenience, it may be remembered that lines 1–215 are from Chapter 3 ("Early Written Texts"), lines 216–960 from Chapter 4 ("Recordings of Natural Speech: Cane Walk"), lines 961–1338 from Chapter 5 ("Recordings of Natural Speech: Other Areas"), and lines 1339–1562 from Chapter 6 ("Modern Texts from Diverse Domains").

ARTICLES, INDEFINITE

a, o(n); 'a(n)': 65, 101, 122, 139, 156, 162, 164, 165, 166, 167, 168, 169, 172, 175, 178, 181, 195, 211, 213; 256, 263, 284, 287, 409, 428, 431, 432, 437, 441, 443, 450, 451, 452, 458, 519, 566, 580, 603, 611, 613, 616, 628, 630, 631, 632, 642, 643, 647, 652, 659, 664, 669, 680, 685, 690, 706, 712, 714, 721, 722, 725,

733, 741, 748, 751, 755, 760, 765, 767,
768, 778, 787, 794, 809, 810, 830, 838,
839, 857, 885, 891, 895, 934, 940, 947,
952, 960; 963, 965, 966, 976, 978, 982,
985, 986, 988, 990, 1001, 1004, 1021,
1029, 1043, 1052, 1193, 1222, 1225,
1254, 1265, 1266, 1267, 1270, 1282,
1285, 1289, 1290, 1328, 1335, 1336;
1339, 1343, 1347, 1348, 1353, 1377,
1394, 1403, 1415, 1418, 1443, 1444,
1446, 1451, 1452, 1454, 1474, 1477,
1478, 1484, 1488, 1493, 1495, 1502,
1508, 1514, 1516, 1531, 1532, 1535,
1540, 1542, 1552, 1557, 1562

wan, won; 'one,' 'wan' (unstressed,
noncontrastive): 15, 17, 31, 52, 134,
158; 216, 217, 226, 232, 256, 264, 291,
297, 331, 333, 361, 362, 363, 365, 368,
391, 421, 468, 556, 567, 773; 1069,
1080, 1092, 1114, 1117, 1119, 1123,
1124, 1207, 1218; 1386

Ø (zero article; including but not
limited to nonspecific noun phrases):
991, 1030, 1040, 1082, 1095, 1097,
1098, 1100, 1221, 1243, 1261; 1385,
1401, 1498

COMPLEMENTIZERS, INFINITIVAL

fu, fi; 'fo('),' 'for': 12, 13, 15, 31, 32,
39, 52, 59, 130, 133, 142, 152, 166,
171, 173, 183, 201; 219, 227, 233, 241,
252, 254, 280, 293, 294, 313, 316, 322,
323, 324, 334, 358, 419, 425, 427, 437,
439, 454, 462, 464, 466, 495, 551, 552,
555, 567, 578, 581, 680, 741, 767, 950;
992, 1109

gu; 'go': 329, 335, 421, 489; 1116

(t)u; 'to': 25, 96, 101, 162, 176; 287,
288, 292, 294, 302, 383, 405, 414, 421,
422, 436, 437, 450, 517, 558, 583, 596,
602, 606, 621, 627, 631, 642, 648, 649,
653, 662, 674, 675, 677, 698, 707, 709,
721, 722, 723, 726, 733, 734, 737, 743,
757, 766, 780, 788, 790, 798, 800, 807,
859, 876, 900, 907, 908, 909, 915, 921,
923, 926, 928, 930, 938, 940, 941, 944,
945, 948, 956, 957; 962, 986, 992,
1021, 1028, 1034, 1035, 1045, 1049,

1095, 1096, 1159, 1200, 1207, 1253,
1270, 1273, 1278, 1281, 1290, 1292,
1293, 1321, 1336, 1337; 1343, 1347,
1370, 1377, 1378, 1380, 1414, 1415,
1416, 1431, 1438, 1444, 1450, 1463,
1464, 1471, 1474, 1479, 1483, 1485,
1495, 1499, 1502, 1503, 1509, 1520,
1528, 1530, 1537, 1542, 1543, 1547,
1557, 1561

Ø (zero): 60; 303, 360, 389, 412,
567, 653, 690, 728, 729, 739, 756;
1096, 1135, 1136, 1149, 1150, 1160,
1186, 1188, 1208, 1210; 1352, 1360,
1382, 1384, 1436

COMPLEMENTIZERS, SENTENTIAL/NONINFINITIVAL

(d)at, (d)ot; 'dat': 31, 167; 218, 220,
240, 344, 516, 657, 674, 786, 793, 941,
949, 954; 1236; 1444, 1463, 1464,
1473, 1476, 1477, 1478, 1484, 1513,
1518, 1523, 1525, 1542, 1560

(h)ou: 218, 220, 240

let: 218

mek: 383

se(e), si(i); 'say' (preceding indirect or
reported speech): 128, 167; 495, 685,
687, 691, 727; 730; 1077, 1084, 1091,
1092, 1129, 1165, 1196, 1211

Ø (zero): 279, 282, 283, 340, 386,
387, 519, 590, 597, 601, 602, 620, 741,
779, 787, 790, 829, 834, 937; 1028,
1031, 1039, 1040, 1041, 1199, 1236,
1241, 1253, 1321; 1362, 1391, 1521,
1558

CONDITIONALS/ HYPOTHETICALS

Protasis-only or dramatic conditionals: 847, 979, 1331–32

With *if*; 'if': 30, 146, 152; 294, 297,
323, 331, 333, 349, 406, 422, 652, 660,
740, 747, 793, 798, 847, 898, 907, 908;
965, 979, 1007, 1048, 1057, 1070,
1071, 1077, 1146, 1187; 1331–32,
1345, 1414, 1419, 1439, 1440, 1455,
1459, 1523, 1529, 1533, 1554

Without *if*, but including *aaz*, 'say'

d(h)ooz; 'dose': 184; 704, 900, 912; 1463, 1546

EMPHATIC AFFIRMATIVE: *na, n(o)* (in sentences with rising intonation): 239, 466; 1073, 1099

EVIDENTIALS (in narrative): 482, 970

EXISTENTIALS

With 'be' (inflected forms), preceded by 'there' (*d(h)eer, di, d(e)*): 118; 659, 668, 953, 954; 1046, 1225

With 'got' (*ga(t), gOt, ge(t)*), preceded by an impersonal or indefinite pronoun (*di, dee, dem, ii, it, yu(u), wi(i)*): 251, 290, 368, 409, 484, 516, 582, 685, 717, 745; 996, 1027, 1052, 1311; 1355, 1439

With 'had' (*ha, ad*), preceded by an indefinite or impersonal pronoun (*de, di, wi*): 256, 670, 714, 722, 725, 765, 802; 968, 1008, 1308 (1011: J)

NEGATIVES

en, in, on; 'ain't,' 'ent': 112; 260, 282, 535, 653, 749, 827, 848; 965, 997, 1037, 1158, 1160, 1168, 1169, 1170, 1171, 1195, 1196, 1200, 1315, 1324, 1329; 1345, 1438

k(y)aan(t) and other negative modal forms, *kun, mosn(t), wu(d)n, wun(t)*; 'shouldn't': 186; 345, 350, 431, 452, 550, 596, 652, 701, 709, 742, 836, 843, 859, 926 (272, 434, 700: J); 1031, 1044, 1103, 1133, 1186, 1187, 1221, 1250, 1251, 1335; 1474, 1527, 1530, 1541

na, no; 'no' (preverbal or pre-"adjectival" negator; in modern texts, usually with short vowel): 5, 6, 30, 39, 58, 64, 68, 145, 157, 203; 220, 221, 258, 263, 266, 279, 296, 322, 333, 335, 336, 341, 342, 343, 369, 372, 373, 374, 375, 383, 385, 386, 389, 394, 395, 400, 404, 413, 425, 448, 451, 455, 462, 464, 468, 485, 516, 531, 537, 541, 576, 584, 721, 739, 746, 772, 904, 913, 928, 958; 963,

1068, 1084, 1087, 1088, 1106, 1121, 1126, 1128, 1131, 1134, 1139, 1143, 1145, 1148, 1149, 1150, 1153, 1156, 1163, 1164, 1167, 1178, 1179, 1204, 1208, 1228, 1244, 1327; 1351, 1356, 1357, 1360, 1362, 1382, 1384

nat, nOt; 'not,' and contracted forms of nonmodal auxiliaries, including *di(d)n, doon(t), dozn, (h)adnt, wuzn(t)*, 'isn't,' 'wasn't': 134, 141, 171; 586, 590, 591, 616, 632, 642, 667, 674, 675, 695, 703, 704, 729, 731, 764, 786, 787, 802, 820, 879, 898, 924, 928, 929, 959, 960; 984, 1034, 1244, 1279, 1311, 1315; 1414, 1459, 1502, 1507, 1530, 1531, 1532, 1537, 1541, 1559, 1561

neva, nevo: 356, 361, 398, 399, 649; 985 (1274: J); 1446

noo, no; 'no' (prenominal, preadverbial, or independent negative particle; in modern texts, usually with long vowel): 58, 90, 112, 119, 121, 136, 157, 172, 179, 193; 267, 276, 305, 322, 374, 395, 455, 456, 484, 507, 535, 683, 714, 721, 786, 868, 909, 953; 984, 1008, 1025, 1046, 1087, 1106, 1170, 1279, 1512

PASSIVES

With forms of the English copula *bii*: 134, 186, 207; 606, 783, 829, 865, 879, 883, 886, 890, 914; 1254, 1265, 1268, 1279; 1453, 1502, 1517, 1518, 1522, 1523, 1524, 1527, 1536, 1540, 1542

With *ge(t)*: 296, 298, 934, 956, 957; 1466 (1023, 1024: J)

With *Ø* (no *bii* or *ge(t)* auxiliary and no participial suffix; the unmarked Creole passive): 72, 177; 362, 370, 372, 506, 570, 571, 752, 761, 950, 958 (536: J); 1001, 1003, 1030, 1073, 1074, 1099, 1109, 1111, 1123, 1125, 1128, 1135, 1139, 1147, 1149, 1152, 1159, 1163, 1164, 1300

Generalized indefinite actives (usually with impersonal pronoun subjects like *dem, di*, 'they,' 'you'; see Weiner and Labov 1981): 279, 283, 287, 294, 302, 305, 322, 327, 332, 342, 343, 405,

26; 226, 232, 256, 714, 722, 725, 745, 953; 1027, 1197, 1201, 1209, 1229, 1291, 1304

SERIAL VERB CONSTRUCTIONS

Conventional types (directional, instrumental, purposive, etc.; *see* Alleyne 1980; Huttar 1981): 331, 367, 369, 372, 383, 386, 387, 421, 422, 616, 776, 844, 919, 920, 921; 1071, 1078, 1090, 1100, 1105, 1110, 1127, 1134, 1221; 1352, 1403

Simultaneous verb phrase type: 532, 546, 549, 555. *See also* Serial verbs in the General Index

TENSE-ASPECT MARKERS

a, *bina*, *o*; 'a,' 'da' (nonpunctual; iterative or continuative): 114, 126, 129, 132, 133; 226, 232, 254, 267, 270, 271, 277, 293, 303, 325, 327, 338, 342, 343, 360, 366, 375, 393, 394, 400, 411, 439, 448, 457, 465, 467, 471, 474, 494, 546, 549, 558, 565, 573, 717, 746, 772; 1061, 1063, 1066, 1070, 1085, 1109, 1115, 1116, 1117, 1122, 1123, 1124, 1127, 1128, 1130, 1132, 1144, 1145, 1152, 1154, 1155, 1156, 1163, 1164, 1166, 1167, 1176, 1177, 1178, 1204, 1209, 1215, 1216, 1218, 1229, 1230, 1239, 1242, 1248; 1351, 1352, 1353, 1366, 1382, 1384

(b)in, *biin*, *in(a)*; 'been,' 'bin' (anterior or past): 50, 51, 53, 54, 129, 134, 138, 142, 146, 147, 148, 150, 165, 170; 216, 217, 251, 266, 306, 312, 322, 325, 352, 359, 361, 362, 365, 368, 378, 379, 391, 492, 493, 494, 502, 521, 523, 526, 531, 532, 543, 567, 570, 571, 576, 762, 765, 766, 913; 973, 1055, 1069, 1074, 1127, 1128, 1151, 1214 (1002:J); 1382, 1384, 1385

di(d), *di(d)n*; 'did(n't)' (anterior or past): 167, 174, 179; 284, 565, 590, 591, 642, 752, 761, 763, 764, 770, 786, 959, 960 (513, 514, 518, 525, 712,

784:J); 1007, 1034, 1057, 1198, 1292, 1300, 1311, 1315, 1331 (961, 1006, 1011, 1023, 1024: J); 1502

don, *dom*; 'done' (completive): 149, 182; 221, 228, 235, 241, 245, 383 (856: J); 983, 1082, 1114, 1122; 1362

(d)oz, *(o)z*; 'does' (habitual or iterative): 258, 280, 287, 288, 290, 291, 302, 305, 356, 363, 365, 560, 664, 687, 715, 730, 732, 751, 761, 764, 812, 904 (272, 286, 289, 300, 750: J); 1021, 1051, 1055, 1208, 1321, 1325, 1326; 1440

gu(n), *goo*; 'go,' 'goin',' 'going,' 'gwine' (irrealis or future): 148; 330, 332, 360, 372, 387, 412, 413, 415, 421, 423, 453, 495, 561, 576, 717, 720, 737, 743, 744, 745, 747, 920; 967, 970, 999, 1031, 1037, 1038, 1042, 1057, 1067, 1111, 1129, 1136, 1139, 1147, 1148, 1149, 1186, 1188, 1206, 1211, 1212, 1213, 1219, 1220, 1223, 1228, 1233, 1234, 1236, 1244, 1247, 1250, 1281; 1360, 1377, 1414, 1416, 1436, 1438; 1528

(h)av, *haz*, *(o)v*; 'has,' 'had,' 'hasn'(t),' 'haven't' (perfect auxiliary): 91; 786, 787, 940, 956, 957; 1346, 1468, 1484, 1534, 1558, 1560

so, 'sa' (irrealis or future): 131, 150, 158; 1071

(wi)l, *wu(d)n*; 'will,' 'won't,' 'wouldn't' (irrealis or future): 709, 742, 942; 1044, 1281, 1283; 1389, 1419, 1453, 1454, 1459, 1474, 1542, 1543, 1546, 1554

TOPICALIZATION

With *a*/'da' or *iz*/'is' (involves clefting): 108, 137, 213; 260, 351, 468, 561, 817; 972, 995, 1057, 1190, 1333; 1445

Without *a*/'(d)a' or *iz*/'is' (involving fronting only, including 19th-century examples that may involve transfer of Bhojpuri object-verb sentence structure): 191, 198, 199, 215; 270, 287; 1055, 1106, 1176, 1197

Index of Personal Names

In this Index and the Subject Index an "f" after a number indicates a separate reference on the next page, and an "ff" indicates separate references on the next two pages; "passim" is used for clusters of references in close but not consecutive sequence. Only passing mentions of text speakers and writers are listed in their entries; the main discussions are omitted. In-text bibliographic citations and citations of works as such are not indexed.

Park, Mungo, 82
Persaud, Arnold, 205, 225
Pinckard, George, 32f, 53–57 passim, 90,
  94n, 100ff, 144, 151, 294
Postma, Johannes, 43–49 passim

Quow, *see* McTurk

"Radio announcer," 216, 279
Raleigh, Sir Walter, 42
"Reefer," 129, 136, 157, 176, 190f, 209,
  226, 234, 251
Reinecke, John E., 114
Reisman, Karl, 36, 59n
Rickford, Angela, 165
Roberts, Peter A., 136
Robertson, Ian E., 45, 96, 291f, 300
Robinson, R. O., 301
Rodney, Walter, 48n, 67, 292
Ross, John R., 17, 29
Roth, Vincent, 91, 96, 99
Roth, Walter E., 114

St. Clair, Thomas S., 32, 54–56 passim,
  83–89 passim, 97–102 passim, 111
Salkey, Andrew, 301
Sankoff, David, 29
Sankoff, Gillian, 23
"Sari" (Cane Walker), 74
"Schoolteacher," 279
Schriffrin, Deborah, 186, 299
Schuler, Monica, 60
Selvon, Samuel, 264, 301
"Seymour" (Cane Walker), 75
Seymour, A. J., 264
"Sheik," 191, 197–99 passim, 207–9 pas-
  sim, 226f, 269

Simms, Edward, 52
Slobin, Dan I., 3
Smith, Rev. John, 70, 99
Smith, Michael, 258, 264
Smith, Raymond T., 58, 59n, 73f
Solomon, Dennis, 253
Speirs, James, 261
Stewart, William A., 84, 288, 293
Sutcliffe, David, 21
Szwed, John, 245

Tabouret-Keller, Andrée, 30
Thomas, Dylan, 221
Thomas, J. J., 219
Tinne, J. E., 66
Todd, Loreto, 105
Traugott, Elizabeth C., 227
Turner, Lorenzo D., 89, 144
Tyndall, Belle, 268

"Ustad," 17, 191

Valdman, Albert, 289
Van Berkel, Adriaan, 46, 114
Van Sertima, J., 17, 295

Waletzky, Joshua, 186
Warner-Lewis, Maureen P., 61, 246
Washabaugh, William, 23–26 passim, 31,
  289
Whinnom, Keith, 220, 222
Winford, Donald, 31, 158, 291
Wolfram, Walt, 185, 190
Wolfson, Nessa, 189, 299

Yansen, C. A., 93, 109, 275

Subject Index

Library of Congress Cataloging-in-Publication Data

Rickford, John R., 1949–
    Dimensions of a Creole continuum.

    Bibliography: p.
    Includes indexes.
    1. Creole dialects, English—Guyana.   I. Title.
PM7874.G8R53   1987   427'.9881   87-10065
ISBN 0-8047-1377-4 (alk. paper)

47505

10^3